A Dutch Family in the
Middle Colonies, 1660–1800

A Dutch Family in the Middle Colonies, 1660–1800

Firth Haring Fabend

Rutgers University Press
New Brunswick and London

Library of Congress Cataloging-in-Publication Data

Fabend, Firth Haring
  A Dutch family in the middle colonies, 1660–1800 / Firth Haring
Fabend.
      p.   cm.
  Includes bibliographical references and index.
  ISBN 0-8135-1627-7
  1. Dutch Americans—New York (State)—Rockland County—Social life
and customs. 2. Dutch Americans—New Jersey—Bergen County—Social
life and customs. 3. Haring family. 4. Rockland County (N.Y.)—
Social life and customs. 5. Bergen County (N.J.)—Social life and
customs. 6. Rockland County (N.Y.)—Biography. 7. Bergen County
(N.J.)—Biography. I. Title.
F127.R6H37 1991
929′.2′0893931073—dc20   90-37644
                                                              CIP

British-Cataloging-in-Publication information available.

This work is dedicated to the memory of my parents, James F. Haring and Elizabeth Haring.

It is dedicated as well to my daughters, Caroline and Lydia, in the hope that they and their descendants, like their forebears, may also know the joy of family, the love of country, and the grace of God.

It is dedicated, too, to the 770,000 Haring descendants alive today, whoever and wherever they may be.

And finally, it is dedicated to "them"—the men and women whose lives I have here uncovered, whose privacy I have invaded, and whose long sleep I have disturbed. May they now return to their twice well-earned slumbers and rest again in peace.

Contents

Figures

Tables

Preface

Family history, especially of Middle Colonial farming-class families, has been sorely neglected. Few studies exist that identify a particular family of the middling sort in any of the thirteen colonies and examine it in a systematic and scholarly manner over the course of the colonial period. Yet, to locate and reconstruct such a family over four or five generations is to discover a wealth of information about how ordinary seventeenth- and eighteenth-century Americans weathered the immigrant experience, established themselves in a community, took part in the social, political, economic, and religious life of their time, coped with a century and a half of enormous social change, and adjusted to conditions in the new republic.

This aspect of our national experience has been passed over because of the difficulties in getting at obscure middling families. Such families did not leave the rich store of diaries, letters, journals, and account books that offer insight into colonial families of the "better sort"—the Beekmans, Gansevoorts, Livingstons, or Schuylers, to name only a few that have been investigated. To gain a sense of the middling sort requires a different approach, and a difficult one. Their lives must be reconstructed through the public record: church and cemetery records, deeds, wills, inventories, court, town, tax, and military records—a task more easily described than carried out. Yet it is here carried out, for it is important that we deepen our understanding of the lives of those ordinary folk who populated and shaped early America—and whose descendants populate it still in great numbers. Of the Haring family, the subject of this study, for instance, it is conservatively estimated that there are alive today some 770,000 descendants.

The Haring family is ideal for such a study. Its beginnings in Manhattan in the 1660s are documented in the records of the New York Dutch Reformed Church; its decision to leave New York after the British conquest and resettle on land on the west side of the Hudson River is a matter of record; its motives for leaving New York are clear; it stayed in one place—Orange (now Rockland) County, N.Y., and Bergen County, N.J.—for the entire eighteenth century (indeed, it is still there); and its experience and behavior can be traced in surviving church, land, town, tax, court, military, and probate records for the entire period under consideration. As a bonus, a number of the houses the family built and lived in over the course of the eighteenth century still stand—rich primary sources in themselves.

John Pietersen Haring emigrated to America in the 1630s from Hoorn, in West Friesland, then part of the Province of Holland and West Friesland (today the Province of North Holland). A scrutiny of the records pertaining to Haring in this country discloses that he had four sons, eleven grandsons, twenty-nine great-grandsons, and seventy-five great-great-grandsons, almost every one of whom can be traced in the public records of New York and New Jersey. (He also had an equal number of female descendants, of course, but as daughters and granddaughters marry, they become identified primarily with their husbands' families—and thus are difficult to trace vertically.)

As we explore the records of these 120 men and their wives and children, their politics, religion, inheritance practices, domestic life and, of course, their hopes and dreams, successes and failures over the course of five generations, a textured and satisfying portrait emerges of a colonial American family.

And yet the picture that emerges out of the great welter of records is in one respect puzzling, for it is one of a Dutch family whose retention of its Dutchness over many generations in America may suggest a deep ambivalence toward America and toward becoming American. On the one hand, the Harings and the Dutch farmer in general were exemplary Americans. In an age when what has been called the yeoman ideal served as a resonant vision of American society, they were indeed ideal yeomen: their farms were models of good husbandry, their families were healthy, their housing stock was excellent for the period, their diet was nutritious, their life expectancy long, and their fertility levels high. They prospered, provided well for their offspring, served as officers in their churches and in their colonial militias, shouldered the main burden of administering their town and county governments, and participated in a significant way in province-level political affairs. To men like them adhered a certain moral luster. Indeed, Thomas Jefferson saw in their example a model for the nation. "Those who labour in the earth," Jefferson wrote in a much-quoted passage from his *Notes on the State of Virginia* (1785), "are the chosen people of God . . . whose breasts he has made his peculiar deposit for substantial and genuine virtue." Cadwallader Colden declared at midcentury that, in the whole society, farmers were the most useful and the most moral. And St. John de Crèvecoeur, an Orange County, N.Y., farmer, described America in 1782 as a "people of cultivators . . . united by the silken bands of mild government, all respecting the laws . . . because they are equitable. . . . We have no princes, for whom we toil, starve, and bleed: we are the most perfect society now existing in the world."

On the other hand, though, after the Revolution, the Harings and other Dutch farmers in the Hackensack and Hudson valleys were demonstrably less prosperous than their forebears had been, and far less visible in the colonial assemblies where they had been prominent in earlier generations. In fact, with the exception of Martin Van Buren, also of a middling farmer family, it is difficult to think of any representatives of the middling Dutch who played any part at all on the state or national scene during the first half of the nineteenth century. Further, these people were perceived by observers as Dutch, not American, although they had been in America for a hundred and fifty years. When Washington Irving, born in 1783, came in 1820 to write of his Hudson Valley neighbors, he saw quaint Dutchmen in calico pantaloons, not the American frontiersmen, politically minded farmers and, as we will see, radical patriots (or loyalists) of the previous two centuries. *They* had retired after the Revolution into "Dutchness."

What accounts for the withdrawal of the Dutch American farmer from the stage of the new republic? Had his persistent Dutchness made him unassimilable? If so, what, in fact, could Dutchness have been to a "Dutch" family after five generations in America? For the Haring family and other Dutch American farming-class families like them, was Dutchness at the end of the eighteenth century a defense against the painful process of change from an agricultural to a commercial society? Did all that they treasured of security and stability, of freedom and independence, of the familiar ways of their fathers lie in something that had been Dutch before it was American? Did the nineteenth-century descendants of the Dutch families, harking back to a remembered golden age, reinvent their Dutchness? And if so, how accurate was their memory of that bygone era? Or were the Dutch in America ambivalent from the beginning about America and about becoming American?

Answers can be forthcoming only by first looking closely at a Dutch American family of the middling sort, reconstituting it in the only way possible, through the public record, and examining its structure, values, beliefs, aspirations, expectations, and history—the totality of its experience in America—from New Netherland to the new republic.

Acknowledgments

Literally dozens of historians and librarians have helped me over the past seven years in tracking down the public records and in locating the appropriate printed sources to complete this study. But the person to whom I owe the greatest debt is Patricia U. Bonomi—both for her initial enthusiasm for the project and for her consistent encouragement and generous support and direction as it proceeded. The difficult challenge of rendering meaning out of a seeming chaos of information was assisted enormously by her astute guidance and unflagging confidence. I thank her!

Also most encouraging and helpful over the years have been Paul R. Baker and Kenneth E. Silverman of the New York University Graduate American Studies Program. The final manuscript reflects their helpful reading of an earlier version, as it does the insightful comments of Thomas Bender and David Reimers. Herbert Rowan, Oliver Rink, and David Steven Cohen also made excellent suggestions for improvements that are incorporated into this revised version of my doctoral dissertation.

Other readers of individual chapters or parts of chapters whose comments appreciably improved the final result are David E. Narrett, Claire K. Tholl, and Thomas B. Demarest. Among local historians, I owe the greatest debt to Howard I. Durie. His patience and generosity smoothed my way countless times. To Sally Dewey of the Tappantown Historical Society, the Reverend James Johnson of the Tappan Reformed Church, and to E. Haring Chandor I owe particular gratitude for providing me with access to important sources of information.

The staffs of the New-York Historical Society, especially Thomas Dunnings, the New Jersey Historical Society, the New Jersey State Library and Archives, the New York State Library, the New York Public Library, Bobst Library at New York University, the Columbia University libraries, Queens College Library, the New Jersey Room of the Alexander Library at Rutgers University, the New Jersey Room at the Newark Public Library, the

New York Genealogical and Biographical Society Library, the Rockland Room of the New City, N.Y., Free Library, the Historical Society of Rockland County, the Stevens Institute of Technology Library, the Johnson Library in Hackensack, N.J., and the Rosenbach Museum & Library in Philadelphia patiently and cheerfully produced innumerable documents and printed sources for me. Besides Mr. Dunnings, I thank for particular kindnesses William C. Wright, Larry Hackman, William Evans, James D. Folts, Christine M. Beuregard, John D. Stinson, Brent Allison, Leo Hershkowitz, Charles Cummings, Yvonne Yare, John Scott, Katherine Fogerty, and Jane G. Hartye. And for particularly fine copyediting, I thank Charles B. Purrenhage.

For a research grant in 1985 I am grateful to the New Jersey Historical Commission, and for the decisions of the judges of the 1989 Hendricks Manuscript Award of the New Netherland Project and the judges of the 1989 New York State Historical Association award I will always be grateful.

Finally, I have my family to thank: Carl, Caroline, and Lydia for sustaining me over the long years with their loving support, encouragement, and good humor.

Part One

THE FIRST AND SECOND GENERATIONS

Chapter One

New Netherland Beginnings

On May 18, 1662, in the Out-ward of Manhattan, north of Wall Street, an obscure Dutchman took a bride in the recently constructed chapel on Peter Stuyvesant's "bouwerie," or farm. The bridegroom was John Pietersen Haring, whose parents had emigrated from Hoorn, the Netherlands, in the 1630s. The bride was Grietje Cosyns, born on Manhattan Island in 1641, the daughter of Cosyn Gerritsen van Putten and his wife, Vroutje.[1]

John and Grietje were married by Dominie Henricus Selyns, minister of the Dutch Reformed Church in New Amsterdam and the first pastor of the new chapel on Governor Stuyvesant's farm. Selyns has given us a brief account of the Bouwery Village in the 1660s: It is a "place of relaxation and pleasure," he wrote, where "people go from the Manhattans [i.e., 'downtown'] for the evening service [on Sundays]. There are there forty negroes, from the region of the negro coast, besides the household families."[2]

The Bouwery was one of two farming villages in the Out-ward—the rural district north of Wall Street. The other was Harlem, farther to the north, settled in 1661. The Bouwery was definitely an *aardig* (pleasant) place to live in the late seventeenth and early eighteenth centuries. Maps show it as an area of gently rolling meadows—with views of the East River and Hudson River possible from almost any hill or knoll—ponds, streams, marshlands, sandy beaches, and fields dotted with neat palisaded farmhouses, barns, and hayricks. South of Wall Street, the thriving little city was described as "built most of Brick and Stone, and covered with red and black Tile [roofs. It] gives at a distance a pleasing Aspect."[3] (See Figure 1.1.)

In general, New Netherland was, according to one testimonial,

Figure 1.1. New York in the 1660s: The Prototype View. Courtesy Museum of the City of New York.

4

under the best clymate in the whole world; . . . seed may
bee thrown into the ground, except six weekes, all the yere
long; there are five sorts of grape wch are very good and
grow heere naturally, with diverse other excellent fruits
extraordinary good, and ye fruits transplanted from Europe
far surpasseth any there; as apples, pears, peaches, melons,
etc. [T]he land[,] very fertile, produceth a great increase of
wheat and all other grane whatsoever; heere groweth tobacco very very good, it naturally abounds, with severall
sorts of dyes, furrs of all sorts may bee had of the natives
very reasonable; store of saltpeter; marvelous plenty in all
kinds of food, excellent veneson, elkes very great and large;
all kind of land and sea foule that are naturally in Europe
are heere in great plenty, with severall other sorte, ye
Europe doth not enjoy; the sea and rivers abounding with
excellent fat and wholesome fish wch are heere in great
plenty.[4]

The optimal strategy of a young man in this Edenic-sounding
place was to acquire land and a primary source of income, marry
a woman with a good marriage portion, meet the people who
would put opportunity in his path, and accumulate a nest egg
that would provide him with a certain freedom of action. By marrying Grietje Cosyns, John Pietersen Haring did well indeed. Although she was only twenty-one, Grietje was already a widow,
and one with assets to her name. Within twenty years, this couple
(now parents of seven children), along with nine other families,
would have prospered enough to be able to purchase cooper-
atively some sixteen thousand acres of land in the Province of
East Jersey—the Tappan Patent.

A FIRST-GENERATION ROLE MODEL

In 1683, the Tappan patentees left Manhattan Island to start a
new life in the wilderness across the Hudson River. For managing his affairs up to this point, John Haring had in his father-in-
law, Cosyn Gerritsen, an energetic example of how to succeed in
seventeenth-century New York. In the 1630s, young Dutchmen
like Pieter Janszen and Cosyn Gerritsen, John Haring's father and
father-in-law, were persuaded to emigrate to New Netherland
by the promise of the home government and the Dutch West India Company to supply those who wished to farm with as much

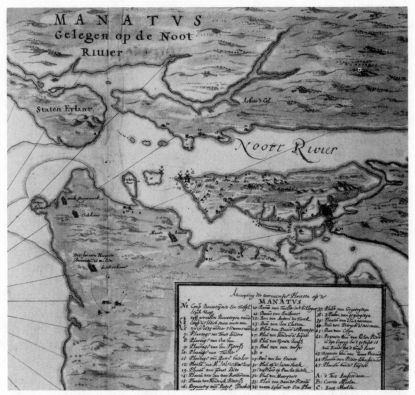

Figure 1.2. New Amsterdam in 1639: The Manatus Map. Cosyn Gerritsen's farm is no. 41, "Bou von Cosyn." Courtesy Geography and Map Division, Library of Congress.

tillable, pasture, and hayland as a man with his family could work: "from twenty to thirty morgens [40 to 60 acres] upon condition that [this land] . . . within two years . . . be brought into cultivation."[5]

Cosyn Gerritsen acquired his first property in New Amsterdam under these terms. His farm, or "bouwerie," appears as no. 41 on the Manatus map, "Manhattan Lying on the North River," made in 1639.[6] (See Figure 1.2.) The policy of the Dutch West India Company was to allow a colonist to hold and occupy his land without paying anything for it for ten years (Article 22), calculating these years from the time the land was "first sowed or mowed." Since Cosyn Gerritsen's formal patent dates from 1647, he had first "sowed or mowed" Bouwerie no. 41 as early as 1637 and had erected at that time the combination house-barn structure that appeared on the Manatus map two years later. The farm was approached along "Cosyn Gerritsen's Wagon Way," known today as Astor Place and Eighth Street.[7]

By 1662, when his daughter married John Haring, Cosyn Gerritsen had lived for a generation in New Amsterdam, and his activities there, as reconstructed from the public record, illustrate the ways in which, in pursuit of betterment, the earliest Dutch farmers rose.

Determined to succeed in the New World, Cosyn Gerritsen had prepared himself in three ways. He farmed. He had a second occupation as wheelwright (thus "Cosyn Gerritsen's Wagon Way"). And he dabbled in real estate. Both enterprising and business-minded, this seventeenth-century farmer used his land not only for subsistence, but, buying and selling it, as a way to enhance his economic status and to advance his family's opportunities and position.[8]

Among landowners in early Manhattan, activity in real-estate speculation was widespread. Even small farmers like Gerritsen were soon selling parts of the farmland they had received free as colonists, subdividing and selling their separate house lots, and purchasing other lots with the proceeds. In short, they were participating in the Manhattan real-estate market in miniature reflection of the large-scale speculation taking place in the hinterlands by the great land barons of the day: the Philipses, Van Cortlandts, Schuylers, Livingstons, and others.

Land deeds document how Cosyn Gerritsen purposefully managed a slow but steady improvement in his economic status as he bought and sold property. Besides his 78-acre bouwerie, almost exactly on the site of New York University and Washington Square Park today, Cosyn Gerritsen had been granted in 1647 a 5-acre house lot plus a smaller, separate lot on the west side of "ye Great high way"—Broadway. In 1651, he divided the larger of these two lots, selling one part to Hendrick Hendricksen and a house and lot to Matys Capito. These properties appear on the Castello plan as houses no. 13 and no. 14 (see Figure 1.3). The subdivision left Cosyn the smaller of the original two lots on Broadway for himself. In 1656, he bought from his neighbor Teunis Nysen a lot that was bounded by his own land. And, sometime "before 1665," he came into possession of a 10-acre lot and farmhouse that he had probably had his eye on for many years. This house, built in 1633 for Director General Wouter Van Twiller, appears as no. 10 on the Manatus map, just to the northwest of Cosyn's farm, and its acquisition by Cosyn was

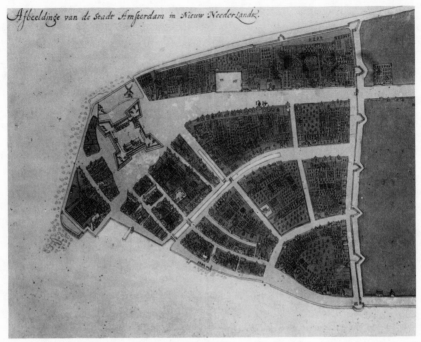

Figure 1.3. New Amsterdam, c. 1660: The Castello Plan. Courtesy Museum of the City of New York.

undoubtedly the jewel in his small crown. (Cosyn Gerritsen probably moved his family into the Van Twiller homestead in about 1660, as his old house on Broadway was that year occupied by another party.)[9]

When they married in 1662, then, John P. Haring and his bride had in Grietje's father a model for success and could comfortably anticipate their own prosperous future in a New Netherland where opportunity under the Dutch government seemed boundless and ensured. Within two years of their marriage, however, New Netherland was conquered by the British, and the future of the Dutch farmer in Manhattan dimmed.

THE AMERICAN DREAM, 1664

Scholars disagree as to how dark the New York Dutchman's prospects were in the last decades of the seventeenth century. Thomas Archdeacon contends that it had become sharply clear by 1674 that the Dutch and their descendants were going to have to be content with a much smaller share of the city's leadership and trade than they had originally expected. Archdeacon's comparison of tax rolls for New York in 1677 with those for 1703 show that in this interval the Dutch declined dramatically from economic and social dominance, by 1703 comprising 58 percent of the city's population but 52 percent of the bottom economic groups. The same two assessment lists show the English and French in 1703 residing in the best new neighborhoods of the city, while the Dutch were increasingly having to resort to old poor and new marginal areas. By the end of the eighteenth century, 80 percent of the families in the city's poorest district were Dutch, while English and French "gentlemen" and "merchants," the top two elite occupational designations of the period, outnumbered Dutch gentlemen and merchants in 1703 by sixty to thirty-six. Increasing numbers of Dutch worked as cartmen, blacksmiths, carpenters, coopers, cordwainers, silversmiths, and yeomen—all good occupations, but by no means at the top of the ladder.[10]

On the other hand, Joyce Goodfriend, using a different method for analyzing the tax lists and focusing on those of 1695 (as compared with Archdeacon's of 1677 and 1703), finds that the years from 1664 to 1700 were a period of gradual adaptation and adjustment by the old settler families to slowly changing conditions. The Dutch in Goodfriend's "conquest cohort" were losing ground to other ethnic groups, but gradually, not dramatically. In 1695, three decades after the conquest, the Dutch, representing 58 percent of the population, still owned 59 percent of the city's taxable wealth. The English, at 29.5 percent, owned 28 percent of the wealth; and the French, at 11 percent, owned 11 percent of the wealth—a remarkably equitable division of resources. By 1703, however, one of the main indexes of wealth in the period—slave-owning—shows the Dutch in the bottom position relative to their numbers in New York City and relative to the English, French, and Jews.[11]

A study of the farming village of Harlem, at the north end of Manhattan, documents that children of the original settlers there left Harlem in droves after the British conquest. But whether they left because of disappointing prospects in the city or for more positive reasons is debatable. Riker's genealogical accounts of the Benson, Bogert, Brevoort, Bussing, Delamater, Dyckman, Haldron, Kiersen, Kortright, Low, Mantanye, Myer, Nagel, Oblenis, Parmentier, Tourneur, Vermilye, Vervelen, and Waldron families show children flocking to New Jersey and New York across the

Hudson in the late seventeenth century.[12] It is more accurate to say that, like the Tappan patentees, the Harlem families viewed themselves not as leaving an unpromising future in the city, but rather as going forth to embrace the marvelous opportunities offered by relatively cheap and very abundant land in the country.

A NEW GENERATION, A NEW DREAM

From what can be learned of John Pietersen Haring's activities after his marriage to Grietje Cosyns, he was among those Dutchmen who continued to prosper, at least in a modest way, after the conquest. He had long since acquired land adjoining his father-in-law's farm in the Bouwery.[13] He was a member of the Dutch church. And both in 1673 and 1674—when the Dutch briefly regained control of New Netherland from the English—he was elected a "schepen," or public official, for the Out-ward. Schepens received a salary for their services, and they, as well as the "schout" (sheriff), burgomasters, clergy, and military and civilian officers (and their male descendants) also enjoyed the so-called Great Burgher Right, entitling all who held it, and no one else (unless they paid fifty guilders for the privilege), to practice a trade, carry on business, vote, and run for office.[14]

John and Grietje Haring had seven children together between 1664 and 1681. Their four sons and three daughters were Peter, born in 1664; Vroutje, 1667; Cosyn, 1669; Cornelius, 1672; Brechtje, 1675; Marytie, 1679; and Abraham, 1681. The baptisms of all but Peter are published in the records of the New York Dutch Reformed Church.[15]

Within twenty years of his marriage, then—and during the first two decades of the British period—John Pietersen Haring had acquired land, probably followed a trade, fathered seven children, affiliated with the city's first and foremost church, participated in government and, as a schepen, enjoyed the privileges of the city. He had, in other words, achieved a modest but respectable place in the city's society, below the great landed and merchant families but above the mass of unpropertied "mechanics" and tenant farmers.[16]

He had also been accumulating enough capital to leave New York for greener pastures. The advent of the British had coincided with a shortage of land on Manhattan Island, and the pres-

10

cient Dutch farmer in New York had foreseen that land would continue to become ever scarcer and more expensive. Yet land was, as we saw in the case of Cosyn Gerritsen's rise, one of the keys to prosperity in seventeenth-century New York. The farmer prized it as more than merely an arable stake, and more too than something to pass on to his children. He prized it for the speculative opportunities it allowed him; as he knew, trading in real estate was a tested means by which a man could improve his economic position.

In 1681, the year after his seventh and last child was born, John Pietersen Haring and two of his neighbors in the Out-ward signed a deed to purchase from the Tappaen Indians a tract of land across the Hudson River that came to be known as the Tappan Patent.[17]

That John Pietersen Haring would want to leave the place he had called home for twenty years, his wife's family, his property, his trade, his church, his role in city affairs, his children's best chance for an education and, putting all at risk, strike out anew in the dense, wolf-infested wilderness to the west is testimony both to his optimistic assessment of the future he foresaw for himself and his children away from New York and to his dissatisfaction with circumstances in New York.

Contemporary promotional literature described the area across the Hudson River as "plentifully supplied with lovely Springs, Inland Rivers, and Rivolets; in which are great store, and various sorts of very good Fish, and Water-Fowl, much bigger, fatter, and better Food, than . . . in England." Timber was, of course, in plentiful supply—to the point of being an encumbrance on the land, but there were also "great quantities of open Ground by Nature, as well fit for Arable, as Meadow, and Pastorage for Sheep, Cows, Oxen, and Horses; which are . . . as large and good as the English." Deer, swine, wild turkeys, pigeons, and all sorts of landfowl were free for the taking, as were sturgeon, lobster, oysters, and many other "Sea-Fish"; and rivers offered opportunity for considerable trade in wheat and flour, beaver pelts, tobacco, iron, fish, pork, beef, salt, corn, tanning, masts, and the building of vessels.[18]

In this teeming and fertile wilderness, the Harings and their friends would have land to farm, land to leave to their children and grandchildren, and excess lands to sell for profit. And once the ground was cleared and cultivated, they would have an opportunity to sell their surplus produce to the flourishing city downriver, imitating again on a small scale what such colonial New York merchants as Frederick Philipse, Stephanus and Jacobus Van Cortlandt, and Robert Livingston were already doing on a great one: acquiring land in the countryside and milling grain for domestic and overseas sale.[19]

The ambitions of the Harings and their fellow farmers in 1685 provide a sharp contrast to Thomas Jefferson's rather wistful view in 1785 of the ideal yeoman as a subsistence farmer content to cultivate a small patch of land while his contact with nature improved his character and inspired him with a love of republican government. Their ambitions are more in line with Jefferson's more realistic acknowledgment, also in 1785, that his vision of America as an agricultural society was a "theory only."

In fact, far from wishing to endure a condition of subsistence, it was the plan of the Harings and the other Tappan settlers, according to a historian who in the 1880s interviewed their descendants, "to build a city which should eclipse all rivals in the Colony save its neighbor, New York." This project does not seem absurd, he commented, given the "wonderful agricultural resources of the Hudson Valley . . . and the enormous profit to be obtained with the Indians in furs." Trade with the Indians was drawing to a close in this area in the last decades of the seventeenth century, but there were growing opportunities to sell wheat, produce, and lumber through middlemen to the Atlantic markets. The southern tip of the Tappan Patent lay close enough to the head of navigation on the Hackensack River that men familiar with the canal system of the Netherlands could easily envision building a canal through the marshes (where the Oradell Reservoir is today). Then, rather than shipping down the Hudson to New York—where port duties were a barrier to profit—they could transport their farm surpluses and timber down the Hackensack River to markets in East Jersey's free ports—not an illogical scheme, considering that the patentees believed the land they were acquiring lay in the Province of East Jersey.[20]

Beyond their economic motives for leaving New York, the Harings and their coventurers—thirteen families in all—also had religious and political reasons for moving away from the city in the 1680s. As dissenters in the Dutch Reformed Church, they were at odds with their ministers. Moreover, as people accustomed to the constitutional rights and liberties the Dutch had had in the Netherlands, they were at odds also with James II, the Roman Catholic king of Great Britain, and with the Catholic governors

James sent to administer his colonies in America. In Tappan, they believed, they could prosper economically, form a church along the lines of their Pietist beliefs, and govern themselves in a township protected by the conditions of their patent. Not of least importance, they could build a community of like-minded friends centered around the family life so dear to the typical Dutchman.

Chapter Two

"A Cartaine trackt of Landt named ould tappan"

In exploring why nineteenth-century observers—Washington Irving, for one—considered families like the Harings to be Dutch, two hundred years after their arrival in America, I have suggested that Irving's nineteenth-century Dutch-descended neighbors in the Hudson Valley may have reverted to a remembered Dutchness of a golden age in America, of an age when an ideal yeomanry—their ancestors—had tamed and cultivated the wilderness, lived in harmony and peace with their neighbors, and practiced equality and justice.[1] But how accurate a memory of the settler experience might this have been? How smooth in fact was the Dutch farmer's access to his wilderness land? How peaceably did he interact with his neighbors? How golden was the golden age his descendants remembered? An unsentimental look at the record suggests that settlement, far from being a smooth and harmonious process, was marred by disappointment, duplicity, bitter compromise, divisiveness, and—in the widespread use of slave labor to clear and work the land—irony.

The process of acquiring land in seventeenth-century New York and New Jersey was a complicated one, involving much red tape, time, and expense. In 1809, Washington Irving's satiric history of New York depicted the Dutch farmer as bilking the Indians out of as much land as he could throw his capacious pantaloons over, but the reality in 1680 was far different.

The buyer first had to scout the hinterlands to locate a suitable tract. Then, if the land he wanted was "owned" by Indians, as the Tappan land was, the buyer had to ascertain whether or not the

14

Indians would sell it, negotiate the terms with them, and obtain "Leave . . . from the Governour" to purchase it from them. If seller and buyer came to terms, and if the governor gave permission, the license was filed, the land was surveyed by the surveyor general, and a deed was drawn up. The buyer with his documents then went before the governor to petition for a formal grant, or patent. Finally, he reappeared before the governor to receive official confirmation.[2]

Expenses included travel time to scout possible locations, perhaps the hire of a translator to negotiate with Indian owners, plus travel expenses to the seat of government, the cost of surveying the perimeter of the parcel, legal fees, and various other costs related to securing the governor's approval. Thus, the purchase of land was an expensive undertaking for men of ordinary means, and groups were formed to share the costs.

Thirteen men joined John Pietersen Haring in purchasing land from the Tappaen Indians. As the moving spirit behind the venture, Haring purchased three of the total sixteen shares, one of which entitled the owner to about a thousand acres. The other thirteen men, who each purchased one share, were two Blauvelts, three Smiths, two De Vries, and Claes Manuel from the Bouwery as well as five men from settlements in New Jersey: Cornelius Cooper, Garret Steynmets, Ide Van Vorst, John Stratmaker, and Staats De Groot.

According to the Indian deed, the patentees agreed to give the Indians 100 fathoms of white wampum, 75 fathoms of black wampum, 15 guns, 4 pistols, 15 blankets, 16 kettles, 1 great kettle, 40 yards of duffel cloth, 10 yards of another kind of coarse cloth, 3 coats, 8 great hoes, 8 small hoes, 40 pounds of gunpowder, 50 pounds of lead, 10 shirts, 12 pairs of stockings, 1 cutlass, 1 trammel, 3 wedges, 2 gallons of rum, 4 casks of beer, 40 knives, 2 adzes, and 15 axes.

What they got in return was a territory the size of Manhattan Island in the eighteenth century: about sixteen thousand acres of fertile and well-watered wilderness teeming with game and fish, and broken by only a few Indian trails, perhaps a few natural meadows that did not need clearing, and a few scattered areas the Indians had cleared for their own purposes. Eight miles long from north to south and about two miles wide from east to west, the Tappan Patent lay in the valley between the Hudson River on the east (though not on the river) and the Hackensack River on the west. Suited for both farming and trading, it was entered by boat from the Hudson River—through property owned

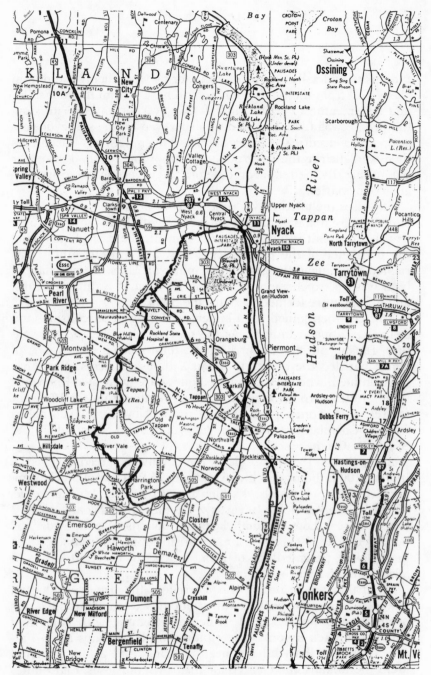

Figure 2.1. The Tappan Patent. The western boundary of the patent was the Hackensack River; the eastern boundary was the Nyack Range.

by other parties—at the mouth of Tappan Creek. On the south, it was within striking distance of the head of navigation on the winding Hackensack River. (Today, the New York State communities of Tappan, Orangeburg, Blauvelt, and Sparkill and the New Jersey communities of Northvale, Norwood, River Vale, Old Tappan, and Harrington Park lie within the perimeter of the patent. See Figure 2.1.)

To own sixteen thousand acres of land suitable for both farming and trading far exceeded the wildest dreams these men of ordinary means could have had for themselves in Europe (or in Manhattan). But before they had signed the final papers to secure its ownership, a series of setbacks, disappointments, and personal tragedies began to overtake them. The first of these occurred on December 7, 1683, when, eighteen months after signing the deed with the Indians, John Pietersen Haring died. That same month, the heads of two other families in the venture also died: Ide Van Vorst and Gerrit Blauvelt. And a fourth was soon to follow. Cornelius A. Smith died sometime "before 1686."[3]

To complicate matters, at almost exactly the same time, jurisdiction over the Tappan land, which the patentees had believed was in the Province of East Jersey, fell into doubt. When Governor Thomas Dongan claimed the territory for New York, he not only confounded the patentees' trading strategy, but set the scene for rancorous border disputes that were not settled until 1769.

"PAYING NOE CUSTOM . . . WEE ARE LIKE TO BEE DESERTED"

One of the patentees' intentions in moving from New York to what they thought was the Province of East Jersey was to avoid New York port duties by trading wheat, timber, and agricultural surpluses through the free ports of Perth Amboy, Burlington, and Philadelphia—all accessible to them from their vantage point on the Hackensack River. But the Common Council of New York had other ideas. It coveted the trade of New York's sister province across the Hudson River, and on March 7, 1684, the mayor and aldermen of New York moved to frustrate East Jersey's (and the patentees') trade ambitions. As the "unhappy Seperation of East Jersey [doth] Diverte the Trade of this Province," they pointed out to Governor Dongan, "Wee doe humbley Suplycate your Honor [to] Represent the Same unto his Royall Highness . . . And Desire

17

that East-Jersey may be ReAnnexed to [New York] . . . Again by Purchas Or Other wayes."[4]

Governor Dongan agreed. In a report to the Privy Council in London on the state of the Province of New York, he urged that not only East Jersey but also Connecticut, Rhode Island, three counties in Pennsylvania, and West Jersey be annexed as well. As for East Jersey, he wrote:

> it being situate on the other side of Hudsons River and between us and where the river disembogues itself into the sea, paying noe Custom and having likewise the advantage of having better land and most of the Settlers there out of this Government. Wee are like to bee deserted by a great many of our Merchants whoe intend to settle there if not annexed to this Government.
>
> Last year two or three ships came in there with goods and I am sure that the Country cannot, noe not with the help of West Jersey, consume one thousand lbs. [sterling] in goods in two years soe that the rest of these Goods must have been run [i.e., smuggled] into this Government without paying his Majesty's Customs, and indeed theres noe possibility of preventing it.
>
> And as for Beaver and Peltry, its impossible to hinder its being carried thither. The Indians value not the length of their journey soe as they can come to a good market which those people can better afford them than wee, they paying noe Custom nor Excise inwards or outwards.[5]

As part of the Province of New York rather than of East Jersey, Tappan was no longer as economically attractive as it had been to the men who had hoped to trade through East Jersey's free ports, and three of the Tappan shareowners from East Jersey now defected from the venture: Cooper, Stratmaker, and Steynmets either sold their interest in the Tappan land or retained it for their children to settle on when they married.

With its leadership depleted, Tappan was a smaller community at the beginning than its founders had envisaged. And it was poorer: now short on labor and capital, its chances for development were sharply curtailed. Those who built the first temporary houses on the land were probably the two sons of Gerrit Blauvelt, Adriaen Smith and his surviving son Lambert, John De Vries and Claes Manuel, and Staats De Groot. After Haring died, his widow, Grietje, returned temporarily to the Out-ward. When she remarried an Out-ward neighbor and widower, Daniel De Clark, in 1685, she moved again to Tappan with him, the seven Haring children, and De Clark's son.[6]

Tappan was also, demographically speaking, a younger community than it had expected to be. Most of the "patriarchs" of Tappan were very young men, some of them barely out of their teens. The eldest Haring son, Peter, who was assigned one of his father's three shares, was living in Tappan by September 1687, when he signed the oath of allegiance to the British king.[7] Peter [21] was twenty-three and married.[8] His younger brother Cosyn [23], who was only fourteen when their father died, was assigned the second of the three shares. He married in about 1692 and probably built his first house that year, at age twenty-two. The third and fourth Haring brothers, Cornelius [24] and Abraham [27], began to establish their families on the land in 1693 and 1707, when they were twenty-one and twenty-six. Even De Clark was young. At about thirty-one years of age in 1685, he was thirteen years Grietje Haring's junior.[9]

EARLY TRADING ACTIVITY: A "PASSAGE THRO THE MEADOW"

The patentees' slow start toward their goal of economic betterment was exacerbated in the 1680s and 1690s by official economic policy that furthered not only New York's welfare over East Jersey's, but also English merchant interests over Dutch. Governor Dongan's new laws regulated exports and imports, ended any legal trade between the city and Amsterdam by forbidding the entry of foreign vessels into New York City, and in general made it harder to engage in the smuggling activities between New York and Amsterdam that had characterized the decade immediately following the British conquest of New Netherland. But despite stricter mercantile regulations, wars, French piracy on the high seas, and higher taxes, a brisk sloop trade flourished on the Hudson River, with merchant ships visiting settlements on both banks of the colony's main north-south artery in order to obtain country goods, lumber, furs, and hides from farmers and trappers.[10]

With the ports of New Jersey effectively closed to them, the patentees' next best hope was to trade down the Hudson River, to which their natural access was the Tappan Creek. But here again, their way was not clear. Standing between them and the Hudson

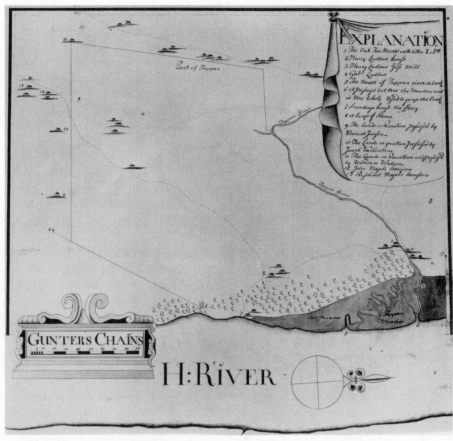

Figure 2.2. Tappan in 1745, by Philip Verplanck, Surveyor. Courtesy Palisades Free Library.

were, suddenly, one George Lockhart, a physician and merchant trader of New York City, and Frederick Philipse. Philipse, one of the members of the Common Council who had urged Governor Dongan to annex East Jersey to New York, was a New York City merchant who by 1674 had become the richest man in New York Colony and the proprietor of Philipsburgh Manor, across the Hudson River from Tappan. Lockhart, like Philipse a favorite of Governor Dongan, was granted a tract of 3,000 acres adjoining the Tappan Patent on February 7, 1685—just a few months after this land was claimed by New York, and before the Tappan patentees' grant was officially confirmed. Two weeks later, on February 20, Lockhart conveyed the first of two choice parcels of this land to Philipse, an entrepreneur with an eye for new opportunities.[11]

Lockhart's land extended from the mouth of the Tappan Creek south along the Hudson River for two miles and three miles west along the creek "into the woods"—a parcel of six square miles shown on a map made in 1745 (see Figure 2.2). The piece Lockhart sold to Philipse consisted of 67 acres of choice meadowland where the creek met the river. The two men planned to "collaborate during the next seven years for the further and better conveying and assuring" of this land. Philipse, who had "lived on [the] eastern half" of it in 1684, no doubt while overseeing the construction of mills and other improvements, may have begun cutting at this time the "passage thro the meadow . . . now wholy used to go up the Creek" (no. 6 on the map).

Philipse's decision to develop property adjacent to the Tappan Patent was a logical extension of his varied commercial ventures. His mills on the east bank of the river were highly profitable, and his presence on the west bank would give him ready access to the produce and trading goods of the Tappan patentees. As a Dutchman with firsthand knowledge of the Dutch talent for farming, he could be sure that the Tappan people would be a reliable source of supply for grain and lumber—raw material he could process on the spot for resale in the "Sugar Islands" and London.

New York City merchants had enjoyed, since 1670, an exclusive monopoly over the Hudson River carrying trade, and in 1680 the city had received in addition the flour-milling monopoly. Thus, Philipse's demand for grain to mill was as boundless as his markets were far-flung. Detailed shipping records at the Public Record Office in London document the Hudson River sloop trade in the seventeenth and early eighteenth centuries and reveal that Philipse and, later, his son Adolph owned at least seven ships that carried Hudson Valley flour, produce, lumber, and horses to the West Indies, returning with sugar, rum, wine, spices, and slaves. On the eastward leg of their triangular trading empire, the Philipse ships sailed with peltry, hides, and produce to London and Amsterdam.

The Lockhart-Philipse plan to develop the area south of the Tappan Creek seems to have been, if anything, a limited success. For an explanation, we might look to the Dutch farmer's political views in the 1680s and to his traditional conception of society as essentially of two classes—"them," the upper classes, and "us," the people. The Harings and their friends already resented Philipse, who as a member of Governor Dongan's council had urged Dongan to annex East Jersey to New York in 1684, thus thwarting their plan to trade down the Hackensack, and they would have been averse to doing business with him or anyone whose connections to the patronage of British governors and the privileges of high office gave him unfair advantages. Their resentment would erupt into open enmity within a few years. In 1689, when the people of New York revolted against the British Crown, Philipse sided with the government, while the Harings and their fellow settlers in Orange County supported Jacob Leisler.[12]

AS THE RIVER RUNS

Slowed initially by the unexpected depletion of their leadership ranks, then stymied by the economic policies of Governor Dongan, the patentees faced yet another setback to their prospects in a serious assault on the legality of their patent. As their farms prospered, envious hearts coveted the flat, fertile fields and propitious sites on the Hackensack River, and in 1717 Lancaster Symes, an ambitious land-grabber with connections in high places, purchased property from John McEvers adjoining the Tappan Patent on the west and laid claim to a strip of land east of the Hackensack River that the patentees had assumed was theirs.

A vagueness in the language describing the western boundary of the Tappan Patent was at the root of the problem: the boundary was to proceed northerly along the Hackensack River "to a place called the Greenbush." But the description neglected to add the crucial phrase "as the river runs," and the Greenbush was nearly a mile east of the winding river. Symes seized upon the crucial omitted phrase and claimed title to a piece of the patent seven miles long from north to south and from a third of a mile to a mile wide—a fertile area along the Hackensack where patentees had settled over the years and improved the land in good faith that they owned it.

"Divers variances, suites, controversies, debates and demands" ensued and continued for nine long years between the patentees and Symes and McEvers (who supported Symes's suit). Unable to settle the matter themselves, in 1725 twenty-seven of the Tappan freeholders finally resorted to the law and hired Richard Edsall, a surveyor and attorney, to "preserve the patent of Tappan." New York's Deputy Surveyor Robert Crooke was dispatched to take official measurements of the disputed line. After nearly a decade of controversy and litigation—with lawyers' and surveyors' fees to pay—a settlement was finally reached, and it was a costly one for Tappan. In return for a deed from Symes for the land in question, the freeholders agreed to pay him the enormous sum of £500—more than the value of the goods they had initially paid the Indians for the whole territory.[13]

SLAVES: THE MACHINE IN THE GARDEN

Finally, slavery presented its own ambiguities. Contemporary descriptions of eighteenth-century America as an asylum of freedom and unlimited opportunity were belied by the existence of slavery and sharp class distinctions. These were not referred to, of course, in the glowing promotional literature about America, which invariably portrayed it as a classless society of boundless chances for self-betterment. In reality, a privileged elite sought and received favor from the British Crown. A developing middle class began to prosper, by dint of industry and their own ambitions, while resenting the favoritism shown their social betters. And a huge and growing lower class, of which slaves occupied the bottom position, found America to be a place neither of opportunity nor freedom, whether economic, social, or political.

Tappan, which seems on one level to have been a near-utopian community where blacks and whites owned land side by side, was, in fact, as will be shown presently, economically multilayered and socially stratified. Its most affluent inhabitants prospered on the labor of their slaves.

Although the Harings and their fellow patentees in Tappan smarted at the high-handed behavior of their social betters, they very likely purchased slaves from these same men, for the merchant Jacobus Van Cortlandt, Frederick Philipse's son-in-law, was a major trader dealing in that commodity. In 1699 alone, Jacobus's sloops and brigantines, loaded with Hudson Valley flour, bacon, bread, butter, apples, garden seeds, nuts, cornmeal, shallots, and smoked beef—some of it purchased no doubt in Tappan—sailed to Antigua, Curaçao, Madeira, Jamaica, and Carolina—and with cornmeal, lumber, cowhides, and beaver to London. English spirits, Holland duck, household goods, money, rum, sugar, and slaves flowed into New York on the return voyages of Jacobus Van Cortlandt's ships and on those of other merchant traders.

Slaves were a convenient source of labor in the grueling work of opening virgin land to cultivation, and of slaves there were often so many in New York "from Madagasco & other parts" that sales were slow, "specially [of] those that are ould and defective." Off the ships of New York merchants, scores of young, healthy men and women ended their long journey from Africa clearing forests in the Hudson and Hackensack valleys. In 1702, a census of Orange County would count 20 adult slaves and 13 children, almost three-quarters of them owned by Tappan patentees. In 1712, there were 30 adult slaves in the area and 13 children; in 1731, 132 adult slaves and 52 children.[14]

If the pious and republican-minded Dutch farmer in the Hackensack and Hudson valleys experienced ambivalence about America, as I suggest, perhaps one source of his ambivalence related to his participation in a system of labor dependent upon human exploitation. Although they were a convenience (from the farmer's point of view), slaves were not essential to the opening of the American continent. Men could clear their land without slave labor, though with much more difficulty, of course. But circumstances—the sheer quantity of land that could be acquired in America, the incredible difficulty of clearing it, and the relative ease with which it could be cleared using slave labor—often overcame moral and republican scruples. After all, many a landowner reasoned, he was using the labor of a race that was considered not fully human, thus not truly his "brother" in the biblical sense.

For Dutch farmers in the New World, the ideal of colonial America as an asylum of freedom did not extend to the slaves who helped make their prosperity happen—any more than Dutch merchants in the Netherlands scrupled to trade in this commodity or, indeed, any more than planters did in any colony. A century after the first slave appeared in Tappan, Thomas Jefferson, owner of nearly two hundred slaves, would ponder the ironies of an America where all men were created equal, even though some men could own other men. No doubt the pious Dutch farmers in Tappan had considered the same contradiction for a century. By the time Jefferson agonized over the discrepancy between his beliefs and his practices, the Harings and the other original settlers of Tappan were in their fifth generation on the land, and the fifth-generation descendants of the original slaves were still laboring in their fields.

In sum, in Tappan, the ecstatic raptures of the promotional literature about America were belied by the realities of settling the land. Far from the idyllic union of happy farmer with his fruitful acres, the settlement of the Tappan Patent was fraught with personal tragedies and riven with disappointment, duplicity, and divisiveness. The yeoman at his plow had reason to harbor deep resentment toward an arrogant, land-grabbing upper class; at the same time, though, he had to contemplate the ironies of his own position, flourishing upon the labor of slaves.

THE CONCEPTUALIZATION OF TAPPAN: AN OLD WORLD MODEL

In the development of rural America during the seventeenth and eighteenth centuries, the way in which a particular community structured itself depended to a significant extent on the opportunities offered by the environment—the land, its quantity and its quality. But geographic factors alone do not explain the myriad types of communities that formed in colonial America. Also important was how the original founders conceptualized the community they wanted to create. Many clearly wanted to reproduce communities in the New World modeled on Old World prototypes.

In Andover, Mass., for instance, land was distributed by the town's English founders on the basis of English economic and social distinctions. It was understood that there was to be a hierarchy of rank and wealth among Andover families, as in England, rather than an equal sharing in the land. The size of Andover house lots ranged from a maximum of 20 to a minimum of 4 acres, depending on the economic and social standing of the assignee, and the size of the house lot governed the size of all subsequent allotments of land. In Sudbury, Mass., too, age and rank commanded respect, and in regard to the distribution of land, "egalitarianism was suspect."[15]

In Dutch communities, the Old World model was very different: egalitarianism in the distribution of land was not suspect but, rather, the ideal. The absence of a feudal tradition in the Netherlands and the presence of one in England seems to explain the different patterns that took hold in New Netherland and New England. Europe's evolution toward feudalism in the age of Charlemagne had been counteracted in the Netherlands by the existence of a class of free farmers. The village had been the basic social unit in the Netherlands as early as the fifth and sixth centuries, with arable land traditionally divided among the inhabitants, and pasture, heath, and forest held in common. Although a hereditary noble class existed, as well as a small class of bondsmen bound to the soil, the mass of the Netherlandish people were free.[16]

These traditions were reinforced, it has been suggested, by the vast undertaking of the Dutch, begun perhaps as early as the eighth century, to convert their western marshland into arable, for this effort required the full use of all available labor and thus created a freedom of movement of peoples that "forcibly loosened" those social and economic ties which normally hold the classes in their place. Dutch social and political freedom can thus be said to have had its ancient origins partly in the necessity for cooperative action in a coastal people's monumental battle against the sea.[17]

The eastern and northern parts of the Netherlands had their own history of independence and democracy, also a model for the Dutch who emigrated to New Netherland. In the late Middle Ages, territorial lords usurped the privilege of letting out rights to woods and wastelands that had traditionally been freely used by all, nobles and peasants alike. But the authority of the lords was circumscribed, for the law obliged them to assign the rights to these lands to the common people who were already living on them. Thus, the peasants of the Netherlands had an autonomous relation to the land at a very early date in their history. In the forested northern and eastern parts of the country, as one historian has put it, "feeling[s] of local comradeship" began to develop among the people after their success in chastening their would-be landlords. Mutually cooperative village communities, including all the inhabitants in the area, whether related or not, began to spring up. Democratically included in these nascent communities were millers, bakers, blacksmiths, and so on, who could perform services for farmers, who in their turn produced the foodstuffs and textiles the millers and blacksmiths required. In other words, not only autonomy, inclusivity, and what has been called a kind of "rural democracy" were present very early on in Dutch society, but also the division of labor necessary to the development of capitalism.[18]

The rights and obligations of the members of these rudimentary villages, both on the coast and in the woodlands, were based on custom and oral tradition more than on written law, and if obligations were not observed by all, customs existed to encourage order and discourage antisocial behavior. These "little circles of relations and neighbours" helped one another in trouble, instituted processes to settle their disputes, hired the "professionals" they needed (e.g., herdsmen and sextons), supervised their own roads, fences, and animals, and in general set a pattern of communality, cooperation, and self-rule that served as an ideal and model for generations of descendants, even in the New World.[19]

To put a fine point on the significance of this ancient model of Dutch community, one can say that the Dutch who sailed to the New World in the dawn of the modern era approached America with a collective memory, one might almost say an archetypal imperative, of what the ideal society should be. The social unit they best understood and most revered was that of a band of families related by ties of blood and neighborliness, guided by principles of inclusivity, democracy, cooperation, communality, and equality, accustomed to autonomy in relation to their land and to the larger community of government, long used to worshiping freely, and inspired by the ancient tradition of their ancestors' success in overcoming not only social forces such as feudalism, but also natural forces. In the Netherlands, they had tamed the howling sea; in the New World, the howling wilderness would not seem so formidable.

Cooperative action, communal spirit, the idea of a community of like-minded, goal-oriented friends acting together—these welded the Harings and their neighbors into a community in Tappan capable of withstanding the adversities of the pioneer period; or at least this is the model their nineteenth-century descendants may have come to revere as the actuality. But was it the actuality? Certainly Tappan seems to have been conceptualized from the outset as a multigenerational community of neighborhoods of family farms, with "community" being the operative word. The language of the patent specifically authorized the settlers to form a township—that is, the land was granted to them not for speculative purposes, as were many grants of the era, but for the establishment of a settled town with the rights and obligations special to it—and form a township they did.[20] But did they do so as equitably and harmoniously as this model would have it? For an answer, let us look at how they allocated their land.

THE ALLOCATION OF LAND

There was no fear of Indian attack by the 1680s in Tappan, and because the patentees envisioned their community as one that eventually would comprise neighborhoods of family farms, they did not cluster their houses, as New Englanders did, around a village square and travel back and forth to their outlying fields. Rather, with an eye to the future, they spread out on the land, built their houses and barns on it in a seemingly random pattern, probably much influenced by the ease with which a particular portion of the land could be cleared of rocks and trees, and farmed directly from this base—the homestead farm. The unused surrounding land between their farms they reserved for sons and grandsons. Thus they traveled from their farms to the town for sacred and secular matters, rather than living side-by-side on streets in the town, as New Englanders did.

In the Middle Colonies, the so-called open-field system was never popular. (Even in New England, the open-field system was abandoned early—in Plymouth by 1645, in Sudbury by 1655, and in Andover by 1662.) Once the threat of Indian attack was gone, settlers in New York, New Jersey, Delaware, and Pennsylvania demonstrated a preference for living on individual farms rather than in towns. In Pennsylvania, even churches and public buildings were dispersed in a seemingly haphazard way instead of being organized around a central green.[21]

In Tappan, members of the first generation gathered in kinship groups in three main areas: the Blauvelts at the northern end of the patent; the Harings and Daniel De Clark, as manager of the Haring estate and the new leader of the group, at the southern end and northward to the center, where church, jail, and courthouse were soon to appear; and the Smiths at Orangeburg, northeast of Tappan and southeast of Blauvelt on today's map (see Figure 2.1).

The settlers distributed their land in two divisions, one in 1704 and one in the early 1720s, undistributed land being held in common in the interim. Between original settlement in the 1680s and the first formal division in 1704, when deeds were issued, they apparently held the land only by oral agreement with each other.

Initially, and in both of the formal divisions, land was allocated by type: pasturage, woodland, fresh meadow, salt meadow, and swamp, each shareholder receiving an equal portion of each. Relatives were allocated adjoining lots of each type and built their homesteads on the pasturage, handy to field, livestock, and each other. They could thus travel together to adjoining woodlots, on Clausland Mountain, and to adjoining salt and fresh meadows, near the two rivers, for ease in sharing the work of felling and hauling timber and cutting, baling, and delivering hay to their cattle. Of the thousand acres that each shareowner was eligible to receive, he got only about one-fourth at first and probably cleared and cultivated only enough of that to support himself and his family.

Although the patentees distributed about a quarter of the sixteen thousand total acres immediately, they did not issue deeds to the individual owners for twenty-one years (1704); and although they had surveyed the perimeter of the boundary initially, in order to get the patent, they did not undertake internal surveys of their individual allotments for some thirty-eight or forty years—more than a generation.

Why did the settlers refrain for so long from formalizing legal arrangements? They had several reasons. First, ancient tradition in the Netherlands, as we have seen, was to hold land in common. But beyond this was the matter, in the New World, of a new law. Beginning in 1691 with the Judiciary Act, the legal system of New York Province was abruptly anglicized, and English common law (albeit often with American interpretations and innovations) came into force, supplanting Roman-Dutch law. At the stroke of William III's pen, legal precedents based upon the Roman-Dutch system and the Bible Codes of emigrants from New England were eliminated, and courts were set up based on the English system. The sudden change in law and courts threw legal affairs into a state of "dishevelment" for some time, and one of the grey areas concerned the division of lands among and between joint tenants. Even though conveying land by allotment was a common practice in all the colonies, it was a practice not recognized by English law until 1726. By that year, it had become painfully clear, the "Ignorance of [earlier] times" on this point had to be overlooked, the "Confusion the Contrary would introduce" finally persuading the authorities that adherence to the letter of the law was fruitless.[22]

The Tappan patentees' delay in putting their land titles into proper legal form may also have had another basis in a far more subtle condition: perhaps they understood instinctively that surveying their individual holdings might reveal unintended inequities in the quality and quantity of the parcels, inequities that would then sow discord. If the evolution of a community of neighborhoods of family farms was the social ideal they were pursuing, a survey was certain to bring uneven allocations to the attention of neighbors who were also brothers, cousins, uncles, and in-laws. Despite their best efforts to distribute land as fairly as possible, some lots would inevitably prove to be superior to others: flatter, better watered, closer to transportation, more fertile, less rocky, and so on. In other words, in Tappan, the apparent indifference to

29

deeds and surveys may have been, in part, an expedient, a sublimation of an anxious awareness that peace and accord had to last for several generations if the group goal of harmonious neighborhoods of family farms were to be realized.

In Flatbush, a Dutch American community on Long Island, farmers had chosen their sites publicly by lot to ensure fairness. Even so, it appears that the various sites differed in size by as much as 15 percent.[23] Yet, no challenges to the divisions were made. In an intimate community with a finite quantity of land, it was important to suppress social and economic differences and put a harmonious face on things. The seeming indifference to marginal variations in the Flatbush lots may have been based not on a love of harmony for its own sake, then, but on a fear of the consequences of self-assertion and competition. The same mentality may well have been at work in Tappan.

In any case, the inhabitants of Tappan were fully aware of the unhappy results of boundary disputes. Besides their own long conflict with Lancaster Symes, and the dispute between New York and New Jersey that was to exercise them for three generations, they knew of boundary disagreements that roiled families and friends in Marble Town and Hurley, in Ulster County, and in those Long Island communities with which they had direct and frequent communication. Newtown's conflicts with Flatbush, Jamaica, Brooklyn, and Bushwick continued for nearly a century and were well publicized; and Jamaica contended with Flatbush, Flushing, Newtown, Hempstead, Flatlands, and Brooklyn for decades. Among Connecticut towns, boundary disputes were rife, and they were endemic in parts of Massachusetts. Word of these, too, had of course penetrated to New York.[24]

Tensions are perhaps inevitable whenever people have to face circumstances that limit their opportunities or circumscribe their potential. But the patentees, who had removed to Tappan to improve their lives, knew that cooperation among them, harmony rather than belligerency, was in the best interest of their advancement, and they prudently avoided as long as they could the one occasion sure to produce dissension in their midst.

THE FIRST DIVISION: "BEGINNING AT A ROAD UNDER THE HILLS"

By 1704, however, the potentially divisive moment could be put off no longer. Deeds had to be issued, for by then changes had

30

occurred in land ownership that required an attempt to sort out the various parcels. Eight of the original patentees had by 1704 either died, sold their shares, or subdivided their sites.

It was decided that year to make the first of two formal divisions of the land and to issue deeds for it to the eight living patentees and to the seven other owners who had either inherited or purchased shares from the original owners. (John De Vries, Jr., now owned two shares, having inherited his father's share.)

Even at this time, however, although deeds were issued, the patentees hesitated to make a survey, and none was made. The 1704 deeds merely confirmed each owner in his original home lot and laid out and distributed hundred-acre lots on the east bank of the Hackensack. Mountainland, the choicest fresh and salt meadow, as well as badlands, swamps, and uncultivatable places, were, as mentioned already, distributed in such a way that every patentee got an equal share of each of the various types. As a result, the shareholders owned land all over the patent. Cosyn Haring, for example, received in 1704 the deed to 100 acres "beginning at the road under the hills," in present-day Old Tappan, N.J., 50 acres on the north side of the hills in the Greenbush, 100 acres at Greenbush, 50 acres on the west side of Old Tappan, and 4 acres of fresh meadow, for a total of 304 acres in five locations.

All told, the land deeded in 1704 amounted to 4,112 acres (or about a quarter of the entire patent) with each proprietor receiving between 250 and 300 acres, depending on the quality of his particular share. The balance of the land was held in common until 1721, when agreement on the final division was reached. "The descriptions of the parcels conveyed [in 1704]," Budke wrote, were "so utterly . . . inadequate that it will never be possible to plot [them] out."[25] Without a survey, the area of the various plots could only be estimated. In some cases, adjoining owners' names were supplied; in others they were not. Courses and distances were not always given, and locations were only vaguely described ("Beginning by a white oak tree," etc.).

But even though a survey was not made, disharmony and dissatisfaction arose anyway: as had been feared, the deed descriptions themselves drew attention to individual variations in terrain, soil quality, water sources, and drainage that made one piece of land more valuable than another. To avert tension and conflict, to preserve the ideal of community harmony, an expedient was hastily devised and a provision was appended to each release. Anyone who had a "doubt or scruple that [he or they] should not have their just dividend and proportion of lands" was invited to have the land surveyed at his own expense. "And what land should be found . . . short . . . he or they shall receive out of the undivided lands and what land he or they shall have more than [their share] . . . shall be for the benefite of all the patentees."[26] With a stroke, conflict was again avoided, for the expense of surveying the land would far outweigh any possible benefits of an added measure of it.

THE SECOND DIVISION: "TO EACH THEIR EQUAL PROPORTION"

In 1721 the patentees engaged Richard Edsall to draw up the papers for the last division of the common lands. By now, only five of the original patentees were alive. These five—Daniel De Clark (husband of J. P. Haring's widow, Grietje); the brothers Peter and Cosyn Haring (now fifty-five and fifty-two years old); Lambert A. Smith; and Johannes Blauvelt—"thought fitt to make an equal division of all the land of the township of . . . [Tappan and to give] to each patentee and assignee their equal proportion."[27] Besides the five patentees, land was allotted to twenty-two other men who by this time owned rights in the common lands, including the two younger Haring brothers, Cornelius and Abraham, who had long been living on it.

In this division, the patentees again received some of each kind and quality of land. Peter Haring received 168 acres at Schuyer Clove, 53 acres at the Hemp Meadow, 178 acres at Dorratakes, 236 acres on the Dwars Kill (Tappan Creek), half of mountain lot no. 14 north (33.5 acres), and mountain lots 6 and 7 north (134 acres) for a total of 802.5 acres.[28]

His brother Cosyn received one parcel of 469.5 acres (bounded by twenty-six different courses), 81 acres at the Hemp Meadow, 150 acres at the Greenbush, half of mountain lot no. 14 north (33.5 acres), and 28.5 acres of mountain lot no. 3 south, for a total of 762.5 acres.[29]

The third brother, Cornelius, forty-nine years old in 1721, had long since been entitled to his right in his father's original three-sixteenths of the land, and he was allotted 346 acres on both sides of the Tappan Road, between the lands of Peter and Cosyn and adjoining the lands of his younger brother, Abraham, as well as 30 acres at the Hemp Meadow, 16.5 acres in mountain lot no. 10

south, 33.5 acres in mountain lot no. 8 south, and 28.5 acres in mountain lot no. 3 south (total: 454.5 acres).[30]

Abraham, forty years old in 1721, received 184 acres on the Tappan Road (next to a lot of 108 acres he had purchased from the patentees in 1721 to enable them to pay the fees of the surveyor) as well as 51 acres at the Hemp Meadow, between the lots of Cornelius and Cosyn and adjacent to the land owned by Peter, and two mountain lots—268 acres in all.[31] (The discrepancy in the unequal amounts the four brothers received can be accounted for in only two ways: either earlier allotments were unrecorded, or cash differentials were paid to Cornelius and Abraham. It would have been contrary to Dutch inheritance practice in this era, discussed in Chapter 6, had the four brothers not shared equally in their father's estate.) It is clear that, by brother situating himself next to brother, the groundwork had been carefully laid by the first generation so that sons and grandsons, cousins and second cousins, could be neighbors a century later.

And they were. By the time the patentee generation had grandchildren, the original vision of the first settlers was realized. Whole neighborhoods of farms owned by members of the same family had evolved, with fathers, sons, brothers, uncles, cousins, and in-laws living near one another on clusters of family farms. When a family was very prolific, the clusters came to be named after the family. In the cluster called Harington Township, the 1779 ratables show twenty-five separate Haring taxpayers or heads of families, all descendants of the original four brothers.[32] These twenty-five families were themselves clustered in miniclusters: Peter's descendants lived on what is today Tappan Road in Norwood; Abraham's, farther up Tappan Road in Northvale; Cosyn's on today's De Wolf Road in Old Tappan; and Cornelius's to the west on Rivervale Road (see Figure 2.1). In Orangetown Township, over the border in New York State, the 1779 ratables show nine Haring taxpayers, all related and all more or less around today's hamlet of Tappan. The same pattern developed in the other patentee families. Blauvelts, for instance, lived for generations on farms in what came to be called first Blauveltville, today's Blauvelt, N. Y.[33]

This settlement pattern, which was inspired by an ideal of family coherence and which was based on a tradition long associated with the Netherlands—equal treatment of heirs—was also practical and functional in that it provided family members with the economic advantages of being able to share among themselves such capital-intensive commodities as oxen and slaves and such labor-intensive undertakings as field clearing and house, barn, and fence building.

But this is to get ahead of the story. By the early 1720s, all of the original land had been allocated, just in time to coincide with the coming-to-marriage age of the children of the patentee generation.

Chapter Three

First Families

About twenty years ago, the work of historical demographers made it possible to begin to revise earlier notions of the colonial family's basic characteristics. Men and women did not marry at such an extremely early age as had been thought. Parents often had a large number of children, but not all parents did. Infant mortality and mortality of mothers in childbirth were high, but not extremely high. Many, not few, colonists lived to old age, and communities contained many fewer widows and widowers than was previously thought. Most strikingly, the typical family, which had been described as extended, was found to have been predominately nuclear.[1] How does the Haring family fit into this picture?

With their father dead untimely and their mother remarried, the seven Haring children constituted the first generation of the family in Tappan. Records show that they married young, they had many children (many more than their corresponding generation in the Netherlands), they lived in nuclear households, they experienced the death of some of their children, and all but one of them lived into very old age.[2]

MARRIAGE: A MATTER OF FIELDS, AND OF FEELINGS

Marriage was viewed in Tappan and in other eighteenth-century American communities—and in the Old World as well—as an economic, social, and cultural alliance, both of whose partners brought to it things of material and nonmaterial value. The material things were usually land on the part of the husband, cash or goods on the part of the wife. The nonmaterial contributions were a common core of beliefs, a shared system of norms and values, and a set of mutual expectations. Just as intermarriage of leading families in the city cemented political factions, preserved fortunes, and extended and strengthened social networks, so in rural areas marriage was intended to have the same happy effects on a smaller scale.

Dutch families in particular were "wholeheartedly devoted" to improving their fortunes through opportune marriages, and it was taken for granted that children would marry to the family's advantage—within reason. In his panegyric on marriage, the seventeenth-century Dutch poet Jacob Cats wished for "A wife not rich or mighty grand / But like to me in goods and land." No evidence exists for any formal parental intervention or attempt at arrangement, but marriage between the children of neighboring farmers in the seventeenth, through the eighteenth, and into the nineteenth centuries in Tappan is so prevalent as to seem virtually to prove that marriage there was indeed a matter of "goods and land." Yet, no evidence exists either for absconding spouses, wife abuse, adulteries, legal separation, or divorce, suggesting also that the next-door neighbors found each other quite acceptable as marriage partners.[3]

Among European nations, the Dutch revered family and household as the source of moral authority, and a properly run family as a microcosm of the properly governed commonwealth. In his study of the collective personality of the Dutch, Simon Schama states that the goal of the individual Dutch family in the seventeenth century was to produce within itself a "prospering Christian peace" and to further the creation of more virtuous households like itself.[4] Although the Harings left no such words of their own to tell the modern researcher that family was the cornerstone of the community they hoped to construct in Tappan, church marriage and baptismal records are an adequate and eloquent testimony to that fact.[5] What sorts of spouses did the seven Haring children choose, and upon what considerations were these choices based? Predictably, all seven chose spouses of similar economic and social background—that is, from families with the ability to acquire substantial real estate and to own slaves and whose male members, in addition to being prosperous yeomen, were also judges, militia officers, deacons, elders, and so on.

"LIKE TO ME IN GOODS AND LAND"

Eldest brother Peter Haring [21] married Grietje Bogert, the eldest daughter of a schepen, chosen from among the "most discreet and proper persons" in Harlem Village for that position.[6] Second brother Cosyn [23] married Maretie Blauvelt, a sister of the two patentee Blauvelt brothers. Third brother Cornelius [24] and his sister both married Flierbooms, themselves siblings, the daughter and son of Matthew Flierboom of Albany, a schepen of that community.[7] Two other Haring siblings, youngest brother Abraham [27] and his sister Brechtje, married Talmans, who were first cousins to each other and whose family owned a large tract of land north and east of the Tappan Patent.[8] The seventh sibling, Vroutje, married Teunis Quick, a prosperous New York baker.[9]

All seven marriages had in common, also, some connection or other of blood: the Haring, Blauvelt, and Bogert families were related through marriages undertaken in previous generations. In four cases, siblings in one family married opposite-sex siblings or cousins in another; and in the seventh case, the bride married her uncle's brother-in-law.[10]

This pattern suggests that a consolidation of already established marital connections was an important goal of the Haring family, and that exchanging siblings in marriage was another goal. Both strategies made good economic sense. Such marriages produced an advantage to both families as bride wealth and land, which would otherwise have been lost to the two families, were instead reimbursed to them, as it were, in the exchange.

Such marriages also reinforced the kinship bonds established in the initial union, especially when the families of new in-laws were encouraged to cement their new ties with Tappan by purchasing land there. For example, Jacob Flierboom bought land from his brother-in-law Cosyn Haring in order to start a farm next door; Peter Haring's brother-in-law Gysbert Bogert bought land from the Smiths and began to raise his family in Tappan; and Garret Blauvelt sold land to his brother-in-law Ralph Van Houten. Other patentees sold land to Haring, Blauvelt, and Bogert in-laws: the widow and son of Staats De Groot sold to Johannes Meyers, a Bogert in-law, and to Jacob Flierboom, a Haring in-law; and the widow and children of John De Vries sold to Jacob Flierboom—to cite just a few cases of a prevalent pattern.[11]

Thus was the stage being set for marital alliances among the third-generation children. Looking ahead for a moment, of the thirteen third-generation Haring males who survived to marry, six married either a Haring, a Blauvelt, or a Bogert woman, and five of their eighteen sisters married either a Haring, Blauvelt, or Bogert man.[12]

On the other hand, that only one of the original seven Haring children in Tappan (Cosyn) married into a fellow-patentee family suggests that another goal of the family was to widen its network of alliances.[13] This, too, made sense—genetic sense—for it served to expand the marriage pool. And again, looking ahead to the third generation, the tendency to widen the network of alliances also remains clear: seven third-generation Haring men, or 53 percent, and thirteen of their sisters, or 72 percent, married into families not previously related to their own. That men were much less likely to do so than their sisters suggests that males bore a larger economic responsibility for protecting the family's stake than did females and, thus, were less able to exercise freedom in choosing a spouse. The corresponding generations of Smiths and Blauvelts, already related to each other by marriages undertaken in the Out-ward, followed·the same patterns. One of the Smith brothers married a Blauvelt woman in Tappan, and one of the Blauvelt brothers married a Smith woman; but the other two Blauvelt and Smith brothers went beyond the boundaries of the community for their wives.[14]

Cousin and close-friend or in-law marriages were not unique to Tappan, to towns settled by Dutch Americans, or to towns settled by those of other ethnic backgrounds. In all new communities, there was a strong disposition to use marriage to strengthen roots already put down and to fortify an already coherent social universe.[15]

Whether they married in or out, the Harings and the other settlers quickly established a wide network of kinship connections, and thus a wide source of support, cooperation, loyalty, and sharing in times of need and joy. Again, they had good reason to do so, for with a wide kinship network they had more men and women to choose among not only for marriage partners, but also for baptismal witnesses, guardians for orphaned children, administrators of estates, and witnesses and executors of wills. Older kin were a source, too, of advice and counsel, and of loans, mortgages, and other types of financial aid in this prebanking era. Moreover, in a time when education of the next generation was more likely undertaken not so much in formal schools as in the church, the community, and (mainly) in the home by family members, the close bonds of kin ensured the smooth and efficient transmission of both practical knowledge and shared values.[16]

Because land was plentiful, the Haring brothers had no reason to prolong their bachelorhood. The average age at which they married over the two decades 1687–1707 was 23 years, 1 month.

The average age of their wives at marriage was 22 years, 4 months. Although averaging suggests a marrying-age pattern for this generation of the family in which a young man in his early twenties chose a wife a year or so younger, a look at the individual ages suggests that this "pattern" was true in this family in only two out of four cases. Both Peter and Cosyn married women who were just a year of so younger than they, but Cornelius married at 19.3 to a woman five or six years his senior, and Abraham, who waited until he was 25.7 to marry, chose a wife who was six years younger. Two of the Haring sisters married at age 20 to men who were nine years older. Children apparently exercised a considerable independence in regard to the age at which they married and the families they married into. They chose spouses from nonrelated families, from outside the patentee circle, and even from as far away as Albany; but their spouses were always from families of concomitant economic status—and, of course, families willing to affiliate with the Dutch Reformed Church, where all marriages, without exception, are recorded.

This generation of males in Tappan married a little younger than the corresponding generation in New York City—but a good deal younger than men in three Massachusetts communities. Brides were slightly older in Tappan than in New York City, but almost exactly the age of brides in the Massachusetts towns.[17]

In New England towns marriage appears to have been correlated with economic factors, men postponing this life event until they could support a family, or until their fathers would enable them to do so.[18] In Tappan, where four of the original thirteen fathers had died before settling and where three or four others did not settle for other reasons, a strong paternal influence was absent in the beginning, and sons seem to have married as soon as they pleased. Since the land was theirs and was abundant, it was to their advantage to start working it as soon as possible, to build a house, and to find a wife as helpmeet.

"FINE CHILDREN AND ALMOST EVERY HOUSE FULL"

Thereafter, children came in abundance, too, as they seemed to in other Dutch families in the colonies. Children "multiply more rapidly here than anywhere else in the world," Dominie Henricus Selyns wrote of New Amsterdam in the 1680s. It was an observation supported by William Penn, who described the Dutch on the

Delaware River as having "fine Children, and almost every house full; rare to find one of them without three or four Boys, and as many Girls; some six, seven, and eight Sons."[19]

Among them, the 7 Haring children had 65 children, an average of 9.3 per family. These 65 were born over a long period ranging over forty-six years—from 1688 for Peter's first child to 1734 for Abraham's last. The childbearing years of their wives ranged from about fifteen to twenty-six years, and children were born with the frequency and regularity predictable in an era when reliable methods of birth control were unknown.

Peter's 12 children were born over a period of twenty-two years, at an average interval of 22.6 months. His wife, Grietje Bogert, bore a child less than every two years for probably as long as she was fertile.

Cosyn and his wife, Maretie Blauvelt, had 8 children over a period of fifteen years at intervals from 9 months to 39 months. Maretie averaged a birth every 22 months, exactly the same as her sister-in-law. Unless she had unrecorded births after 1709, Maretie bore children from the age of 23.8 until she was 39.

Cornelius Haring and Cattryn Flierboom had 8 children, 4 sons and 4 daughters, all of whom survived to adulthood. The 8 were born over a period of about seventeen years from an unrecorded month in 1692 until January 1709, with an average interval between births of 25 months. Cattryn's last child was born when she was about age forty-one.

The youngest brother, Abraham Haring, married Dircktie Talman on June 25, 1707, when he was twenty-five years and seven months old and she was two months short of twenty. This couple had 13 children born over a period of twenty-six years, at intervals ranging from 16 to 53 months. A 53-month interval is long in this era, especially for Dircktie, who gave birth within two-year intervals—in 1708, 1710, 1712, 1714, 1716, 1717, 1718, and 1720, and also 1724, 1726, 1728, 1732, and 1734. Gaps longer than about 20 or 22 months may be evidence of unrecorded births or stillbirths in 1722 and 1730.

"ENJOYMENT PRECEDING MARRIAGE"

Dircktie was especially fertile among a fertile population, conceiving probably even before marriage, for her first child was born eight months less one day after her wedding day. Possible prenuptial pregnancies may be suspected also in the case of Peter and Grietje, whose first child was born almost exactly nine months to the day after their marriage. The marriage dates of the other two brothers, Cosyn and Cornelius, are unrecorded—a circumstance that too may be evidence of pregnant brides. (In regard to their three sisters, unreliable or incomplete records make the question impossible to address.)

Attitudes toward prenuptial pregnancy among any group of preindustrial people are not easy to discover, but a general absence of comment and the perhaps purposeful failure to record a marriage date or a birth date suggest that premarital sexual activity was condoned in Tappan so long as the partners married, and was in fact tactfully obscured if pregnancy occurred. In many colonial communities, there appears to have been a general toleration of premarital conception, and, provided that they married, couples were not punished.[20]

Premarital pregnancy, defined as the "conception, before marriage, of the first post-maritally born child," has fluctuated widely in America—from a low of 10 percent in the seventeenth century to a high of about 30 percent in the mid-eighteenth, falling below 10 percent in the mid-nineteenth century, and rising to 20 or 25 percent today. The trends, it has been suggested, relate to successful attempts by society (mainly the church and the parental generation) to control the sexual behavior of its members. According to this theory, the surges relate to a weakening of external controls as authority of church and parents is questioned by the young.[21]

It was one late-seventeenth-century minister's opinion that external controls on premarital behavior, in New York at least, were not effective. The Reverend John Miller, an English Episcopalian clergyman touring New York Province in 1695, commented that "those who in earnest do intend to be married together are in so much haste, that, commonly, enjoyment precedes the marriage, to which they seldom come till a great belly puts it so forward, that they must either submit to that, or to shame and disgrace which they avoid by marriage; ante-nuptial fornication, where that succeeds, being not looked upon as any scandal or sin at all."[22]

If the first post-maritally born children of the four Haring brothers were conceived before marriage, as seems likely, it may be suspected that in the absence of an older parental generation in the community, or an organized church until 1694, the young people of the community set their own standards of sexual conduct. On the other hand, they may simply have adopted the standards of a wider community or continued an old tradition. From sparse data on the Netherlands in the same era, it is estimated that "early" births were connected to 14.3 percent of marriages in the Gelderland region between 1666 and 1730. In coastal villages, premarital sex "was not reckoned shameful when it was certain that the lovers were true and steadfast and would make a good marriage." Ministers in Middelburg, the heartland of Dutch Pietism, severely reprimanded those who indulged in sex before marriage, but allowed the marriage to take place. They had little choice, it appears. At the Hague, earlier in the century, the synod had lamented that scarcely four out of forty young persons married "with decent conduct."[23]

If premarital enjoyment resulted in an illegitimate birth, however, sanctions in the Netherlands and in Tappan were swift and sure. In April 1703, at the first session ever held of the Orange County Court of Common Pleas, the courtroom was discreetly cleared, and the following presentment was read: "Wee the Jurors for our Sovereigne Lady ye Queen upon our oaths Doe present Katherine [——] of Haverstraw single woman for haveing and beareing A Bastard male Child which as yet she hath not fathered [i.e., named the father of] and with which the County may Come to be burthened."

A warrant was issued for the arrest of Katherine, a woman of twenty-two, that she might "be proceeded against according to the law in the case," and in July she went before the clerk of the court to swear "upon the holly Evangelist of Almighty God" that the father of the child begotten of her body was one Henry Tenike. Henry, Katherine swore, had promised to "give her an estate to maintain her and her Children Likewise to marry her if she would consent to Ly with him." Katherine was illiterate and poor. Haverstraw was too far from the school of the Tappan Reformed Church for children from that settlement to attend, and she had not even learned to write her own name by age twenty-two. Her family was not far from the bottom of the economic ladder. They gave only three florins total to the support of the church in the first thirty years of its existence, and her brothers were frequently in court, charged with horse theft and the like. Clearly, Katherine had been duped and taken advantage of by Tenike, a scion of the Ten Eyck family and in later years a delegate to the New York Provincial Assembly. But this was of no interest to the court, which was concerned only that the child should not have to rely on the county for his support. Bastards put a strain on the public purse, and the public purse took precedence over the private predicament. Henry was ordered to "stand committed" unless he produced the means to provide for his son.[24]

"MOTHER, WHY DO YOU CRY SO?"

Life was precarious in Tappan. Of the forty-two children born to the four Haring sons, thirteen, or 30 percent, died in infancy or youth. "In the Spring," the Orange County physician Cadwallader Colden observed,

> the people are subject to Pleuresies and inflammatory fevers. . . . The country people and such as are most exposed to the cold are more liable to these Distempers. . . . The months of July, August or beginning of September are the most sickly months in the year more people being sick and more children dying than in all the rest of the year. The Epidemical Diseases are intermitting Fevers, Cholera Morbu and Fluxes. . . . In the beginning of Winter People are in danger of Rheumatic pains and in February to Bastard Pleurisies. . . . We have few consumptions or diseases of the Lungs . . . but if there be ulcers formed they die in a little time.[25]

Measles, a serious and often fatal disease among an unimmunized population, struck adults and children alike throughout the colonies in 1713. In 1718, smallpox returned. And wherever there were swampy areas, as there were all over the Tappan Patent, malaria and yellow fever, mosquito-borne diseases, were dreaded and regular visitants. Recorded epidemics of measles again in 1729, smallpox in 1731, and yellow fever in 1732 claimed their melancholy tolls in New York and in Tappan, whose inhabitants, just a morning's sail up the Hudson, were in frequent contact with the city.

Country children did not die from disease in such numbers as children in the city, where crowding, open sewers, and general filth fostered the spread of germs, but rural children were exposed to other hazards. They drowned in rivers, lakes, ponds, and wells; fell to their death from trees and haylofts; succumbed to snakebite, bee stings, and tetanus; were trampled by runaway horses; and perished by fire and the fast-spreading rabies of mad dogs and woodland animals. In addition, of course, respiratory infections, ruptured appendixes, and other common medical emergencies claimed their toll in city and country alike.

Although child mortality in this generation of the family was high, the adults lived long lives, Peter dying at age eighty-six, Cosyn at seventy-four, Cornelius probably in his late seventies, and Abraham at ninety. The four wives also lived into their seventies, Abraham's wife Dircktie Talman to age eighty-one—a remarkable comment on the sturdiness of this pioneer generation. In the decades 1690–1709 in Virginia, 60 percent of all children had lost one parent by the time they were thirteen.[26]

Of the three Haring sisters, only one death date is known. Brechtje Haring, Teunis Talman's wife, died at age thirty-three, a month after giving birth to a set of triplets, who were taken to the Tappan Reformed Church to be baptized the same day their mother died, January 12, 1709. Two of the triplets soon followed their mother to the grave.

Infant death—the special nightmare of Dutch parents in the seventeenth century—is depicted in a woodcut of the era showing a sinister horned and tailed figure of death stealing a newborn from its crib. It was a nightmare familiar to the Harings. Between 1688, when the first child of the third generation was born, until 1734, when the last was born, seven Haring children out of sixty-five born alive are recorded as "dying young"—that is, probably before the age of one. Although this is not an extremely high number, looking at these seven infant deaths individually suggests some of the special problems of an era when knowledge of birth control was minimal, pediatric care primitive, and antibiotics unknown. The death of two of Brechtje's triplets can probably be attributed to low birth weight, associated with multiple births and often fatal, even today. Cosyn and Maretie's third child, a son, was baptized exactly nine months after their second child was born, indicating that he may have been either premature or simply too puny to live because of his mother's weakened physical condition from her immediately previous pregnancy. No special circumstances are discernible in the case of the fourth infant death in this period. Peter and Grietje's unnamed fourth child was born a comfortable two years and eleven months after their previous child. But this relatively long gap between births may indicate an unrecorded birth or stillbirth in the interval, in which case maternal ill health may again have been the culprit. (Within eight months of this fourth birth, Grietje gave birth yet a fifth time.)

The last three of the seven infant deaths in this generation were children of Abraham and Dircktie Haring. Three babies born to this couple in a period of two years and two months died in quick succession. The first two were born only nine months apart.

It is difficult to imagine even extremely hardy pioneer women enjoying the rigors of many, many years of pregnancy, interrupted if at all by months of nursing, punctuated by painful labor, and always haunted by the specter of death—the mother's as well as her child's.[27] Even in a society where large families were the norm and were valued, wanted, and needed for practical reasons, at least some women must have dreaded the cyclical round of conception, pregnancy, labor, parturition, nursing, and again conception. If there is any suggestion of resistance to the cycle, it may lie in the interesting fact that among the four Haring wives and two Haring sisters who survived to at least age thirty-eight, four stopped childbearing at ages thirty-eight, thirty-nine, forty-one or forty-two, and forty-three. Two of their husbands, even more provocatively, were only thirty-seven and forty at the time of their wives' last pregnancies. Did these women suddenly begin to practice some successful form of birth control?

Their average age at last birth coincides with the average age of eighteenth-century women in Germantown, Pa., at the birth of their last child (40.2 years). One contemporary observer of this phenomenon inquired into its causes, "but none could give me a good answer," Peter Kalm reported. "The women . . . seldom or never have children after they are forty or forty-five years old, some leave off in their thirties. . . . Some said it was owing to the affluence in which people live here. . . . Some ascribed it to the inconstancy and changeableness of the weather."[28]

One modern observer believes that the early age of the mother at last conception and progressively longer intervals between conceptions are "plausible indications" not of fickle weather, but of contraceptive practices, a conclusion that seems warranted, given the small mean household size (4.75) in the Netherlands during the corresponding period. The biology of reproduction was well known in the seventeenth century. A popular obstetric manual, *Het Kleyn Vroetwyfs-boeck* (The Little Book of Midwifery), gave explicit advice on conception methods. And an "extraordinarily frank" sex manual, *Venus Minsieke Gasthuis* (A Picture of Love within the State of Marriage), published in Amsterdam in 1687, had gone into seven editions by 1715. Whether these inexpensive and popular works reached Tappan is not known, but they did contain the kind of interesting and practical information about sex that tends to get around.[29]

THE VALUE OF CHILDREN

In colonial settlements, couples had many children because the labor that sons and daughters could provide in their gender-structured tasks—clearing, tilling, cultivating, harvesting, chopping wood, hunting, fishing, and fowling for boys and spinning, weaving, cooking, cleaning, and child care for girls—was a recognized and highly valued asset. Children were also a valued source of economic and emotional support in old age. Childless couples were forced either to shift for themselves or hope that a niece, nephew, or neighbor would be willing and able to look after them. Also, a son could bring luster to the family by attaining some level of distinction in his chosen vocation, or in his activities in public or church affairs. Finally, sons and daughters could enrich a family and enhance its social status by making favorable marriages.

A family's hopes for rising in the world could be fulfilled by its offspring. On the other hand, they could also be thwarted. If there were too many children to provide for, or if the children were sickly, feebleminded, or ne'er-do-well, or if they married badly or died before reproducing, the family in a sense died too. Children were a gamble. They might pay off, but they might not.[30]

One father in Hackensack, not far from Tappan, put an exact price on the value of his daughter and gave a precise name to the source of her value to the household: "Servant." In 1747, in the Bergen County Court of Common Pleas, Jacob Van Wagoner complained that Cornelius Van Boskirk "unlawfully did Ravish and Deflower and Carnally did know [Jacob's daughter] then for a long time unlawfully did frequent [by climbing in through her bedroom window] . . . and impregnate and get [her] with Child so that . . . Jacob the service of . . . his Daughter and *Servant* . . . for all the time . . . and long after totally did loose and . . . Jacob with all his family by that Occasion unto Great Scandal and Infamy and Impoverishment did fall."[31] Jacob demanded restitution in the amount of £200, and a sympathetic jury awarded him the same.

Even though the Dutch family tenderly valued children for their own sake, it is nonetheless clear—considering the labor-intensive nature of farmwork, the necessity to arrange one's security in old age, and the importance to a family of its economic and social standing and aspirations—that an important aspect of a child's value was an economic one.

THE NUCLEAR FAMILY
IN TAPPAN, 1702

A census of Orange County taken in 1702, fifteen years after the Harings settled in Tappan, reveals that all of the forty or so households in the county were nuclear families, not extended and not "stem" families. Married couples, that is to say, normally lived with their children, apart from all other relatives. (A "stem family," as opposed to a nuclear family, occurs when a son marries and moves in with his parents, raises the next generation, and inherits the homestead. There is evidence of stem families in the Haring third, fourth, and fifth generations, but not in the settler generation. Use of the term "extended family" in this work refers not to the trigenerational stem family, but rather to the network of households of related kin living in the community.)[32]

In the census of 1702 (see Figure 3.1), four separate and nuclear Haring households are discernible. (We will consider only Haring male-headed households. Haring women, once married, formed new families with their husbands.) Peter Haring, age thirty-eight, lived with "His Wiffe, 1 Child [i.e., a son, and] 5 gerlls" (daughters). Cosyn, thirty-three, had a wife, 2 sons, and 2 daughters. Cornelius, thirty, had a wife, 1 son and 4 daughters. Daniel De Clark, with the Harings' mother and two children, constituted a fourth "Haring" household—which possibly also included the youngest Haring brother, Abraham, age twenty-one, who was not yet married. (Abraham and his stepbrother Jacob d Clerque are listed immediately after the De Clarks and may have lived under the same roof or in bachelor quarters on the property.)

Only in old age in this community—as in most colonial American communities—were parents likely to live with a married child, although never-married adults, orphaned, disabled, or otherwise helpless kin, and the widowed often shared a roof with their relatives. As the Harings' father was dead and their mother remarried, they did not have to confront this particular problem. If they had been faced with it, Grietje Cosyns Haring De Clark no doubt would have made her home with one of her seven children.

Three Tappan widows were able to fill a vacancy in their married children's households in 1702, at the same time as they found

47

LIST OF THE INHABITANTS IN THE COUNTY OF ORANGE. 1702.

	Males from 16 To 60.	Males men Above 60:	ffemale women	Males Childeren	ffemales children	Males Negros	ffemales Negros	Males negros Children	ffemales Negros Children
	William Merritt		Margry His Wijff			4 Men	1 Women	1 Child	2 Gerls.
Daniel D. Clerque .			Geretje His Wijff	1 Child .	1 Mayd	1 Men	1 Women	1 Child	1 Gerl .
Jacob d Clerque .									
Abram Hearingh .									
Thomis Van Howtten			Trijntje His Wijffe	1 Child .	6 Mayds		1 Women	1 Child	
Roloff Van Howtten									
Claes Van Howtten									
Hendrick Geritssen			Mary His Wijfe .	3 Children					
John Hendrickssen .									
Herman Hendrickssen									
Geridt Hendricssen .									
Lambert Arianssen .			Margrit His Wiffe	2 Childeren	4 gerells				1 gerell
Geridt Lambertzen .									
Lowe Reynerssen .	Reyn Janzen .		Lysbeth His Wijffe	1 Child .	1 gerell				1 gerrell
Thonis Taelman .			Brechtie His Wyffe		3 gerells	2 Men			
			Dirckje A Widow				1 Women		
Caspar Janssen . .			May His Wyffe .	3 Childeren					
Johan Classen . .			Trijntie His Wyffe		3 gerells			1 Child	
Johanns Gerissen .			Cathrin His Wiffe	6 Childeren	2 gerells				
Jacob Cool . .			Barbara His Wiffe	2 Childeren	2 gerells				
Coenrat Hanssen . .			Leuntje His Wiffe	1 Child .	1 gerell				
Reijnier Mijnerssen			Mary His Wiffe .		1 gerell			1 Child	
Dirck Straat .			Tryntje His Wiffe	1 Child .	1 gerell			1 Child	
Cornelis Hearingh .			Cathe His Wiffe	1 Child .	4 gerls .	1 Men			
Cosyn Hearingh .			Mary His Wiffe .	2 Childeren	2 gerls .		1 Women		
Jacob Flierboom .			Marlj His Wiffe .		1 gerll .				
Samuel Conklijn .			Hanna His Wiffe .	1 Child .	3 gerells	1 Men			
Abram Blauvelt . .			Gritje His Wiffe .	4 Children	3 gerlls				
John: Waard .			Gritje His Wiffe .		3 gerlls				
Isaac Gerissen . .			Mary His Wiffe .	1 Child .					
Pieter Hearingh .			Gritje His Wiffe .	1 Child .	6 gerlls	1 men			
Jeremiah Ceniff . .			Anna His Wiffe .	3 Childen	3 gerlls				
John D'puy .			Janneke His Wiffe	3 Childeren	3 gerlls				
John: d'fries . . .			Ariantje His Wiffe	2 Children	2 gerlls				
Gerritt Huijbrechts									
John: Meijer .			Antje A Wedow .	2 Childeren	3 gerlls	1 Men			1 Gerll
Poulus Tjurckssen .									
John: Hey . .			Trijntje A Wedow		2 Gerlls				
Melchert Casperssen			Gertruyt His Wife	2 Children	2 Gerlls				
Jeurian Melgertssen									
John: Perre . . .			Sara His Wiffe .	1 Child .	3 Gerells				
Jemes Weller . .			Bethe His Wiffe .	3 Childen					
Isaac Brett . .			Magdalen His Wiffe		1 Gerlls				
Will: Juell . .			Sara His Wiffe .	2 Children	4 Gerlls				
Will Juell Juner .									
		floris Crom .	Lyne His Wiffe .	1 Child .	2 Gerells				
Willem Crom . . .			Geritje His Wiffe	1 Child .					
Ariam Crom . .									
Gysbert Crom . .									
Albert Mimelay . .			Meenske His Wiffe		6 Gerlls	1 Men		1 Child:	
Cornlis Coeper . .			Altje His Wiffe .	4 Children	7 Gerlls	1 Men	2 Women		
			Sara Crab Widow	2 Children	1 Gerll				
Edward Mek . . .									
		frans Wey .	Indian w : His Wiffe						
		Dirck Storm .	Mery His Wife .						
Coms to 49 men . .		Coms to 5 men	Coms to 40 Wiffe	Coms to 57 Childr:	Coms to 84 gerlls	Coms to 13 men	Coms to Women	Coms to 7 Childes	Coms to 7 gerels	Coms to 6 gerels

In the Countij Orange the 16th Day of Junij 1702. This ji a Trew ACount off all the Males and ffemales off Men Women and Childeren

WITNESS OUWER HAND . . . .   WILL MERRETT
                                          DANIEL DE KLERCK

Pr: Order of the Justices
the paes   Dit is ℟ het marck van   } Justices.
          D. STORM CI.:

[Endorsed] This is a Trieuw Acount of the County Orange.   THEUNIS ROELOFFZEN VAN HOWTEN
                                                            CORNELIS CLASEN

Figure 3.1. Census of Orange County, N.Y., 1702.

shelter and companionship by being with or near their sons. Although the widow Sarah Crab lived alone with her three young children, Dirckje Talman lived with or next door to her married son, and the widows Antje Meijer and Trijintje Hey lived with and probably kept house for their widowed sons. Reyn Janzen, a widower, lived with his married son.

48

A MIXTURE OF MANY NATIONS

Marriage, census, and other information gleaned from the public record about the Harings and their fellow settlers in Tappan challenges the familiar stereotype of the rural "Dutchman" in the Hackensack and lower Hudson valleys as a clannish Hollander moving away from New York to preserve his Dutchness in an isolated ethnic enclave. If Manhattan was a melting pot in the seventeenth century, Tappan was a melting pot, too, and from the beginning of settlement. Support for the idea that the Haring family's move transcended ethnic considerations comes most strikingly from the fact that, of the other families from the Outward who joined it in removing to the Tappan Patent in 1683, three were not Dutch, not even European, and not even Caucasian. They were free blacks—the De Vries and the Manuels—who owned their own land in New Amsterdam, whose farms there adjoined the farms of some of the other patentees, and who like them were members of the New York Dutch Reformed Church. The Tappan Patent may have been the only settlement in colonial America in which blacks and whites alike shared in the ownership of land.

Additional support that the patentees did not resettle in Tappan in an attempt to flee the melting pot of New York comes from another quarter too: When they got to Tappan, the patentees readily sold surplus land to outsiders, and they showed no resistance to marrying into families with French, German, Scandinavian, or even British backgrounds. Economic factors were more important than ethnic ones in choosing marriage partners.

It has been amply demonstrated that the Dutch in seventeenth-century America were not, in fact, nearly so Dutch as they seemed.[33] Many of the Dutch were actually ethnically disparate people who were considered Dutch because, for a generation or even two, they had lived in the Netherlands, a haven in the seventeenth century for political, religious, and economic refugees from all over Europe. If life was unkind to them in the Netherlands, America held out another new promise.[34] In the meantime, they had acquired the ability to speak Dutch and had often affiliated with the Dutch church. When they arrived in New Netherland on ships from Dutch ports, they were "Dutch" in name, though often not in fact. They had also assimilated much of Dutch culture, habits, manners, and customs, and they tended to retain this culture as their own, even in America.

49

As the fabric of the Haring family's life is investigated, it becomes apparent that the Dutch freely borrowed from other continental cultures and from the ruling English culture as well. The "Dutchness" of the society the settlers created in Tappan was thus a hybrid phenomenon: a new American thing, not a replica of an old Dutch one. This, of course, renders all the more curious the persistence of Dutchness into the nineteenth century in the Hudson and Hackensack valleys and lends force to the notion that the Dutch farmers and their descendants were, at least on some level, ambivalent about America and about becoming American.

THE SLAVE FAMILY IN TAPPAN

Free blacks were an important part of the Tappan community from the beginning, but the ideal of family life enjoyed by the Harings and their friends was not permitted to the slave population of Tappan. Thirty-three "Negros"—13 adult males, 7 adult females, 7 boys, and 6 girls—were among the enumerated inhabitants of Tappan in 1702. But the census documents that only two slaveowners, William Merritt and Daniel De Clark, owned what could have been a complete slave "family"—defined here as containing at least one adult male, one adult female, and one child.

Most black families were split up—albeit, one would like to believe, in at least some cases with an effort to keep them within one larger owner family. For instance, Cornelius Haring owned a male slave; his brother Cosyn, on an adjoining farm, owned a female one; and these two slaves may have been husband and wife. In three cases, an adult slave and a slave child (possibly parent and offspring) lived in the same free family; but three slave boys and two slave girls were owned by free families that owned no adult slave, and some families owned adult slaves, but no children. Whether any attempt was made to keep siblings together cannot be determined. The only known free-black male in the county in 1702, the patentee John De Vries, did not himself own a slave.

This glimpse into Haring demographics reveals the family to have been a kinship network of separate households situated in close geographic proximity to one another and to kinship networks of other families often related to it by ties of blood and marriage. This form of organization was functional: as each family member found shelter and nourishment under his or her own family's roof, so did the many individual families derive benefits

50

from their association under the larger umbrella formed by all of the families in the cooperative venture.

Finally, it must be repeated that although this study concentrates on the male lines, Haring women are important for the purpose of describing how a large and growing family in early America acted. The sisters did not simply disappear from the scene, or become extraneous to the family's character. For the most part, they, like their brothers, settled in Tappan or in nearby Bergen County, N.J., marrying into the same families that their brothers, uncles, and nephews married into as well as into the families of other large landowners and of newcomers to whom the original families sold land. Sometimes, the children of Haring women married their brothers' children—their first cousins. In many more cases, their grandchildren married their brothers' and sisters' grandchildren—their second cousins. In this way, the family enlarged itself in overlapping circles of cousinships and deepened itself in increasingly complicated relations to the land, as women saw their own descendants, both male and female, come into the ownership of property that, but for the fact of gender, might have been their own to bequeath. And, as we will see in the next chapter, women—wives, mothers, and daughters—were very important as the practical and emblematic keepers of hearth and home.

Part Two

THE SECOND AND THIRD
GENERATIONS

Chapter Four

"A Gallant Plentifull Country"

Were Thomas Jefferson to "indulge his own theory" of the yeoman ideal of America as an agrarian paradise, "all our citizens would be husbandmen" happily plowing their long, neat furrows. But the reality of a farmer's life, as Jefferson himself knew from personal experience, was far from idyllic. Before the plow could turn the neat furrow, the hideous wilderness had to be tamed.[1]

The "gallant and plentifull country" extolled in seventeenth-century promotional literature enticed settlers like the Harings with a wealth of opportunity that could be realized only at great personal risk and with a staggering amount of hard labor. By brute force land had to be cleared, a crop or two planted immediately to ensure a source of food, and shelter erected against the elements and the wildlife. And all three tasks had to be accomplished nearly simultaneously. Settling into the American wilderness was, literally, a radical experience in that it went to the root matter of human existence: survival.

CLEARING THE LAND

Tappan lay close enough to Manhattan that the patentees in 1683 could leave their wives and young children in the Out-ward while they and their older sons spent a spring and summer feverishly clearing land and planting fields. In his first season in Burlington, in East Jersey, a contemporary reported on his activities: "I shall have fenc'd and clear'd a Quarter of a Mile this Summer. I have set Four Acres of Indian-Corn; and in the Fall, I shall Plow Twelve Acres of Wheat, and Six of Pease."[2]

Planting the first survival crops had to be preceded by land clearing, the methods for which varied depending on the type of timber on the land. In the lower Hudson Valley, where beech, birch, basswood, maple, and butternut were plentiful, farmers were advised to cut trees into logs of about twelve feet, to set aside enough for fence rails and fuel, and to pile the rest in heaps to burn, using the ashes as fertilizer. Then, before the land could be plowed, harrowed, and cultivated, underbrush had to be cut and burned or otherwise cleared away. On land covered with scrub oak, which was considered the most difficult type to clear because of the oak's deep and persistent root stubs, the farmer was advised to cut, plow, and harrow "as well as you can," then put in a crop of wheat or rye, and the following July or August cut the oak sprouts and try to uproot the stubs. To get rid of the stubs and sprouts, the farmer could confine sheep to small portions of a field in turn, where they would eat the sprouts in two days and eventually "subdue" a large field in this manner.[3]

Land could be cleared only gradually, and it was a despised, laborious task that was literally never done, for a cleared field could revert to bush in a single year and could be a full-grown forest again in twenty. A melancholy testimony to the depredations of nature and the necessity for the farmer's unceasing labor is found in the description of a Hudson Valley farm neglected for only one year. In 1755, the administrators of the estate of Rachel Wileman, a widow and lunatic, urged the court to let them sell it in that "no Rents or Yearly profitts [are] arising out of the . . . Lands to pay the Annual Intourest that will become Due, that the parsonal Estate is Dwindling away, and the fences and Improvements on the farm [are] going to Decay[,] that there is no Crop Sown this fall to Support Labourers and Negroes to Repair the fences and Take Care of the Improvements and there is no Sufficient provision made for keeping the Stock this winter."[4]

In a nutshell, these were the life tasks of the Haring brothers as they took up their Orange County lands: to clear and plant their acres, and to keep doing so year in and year out, so that they could sell enough of their surpluses to make a "Yearly profitt," so that in turn they could maintain their improvements, feed and shelter their families and their workers and *their* families, and feed and shelter their livestock. Only when the farmer could make a return on his investment could families survive and prosper. If he lost money, he failed and disappeared from the scene. If he broke even, he might stay or not, but his existence would be a subsistence one. He could count himself among those who would rise only if he could sell his surpluses. For only in this way could he afford to develop and improve his holdings, purchase seed, tools, livestock, and slaves; hire labor; and acquire the niceties to make his life more comfortable than that of his poorer neighbors. That the Haring brothers succeeded in this direction can be judged on one level by the houses, barns, and outbuildings they constructed.

BUILDING HOUSES

During their first frantic season at Tappan, the Harings and their fellow patentees may have "nestled rather than dwelt" in temporary pits dug in the ground, cased around inside with timber and bark, and roofed with bark laid over raised spars. Pit shelters were known in Europe from the Middle Ages, and this is how the first settlers in both New Netherland and New England are known to have lived until they could build more permanent housing.[5]

Recent archaeological excavations of a number of seventeenth-century house sites in Dutch-settled communities in New Netherland have uncovered pit houses with floors and walls of wooden boards in direct contact with the earth. As they were able, the settlers built a more permanent abode above the pit. Excavators of a house site north of Albany discovered a wood-lined cellar hole dating from the 1670s, brick footings to support the above-ground structure built over the hole, and wooden steps leading into the cellar. Another such house, built by an ordinary citizen of Albany in about 1651, indicates that the settlers appreciated comfort and aesthetic qualities even in very simple domiciles. In the archaeological rubble of this house were found delft tiles and glazed, leaded windows with enamel-painted decoration.[6] In Tappan, families long used to the comforts of life in New Amsterdam and New York would have constructed above-ground houses as soon as they could. Although no literary or archaeological evidence exists to indicate exactly what the settlers first built in Tappan, by 1700 at least one of them, Daniel De Clark, had erected a handsome stone and brick house, still standing

By as early as 1628, farmers in New Netherlands were building above-ground farmsteads large enough to house under one roof both the farmer's family and his livestock. Like the pit house, the combination house-barn was a transient architectural form. Evidence for it comes primarily from contracts. One contract from

1641, between farmer Joannes Winckelman and his carpenters for a "bouwhuys" in the Achter Col Colony on the Hackensack, not far from Tappan, calls for a timber building ninety feet long and twenty-four feet wide, with two "aisles," also ninety feet long, and nine and ten feet wide respectively, appended to the sides. The aisles were to contain stalls for farm animals. The family would live in the central portion. There were to be three doors in each aisle, according to the specifications, and at the end of the building a wide wagon entrance above which was to be an "opening to pitch hay and straw in." The contract specified windows and a stairway "straight up to the garret," part of which was to be used as a family sleeping-and-storage area. Such houses as this had a long history in the Netherlands.[7]

The first "real" houses in New Netherland were built of timber—the side walls of horizontal boards or clapboards. Building contracts and deeds document three types of house by the middle of the seventeenth century: the narrow, single-side-aisle house; the two-aisle house; and the three-aisle house. The side aisles, it is conjectured, were used as halls for built-in beds. Anchor-beam construction permitted interior partitions to be placed according to the family's needs.[8]

In Tappan, the first documented houses were vertically organized structures of roughly eighteen square feet ($18' \times 20'$), comprising a storage cellar, a ground-level living-sleeping-cooking area, and an overhead garret reached by a ladder. Some of the poorer among the earliest inhabitants undoubtedly lived in such lowly one-room dwellings throughout their life on the land. But settlers of greater means lived accordingly. Investigation of the Tappan area has revealed a variety of house types there suited to every pocketbook.

A comprehensive survey of the early houses in Bergen County has identified several basic house configurations, ranging in style from the very simple to the very comfortable. For the seventeenth and eighteenth centuries, these include the one-room house, the two-room/twin-door house, and the four-room/twin-door house as well as the more elaborate two-room/center-hall house, the four-room/center-hall house with gable-end chimneys, the four-room/center-hall house with interior chimneys, and two-and three-room side-hall houses.[9]

The basic one-room unit, the simplest, most economical module, was built in all the colonies by all settlers, not just those in New Netherland. It was built in Tappan, sometimes with a side extension, consistently from the late seventeenth century through the eighteenth century. The two-room/twin-door model began to appear, according to the "Stone House Survey," in the first half of the eighteenth century. However, with one possible exception, discussed below, no twin-door houses erected before 1740 are extant. Clues to their having existed earlier come mainly from sketches found on survey maps.[10]

Twin-door houses are rare in the Netherlands, but they were quite common in rural areas settled by the Dutch in New Netherland, particularly in the Hackensack and Hudson valleys. Their function is not explicitly stated in any known document, but as families were much larger in New Netherland than in the Netherlands during the comparable period, logic suggests they may have been designed either to accommodate two generations of the same family or to serve the habits and needs of one large family with offspring ranging in age from infancy to adult. Most two-room/twin-door houses were built as such, although some were created by the addition of a second unit to one already standing. Likewise, most of the four-room/twin-door houses were built as such, while a few were created by extending the house at the rear.

HARING HOUSES: THE FIRST GENERATION IN TAPPAN

The house in Tappan that was considered the most suitable for General George Washington to stay in on four occasions during the Revolution was built by the Harings' stepfather, the patentee Daniel De Clark, in 1700 (see Figure 4.1). Built on the two-room/center-hall plan, De Clark's house is still standing, the year of its erection, 1700, set in brick into the west-facing façade. Of stone and brick, with a "medieval-style," steeply pitched gable roof, its central hall is flanked by two good-size rooms, each with two windows on the front and one window on the rear. The room on the left, with plaster walls, hand-hewn ceiling beams, brick floor, and a large, utilitarian fireplace, served as a kitchen. The room on the right has a planked flooring and a fireplace inlaid with nearly a hundred purple Dutch tiles depicting biblical scenes. A staircase off the center hall leads upstairs to another hall and two bedrooms. A circa-1840 painting of the house (Figure 4.1) shows a wing on the north end, possibly a kitchen wing.[11]

The fireplace was the hub around which rural farm life revolved. Used both for cooking and for heating, fireplaces in Orange and Bergen counties were customarily located on the

Figure 4.1. House of Daniel De Clark, 1700. Oil on canvas by Cornelius L. VerBryck, c. 1840. Photo courtesy Lynn S. Beman.

Figure 4.2. Kitchen, De Clark's House. Courtesy Tappantown Historical Society.

interior of gable-end walls, as in De Clark's house (see Figure 4.2). In New England, because of the more severe winters, the fireplace would be placed at the center of the house; in the southern colonies, outside the house altogether. The weight of the hearth or chimney, whether of the jambed or jambless type, was received in the cellar by massive stone arches. The jambless fireplaces of the Dutch, though, were "built in an unusual way . . . [and] consisted of nothing more than the wall of the house. . . . There were no projections [jambs] on the sides of the fireplace, so it was possible to sit on all three sides of the fire and enjoy the warmth equally." The disadvantage of the unjambed, undampered fireplace, of course, was that there was nothing to prevent smoke from entering the room when the house doors or windows were opened.[12]

A visitor to Manhattan in 1704, just four years after De Clark's house was built in Tappan, described the interior of a Dutch house there as

neat to admiration, the wooden work, for only the walls are plastered, and the Sumers and Gist[s] [beams and joists, or ceiling supports] are plained and kept white scower'd as so is all the partitions. . . . The fire-places have no Jambs [as in English style]. . . . But the Backs run flush with the walls, and the Hearth is of Tyles and is as farr out into the

61

Room at the Ends as before the fire, [which] is Generally Five foot. . . ."[13]

A brick baking, or "beehive," oven projected through the wall to the outside of the dwelling.

The early houses in Tappan had gable roofs—like De Clark's. The famous gambrel roof did not appear before the mid-eighteenth century and was intended to enlarge the headroom in the upper story and to make private the sleeping quarters of the family. The gambrel roof has no prototype in the Netherlands, contrary to common opinion, although it does have one in England— a reminder of the cultural borrowing so common in the lower Hudson and Hackensack valleys, where Dutch and English lived as neighbors.[14] (In the upper Hudson Valley, where the Dutch were more isolated from the English, the gambrel roof is far less common than in the area where the Harings settled.)

The house plan that De Clark chose in 1700, the two-room/ center-hall style, may have been widely used by the earliest settlers, though only, of course, by those of means, as its two spacious halls were a luxury requiring extra building materials and labor that only the more affluent could afford. Nevertheless, it was a form familiar to all the settlers, for it was in popular use in rural areas throughout the seventeenth-century Netherlands.[15]

Evidence from two wills and from the financial records of the Tappan Reformed Church suggests that the four Haring brothers, like their stepfather, were among those men able to build relatively large and comfortable homes in Tappan. In his will, written in 1733, Cosyn Haring [23] refers, in fact, to ownership of two farms, equipped with all the usual barns and outbuildings—one "old" one, where his only son lived, and one "where I do dwell at present." Evidently Cosyn had become prosperous enough by the time his son married in January 1718 to build or buy a second house and accompanying farm buildings for himself, letting his son take over the first.

Cosyn's youngest brother, Abraham [27], writing his will at age forty-five in 1752, specified that his widow was to have her "choice of one of the best rooms" in the house. That is to say, she was to have not just "a" room or "the" best room, as owners of a small and simple house might indicate, but a house with (at least) two best rooms.

And their eldest brother, Peter Haring [21], was reimbursed by the Tappan church for ten years—from 1714 to 1724—for boarding the minister on his quarterly visits. As Peter had a wife, eleven children, and a number of slaves, and was for many years a judge of the court of common pleas and a member of the New York Assembly, it can be assumed that he had the need and possessed the means to have had one of the largest and most comfortable houses in the community.[16]

From these clues—that De Clark built a center-hall house in 1700, that Cosyn owned two separate and substantial "plantations," as he called them, apparently by as early as 1718, that his brother Peter Haring's house was chosen as the best in the community for the minister's comfort on his quarterly visits, and that Abraham had a house with at least two best rooms—it is safe to conclude that the fourth brother, Judge Cornelius Haring, who appears on other evidence to have been the most affluent of the five relatives, also lived in a substantial house.

THE TWIN-DOOR HOUSE

The twin-door house, as noted above, was popular in Tappan in the eighteenth century, and several associated with the Haring family exist today. A four-room/twin-door house long considered to have been Cosyn Haring's, but now thought to have been improved by his son and perhaps his grandson, is still owned by Cosyn's descendants. Facing east-southeast on De Wolf Road in present-day Old Tappan, it is built of native sandstone cut in blocks twenty inches thick.[17] (See Figure 4.3.)

Almost square (36' 2" × 35' 3"), with a gambrel roof and two exterior front doors, the house today is of one and a half stories, but the upper story is divided into two floors, a convenience permitted by the gambrel construction. Planks laid on the wind-beams divide the under-roof space into a conventional "upstairs," for bedrooms, with an attic over them. The attic, or garret, served as important storage space in the house. In a Haring house of similar size and construction, built in nearby Pascack by Abraham G. Haring [592] in about 1790, the contents of the garret were described by a descendant:

> Nuts of all kinds were there stored in baskets and bags, apples and pears in their season, [and] bags of dried apples and beans. Spinning wheels, . . . spare ribs and sausage, bacon and hams, bundles of broom corn for brooms and field corn on the cob for the next year's planting, garden seeds and herbs of many kinds, boxes and barrels and chests, and

Figure 4.3. Twin-Door Haring-DeWolf House. Courtesy Library of Congress.

irons and drums, sleigh bells large enough to be heard a mile distant, harness, tin horns, robes and whips, stepladders and stoves, candle moulds and sausage stuffers, hand sleds and cradles. . . .[18]

The wing on the left of the Haring-DeWolf house may have replaced an earlier wing or even a self-contained dwelling that was used as a kitchen after the main structure was built. A feature of Dutch houses from the Middle Ages was the detached kitchen, or "kitchen in the garden." In describing the sandstone house built by his great-grandfather, John J. Haring [8131] recalled that "nearly every house [like it had] a small, square, stone structure known as the out-kitchen." In the boyhood of his great-grandfather, who was born in 1755, "these kitchens were largely appropriated to the use of the colored people." When the day came that "funeral sermons were preached over the old slaves . . . the out kitchen continued for years following to present the scenes of family laundering and cooking."[19]

The two front rooms in this twin-door house communicated by an interior door, and both served as living-eating-sleeping rooms, while the two smaller rooms behind them were used either as bedrooms, birthing rooms, storage areas, or all three. As mentioned above, two families or two generations of a family could share a house on this plan, with the separate outside entrances and the communicating interior door between the two front rooms providing privacy for both. On the other hand, one large family could spread out in it. Access to the upper rooms in this house was by a set of steep stairs, and to the cellar by an exterior entrance and bulkhead stairs. Like the twin-door façade, this last feature was rare in the Netherlands, except in Zeeland, but quite common in rural Dutch houses in America.[20]

Characteristics of the Dutch farmhouses in eighteenth-century Bergen and Orange counties are the extended eaves, seen in Figure 4.3. Eaves, which serve an obvious utilitarian purpose, are of ancient origin. Etymologically, the word has roots in Old English, Old Frisian, Flemish, Old High German, and Old Norse and is defined as the edge of the roof of a building, or the edge of the thatch overhanging a haystack. In houses with mud-mortared walls, like those of the Dutch in the Hackensack Valley, and with exterior openings into the cellar, longer eaves were a more effective shield from the rain. Very long eaves were supported by columns, posts, or pillars. One traveler through Bergen County in 1778 commented on the stone houses and their pillared "airy piazza[s]"—the roof of the piazza or veranda being, of course, the extended eave. Even more interesting, recent research on the Jan Martense Schenck house, built in Brooklyn, circa 1675, reveals that its open veranda was originally a closed-in side aisle.[21] Thus, it seems that the side aisle used in rural Dutch architecture in the days when man and beast sheltered under the same roof, and later specified in the New Netherland house contracts, continued to evolve. Like the "kitchen in the garden," the veranda became both another room out-of-doors, serving both to expand the living, working, and storage areas of the Dutch settler's crowded house and to keep out the fierce summer sun of the forty-first latitude.

A four-room house the size of the Haring-DeWolf house was an ambitious undertaking in the early eighteenth century. Cadwallader Colden of Orange County built a smaller house (Colden's was 24' × 33') in 1732 and employed two men for three and a half weeks to dig an eight-foot-deep cellar, two carpenters and an apprentice for another three weeks to frame out and raise the house, and the carpenter and his apprentice another six weeks to finish the siding and roof and the interior plastering and woodwork.[22]

In time, the compartmentalization of space, with its separate wing or room for cooking and its separate rooms for sleeping, eventually became a standard feature even of mean dwellings. But although the Harings probably cooked in an area designed specifically for the purpose and may have had separate bedrooms earlier than many eighteenth-century families, the contents of their inventories, and the inventories of other Dutch-descended families in the area, make it clear that they also continued to use the main downstairs rooms for eating, living, and sleeping throughout the entire eighteenth century—perhaps a testimony to the persistence of their ideal of family cohesion and intimacy.

INTERIORS

No firsthand descriptions exist of the interior furnishings of Hackensack and lower Hudson Valley houses from the early eighteenth century, but wills, inventories, and other written evidence indicate that these houses and their simple, utilitarian appointments were passed down from generation to generation. Each new bride, of course, also contributed her "outset" (home furnishings for setting out on married life) to the household, so that worn-out furniture was continually replaced—with items of the same design. Thus, the contents of the brothers' houses in, say 1720, can be known rather closely from an inventory made in 1798 at the death of Cosyn's grandson, Johannes [451], who was born in 1720! With few exceptions, all of the furnishings in Johannes's house when he died in 1798 and all of the tools and implements in the barns had been available to the prosperous farmer in the early part of the eighteenth century; and, from what can be deduced about the four Haring brothers' relative economic standing among the inhabitants of Orange County, they were among those most able to have afforded them.[23]

First, it is clear from the groupings in Johannes's inventory that the two main rooms on the first floor of his house were still being used in 1798, when the inventory was made, as multipurpose chambers, with eating, sleeping, and everyday activities in general being conducted in both rooms, although the cooking operations probably took place in a wing off the main room or in a freestanding structure designed for that purpose. Some members of the family slept in the smaller rear rooms and in the chambers on the second story.

Kitchen equipment was of iron and stone manufacture and included several iron pots, a griddle, two tea kettles, four stone pots, four stone jugs, tongs, pans, pails, kegs, and sieves. A buttermilk cask, the tea kettles, a coffee mill, and a decanter with wine glasses indicate that the family enjoyed a variety of beverages. They ate off pewter plates, probably with spoons only, for no other cutlery is mentioned. Food was brought to the table on pewter platters and in earthenware bowls, and tumblers and tankards held their libations. Some of the appointments of a typical kitchen can be seen in Figure 4.4.

The two main rooms in Johannes's house contained between them three bedsteads, four small chests, a stand, fourteen chairs, a table and benches, one large chest, a common table, an oval table, various small trunks, a set of fire tools (andirons, tongs, shovel, and bellows), a stove (one item not available in the early part of the century), and a large Dutch cupboard, or "kas." Some of this furniture, such as the massive kas shown in Figure 4.5, would have been made by local artisans after Dutch prototypes and were a standard part of the outset of every young woman whose parents could afford to provide one. A looking glass, six silver teaspoons, and an eight-day clock worth the large sum of £20 were luxury items available only to the more prosperous members of the farming class, although other nonutilitarian

67

Figure 4.4. Kitchen, House of John A. Haring [5208]. Originally this was the kitchen of a one-room sandstone house built on Haring land, c. 1776, and later incorporated into an expanded house, still standing in Rockleigh, N.J. Photo, c. 1912, from Emma Winner Rogers, *The Journal of a Country Woman* (New York, 1914).

Figure 4.5. An Eighteenth-Century Bergen County Kas. Photo courtesy Bernard & S. Dean Levy, Inc., New York.

articles, such as rugs and curtains, are not mentioned. Women's work is easily identified as spinning and weaving (in addition to all their other domestic occupations) by the presence of three spinning wheels, a loom, two hetchels (iron-toothed instruments for combing flax and hemp), and quantities of flax, tow, woolen yarn, tow thread, and wool cards.

THE KAS

In 1778, one observer of the Dutch in Bergen County described such furnishings as "of the most ordinary kind, and such as might be supposed to accord with the fashion of the days of Queen Anne." In a Dutch American household, however, at least one of these items, the kas—massive, stately, paneled, corniced, and sometimes painted and decorated—was hardly "ordinary." Both physically and symbolically it was the largest and most imposing piece of furniture in the house.[24]

The kas, a particularly enduring form among the Dutch in America, was made by them (and their descendants) from the seventeenth well into the nineteenth century. Its significance went beyond utility into the realm of the symbolic, and on several levels. The commodious cupboard, its ample and well-stocked interior bursting with linens, blankets, petticoats, and porcelain, represented the householder's plenty and was a conspicuous testimony to his industry and affluence. On another level, the kas represented a symbolic link with tradition, for the design was remembered by the Dutch in America from their past in the Netherlands. Moreover, as a traditional part of the bride's outset, or dowery, the kas had a symbolic association with wife, mother, hearth and home. Some renditions of this cupboard were even painted and decorated with pomegranates, a traditional fertility symbol. Like cozy, curtained feather beds, lovingly woven coverlids, pewter bowls, dishes, cups, and decorative, carved spoon racks, the idea for and memory of these ubiquitous items in Dutch American inventories traveled with the settlers from their Netherlandish seventeenth-century past into their American future. The persistence of the kas—and of other enduring domestic objects—was, as one investigator of Dutch material culture in American has noted, consistent with the desire that one's "home" continue without change from generation to generation.[25] The house in Figure 4.3, still owned today by descendants of Cosyn and Johannes Haring, contains in the east front room an eighteenth-century sweet-gum kas.

Excavation of a Tappan house site would undoubtedly uncover the same types of household artifacts found in abundance at excavated sites in other Dutch-settled areas of New York: common, undecorated, lead-glazed redware pipkins; pans, colanders, frying pans and pitchers; slip-decorated redware, glazed and decorated earthenware; stoneware drinking vessels and jugs; and majolica, faience, and Ming-influenced tin-glazed bowls and plates. Metal utensils (particularly pewter, but also brass, copper, tin, and iron), traces of wooden utility and eating vessels, as well as clear- and colored-glass goblets or *roemers*, bottles, beakers, and beads are evidence of the array of consumer items available to the settlers, even in the wilderness and even in the seventeenth century.[26]

BARNS AND BARRACKS

If the Dutch housewife in America clung to her traditional domestic objects and forms, so did her yeoman husband cling to familiar outdoor structures and implements, albeit with variations to suit local conditions. Thus the Dutch barn in New York and New Jersey has its prototype in the Netherlands in the so-called *hallehuis* (or "open house") barn, an aisled H-frame structure, whose sides were designed for cattle, its central nave for threshing—and, originally, partially for human habitation—and its overhead loft space for grain storage. Large doors at the gable end allowed loaded wagons to pass directly onto the threshing floor and out again.[27] (See Figure 4.6.)

A reconstructed perspective view of Winckelman's ten-bent, ninety-foot-long barn of 1641 underscores its resemblance to eighteenth-century New York and New Jersey Dutch barns, a few of which are still standing. On the other hand, John Fitchen found Old World and New World Dutch barns to differ in no fewer than sixteen ways! Like its owner-builder, the Dutch barn looked to the past as well as to the future; it remembered its origins and adapted to its new environment.[28]

The Dutch American barn of the Hudson and Hackensack valleys was much remarked upon by travelers through the area, and the barn of Abraham Haring [27], on the main road from Tappan to Hackensack (Tappan Road), was probably among those most admired by passersby, for Abraham's will reveals that his widow was to have "roome in [it] for ten Head of Cattle," still leaving ample space for the cattle of the son who lived on the farm and inherited it. (A typical poorer testator might be able to leave his wife only one "milch cow" and no stable space.)

At the same time that Abraham was writing his will (1752) and describing his handsome barn, the Swedish naturalist Peter Kalm, traveling (1748–1751) through the Hudson Valley down toward Trenton, New Brunswick, and Princeton, N.J., described the Dutch barns he saw. They were, he wrote,

71

Figure 4.6. Bergen County H-Frame, Dutch-Style Barn. Courtesy C. K. Tholl and Bergen County Historical Society.

very large almost the size of a small church; the roof was high, covered with wooden shingles, sloping on both sides, but not steep. The walls which supported it were not much higher than a full grown man; but on the other hand the breadth of the building was all the greater. In the middle was the threshing floor and above it, or in the loft or garret, they put the unthrashed grain, the straw, or anything else, according to the season. On one side were stables for the horses, and on the other for the cows. The young stock had also their particular stables or stalls, and in both ends of the building were large doors, so that one could drive in with a cart and horses through one of them, and go out at the other. Here under one roof therefore were the thrashing floor, the barn, the stables, the hay loft, the coach house, etc.[29]

The Dutch stored grain in their barns, but hay in hay barracks, which are mentioned in virtually every deed of the period from Dutch-settled areas and which were so useful that they were adopted by farmers of all ethnic backgrounds. (Cadwallader Colden refers to his barracks many times in his farm journal.) These unique structures were considered "Excellent for the pre-servation of Corn & in some degree defends it from Vermin." By means of pulleys, ropes, and winches, the adjustable roof could be raised and lowered against the "hasty rains . . . common hear in Summer"; and if the bottom "room" were floored and boarded around, two head of cattle could be sheltered in it.[30]

In addition to large three-aisle barns, sheep barns, and hay barracks, it is known from contemporary references that Haring farms and those like them in the early eighteenth century also had corncribs, smokehouses, springhouses, cider presses, and var-ious small, single-purpose storage coops, sheds, and workshops. A Haring farm in 1730 would have looked, then, very much like the farm in the Van Bergen overmantel, circa 1733, with (moving left to right in Figure 4.7) a barn, hay barracks, farmhouse and, off to the right, smokehouse; scattered here and there (not pictured) were all the other outbuildings characteristic of a busy farm.[31]

Some Haring farms still looked much the same in 1930. That year, the Haring-DeWolf farm in Old Tappan was visited by the Historic American Buildings Survey:

The present farm buildings consisting of barns, corn crib, wood shed, and poultry houses are grouped into a rough

73

Figure 4.7. The Van Bergen Overmantel. Courtesy New York State Historical Association, Cooperstown, N.Y.

semblance to a coutyard in the rear of the house. . . . The farm life has been carried on continuously [here] for over two hundred years. Some of the food supply is still raised on the farm. Water is provided from the well partly by hand pump at the kitchen sink, but mostly from a bucket at the end of the primitive well sweep. The wood is still chopped and stored in the wood shed for the purpose of cooking and heating. The cellar still contains its supplies of pickeled [sic] meat, vegetables, and preserves. Electricity has been installed but the primitive rural life is still in evidence. [HABS NJ-154]

PLANTING THE LAND

To generate the maximum profit from his land, one might expect that the farmer would use the most advanced agricultural methods he could. But contemporary commentators on the farmer in eighteenth-century America found that, far from doing so, he was an indifferent agriculturist—indeed, profligate with his most abundant resource, land. Apparently, the "average" or "above-average" farmer was content with his returns and felt little incentive to improve his methods and techniques in an economy in which the labor supply was short and thus expensive, in which land was plentiful and thus relatively cheap, and in which the range and quantity of goods he might consume with any additional income were not attractive enough to spur special effort or innovation. The anonymous author of *American Husbandry* flatly declared in 1775 that "American planters are in general the greatest slovens in Christendom," and of the New York farmer in particular, he wrote:

The rural management in most parts of this province is miserable: seduced by the fertility of the soil on first settling, the farmers think only of exhausting it as soon as possible. . . . [They] crop their fields with corn [cereal grains] till they are absolutely exhausted; then they leave them what they call fallow, that is, to run to weed for several years, till they think the soil has recovered somewhat of its fertility, when they begin again with corn, in succession, as long as it will bear any. . . . The extent to which this practice is carried would astonish any person used to better husbandry; it is owing to the plenty of land.[32]

On the other hand, the Dutch farmer in America seems not to have been included in such indictments. In New Netherland, in fact, the Dutch were regarded by Governor Dongan, as early as 1687, to be "great improvers of the land," and modern historians concur that the best gardeners and farmers in the American colonies were those who settled along the Hudson, Hackensack, and Mohawk rivers, where the Dutch settled. Peter Kalm, in 1748, thought that the "Dutchmen . . . in the province of New York . . . possess[ed] the greatest and best estates in that province."[33]

If the Dutch in America were good farmers, they had learned to be so in the Netherlands. Dutch agriculture was known to be the best in Europe, because the shortage of land in relation to the population had forced the Dutch farmer to import his grain and to concentrate on cattle breeding and horticulture. He also practiced deep plowing, heavy fertilizing, continuous weeding, crop rotation, and convertible husbandry (i.e., three years of planting were followed by six of pasturing) in order to make the most of his limited resource, land. Great attention was paid to drainage, to manure catching (by stall-feeding livestock, rumps to trough), and to experiments with innovative fodder crops. The Dutch led in market gardening and orcharding in Europe, introduced hops to England in the sixteenth century, developed improved methods of beekeeping, and introduced turnips and clover into the usual grain rotation in order to improve the soil's nitrogen level.[34]

In the Hudson Valley, the benefits of these various practices were understood very early in the eighteenth century. Clover seed, though reportedly unknown in some colonies even as late as the 1790s, was used to advantage by the Orange County farmer Cadwallader Colden—a friend of the Harings—at least as early as 1727 (when he began a farm journal). That year he "sow'd some of the Timothy grass on the upper Bever dam"; in October, hop clover he had sown appeared in the south end of the new field. In March 1728, Colden sowed mixed red and white clover seed, more timothy, and several patches with English clover seed. The following spring, he sowed the "place in the Meadow where the Hassocks are cut of[f]" with clover and timothy, "white cap" clover among the oats next to the timothy grass, clover in the rye field, timothy and white clover at the north end of the "Pease," and red clover in the middle and at the south end of the peas. Colden's efforts to enrich his land with the nitrogen-producing grasses enabled him to sow about 20 acres of wheat the following year with only eight bushels of seed—or two-fifths of a bushel of seed per acre. Land treated carelessly required two and three times as much seed to yield a decent crop.[35]

Contemporary descriptions of the handsome farms in the Tappan and Hackensack areas suggest that the Dutch farmers there, like Colden, also knew how to get the most out of their acreage. Certainly it is clear from Colden's farm journal and from the farm journal kept by the Verplanck family, in Dutchess County up river, that sharing and cooperation on a number of levels were common among the farmers in the Hudson Valley, the best of whom, whatever their ethnic backgrounds, seem to have been conversant with the most efficient techniques of land management. Colden names a dozen or more men, English as well as Dutch, with whom he shared and traded seeds and grafts; among the subscribers to *A New System of Husbandry* by Charles Varlo was Isaac Blanch, a Haring brother-in-law with a prominent farm just a stone's throw from Tappan; and the Verplanck journal meticulously records the published advice of various English agriculturalists. Perhaps some of the Dutch farmers and some of their farming neighbors in the New York and New Jersey river valleys were unique in their progressive attitudes toward agriculture, and perhaps their noted farms were the exception to the rule. James Lemon uncovered no reference to the *use* of timothy grass in southeastern Pennsylvania before 1740, although its value was well known, and he notes that red clover, another seed coveted for its beneficial properties, was hardly known before the 1790s.[36]

In any case, it seems safe to say that Colden on his farm of 3,000 acres in northern Orange County, the Harings on their 3,000 acres in southern Orange County, and Gouverneur Morris at Morrisania, a 3,000-acre estate across the Hudson River in Westchester County, shared a common fund of agricultural information and knew what had to be done to make their farms prosper: "You have a fine field to shew what may be done to profit on a American Farm," wrote a knowledgeable family friend to Morris, "but as much depends on Management, and the Expense properly applied." Good management required Morris (and all farmers who had to be away from their fields for long periods of time) to have a headman on the farm—a "person of abilities, honesty, knowledge and Experience to assist . . . and to direct in your Absence." It was also good practice to keep 200 acres "in constant culture," and it was recommended that this should be "well manured in four Divisions with a change of Crops after the latest . . . manner." If 200 acres were kept in constant culture, and if manured, the writer estimated that thirty-two bushels of wheat, forty bushels of barley, and from two to three tons of clover hay per acre would be produced—enough to supply the farm inhabitants and the livestock, and to have a surplus to sell in the New York markets.[37]

Manuring was one of the keys to agricultural success, and the profit-oriented eighteenth-century farmer was advised to enrich and restore his fields with everything from plaster of paris to animal entrails. The author of the Verplanck journal quotes a farmer in Elizabethtown, N.J., who "ploughed up a gravel hill wch had produced no kind of grass but Indian or poverty grass for some time before it had laid idle being so very poor a soil. . . . [After sowing] about 4 bushells of the plaster of paris [lime] on an acre with the clover seed . . . [the farmer] mowed 3 Tons of good clover hay at 2 Crops that year."[38]

Manures of all kinds were rated according to their economic value. Marl was one of the best, especially for sandy and loose soil, and "whoever finds . . . marle, finds a mine of great value [as] it is one of the best and most general manures in Nature." Clay and "Mud out of Ponds Ditches or Salt Rivers" were excellent for light soils, but had to be mixed with dung or mold and left to lie in a heap for a year. Otherwise, the substance would grow as "hard as mortar" and be of no value. Salt, applied on the winter snows so that it dissolved and soaked into the ground, was another recommended way to increase crop yields ("4 bushels will not be too much" per acre), and seaweed, salt hay, and sedge were "of incomparable excellence" if "fermented, matted, & grown mellow" by mixing them in layers with dung, mold, mud, lime, ashes, and soot. Vegetables, rotten wood, tanner's bark, sawdust, bushes, thistles, and animal flesh, entrails, blood, bones, hooves, "Baggs of their wool or hair," and urine went onto the manure pile—to be mixed in layers with dung and mud until they mellowed into the desired richness.[39] All of this effort, for the farmer who would succeed in America, was necessary in order to obtain that vital "Yearly profitt."

COOPERATION AND COMMUNITY

A profitable farm was described by Mrs. Anne Grant, who spent her childhood in prerevolutionary America and observed harvesttime at Colonel Schuyler's farm in the Hudson Valley, near Albany:

Whenever the corn or hay was reaped or cut, and ready for carrying home . . . a wagon loaded with hay . . . was driven

into the midst of . . . [the] great barn; loaded also with
numberless large grasshoppers, butterflies, and cicadas,
who came along with the hay. From the top of the wagon,
this was immediately forked up onto the loft of the barn,
[and] . . . every member of the family witnessed or assisted
in this summary process; by which the building and thatch-
ing of stacks was at once saved; and the whole crop and
cattle were thus compendiously lodged under one roof.[40]

Cooperation of many hands was essential on a farm the size
of the Harings, in early-eighteenth-century New York, and every
able member of the family, young and old, male and female,
turned out to assist—particularly at harvestime. But paid, seasonal workers were also needed, especially in the busy months
from May to November.

The agricultural year began in March. As soon as the ground
thawed, the farmer sowed his family's annual vegetable garden of
fennel, coriander, lettuce, cress, white poppy, onions, scallions,
garlic, leeks, parsnips, cabbage, carrots, spinich, and bush beans.
In April and May, seeds for savoy cabbage, Indian pepper, Indian
corn, yellow tender beans, kidney beans, and Scotch kale went
into the ground along with artichokes, sage, burnet, sweet mar-
joram, long-headed cabbage, celery, radishes, thyme, peas,
squashes, cucumbers, watermelons, and muskmelons.[41]

In June, on Colden's farm, seasonal workers arrived to prepare
the ground for buckwheat and to plant turnips in the buckwheat
fields at the same time. In the Hudson and Hackensack valleys,
July was the time to mow and gather wheat and hay into barns
and barracks, and in August and September new crops of wheat
and rye were sown. Indian corn was gathered and stored in October, and November was butchering season.

During the year from April 1728 to April 1729, Colden depended on the labor of fourteen hired workers who came and
went to sow, hoe, and mow, to reap, thresh, cradle, stack, and mill
wheat, and then convey it on horseback, sometimes in deep snow,
to Mr. Ellison's store in Newburgh, and to "work at logs" betimes.
Slaves and day laborers did the plowing and harrowing and
toiled on the ubiquitous manure pile.[42]

The owner of a farm the size of a typical Haring farm in the
eighteenth century was, in short, a busy administrator who had
to plan and coordinate everything from the acquisition of seed to
the selling of his surpluses, and schedule the efforts of all the various human beings involved to boot. He also had to deal with his

workers' problems, both physical and emotional. When Colden settled his accounts with John Williams and his man in 1729, he had to dock Williams's pay, for "his mind was so much disturb'd that he Could not work & suffer'd his man to be idle." And in May 1728, at the height of the planting season, Colden's day worker Billy Cranford took sick and could not work. Billy was sick again on June 6, 7, and 8, and Colden, a physician, "gave him a Vomit." He returned to work the following week, but his health was no better, and Colden "let him blood[,] purged him & a Parigoric after it."[43]

The farmer counted on cooperation not only from the artisans, day laborers, and seasonal workers in the area, but also from his fellow farmers. Colden experimented with seeds for various grasses and clovers, some obtained from other farmers, as well as with grafts for cherries, pears, and apples from a dozen farmers both in the Hudson Valley and in Manhattan. An apple he grafted from "Mr. Ryands house in the Bowry Lane" was commended to him as "ye best Apple in the Country . . . [called] a Golden Rennet." And even though they slaughtered some of their own livestock, some farmers, Colden included, also purchased live animals from their neighbors for slaughter. In November 1730, Colden "killed a steer we bought of John Humphreys" and another bought of Phillip Miller. Neighbors were counted on also for breeding one's livestock: "The 7th of May [1729] Bess's two year old black colt took horse of Fosters Natural paceing colt."[44]

ORCHARDS AND KITCHEN GARDENS

Haring wills from the first generation on refer to their orchards, which were of a size to furnish both the table and the market. "Upon almost every farm," according to a Haring brought up in his great-grandfather's eighteenth-century sandstone house in Pascack, near Tappan, "there was a frost-proof apple cellar built of stone, partially under ground, and thatched with straw. Into these the winter apples were placed and the door barred, not to be opened till early spring when the market price suited the owner, and the apples were then quickly shipped to the New York market." Like Abraham Hoagland's farm in the Raritan Valley, farms the size the Harings owned probably included a "large cider house, with mill and press, for home use and for the convenience of the neighbors." Hoagland's farm was well supplied with fruit: "There were all kinds of cherries, . . . thirteen different kinds of pears, also apricots, English strawberries, and all the choicer kinds of apples."[45]

Besides these fruits, orchards of Dutch farmers in the lower Hudson Valley, even as early as 1650, also contained quince, peaches, apricots, plums, berries, almonds, persimmons, and figs. Writes one observer: "I have seen Orchards so loaden with Fruit, I have wondered to see it, their very Limbs torn in pieces with the weight of their Fruit; and most Delicious to the Taste, and Lovely to behold. [Also] Peaches in such plenty that some people took their Carts a-Peach gathering."[46]

From his orchard, then, as from his arable fields and his dairy, the Orange County farmer, with his access to the New York market, could, if he practiced good management, make a tidy profit. His kitchen garden, too, fed family, farmworkers, and the inhabitants of the city. And here women participated in the farm's economy, for "not only the training of children but of plants . . . was the female province." Hardy plants such as peas and beans were grown on poles out in the cornfields among the stalks of corn, but those which required more tender cultivation were cared for by women in gardens close to the house.[47]

In the absence of a farm journal such as Colden's, one can only speculate about the precise contents of the Harings' garden crops in early-eighteenth-century Tappan, or about those of their friends and relations. Their inventories abound with references to wheat, oats, rye, buckwheat, corn, poultry, root vegetables, and beehives, and orchards are almost always mentioned in their wills, as are livestock of all available types. But evidence of the more perishable kitchen-garden items that women tended has vanished from the records, along with any mention of the ornamentals known to have been a characteristic feature of Dutch gardens, whether in the Netherlands, New Amsterdam, Rensselaerswyck, or Yonkers, across the Hudson.

Besides the kitchen garden, women were in charge of the poultry; and keeping the various barnyard fowl healthy was a time-consuming occupation, for they were susceptible to many diseases, including the pip, "cancer in the throat," flux, diarrhea, and lice, and to swellings and sore eyes from pecking at each other and from running into briar patches, cures for all of which are recorded by the author of the Verplanck farm journal. Although most accounts of colonial poultry describe them as skinny and tough, Verplanck family recipes for feeding indicate that the farm wife knew how to concoct stiff dough or pastes of buck-wheat, Indian meal, and bacon to fatten her hens and geese for the table or for market.[48]

One late-eighteenth-century source, accounts kept for the Reverend Nicholas Lansing, pastor of the Tappan Reformed Church beginning in 1786, gives a few details of local diet. The minister was supplied by neighboring farmers with the staples needed by his household, as well as with some treats. Besides the usual grains, which he purchased by the bushel, he bought potatoes and turnips, rye meal, Indian meal, and wheat flour by the hundred weight; pork, mutton, lamb, beef, and veal; codfish, shad, and clams; and butter and cider—all undoubtedly of local origin—as were his purchases of wool, flax, clover seed, and hay. Lansing's supplies of loaf sugar, rice, tea, wine, and rum were procured for him in New York by a member of the congregation acting as his agent.[49]

Profits from the sale of surpluses allowed the farmer who had a healthy balance sheet at the end of the growing season to purchase luxury food items in New York. Chocolate, allspice, pepper, rum, wine, lemons, limes, lime juice, sugar, molasses, tobacco, tea—all were conveyed by sloop and wagon through the eighteenth-century wilderness to the tables of prosperous Orange County farmers. A contemporary of the Harings, Samuel Gale, Esq., in northern Orange County, purchased all of the above-named luxuries in New York through his attorney and agent, William Wickham, and to judge from the quantities he bought, he probably resold some to his neighbors: 4 1/2 gallons of lime juice, 200 "lemmons," 200 limes, 20 pounds of allspice, 30 pounds of coffee, 20 pounds of chocolate, 20 pounds of tea.[50]

DAIRYING

Like Cadwallader Colden in Orange County and Gouverneur Morris in Westchester, the Harings were fortunate in being "handy to the New York market [not only] to dispose of all kinds of Truck besides grain, Hay potatoes and cabbages, but especially to fatten Cattle and Sheep." For the latter purpose "your headman," Morris was advised, "must be constantly buying and selling." Dairying was an integral part of a prosperous farm, and Haring wills and inventories make it clear that the family had followed a system of mixed farming (arable plus dairy) from the beginning, a recommended course not only for the foodstuffs that resulted, and for the pressing need for dung—but, as always, for profit.[51]

In 1742 when Cornelius Haring [24] left his four daughters "all my horses and couse [and] Sheep [and] hogs," he was bequeathing them a valuable asset in eighteenth-century terms. That same year an almanac published in New York calculated the "advantages of Keeping Cows":

Twenty acres divided into three Fields will keep nine Cows, which give each three Gallons of Milk per Day, which is 27 Gallons per Diem; the Whey and Buttermilk of which will keep Ten Swine. . . . By this Calculation a Cow may yield 984 Gallons of Milk per Annum, which Milk will make 200 and a half of Cheese, or else 200 lb. Butter and 100 lb. of Skim-milk Cheese.[52]

The cheese and butter and, when they were slaughtered, the swine that had been fed on the whey and buttermilk, also went to market.

A Haring descendant recorded that in those days

Every large farmer . . . produced and packed his own pork and beef. The surplus buttermilk and the odds and ends from the kitchen were utilized in the pork production, and a horned animal, bought at a low price in the summer or raised perhaps on the farm, was turned to pasture and corn-fed for a month or two in the autumn. About the last week in November . . . fat, dressed porkers were seen hanging in a row in the farmer's backyard. A week or two later, the dressed carcass of beef would be hanging in the farmer's barn.

From his "porkers" the farmer derived salted pork, hams and shoulders for smoking, bacon, sausage, "souse made from the clippings and trimmings," and "choice lard"; from the beef, salted pieces for boiling, ribs to be cooked fresh, and pieces for smoking, headcheese to be sliced and browned, and twenty or thirty pounds of odds and ends cooked, seasoned, and sewed in bags made from tripe and packed in vinegar for slicing and browning for table use.[53]

THE IDEAL YEOMAN: SUBSISTENCE FARMER OR ENTREPRENEUR?

Disagreement exists among scholars as to whether the eighteenth-century American farmer was more interested in protecting the lineal family and the family lands from the "centrifugal forces" of individual enterprise and economic competition, or whether he was an "entrepreneur" who actively pursued a profit by planting enough to generate salable surpluses for the thriving domestic and international markets.[54] Evidence indicates that the Harings as farmers were of both types. In the beginning, they were wholeheartedly entrepreneurial, moving to Tappan with the idea of participating in the market for grain, timber, and produce. As the generations wore on, they continued to be profit-oriented to the extent that opportunity permitted. If opportunity did not permit, they learned to be content with a livelihood closer to the subsistence level rather than abandon the lineal family and the family farms.

Wheat was their "main bent." As early as 1680, wheat was being shipped by sloop from Hudson Valley farms to New York markets. "At the mouth of the creek, on the shore of the river, there are some houses and a redoubt, together with a general storehouse, where the farmers bring their grain, in order that it may be conveniently shipped when the boats come up here," one traveler reported of Kingston, N.Y., in a description that could just as well apply to Tappan. In 1723, New York's Surveyor General Cadwallader Colden reported to London officials on the trade of the province. Exports included beeswax, pork, bacon, beef, butter, candles, hemp, pitch pine, white pine, and iron ore, but the main product shipped out of New York was wheat: "The Staple Commodity of the Province is Flower & Bread which is sent to all parts of the West Indies we are allowed to trade with. . . . [In addition] Several of our Neighbours upon the continent can not well subsist without our assistance as to Provisions for we yearly send Wheat & Flower to Boston & Road Island as well as to South Carolina."[55]

The treasures of the farm were many, but wheat was king. A decade later, in 1734, New York Governor William Cosby also noted that "wheat is the staple of the Province. . . . [I]ts generally manufactur'd into flower and bread, and sent to supply the sugar Collonys. . . . [T]he main bent of our farmers is to raise wheat, and they are like to remain in that way untill the price of it becomes so low, that necessity puts them upon some other way of cultivation."[56]

In 1730, as many as five markets existed within the New York City limits. The most important were the "Fly" (meat and produce) on Maiden Lane; the "Coenties" fish market in the Dock Ward; and the grain market at the foot of Wall Street. After 1741, this main grain market also offered meat for sale, "supplies for this food center coming from the Out Ward and down the North [Hudson] River from Tappan." Another account also describes the traffic between the Tappan area and the New York markets: a "fleet of small boats, filled with foodstuffs, came down the Hudson daily from Hackensack and Tappan on the Jersey shore, usually returning with the flood tide."[57]

The entrepreneurial Tappan farmer—someone, say, like Colonel Abraham A. Haring [336]—sold his surpluses in three ways: to neighbors, to local merchants, and on the New York market. In January 1733, Colden records selling thirty bushels of wheat to a Newburgh storeowner and, in June 1733, eighteen bushels of wheat to nine different individuals in his Goshen neighborhood—in amounts ranging from half a bushel to three bushels. All paid the going price in 1733 of four shillings per bushel.[58]

Wheat prices fluctuated almost daily, affected by supply and demand, which in turn were affected by the seasons, the weather, the success of the crop, price actions by city authorities, and the mood of the farmer—but particularly by political events, as we will see in Chapter 9.

In sum, when the Harings and their fellow patentees decided to leave New York in the 1680s, they chose their new land with an entrepreneurial eye, anticipating Thomas Jefferson's remark to Charles Willson Peale: "I have often thought that if heaven had given me choice of my position and calling, it should have been on a rich spot of earth, well watered, and near a good market for the productions of the garden."[59]

Whether their descendants would succeed or not would depend, however, on more than ambition and geography. As we will see, demographic, social, and political forces were to play a powerful role in the Tappan farmers' fate as the eighteenth century unfolded.

Chapter Five

A Prosperous Minority

By one definition, a "successful" family in a patrilineal society is a family that has enough male children to continue the line. According to this criterion, the Haring family was extremely successful throughout the eighteenth century, although family childbearing patterns changed along with changing economic conditions.

A DEMOGRAPHIC PROFILE

The third-generation Harings who lived to marry included thirteen males, eleven of whom had issue (and seventeen females, all of whom married and bore children). The eleven sons received farms from their fathers at marriage, and they married even younger than their patentee-generation fathers, the average age at first marriage being 22 years, 8 months, as compared to 23 years, 6 months. Wives were younger, too, 19.9 years, compared to 22.7 for the wives of their fathers' generation.[1]

These eleven men had among them 84 children, or an average of 7.6 children each, still a good many by today's standards, but dramatically down from their fathers' generation, the four brothers having produced about 10 each on average. Again, averaging obscures a wide range in numbers. Of the eleven male first cousins who had children, Elbert [310] fathered 16 by two wives, while his cousin Jacob [332] had only 1 child, and she died young. If we leave out Elbert and Jacob, three of the remaining nine third-generation men had 4, 5, and 6 children apiece, whereas three of these men had 8 children each, one had 9, and one, Daniel [330], had 10.[2]

The early marrying age of this generation reflects their fathers' ability and willingness to supply them with the means—land—to support wife and family, but the decline in the average number of children per father can be accounted for by the era's economic realities. Third-generation couples realized that, in order to provide a farm for each of their sons and suitable outsets and legacies for their daughters, they would have to purchase land for their sons without jeopardizing their means to provide for their daughters. Or, they would have to stint their daughters—for it was clear that, by the third quarter of the eighteenth century, when the very numerous fourth generation would begin to marry, all the original patent land would already have been distributed. Land prices were rising as fast as land was disappearing, but the obvious alternative, to buy cheap land far away where it was plentiful, was rejected, for that would require sons to leave the family, perhaps never to return. Thus, family limitation for these third-generation couples was not just a practical necessity. It was also an expression of the extent to which these Harings continued to share their parents' and grandparents' ideal of family closeness, cohesiveness, and communality; and it was apparently accomplished by shortening the childbearing period, increasing the interval between births, and ceasing to reproduce at an earlier age than before.

The fourth, or great-grandchild, generation comprised thirty-two males and thirty-three females as it came to maturity. Twenty-nine of the males married and received inheritances, three married twice, and two married three times—in each case owing to the decease of the wife.[3]

All but one of the twenty-nine male members of the Haring great-grandson generation received farms in Tappan or in adjacent towns from their fathers (and the one who did not, Cornelius [417], received an equivalent amount in cash). Thus, no son of this family through the fourth generation was forced to leave the area to seek his fortune elsewhere. Even in those cases where great-grandsons chose not to derive their main income from farming, they continued to live on inherited lands or on purchased properties in the community.

The average marrying age for men in the fourth generation was 26 years, 6 months, much higher than in their fathers' and grandfathers' generations, but marriage age varied widely. Roelef [4135] signed an "intention" to marry at the tender age of 19 (his bride gave birth five months later). But Jacob [473] postponed matrimony until he was nearly 42, then married a second time, and was still fathering children in his mid-sixties. The age of fifteen brides of men marrying for the first time is known. At 21.2 years, they were six years younger than their husbands, on average.

The twenty-nine fourth-generation men married a total of thirty-seven times—sixteen times to Haring women (seven), Blauvelt women (seven), and Bogert women (twice). (Their sisters married Haring men five times, Blauvelts four times, and Smiths twice.) In addition, some of the other wives were related to their Haring husbands by blood as daughters of Haring, Blauvelt, Bogert, and Smith mothers, and these marital alliances indicate that the old ideals of family closeness, neighborliness, and communality continued to be highly prized. This generation, however, also showed a very marked tendency to broaden its ranks. Besides the families named above, Haring men married into the Auryansen, Banta, Brinkerhoff, Ferdon, Goetschius, Ives, Lent, Livingston, Nagel, Peek, Sickles, Van Emburg, and Verbryck families (with which there was no previous marital connection). In addition, fourth-generation Haring women formed marital alliances with the Blanch, De Baun, De Graw, De Peyster, Eckerson, Jones, Kip, Perry, Quackenbush, Roosevelt, Van Antwerp, Wortendyke, and Zabriskie families. Old cousinships were legion, but new ones proliferated freely.[4]

Of the twenty-nine fourth-generation men who married at least once, three had no children—or at least none who appear in the baptismal rolls of the various churches with which they were affiliated. The total number of children that can be determined as having been born to the other twenty-six is 142, or 5.4 children per father, a further decline from their fathers' average. (This figure includes one set of twins and children by all marriages.)[5]

Mortality continued to be high. Only 100 of the fourth generation's 142 offspring are known to have survived to adulthood. A few others may have eluded notice in the public record, but this is indeed difficult to imagine, if they ever married or ever paid a tax. If a man left the area before marrying or before owning taxable property (even as little as one horse was taxed) and resettled elsewhere, no local record would exist, but apparently this did not happen in this family in this generation. (It is also difficult to imagine anyone who did leave eluding the intrepid genealogists who have pursued the various Bergen and Orange County families for the past century.) Even if as many as 105 of the 142 lived, the twenty-six fourth-generation child-producing males saw an average of only 4.0 of their 5.4 children survive.

These twenty-six Haring couples produced their 142 fifth-generation children over a fifty-one-year period, from 1749 to 1800, most of the births occurring in the 1770s and 1780s. The child-bearing period of their wives can be determined from baptismal records. The range was from 1 year to 27, but average length was 14.7 years, with an average interval between births of 32.4 months—considerably longer than that of the previous two generations. Although at least thirteen of the twenty-six couples produced children over a period as long as that of their parents' generations, the range for nine couples was well below their own generation's average of 14.7 years.

In sum, as their fathers and grandfathers had done, the men of the fourth generation married into a wide range of families, but they married three or four years later and had fewer children over a shorter period of time and at longer intervals.

LAND FOR SONS

The Harings behaved like the grandsons of first settlers in many other small communities of early America: they adapted to changing circumstances. Couples everywhere in those colonies which had been settled early, if they wished to stay in a particular community, had to cope with the diminishing availability of cheap land by postponing marriage and having fewer children.

In New England, founding families often had enough land only for themselves and the next generation; the third and, almost always, the fourth generations had to venture beyond the bounds of the community to buy and clear new lands. When the threshold of "optimal town population" and "maximal morselization" of land was reached, as Bernard Bailyn has put it—which usually happened in the third generation but, if not, then in the fourth generation—the common New England experience was for young couples to move on. It was only by the "comprehensive utilization of the family's initial properties" that the fourth generation could be satisfied on original lands in most New England towns.[6]

In the Middle Colonies, the same pattern is evident, and the exact time when land ran out depended to some extent on how early the town had been settled. In Newtown, N.Y., founded in 1642, land was fully settled by 1700, and those of the third generation who had the means left the community to buy new lands in

New Jersey and New York. Other Newtowners stayed and made do with smaller farms and incomes from second occupations. In Flatbush, N.Y., land was scarce from the beginning of settlement, and few fathers were able to endow more than one son. From the second generation on, children moved away to seek their fortune, often in groups of kin and neighbors. In Pennsylvania, Delaware Valley Quaker fathers in the late seventeenth century accumulated "vast amounts of land" and devised "intricate, demanding strategies" to disburse it to their children, with the aim of providing for all offspring and keeping them from having to leave the family circle in adulthood. Even so, because of land scarcity, Quaker parents even in the settler generation were forced in many cases to purchase land in distant townships and, in some cases, in other colonies.[7]

By the time of the Revolution, prices for land in southeastern Pennsylvania were ten times what they had been in the 1720s and 1730s, but inventories in the same period only quadrupled in value. Thus, the net worth of the "average" or "above-average" eighteenth-century farmer in this area did not keep pace with the rise in land prices, and the lesser sort had to move away where land was cheaper. In New Jersey, many farmers by the time of the Revolution had sufficient land only for their eldest sons. Other sons learned trades or left the area. In six towns studied, only about 25 percent of testators were able to provide all of their sons with land.[8]

The Haring family prepared for the inevitable land shortage it would face in various ways, some members more successfully than others. Some became educated for nonfarm livelihoods, particularly in the law and business. Some learned to improve their agricultural methods to increase yields and profits. Others took up a second line of work—acquiring mills or tanneries, learning trades. Some simply lowered their sights. But none took an obvious course that was often chosen by sons in other communities: no male member of the Haring family left the area for greener pastures until the end of the eighteenth century. In 1769, when the boundary dispute between New York and New Jersey was finally settled, the Harings still owned enough green pastures of their own to forestall the family's dispersal for another generation.[9]

If the four original Haring brothers, Peter, Cosyn, Cornelius, and Abraham, had hoped that their 3,000 acres in the Tappan Patent would yield for their sons and grandsons as many as fifteen farms of 200 acres apiece, their optimism was exceeded by reality. By 1779, ten years after the boundary dispute was settled, land, probate, and tax records reveal that, besides the twenty-five Haring farms in Harington Township and the four in Hackensack, there were another nine in Orange County, thirty-eight in all. These farms were among the largest in the area—nearly a hundred years after settlement.[10]

These Harings were fortunate. The New Jersey economy in the third quarter of the eighteenth century was a subsistence economy, with only 70 percent of the population in Bergen County owning land, and owning on the average only about 80 acres. In an area where a minimum of 51 acres was needed to support a family of six, only 33 percent of the taxpayers in the six East Jersey towns analyzed by Ryan owned more than 50 acres. Farms in the range of 201–300 acres were owned by a "prosperous minority" of only 3.9 percent of the 2,479 taxpayers in these six towns in 1778–1780.[11]

Within Bergen County, Harington Township tax records for 1779 reveal the average farm there (122 acres) to be larger than the average for Bergen County on the whole. Farms owned by those third-generation Harings who were still alive in 1779 were 217 acres on average, nearly a hundred acres larger than either the township average or the average in southeastern Pennsylvania—then the "best poor man's country."[12]

Moreover, tax records do *not* reveal (although wills and deeds do) that the third-generation Harings represented in the tax lists actually owned multiple farms in the two-hundred-acre range. (Farms owned by third-generation men but worked by their sons were attributed to the sons in the tax lists, for it was the sons who paid the taxes on them and who could consume and sell the produce.)[13] Thus, in relation to the population of the six East Jersey towns studied, the third-generation Harings were in the top 1.4 percent—those taxpayers owning from 301 to 500 acres. New Jersey also assessed such property as cattle, slaves, money at interest, gristmills, sawmills, and tanyards; and when all taxables are taken together, every third-generation Haring alive in Harington Township in 1779 was at the top of this top 1.4 percent, occupying an enviable place not only in the community as a whole, but even within the tiny "prosperous minority." The economic position of these men was measured not only by tax assessors, but also by their neighbors in Hackensack, who in 1775 objected to the formation of Harington Township because it would include some of the "most wealthy persons" in the area.[14]

The sons of these men were also among the prosperous minor-

91

ity, although a much wider variation is apparent among members of the fourth generation. In Harington Township in 1779, the Harings were the most numerous family, 33 of them constituting about 9 percent of the 349 taxed in all. Of the 349 polls in the community, altogether 245 were taxed on land and 104 on property other than land. The 25 landowning Harings were taxed on a total of 3,571 improved acres in 1779. Unimproved land was not taxed that year, but in 1785, Harings declared about 52 acres of this description. In Orangetown, the quantity of acreage is not given, but the nine Haring properties taxed there in 1779 probably totaled somewhere between 500 and 1,000 acres. This makes a total of 4,373 acres, estimating 750 acres in Orangetown. In other words, the family had been able to increase its original 3,000 acres by about 40 percent over the course of a century in which economic stratification was growing and the gap between wealthy and poor was widening.[15]

THE UNPROSPEROUS MAJORITY

To set the prosperous minority into even sharper perspective, it is instructive to compare them to some of their neighbors—to leaseholders, for instance. Leaseholders were men who had neither inherited land nor accumulated the means to buy it, but who could at least afford to rent land in the hope of someday being able to scrape together enough capital to purchase it. Leaseholders, tenants or, as they were also called, householders, were a rank below landowners in the pecking order but above "inmates," freemen, and "single men," none of whom either held or owned land. The latter in their turn were above indentured servants and, of course, above slaves at the bottom of the scale. Thus, as a nonlandowning single man might aspire to become a tenant, or leaseholder, the latter might aspire to own his own land.

In what he called both Bayard Manor and Tappan Farms, William Bayard leased property to men who could afford to rent but not own. Bayard granted leases, records of which exist for the years 1766 to 1772, for ten years. The farms he leased ranged in size from 150 to 200 acres; thus they were good farms, three and four times larger than a subsistence farm in one of the East New Jersey towns and at least twice as large as the average Bergen County farm in 1779. During his ten years, the tenant was to build a house and barn on Bayard's land, set out an orchard of a hundred apple trees, and "clear meadow ground to the amount of six acres on an average besides other clearance for corn." At the end of the ten years, Bayard agreed to pay the tenant half the value of his improvements, and then, he admitted, he would either double or treble the rent (a certain number of bushels of "good fine merchantable Winter wheat and two fat Hens" every March) or "turn out the Tenants as he pleased." (Wheat at this time was about six shillings per bushel.)[16]

Valuations on land ranged from sixty to one hundred shillings per acre. Hence, if a man leased, say, 200 acres from Bayard valued at sixty shillings per acre, or £600, at the end of his ten-year lease, Bayard would pay him £300 and either double or triple his rent on a new lease or turn him out, "according as it might happen."

If the latter happened, the farmer with his £300 of capital could then buy a farm of his own. But how large a farm could he buy? In 1773, Bayard sold nine tracts of land in the area in lots of 150 and 200 acres for £3 and £4 per acre. At £3 per acre, the tenant farmer with his £300 would theoretically be able to purchase a farm of 100 acres. But since he would have start-up costs that could preclude spending his whole capital on a farm, he might well have to buy a smaller farm than this—that is, one in the subsistence category of 51 to 80 acres—in order to reserve some of his small capital for expenses. In other words, he was not very well off after laboring for ten years on William Bayard's land. In fact, he found himself firmly ensconced in the "unprosperous majority," even though he had worked Bayard's land for a decade.[17]

In sum, in an area inhabited in this period by significant numbers of subsistence and marginal farmers, unlanded laborers, and tradesmen with small properties, the third- and fourth-generation Harings, with their multiple farms, slaves, livestock, and surplus funds at interest, and with the spare time they had to pursue public life as judges, military officers, assemblymen, and church officials, continued to thrive at the top of the economic scale. They were living as well as any farmer in the country.[18] The careers of two third-generation figures, Elbert [310] and his cousin Abraham A. [336], suggest that luck and the imaginative use of all one's resources were important factors in maintaining this preeminence.

CITY COUSIN

Luck was probably the most important ingredient in determining the prosperity of an eighteenth-century American yeoman—luck to marry well, to a woman with an outset and prospects of a legacy, and the luck to inherit. Of luck, Elbert Haring [310] had a double measure, for twice he married well and at least twice he inherited.

Elbert Haring was the ninth child and second son of the patentee Peter Haring [21] and Grietje Bogert. His parents, who had been married in the New York Reformed Church and who maintained an affiliation with that church for many decades, owned 800 or more acres in Tappan and land in Manhattan—either the old Haring farm, which tax records show was still in the family, or the Bogert farm, which may have adjoined it and been consolidated with it upon the death of Grietje's father, Jan Louwe Bogert, in about 1707.[19]

At age twenty Elbert married Catherine Lent, who bore him three daughters. The sponsors at the baptism of the first of these three infants, in 1727, were Elbert's maternal aunt, Catharina Bogert, and her husband, Elbert Lieverse. Catherine Lent died in 1731, soon after giving birth to her third daughter. A year later, in 1732, Elbert Haring remarried, again in the New York Reformed Church, this time to his first cousin, Elizabeth Bogert—the daughter of his mother's brother, Nicholas (Klaes) J. Bogert, a New York baker and bolter.[20]

Elbert's unusual first name suggests that, from the time of his birth, he had been designated by his parents as an heir or surrogate son of his aunt and uncle, the Lieverses, who were childless.[21] Elbert may even have been brought up by the Lieverses in their home. In any case, tax records show that, beginning in 1727 from the time of his first marriage, he lived next door to the Lieverses in the West Ward.

Upon marrying (second) the Lieverses' niece, his own first cousin, Elizabeth Bogert, Elbert was invited by his recently widowed aunt and now mother-in-law to join the family business. One month after his marriage to Elizabeth Bogert, Elbert was made a freeman of the city, joining as a baker, the trade followed by his new wife's family. Bakers, we recall, were near the top of the economic ladder in early-eighteenth-century New York, just under merchants. Elbert was now in a position to use his strong ties with Tappan to facilitate the movement of wheat from his cousins' farms in Orange County to his in-laws' processing operation in the city.[22]

From the early years of his marriage to Elizabeth Bogert, Elbert furthered his rise in the world by participating in the affairs of the growing city and of the New York Dutch Reformed Church. Starting in 1728, he held two elected positions in the West Ward, as tax collector and assistant alderman, serving for many years on various committees charged with surveying and appraising city-owned property and with laying out roads in developing areas of the city and water lots on the Hudson River.[23]

In October 1741, he became a church master (one rank below deacon) in the Dutch Reformed Church of New York. Church masters, who met once a month, disposed of vacant sittings in the church, made sure nonowners did not occupy seats of owners, and generally attended to an array of practical matters involving church property. Thus Elbert served on a committee to look after the affairs of the Manor of Fordham, a property the church had inherited in 1684 and that over the years had become far more a burden than a benefit: freeholders and lessees were always in arrears on their taxes and rents; lots were always coming up for let or sale; and there were endless squabbles over the use of the common lands and over the rules for the government of the manor. As late as 1760, Elbert was still occupied with Fordham's affairs, although, in the meantime, he had become a deacon and then an elder in the New York church. On several occasions, too, he was dispatched to the Tappan Reformed Church to "adjust matters" in the feud between members of the progressive "coetus" and members of the conservative "conferentie."[24]

In 1750, Elbert's father, Peter Haring [21] died, leaving his Orange County property to those of his children who were living in Orange County, and leaving "all the rest"—presumably whatever he owned in Manhattan—to Elbert. Two years later, Elbert inherited again when his childless uncle-by-marriage, Elbert Lieverse, a New York City "limeburner," bequeathed half of his real estate in Manhattan to five of his brothers' children, and half to Elbert Haring, baker of New York City.[25]

By 1755, Elbert, now the father of four sons and seven daughters, was sufficiently prosperous that he was able to buy enough land adjoining his New York City farm to increase its size greatly. His property (curiously resembling in shape the sails of a windmill) now extended across today's Greenwich Village west to east from Christopher Street to the Bowery (see Figure 5.1). It was a

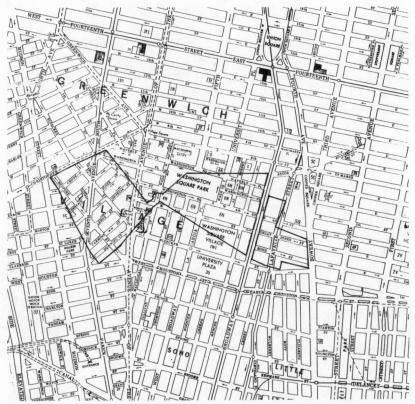

Figure 5.1. Farm of Elbert Haring [310], in Lower Manhattan, 1784. Courtesy C. K. Tholl and Exxon.

good neighborhood. On the Ratzer map of 1767, adjoining property owners were James De Lancey, Esq., and G. and N. Stuyvesant on the south and east; A. Elliot, Esq., and Sir Peter Warren on the north and northwest; and Abraham Mortier, Esq., and Nicholas Bayard on the west and southwest.[26]

When he died in 1773, Elbert, now sixty-seven and a grandfather many times over, lived in a pleasant house off today's Bleecker Street, between Jones and Cornelia Streets, facing southeast. Of three or four stories, the house is described in his inventory as having a central entryway, a kitchen, a dairy, a room above the dairy, a cellar, a little bedroom, a common room, a parlor, a back bedroom and, over all, a garret. There were two barns on the property. On the Ratzer map, the house is shown well back from the road and set off from it by a row of trees with orchards behind.[27]

The lantern-lit entry hall, furnished with a cupboard (was it a kas?) and a small chest of drawers, six chairs, and several pictures, introduced the common room, which contained a table, an easy chair, an elbow chair, twelve leather chairs and, as was customary in a Dutch household, a curtained bedstead complete with all its bedding. Oddly, no cupboard of any type is mentioned in this room. Elbert and his wife probably slept in the common room, whose decorative elements included a clock, worth £10, twelve pictures, a looking glass, fire tools, and various china bowls and plates. A parcel of old books and a large Dutch Bible were the reading material, and a pair of spectacles the means to read.

The main furniture in the English-style parlor, which served as dining room, were two large, round tables and twelve chairs, a cupboard (again, a kas?), two tea tables, and a tea board. Another table with a looking glass over it and two trunks were the other pieces of furniture in this three-windowed room, whose decorative furnishings included a Scotch carpet, twelve pictures, the family's best china and silver, and various tin boxes and canisters. In the cupboard and trunks were stored quantities of bed and table linen, as well as wearing apparel and silver buckles, clasps, and buttons worth £20.

The kitchen was furnished with three tables, four chairs, and all the various instruments of women's work: two lye tubs for making soap, three churns, benches, barrels, beef casks, a cider keg, four butter firkins, "kittles," pans, a waffle iron, two gridirons, a warming pan, smoothing irons, chafing dishes, and so on. To the general domestic clutter of the room were added an old gun, a "stone pott with Rice in it," squashes, frying pans, ladles, shovels, and a box of clover seed, as well as tea kettles, candlemolds, "muggs," and saucepans. Six old pictures and a "small looking glass somewhat broken" adorned the kitchen walls.

In the back bedroom were a curtained bed, six black walnut chairs, a dressing glass, and four chamber pots (two of brass and two of stone). The "little" bedroom, which either was not so little or else was very crowded, contained two double bedsteads with straw mattresses, pillows, bolsters, coverlids, and rugs, as well as "one old bed and a Blanket intended for the Wench."

Although the house was that of a gentleman, by which term Elbert frequently designated himself, the two barns and the barnyards were those of a prosperous yeoman, a term he also often used. An old barn and a new barn sheltered three horses, two bulls, eight cows, four heifers, several calves, and a steer. In the barns also were a wagon and tackling, two pleasure sleds, an old wood sled, two riding chairs, a four-wheeled chaise, two horse-carts and harnesses, plows, and all manner of farming equipment—from a mill for cleaning corn and a corn fan to pitchforks, threshing flails, scythes, a mattock, and a "bryer hook."

When Ebert died, there was Indian corn in the crib, there were "turnips in Holes under the Ground" and potatoes in the cellar, there was grain in the grainery and in the ground, cabbage in the garden, and there were eleven dunghill fowl clucking in the yard. A "stack of wheat" worth £8 stood beside a grindstone. In the barns were horsefeed, hay, barley, straw, and cornhusks—fodder for the stock—and a crosscut saw, various hammers, axes, angles, boards, iron wedges, a sawhorse, and a tar bucket.

Besides this farm and his occupation as a baker, Elbert had several other sources of income. He owned at his death seven other New York properties, on which he collected rents, and he put his surplus money out at interest. In short, he was as imaginative as he could be in capitalizing on all his advantages.

Elbert's career suggests that farming as a way of life was not the ideal of every farmer in the dawn of the new republic. For this yeoman, farming, far from being his ideal, was a sideline—and one he directed none of his children toward. It may be going too far to say that farming held no allure at this point in eighteenth-century New York—at least for any farmer who had an alternative livelihood or a better way to improve his life—but clearly it held little allure for Elbert as a way of life for his children.

Nor did "Dutchness" have the same appeal to a city dweller as it did in the country. On their upwardly mobile path in anglicized New York, Elbert and his wife and children shed many vestiges of their Dutchness. Although they maintained a close affiliation with the Dutch church, and kept to the old Dutch custom of having a bedstead in the common room, the parlor in Elbert's house was English in style—no bed appears—and no furniture in the house was identified by the appraisers as specifically Dutch—most surprisingly, no kas. Except for the Dutch Bible, it might have been the home of a prosperous eighteenth-century New Yorker of English origins.[28]

Even before Elbert's death in 1773, his wife and children had begun to anglicize the Dutch "Haring" to "Herring," perhaps in furtherance of their social ambitions. All six of Elbert's daughters married some of the most up-and-coming young men in New

York—none of them farmers. Catherine married Alderman George Brinkerhoff. Margaret married Alderman Cornelius Roosevelt. Cornelia married the jurist Samuel Jones, a leader of the Federalist party, a member of the New York State convention that adopted the U.S. Constitution in 1788, and the New York State controller for many years. Elizabeth married John De Peyster, Jr., the first treasurer of the city after the Revolution. Ann married Samuel Kip, the great-grandson of Jacob Kip, and spent her married life in the Kip mansion on the East River. Mary married her first cousin, John Haring [415], a patriot statesman and a member of the New York delegation to the First and Second Continental Congresses. And Sarah married a physician, Gardner Jones. Cornelia Street and Great Jones Street in Greenwich Village are named for Cornelia and her husband Samuel Jones (no relation to Gardner), and Jones Street is named after Gardner Jones.[29]

Although Elbert and his family aspired to and achieved the higher reaches of New York colonial society, and although some of them apparently wanted to obscure their Dutch origins, they were clearly ambivalent about deserting the old way of life, for they maintained their ties to Tappan, acquiring there at around the time of Elbert's death a handsome house in the center of town (see Figure 5.2). In 1776, Elizabeth "Herring," Elbert's widow, advertised this property for sale, describing it as "that noted house and lot where Casparus Mabie formerly lived at Tappan, two miles from the North River and 24 from Hoebuck Ferry: It is a convenient stone building, 4 rooms on a floor. There is likewise on said place a good barn, garden and sundry other conveniences." In 1776, when she advertised it for sale, the widow was living "on the premises," perhaps because the lead sash weights of her New York City house had been donated to the patriot cause and melted down for ammunition. Even in this urban and cosmopolitan branch of the Haring family, Tappan retained its value as the symbolic center of family life, and it was to Tappan, when trouble came, that the family repaired. Elbert's widow was joined in Tappan for most of the war years by her married children and saw nearly a dozen of her grandchildren baptized in the Tappan Reformed Church by its patriot minister, Samuel Verbryck.[30]

A COUNTRY COUSIN

Just a stone's throw over the state line from the Tappan church and courthouse and Elbert's country house was the Harington

Figure 5.2. Eight-Room Tappan House, c. 1753. British Major John André was imprisoned in this house while awaiting trial for treason in 1780; he was hanged on a nearby hill. Courtesy Tappantown Historical Society.

Township farm of Abraham A. Haring [336], Elbert's first cousin. Like Elbert, Abraham, the eldest son of the youngest Haring brother, Abraham [27], also benefited by a generous inheritance and a good marriage (to Maria Demarest, a daughter of one of the leading families of Bergen County and a granddaughter of Guiliam Bertholf). By the terms of his father's will, Abraham, as we will see in Chapter 6, was obliged to give his widowed mother one-third of the produce of his large farm and to see that she was comfortably housed and supplied with room in his barn and fodder for ten head of cattle. But these obligations do not seem to have prevented the son from prospering handsomely. The 1779 tax records show him, at age sixty, to be the richest man in Harington Township, with £750 at interest and a working farm of 256 acres. (He owned as well about 500 acres worked by his sons.) At his death in 1791, at age eighty-two, Abraham's inventory shows that he still owned, besides his large farm, eight adult slaves (Cuff, Bett, Sam, Will, Tom, Dina, Hagar, and Cate), eight horses, two colts, ten cows, a heifer, two calves, twenty-six sheep, fourteen swine, fifty dunghill fowl, and three beehives. Although no records have survived to document the wheat trade between the city Harings and their country cousins, one can believe that the fortunes of Colonel Abraham A. Haring [336] and his brother Daniel [342] on the neighboring farm were made by selling their grain surpluses on the New York market, undoubtedly with their relatives Elbert and the Bogerts serving as factors, processors, and merchandisers.[31]

Abraham, like Elbert, also augmented his inherited lands with purchases. At least six, some in New Jersey and some in New York State, are referred to in his will; in all, he owned between 600 and 700 acres. Besides his military commission, the public record shows that he took up an active role in local politics and that he was a deacon and elder in the Tappan church. His resources also permitted him to serve as informal banker to his neighbors. At the time of his death, he was owed £314 on eleven different credit accounts.

In 1791, when he died, this aged widower was sharing his house with a grandson, Abraham [5221], who was designated to inherit it. The house that grandfather and grandson shared is no longer standing, but to judge from the very detailed inventory, it seems to have had at least three major eating and sleeping rooms downstairs, plus an additional two kitchens—probably in wings off the central core—and an upstairs divided into sleeping chambers. It may in fact have been the same large house described in

101

the will of this Abraham's father, Abraham [27], which, as we recall from Chapter 4, designated "one of the best rooms" in the house to the widow. One of the best rooms downstairs in this inventory contained a Dutch-style feather bed with curtains and bedclothes, a table, chest, and dresser, a rug, another feather bed, a cradle, various pewter and earthenware plates and dishes, and an assortment of linens. The presence of the cradle and the extra feather bed mark this room as the living quarters of the grandson and his wife and small children.

Abraham's room—to judge from the presence in it of his clothing, an eight-day clock, sword, cane, and two walking sticks—was furnished comfortably but not so luxuriously as Elbert's best room in New York. It contained a Dutch-style bedstead, a cupboard, two chests, a dining table, common table, and corner cupboard, plates, cooking implements, and a number of looms and spinning wheels. As it also contained (almost incredibly), twenty-two chairs, it must have been a room of large proportions and its occupant a man of many friends. A Dutch Bible and both a Dutch and an English psalmbook were joined in this farmer's small library by an assortment of unidentified books and by Koelman's *Duty of Saints*, *The Young Man's Companion*, Alendin's *Sermons*, Brakel's *Spiritual Life*, and Freeman's *Balance of Grace*, suggesting not only a piety and seriousness of mind, but the error of the notion that the Jersey Dutch farmer of this period barely spoke English.

On the other hand, the remarkably traditional "Dutch" character of this household in 1790, one hundred and fifty years after the Haring family's arrival in America, raises again the question of whether the Dutch farmer was in some way ambivalent about America and reluctant to "become" American. It also raises another question—whether his conservatism was a function of the rural life itself. Perhaps contact with nature, or isolation from the ills of civilization, as Jefferson would have it, was not particularly improving. Perhaps, rather, a country existence closed men to the opportunities for enlightenment and cultural change that they would need to prosper in the early national period.

SHARED COMMUNITY—IN LIFE, IN DEATH

The record yields signs—in the falling birthrate, the persistence of Dutch material culture, and in a trend toward unequal inheritance (to be discussed in Chapter 6)—that the Haring family was experiencing the pressures exerted by changing economic conditions. Nevertheless, for most Harings the decades leading up to the Revolution continued to be seemingly idyllic years of land acquisition, the accumulation of capital, and—on the social side of life—an effort to educate children and participate in the political and religious life of their communities.

There is also ample evidence in wills and other documents that in the affective realm the ideal of family harmony and unity continued to be supported by the third and fourth generations. Even physically the family stayed close together, members of different generations often intimately sharing the same house. Testators whose wives had not predeceased them specified that their widows were to have a room, even a particular room in the house. Cornelius [344] willed the "use of that part of my house (the room with the lintern) as I now use it" in the house he left to his son. (The lintern was a pantry off the kitchen end of a living-eating-sleeping room.) Abraham [336] shared his house with grandson and great-grandchildren. Cornelius [331] specified that his eldest son find "house room" for an unmarried sister. Elbert [310] left "to my niece Elizabeth Bogert, who now lives in my family, £50 when she is married." And, in the early 1770s, John Haring [415] sold his own farm on Tappan Road to his brother and "went . . . to live with his Aged Mother upon the Farm where his Father had lived . . . until she broke up House-keeping."[32]

More often, the family remained close as brothers and sisters on opposite sides of a common fence, as neighbors on adjoining farms belonging to uncles, cousins, and in-laws or, when church seatings were passed down in wills, as worshipers in adjoining pews. Daniel [330] left his "three sitting places in Schralingburg Church" to his five sons and two daughters; and land was now divided with excruciating care, wills spelling out division lines in a manner so precise as to avoid any possible misunderstanding. No longer were such details overlooked, as in the first generation on the land, in the interest of preserving harmony. Rather, they were now carefully attended to in the interest of avoiding conflict.

When tragedy struck and early death took a father from his family, testamentary law decreed that children were entitled to their deceased parent's share of his parents' estate. If a will did not specify who the minor children's guardians were to be, the orphan's court stepped in to appoint suitable persons, usually the closest blood relatives, to oversee the affairs of these children. In one poignant case, the eldest grandson of Abraham A. Haring

[336], David A. [5203], who had himself been orphaned, died intestate in 1801, at the age of forty-one, leaving five children, three from his first wife, also deceased. These three children lived with their stepmother and their two half siblings for a year or two until she remarried, whereupon they petitioned the orphan's court in Bergen County to appoint their uncles as guardians and as the administrators of their property. Blood ties were almost invariably and exclusively preferred to those of other relations in all matters of property, even small ones, and even when the blood relation was three generations removed. When Sarah Haring [4115] died in 1810, for instance, her share of her father's personal estate (about $500) passed, as he had instructed in his will, to his other heirs, her eleven nephews and nieces and great-nephews and great-nieces, the latter being the sixth generation of the family.[33]

Finally, even in death the family shared a symbolic intimacy, renting from the church a black cloth about thirty feet long, the "pall," to drape the room where bier and coffin stood before interment. Generations of Harings in Tappan, along with their friends, neighbors, and in-laws, all rented the same pall—one purchased by the Tappan Reformed Church consistory in 1718 and used until it was replaced in 1812. This symbol of shared community was a palpable source of consolation to the grieving survivors, and its common use over a century was a witness to the strength of the ties that bound community members to one another and to old customs.[34]

Though resonant with meanings consistent with the patentee families' values, the pall must also have seemed to those who draped their loved ones' coffins with it to represent another set of meanings. The pall as symbol was ambiguous, ironic, even prophetic. For if they shared this cloth for a hundred years, during most of those years after about 1730 many of the Harings were at odds with one another and with their fellow congregants in Tappan. As we will see, they fell, initially over religious issues, into disagreement so profound, indeed, as to enshroud families, church, and community in another kind of pall from which it took nearly another century to emerge.

Chapter Six

When Flesh Must Yield unto Death

The last will and testament of an eighteenth-century American farmer was one of the most telling personal documents to which he would in his lifetime put his name. Wills are a rich source of information, nearly unsurpassed for what they reveal about the social and economic status of individual testators, about their fears, hopes, anxieties, and values, and about the evolution over time of family relationships—especially the changing status of wives and children and the treatment of sons in relation to daughters. Eighteenth-century wills also reveal that, as various ethnic inheritance traditions gave way in British America to a more uniform testamentary style, old family values came into conflict with new social forces.[1]

The four Haring brothers postponed writing their wills until they were well into old age. Peter was seventy-two, Cosyn sixty-four, Cornelius seventy, and Abraham seventy-one when it finally seemed to them that the time had come to dispose of their worldly goods.

Why did they wait so long? A reluctance to contemplate death could not have been the reason, for as Christians, death was merely a passageway to another stage of life. Nor could they have been unmindful of their mortality in an era when death was commonplace. Their own father had died intestate at age forty-nine. Perhaps so long as they remained in "good health in body and of good Since memory and Understanding," they felt no urgency to undertake this symbolic stocktaking. Or perhaps they had confidence that, should they die before this formality were undertaken, traditional Dutch inheritance customs would dictate the disposition of their estates in a way that would provide adequately for all their heirs. (The Dutch laws of intestate succession entitled a widow to inherit one-half of the couple's joint property, with the balance devolving in equal parts to their children, regardless of sex.) Most likely, though, the brothers delayed this important step out of ambivalence toward changing laws and customs.

DUTCH INHERITANCE CUSTOMS

Dutch inheritance customs reinforced the value Dutch culture placed upon the family. The testator himself could not detach his wife's portion from her ownership, and although he could bestow small gifts and recognitions as he pleased on one child or another, he could not disinherit a child without an extremely serious reason, nor could he treat his children unequally without good cause. In short, he had much guidance in law and precedent, and little discretion as to who his heirs would be or what portion of his substance they were entitled to. The intended effect of these customs was to preserve the original household if the father died, rather than, as in English common law, to let primogeniture dictate its dissolution by unseating the widow and creating a new household headed by a single heir who inherited all the real estate.[2]

Inheritance behavior, then, expresses cultural values. But when cultural values evolve and change, as they were doing in colonial America, inheritance behavior will also change. It is very clear that the four Haring brothers in Tappan, steeped in the seventeenth-century Dutch testamentary tradition, had by the 1730s become in many ways eighteenth-century American farmers, and as such they adopted the evolving new ways of treating widows and children. Yet a certain ambivalence about these new ways can be discerned in their wills, and this probably caused the four to delay for so long the act of writing their last wills and testaments.

In any case, a reading of the brothers' wills, written in 1733, 1736, 1742, and 1752, reveals that this first generation of the family in Tappan did forsake certain Dutch inheritance customs for English ones and did take up what was to become the mainstream testamentary pattern. They all used the English language for their wills, for instance, whereas in their father's generation, wills of Dutch Americans were composed in the English language by fewer than 50 percent of testators.[3] They departed from the earlier religious style in the progressively secular language of the preambles to their wills. They dispensed completely with the so-called mutual will, a Dutch testamentary convention, discussed below. And the two younger brothers bequeathed directly to their children rather than to their widows, as had been the custom. Still, all four wills exhibit some signs of tension between the old ways and the new.

"IN THE NAME OF GOD, AMEN"

By the early eighteenth century in the Province of New York, most wills, whether the testator was of Dutch, English, or other national origin, followed a general structure and format. In the preamble, the testator evoked God's name, stated the date and place of his testament, often gave his occupation or title, identified his mental health and memory as good, commented upon the state of his physical health, acknowledged the transitoriness of life, regretted his sins, hoped for redemption, and bequeathed his soul to God—some with more, some with less religious language. In the body of the will, the testator directed the disposition of all his worldly goods and in the conclusion appointed one or more executors to see that his wishes were carried out.

An increasing secularization of the religious preambles in New York wills took place as the eighteenth century progressed.[4] The wills of the four Haring brothers, read chronologically, reflect this trend, the language of Peter's and Cosyn's wills in the 1730s being markedly more pious than the two younger brothers' wills, Cornelius's in 1742 and Abraham's in 1752.

Peter, the eldest brother, writing in 1736, is the most pious of the four—at least to judge from his language, whose special fervor recalls the Pietist emphasis on the importance of a personal salvation and of Christ as a personal redeemer. Thus, "Being at present in good health and perfect sound memory & understanding blessed be the Lord for the same but calling to Remembrance the uncertain Estate of this Transitory life and that all flesh must yield unto death whenever it pleased God to call," Peter then commits his "precious and immortal Soul into the mercifull hands of God my Creator hoping through the merits, death and passion of my blessed Savior and Redeemer Christ Jesus to have and receive a full pardon and free remission of my manifold Sins and to inherit Everlasting life."[5]

By midcentury, when Peter's youngest brother wrote his will, a significant number of testators had dispensed with the religious preamble almost entirely. Abraham recommends his soul to God and hopes to be saved "by the alone merits of my blessed Lord and Saviour Jesus Christ," and although he recognizes his good fortune as having come from God, it is not necessarily undeserved but simply something, Abraham succinctly notes, that "god in his Mercy hath blessed me with."[6]

The decline in the religious content of their wills is not a sign that the Haring brothers were experiencing a decline in piety. Rather, as they prospered and enjoyed a surplus of possessions, they were developing new attitudes toward their material goods. There were simply more things to bestow, and they could be bestowed in new ways. The act of writing a will, which had traditionally been associated with the testator's spiritual preparation for death, was evolving, and men were coming to regard a will as an economic tool—an aspect of life on earth, not of life after death.[7]

THE DEMISE OF THE MUTUAL WILL

In the seventeenth century, husbands and wives of Dutch background had held all of their possessions in common. Although they merged their worldly goods into one joint estate, the husband had primary responsibility for managing the couple's property, and by law he could sell it without his wife's consent. Her share, however, was not his to bequeath; and if they made a mutual will, she could will her half as she pleased.[8]

English law was in force by the early 1700s, but the Dutch were not required to abide by English law in inheritance matters, for at the time of the conquest, the English authorities had agreed in the Articles of Capitulation to respect the traditional inheritance customs of the Dutch. Thus, in disposing of his estate, the Dutch testator in early America had four basic options. He could choose not to make a will at all, but let the Dutch customs of intestate succession determine the distribution of his possessions. Or he could follow seventeenth-century Dutch custom and execute a "mutual will" with his wife. In this case, he would be acting on the accepted presumption that their property was owned in common, with his wife entitled to half of the total on his death, their children to the other half. A third option was made possible by the advent of the English common law in New York, for English law did not recognize a married woman as having a legal

108

identity equal to her husband's—or a right to own personal property or to make a will without her husband's permission. The Dutch testator could opt to follow English law and choose any number of ways to distribute his personal property and real estate as befitted the needs of his various heirs. (He could not, however, will less than one-third of his real estate to his widow—her dower right.) Finally, he could recognize his wife's former high status in Dutch law by willing all his property to her—and, after death or in the case of her remarriage, equally among their children. This last is the course followed in the first three decades of the eighteenth century by the majority of New York testators of all ethnic backgrounds.[9]

After the English conquest of New Netherland in 1664, Narrett found that 42 percent of all testators of Dutch origin continued for about three decades to dispose of their property jointly through the mutual will. After 1700, however, almost no mutual wills whatever were composed. Until about 1725, testators chose to leave their widows in possession of their whole estates and to name their wives as executrices of the entire estate during their widowhood. In this generosity to their wives, Dutch testators were not alone. Until 1725, half of all English and French colonists in New York left their widows in control of all or nearly all their possessions.[10]

After about 1725, these customs began to change, even among the Dutch. By midcentury, ethnic Dutch widows had lost significant control over their husbands' property, particularly real estate, and fewer of them were being named in wills as sole executrices of their husbands' estates. These changes occurred first among the wealthy—merchants and professionals—and then among those segments of society—including prosperous yeomen and rural gentry like the Harings—which in many areas of life followed trends set by the wealthy. Now children, rather than widows, began to inherit the bulk of the estate, one reason being that testators, as they became wealthier, could meet their widows' needs more easily and did not have to make their children wait until the widow died or remarried before they could come into control of the land and property.[11]

None of the four Haring brothers executed mutual wills, but the two older brothers, Cosyn writing in 1733 and Peter writing in 1736, observed the traditional high status of women in Dutch law. They made their widows their principal heirs and required the children to wait for their inheritance until their mother had died (or remarried). The two younger brothers, on the other hand, more modern than their elder siblings, left their whole estates to their children, although they did stipulate in very specific terms the children's responsibilities toward their mother.

WIDOWS' ECONOMIC POSITION

Even when children were named as the primary heirs, Haring women of this generation continued to wield great power over their grown children, particularly over sons. Let us look at the wills of the four brothers chronologically.

Cosyn, in 1733, directed that before his children got legal title, his widow and executrix Maretie Blauvelt should have the "Plantation where I do live at present . . . with all its appurtenances . . . Together with all my moveable Estate and with all the profits arising from the same."[12] One's "moveable estate" comprised house furnishings, farm equipment, slaves, livestock, paper currency, notes, bonds, cash and, as the term implies, anything else that moved or could be moved. Maretie got all of this, plus the plantation itself and the profits from it. She also received putative control of Cosyn's other lands—the farm where his only son John [315] lived as well as those lands designated for her surviving daughters and grandchildren. Maretie was seventy-three years old when Cosyn died, ten years after making his will; and since she did not remarry, the farm and the profits arising from it were hers and not legally her children's until she died. It is not known how long she lived, but her three children at the time of their father's death were already fifty, forty-seven, and forty-three, and grandparents themselves. Full independence from parental control was a long time in coming to these elderly offspring, for when the patriarch passed away, he had ensured that the matriarch was firmly in place to continue his authority.

Similarly, Peter Haring's wife, Grietje Bogert, like her sister-in-law, was also made executrix and entrusted with sole management of her husband's estate during her lifetime.[13] Although her eldest son, Abraham [39], was a married man of thirty-two in 1736 when his father made his will and designated him to inherit the home farm, it is noteworthy that Grietje's powers of executrix were shared not with him, but rather, with his uncle, her husband's brother Abraham [27]. The cohesiveness of the first generation of the family in Tappan was an effective instrument of the power and authority that the brothers wielded over their children. Some wives in the 1730s still shared equally in this authority with their husbands.

Even those widows whose children received the whole estate were left in a remarkably strong economic position. The two younger brothers, Cornelius (in 1742) and Abraham (in 1752), in accord with changing testamentary trends, left their whole estates to their children: land to sons; cash, slaves, goods, and livestock to daughters. But they also left detailed instructions to their sons as to how their widowed mothers were to be provided for. Cornelius instructed each of his four sons to give his mother one-tenth of the produce of his farm.[14] As his four sons' farms totaled some 860 acres, they "owed" their mother a very generous living—namely, the produce of as much as 86 acres a year, if they planted every acre (which, of course, no farmer did)—to dispose of as she might.

A CLOSER LOOK

This raises the question of how a widow would dispose of such quantities. The dietary needs and wants of one elderly widow in a rural eighteenth-century community could have been amply satisfied by a small kitchen garden, a few chickens, a milk cow, and a little cash for the purchase of flour, meat, salt, sugar, tea, and so on. If Cornelius Haring's sons planted only a quarter of their 860 acres (i.e., 215 acres) in all crops, legumes and root vegetables included—a conservative estimate—leaving three-quarters of their land fallow, and if each planted, say, twenty of these acres, or a total of 80 acres, in various grains, they could expect to reap about ten bushels per acre, or about eight hundred bushels. (Again, these are conservative estimates. These men probably planted more than only a quarter of their arable land, and their yield per acre was probably somewhat higher.)[15]

Using the standard eighteenth-century ration for soldiers and militiamen, one pound of bread per day and one to three pints of cornmeal a week, it has been estimated that a colonial family of five required thirty to thirty-nine bushels of grain a year (making no allowance for livestock). At this rate, and assuming a yield of ten bushels per acre, three or four acres in wheat could keep a family of five grain-fed for a year. According to these estimates, a widow needed (at the most) eight or nine bushels a year—less than the yield of one acre (more if she had livestock to feed).[16]

Table 6.1. *Women Taxed in Harington Township, Bergen County, N.J., September 1779*

	Improved acres	Horses	Horned cattle	Hogs	Slaves	Riding chairs	Other	Money at interest
Catherina Van Veler	100	2	4	1				
Maria Waling			1					
Margretye Valentine	6			1				
Anna Bogert	200	4	4	8				£262 10s
Efye Cool	115	2	2	6		1		£37 10s
Lea Westerveldt	100	5	6	6				
Elizabeth Van Valer				1				
Brechte Ferdon	200	5	8	8	1	1		
Geertje Haring		1	4			1	Tanyard	£150
Maria Haring	130	4	10	4	2	1		

Name					Tavern
Polly English			1	3	
Elizabeth Enders			2	1	
Rachel Peek	330				
Annatye Demarest	89	2	2	2	
Annatye Sobriskie			1	2	
Elizabeth Cooper	60	2	3	4	1
Sarah Peterson	150	5	8	8	
Antye Baldwin	110	3	4	3	2
Catherine Haring		2	2	2	
Lea Haring	15				
					£203 15s

Source: "A List of the Rateables in the Township of Harington in the County of Bergen with the Assessments Made Thereon in the Month of September 1779," New Jersey State Library.

Such provisions for widows are common in New England wills as well as in those of New Netherland, and their primary aim was to provide a secure source of support for widows. But if Cornelius Haring's widow had a surplus of seventy bushels per year, and she sold her surplus, the income she derived from the sale would have provided her with more than a secure source of support. It guaranteed her financial independence from her children. In fact, it guaranteed her a position as a rather important economic force in the community—a source of food for poor farmers, transients, and hired laborers, and for those tradesmen too busy to farm themselves. From this captive clientele, the income that the widow derived from the sale of her surpluses allowed her to purchase the food items she did not grow or raise, to hire such labor as her children or grandchildren did not supply her free of charge, and to maintain a position as a cog in the community's economic wheel. Even when her spouse did not leave her title to his lands and the power to manage his estate, he left her equipped to function as a significant and independent figure in the scheme of things.

That there was a ready market for farm surpluses and that widows were capable of being suppliers of it is revealed by a look at the tax rolls for the township of Harington, Bergen County, N.J., in 1779—the first year such records are available.[17] Of the 349 polls taxed in this community, 104 owned no land at all, but only livestock, often only a horse or a cow. These 104 persons must have traded or bartered with others in the community for the food they and their dependents consumed. Of the 245 polls taxed on land, 50 owned 50 or fewer acres, when 51 acres has been estimated as the minimum necessary in this period in New Jersey for the subsistence of a family of six.[18] Those in Harington Township with large farms and substantial quantities of livestock could, and no doubt did, serve as suppliers of grain, legumes, dairy products, meat, and cider for the have-nots in the community.

That widows could have been among these suppliers is also clear from these tax records. At least twenty women (some first names are illegible) were taxed in 1779, most of them widows (see Table 6.1). Although eight of the twenty had no land or only a few acres, two of these eight, Geertje Haring and Polly English, supported themselves through the profits of a tanyard and a tavern. Catherina Van Veler, Anna Bogert, Efye Cool, Lea Westerveldt, Brechte Ferdon, Maria Haring, Rachel Peek, Annatye Demarest, Elizabeth Cooper, Sarah Peterson, and Antye Baldwin, with farms ranging in size from 60 to 330 acres, and with 51 horned cattle and 50 hogs among them, were most probably important market providers.

"A GARDEN SPOTT OF GROUND"

The youngest Haring brother, Abraham, also adopted the modern custom of leaving his whole estate to his children, but in his will, as in Cornelius's, Abraham's care to spell out exactly what he expected his sons to do for their widowed mother betrays a certain anxiety with the new and changing ways.

To his "dearly beloved wife" and executrix Dircktie Talman, for example, Abraham gave not only the "Choice of one of the best rooms in my Dwelling House," as we saw in Chapter 4, but also "a Garden Spott of Ground and Roome in my Barne for ten Head of Cattle, and one third part every year of all the Apples that my Orchard shall produce." He also instructed that "Wood sufficient for one fire place [and] Fauder for ten head of Cattle and six Sheep . . . be delivered to her at my Dwelling House by my twoe sones Abraham [336] & Daniel [342], one third part of all the winter and Summer Graine and Flax that shall [be] raised of all or any [of] the Lands heretofore given . . . be delivered at my Dwelling House Clear and Free for her Use during her [widowhood] and likewise . . . my Sons shall from Time to Time and at all Times procure, give, permitt and allow [her] free pasturage for ten Head of Cattles, Six Sheep and Twoe Hoggs."[19] Not only the widow's economic concerns were considered, but also such practical matters as the delivery to her door of fuel for her fire and fodder for her livestock.

Dircktie, like her sisters-in-law, was left a prodigious quantity of livestock for a widow's simple needs; and with one-third of the flax and various grains from her sons' three 200-acre farms and one-third of the orchard's apples, she probably could have fed and clothed an entire neighborhood. It has been estimated that orchards in Pennsylvania containing 100 to 150 trees were common—with one tree yielding four to ten bushels of apples, or from a third to a half a barrel of cider.[20] If Abraham's orchard contained 100 trees, and it probably was larger, it would have yielded perhaps six hundred bushels of apples, or about fifty barrels of cider—of which his widow was entitled to one-third. A widow might consume about two and a half barrels of cider herself in a given year, leaving her some fourteen barrels to sell.

Dircktie Haring's ten head of cattle, assuming a weight of 450 pounds per average dressed carcass, would have allowed her, if she desired to slaughter all ten in one year, to consume a pound of red meat herself every day for a year and to have 3,135 pounds of meat left to sell, not to mention what her six sheep and two hogs would yield.[21] By slaughtering and selling only one or two beasts a year and letting the others reproduce in order to keep the ranks filled, she had her own food, an income, and protected capital.

The wills of the four Haring brothers reflect the strong desire of these testators to fulfill law and custom in providing for the support, comfort, and independence of their widows. But the wills reveal more than mere testamentary obligation to a possibly helpless woman in her dotage. Between the lines, the testator's affection and gratitude for his "dearly beloved wife" is glimpsed as he empowers her, his life's companion, helpmeet, and friend, to administer all that they created together. In the ability of one who had helped him establish his farm in the wilderness, who had borne, fed, clothed, and raised his numerous progeny, who had managed his household for fifty years, and who had seen to his affairs in his absences in the legislature or wherever, he had good reason to have every confidence that she could manage his estate after he was gone forever, and every reason to expect his children to honor her. The widows, daughters, and granddaughters of the sons of the Haring brothers would be treated in a different way.

TESTAMENTARY TREATMENT OF CHILDREN: THE SECOND GENERATION

In New York City, seventeenth-century testators of all backgrounds showed an overwhelming propensity to treat sons and daughters equally at inheritance—despite the Charter of Libertyes (1683), which had instituted primogeniture. Primogeniture was a system of inheritance totally unpalatable to testators of all ethnic and cultural backgrounds in colonial America. Under primogeniture, one member of the family, typically the eldest son, inherited the whole of his father's real estate. The appeal of this system was that the family name could continue to be associated with a particular property for as many generations as could biologically and financially maintain it. But in early America, where land was abundant, testators even of English origins rejected primogeniture in favor of distributing their estate—real and personal—according to the needs of their various heirs. In the countryside, where farming was the main occupation, testators tended to bequeath real estate to sons and goods to daughters—usually choosing to partition both real and personal property as equally as possible along gender lines. Although partitioning a property among all heirs eliminated any possibility of a family name being linked for generations with one large holding, it gave every child in the family a start in life. It was a much more democratic system than primogeniture and better suited to the spirit of enterprise and individuality that informed nascent America.[22]

From 1664 to 1695, more than 88 percent of all New York City's male testators circumvented the law of English primogeniture to distribute their real estate, and 92 percent their personal estate, equally or nearly so among sons and daughters. For the period 1664–1775, the figures are 75.8 percent and 79.2 percent.[23] Although testators of all backgrounds found ways to circumvent the English law requiring them to favor the eldest son over all other children, those of Dutch background were particularly disposed to the expedient of giving the eldest son a token gift "for his birthright"—a stratagem that satisfied the law, yet left the family wealth virtually intact for dispersal among all sons and daughters. Peter [21] left his eldest son his "great Dutch Bible for his Rights of first Born"; Cosyn [23] gave his only son £50; Cornelius [24] gave his eldest son "for his bert Ryt my Great Bible"; and Abraham [27] gave his eldest son a token £5.

No matter how egalitarian a father wished to be, however, his ability to provide for all of his children and for all equally was determined by his means. Some fathers could give a farm to each son. Some were forced to choose among sons. Some could treat daughters and sons equally, and some had to favor sons over daughters. How did the four Haring brothers treat their sons and daughters?

As the four brothers had nearly 4,000 acres among them and only eleven surviving sons to take care of, they were easily able to give farms in the 300-acre range to all eleven third-generation sons. Some third-generation daughters also received land. Cosyn, who had more than 1,100 acres and only one son, willed his daughters land that seems to have been of equal value to that of their brothers. All third-generation daughters in the Haring family received inheritances from their fathers, and all of them and

Table 6.2. *Distribution of Testators' Real Property among Sons and Daughters, New York City, 1664–1750*

	Equal or near equal	All or bulk to sons	Other
1664–1695	88.2%	9.8%	2.0%
1696–1725	80.6	18.3	1.1
1726–1750	65.7	30.4	3.9

SOURCE: Adapted from David Evan Narrett, "Patterns of Inheritance in Colonial New York City, 1664–1775: A Study in the History of the Family" (Ph.D. diss., Cornell University, 1981), table 4.8, p. 231.

all their brothers, following Dutch custom, also received gifts upon marriage—land or the promise of it, plus some cash and livestock for sons, and home furnishings and cash and perhaps some livestock for daughters—in order to establish themselves in their married state.

Few overt references to these gifts or "outsets" can be found, except in wills. In 1752, Abraham [27], for instance, stipulated in his will that his nineteen-year-old, as yet-unmarried daughter Rachel [345] receive "an outset equally as good of all sorts as any of my [three] daughters have had."[24] This is clear evidence that all four of Abraham's daughters were treated equally in relation to one another, but what about in relation to their brothers? Besides their outsets, Abraham also directed that each of his three daughters be paid a "legacy" of £100 by their three brothers in order to compensate the girls for the land their brothers received. But if this testator actually treated his sons and daughters equally, daughters' legacies, when added to the value of their outsets, should equal the value of the land their brothers received. Unfortunately, no quantifiable data exist to indicate how this generation acted on this point.

By the 1730s—when the four Haring brothers began to write their wills—the custom of equal treatment of sons and daughters by New York City testators was beginning to decline, as shown in Table 6.2. But if the same trend was happening in the country— that is, if the four brothers left farms to their sons that were more valuable than the share of the estates (outsets plus legacies) they gave to their daughters—we have no proof, for reliable price information is unavailable.

118

TESTAMENTARY TREATMENT OF CHILDREN: THE THIRD GENERATION

The nine third-generation fathers in this family for whom wills have been found bequeathed each of twenty-eight fourth-generation sons (or grandsons) a farm (the twenty-ninth son got cash instead). Some of these farms were the picturesque, large, and bountiful places so often admired by contemporary travelers in the area. (See Table 6.3 for dates and locations of wills.) Were these men able to leave their fourth-generation daughters (or granddaughters) legacies of equal value? Again, this is impossible to quantify, but there are indications that, by 1770, Haring heirs were being treated quite unequally along gender lines. Changing economic conditions—particularly the disappearance of relatively cheap land—and changing attitudes toward women were the chief reasons.[25]

Even in cases of intestacy, the *intent* of the fathers was clear, for the sons did indeed come into their land. (This was also the law.) Grandchildren, it should be noted, were by law entitled to their deceased parents' share of the grandfather's estate.

In Bergen County, Daniel [330], son of Cornelius [24], had two farms of about 250 acres each which he divided equally among five sons and a daughter. As we see in Table 6.3, six other Haring testators in this generation gave farms to their sons, with legacies and bequests to their daughters, but none of them described daughters' shares as equal to those of the sons. Cornelius C. [331] divided one 200-acre farm and an unknown quantity of other land among three sons, with one daughter receiving 20 acres of salt meadow. The brothers Abraham A. [336] and Daniel A. [342] (sons of Abraham [27] each left three 200-acre-plus farms to their total of six sons and/or grandsons; another brother, Cornelius A. [344], divided one 200-acre farm and other land between two sons.

Among their three Orange County, N.Y., cousins, Abraham [39] (son of Peter [21], had two 200-acre-plus farms to bestow on two sons, and other land (an undetermined amount) for a third. John [326], the eldest son of Cornelius [24], divided his home farm between his eldest and youngest sons, charging them each to pay their sisters £150 (£300 total), and bequeathed 170 acres to his middle son, charging him to pay £100 to his sisters. The differential suggests that the home farm was larger or more valuable than the 170-acre farm that the middle son inherited.

119

Table 6.3. Disposition of Property, Real and Personal, Third Haring Generation

Testator	Will[a]	To Widow	To Sons	To Daughters	Personal Property[b]
Abraham [39]	Orangetown, 1771; Bergen Co., 1793; lib. 33, p. 160.	Mansion house, farm, movable estate & 1 Negro wench while widow.	Eldest: Bible, walking cane, house & farm. 2nd: home farm, lot, 1/4 of residue; he to pay £200 to sisters. 3rd: lot, 1/4 of residue. 4th: already had his share of estate.	Two: each 1/4 of residue; each £100 from brother.	—
Elbert [310]	New York City, 1772; N.Y.C., 1773; lib. 29, p. 27.	All while widow; £300 if she remarries; all silver plate.	Eldest: £55. 2nd & 3rd: each equal of land; each £450; each equal of residue.	Six: each equal of land; each £450; each equal of residue.	Three slaves @ £160; livestock @ £122; real estate; money at interest.
Theunis [311]	Intestate, d. 1771.	—	Two: divide farm of 197 acres.[c]	Two	—
John [315]	Intestate, (?), d. c. 1771.	—	Three.[c]	Five	—

John [326]	Orangetown, 1760; Bergen Co., 1775; lib. L, p. 269.	All while widow	Two: home farm equally. 3rd: "land over the kill."	Four: £100 each	—
Daniel [330]	Bergen Co., 1784; Bergen Co., 1784; lib. M, p. 270.	Deceased	Eldest: £2 & $\frac{1}{3}$ of land at Pascack. 2nd, 3rd, & 4th: home farm equally. 5th: $\frac{1}{3}$ of land at Pascack.	Two: $\frac{1}{3}$ of land at Pascack to one; she to pay £50 to other.	Seven children to share residue (£347) equally.
Cornelius [331]	Bergen Co., 1775; Bergen Co., 1783; lib. 25, p. 283.	All movable estate	Eldest: 26 acres plus lot. 2nd & 3rd: home farm equally.	Four: 20 acres to one; £60 each to three others.	—
Jacob [332]	Orange Co., 1771; Bergen Co., 1779; lib. M, pp. 46, 56.	All during life	No male issue	Deceased (1)	House & lot to a friend; residue to siblings.
Abraham A. [336]	Bergen Co., 1786; Bergen Co., 1791; lib. 32, p. 538.	Deceased	One son: 1 farm of about 200 acres. Three grandsons: 1 farm divided equally. 4th grandson: 1 farm.	One: 23 acres with right to slaves. One granddaughter: £60 to be paid by her three brothers.	£1,888: $\frac{3}{4}$ to male heirs; interest on $\frac{1}{4}$ to daughter.

Table 6.3. (*continued*)

Testator	Will[a]	To Widow	To Sons	To Daughters	Personal Property[b]
Daniel [342]	Bergen Co., 1801; Bergen Co., 1806; file 3361B	£15 yearly	Eldest: £3 and farm, he to pay £200 to sisters. 2nd: land, he to pay £200 to sisters.	Two: £600 equally. Three granddaughters: land, they to pay £200 to aunts.	£122
Cornelius [344]	Bergen Co., 1803; Bergen Co., 1810; file 3490B.	Room, household furniture, 2 cows.	Two: all real estate equally.	Four: £250 each, from brothers.	Residue, equally to all children.

SOURCE: Wills as cited in column 2.
NOTE: The identification numbers in brackets are those assigned in Herbert S. Ackerman's "Haring Family" (bound typescript, 1952).
[a]Place and year written; place and year proved; location.
[b]Estimated from will and inventory.
[c]Though no wills were found for John or Theunis, other evidence indicates their land was allocated as in text note 26, p. 278.

Finally, in New York City, Elbert [310], disinheriting his eldest son, left eight sons and daughters equal portions of his large farm in present-day Greenwich Village, as well as nearly £1,000 in cash to each (when the residue was distributed). Only two of these testators, Daniel [330] and Elbert [310], specifically stated that they were dividing their estates, real and personal, *equally* among their male and female children. One may infer from this that the other third-generation Haring fathers were forced to discriminate between sons and daughters not only in type of property bequeathed, but also in the value of the legacies that daughters received in comparison to the value of the farms their brothers received.[26]

A CLOSER LOOK

In 1771 Judge Abraham P. Haring [39] wrote his will leaving his eldest son, Peter [412], the "house and farm now in his possession," a separate lot and the home farm to another son, Abraham [416]—he to pay £200 to his sisters—and a lot to John [415], a third son. Abraham and John also received one-quarter each of the "residue" of their father's estate. Abraham's two daughters received only £100 each and one-quarter each of the movable estate. A few years later, in 1779, Peter and Abraham were taxed on 140 and 150 improved acres, respectively—the farms they had received from their father. In the same neighborhood, at almost exactly this time, farms were being sold at £3 and £4 per acre. It would seem, then, that Abraham Haring bequeathed his sons farms valued at, say, £450 to £600, while his daughters each received only £100. (It is very unlikely that the daughters' outsets would account for the £350 to £500 differential, as no local inventories, wills, or tax records reveal wealth among women at anywhere near this level.)[27]

Two other cases support the idea that Haring fathers by the 1770s were treating their sons and daughters very unequally. In the first case, in June 1773, Daniel Haring [342] purchased from Willam Bayard 212 acres, for which Daniel paid £848, or £4 per acre. Daniel acquired this property with his son Abraham [4121] in mind. A young married man of twenty-five in 1773, and the father of two children, Abraham built a house on the land and worked it throughout the rest of his life. When Daniel came to write his will in 1801, twenty-eight years after making this purchase for his son, he bequeathed the property to Abraham, requiring him to pay his two sisters, Sarah and Rachel, £200 (£100 each) for it. In other words, some twenty-eight years before, the fair market value of the land was £848, but the value to Sarah and Rachel after their brother had farmed it for nearly three decades was less than a quarter of what their father had paid for it. This differential cannot be accounted for by the size of the outsets Sarah and Rachel received when they married—in 1771 and 1781, respectively—for, again, there is no indication in either Bergen or Orange County tax records that women had wealth on this scale. Rather, it reflects the fact that as the population grew in relation to the availability of land, even "gentry" like the Harings were forced to face their futures with a cautious eye to changing economic conditions and to reevaluate their original hopes for themselves. If they wished to continue their grandparents' vision of living in close-knit neighborhoods of family farms, a more conservative attitude toward land—an increasingly scarce commodity—had to be taken, and sacrifices had to be made at daughters' expense in order to guarantee the futures of their brothers—a strategy facilitated and encouraged by the treatment of women under English law.[28]

Unequal testamentary treatment of sons and daughters is clear in another case. In August 1775, Cornelius C. [331] wrote a will bequeathing his farm of 200 acres—worth about £800—to his two sons John [485] and Abraham [489], but only cash legacies of £60 each to three daughters and a salt meadow of 20 acres to a fourth daughter. The disparity suggests that, although all sons and daughters shared in their father's estate, the shares were not allocated according to any standard of equality. Sons were treated equally in relation to each other, but they were given more than their sisters. Daughters were treated equally in relation to each other, and as fairly and as generously as their fathers could afford. Fathers knew that daughters, of course, would be provided for when they married by their husbands—but, again, according to their husbands' means.[29]

Besides such economic factors as increased demand for a decreasing supply of land, however, what other factors might account for the unequal testamentary treatment of sons and daughters by third-generation Haring fathers? One major consideration was the fact that a son had labored for a lifetime on the farm and had incurred expenses in maintaining and improving it and paying the taxes on it. Also, sons had to assume with the land the obligation to support, shelter, and in general sustain their mother—an economic burden daughters were spared. Still, the

£3,500 differential in the case just discussed (i.e., the will of Cornelius [331]) seems excessive, even after taking account of the rampant wartime inflation in land prices. Perhaps another factor—an intangible one hard to put a value on and even harder to document two hundred years later—was taken into consideration: the opportunities that sons forfeited, vis-à-vis possible alternative careers, by adhering to the family ethic and staying on the farm. In other words, by the 1770s, the farming life may well have lost some of its allure, and perhaps the pot had to be sweetened in order to entice sons to continue the family's tenure on the land and to shoulder the economic burden of their mother's support.

In sum, by midcentury, daughters were still treated equally in relation to one another, but only as fairly and as generously as their fathers could afford in relation to their brothers. In fathers' minds, equality was achieved by daughters marrying men with farms equal to the ones their brothers would inherit. Thus, testamentary patterns can be seen as serving to encourage daughters to find husbands with resources equal to their brothers'—and sons to marry women with attractive doweries and legacies.

FATHERS AND DAUGHTERS

Although most Haring daughters were no longer being treated equally in their fathers' wills by the third quarter of the eighteenth century, they were nonetheless treated well and were provided for by a variety of imaginative means. The will of Abraham A. [336] illustrates the love and concern fathers had for their daughters, at the same time as it illustrates the drastic transformation in women's status that had occurred in the half-century since the original four brothers made their wills.

Writing in 1786, Abraham (the eldest surviving son of Abraham [27]) left his three sons and/or their sons each a large farm and three-quarters of his sizable personal estate. To his only daughter, Sarah, he left the following: 23 acres for the term of her life; the interest on the remaining quarter of his personal estate, with the principal designated for his other heirs at her death; and the children of his slave, Cate. Sarah was allowed neither to control her principal, nor to will it as she pleased, nor to sell her 23 acres.[30]

Sarah's inheritance, in relation to that of her brothers, may seem to us grossly unequal; but Sarah's father was no doubt influenced by the increasingly prevalent inclination in the eighteenth century to consider sons not as more worthy, but as more needy of the family wealth than daughters, who increasingly came to be regarded as the responsibility of their husbands. Married first to Jacobus Blauvelt, who had died intestate in a British military prison in New York City in 1777, and by whom she had two children, Sarah remarried in about 1779 to her widowed second cousin, Captain Abraham A. P. Haring [416], and had two more children with him. At the time her father came to write his will in 1786, Sarah was thirty-seven, and all four of her children were dead. As a hedge against the statistical probability that her husband, seven years her senior, would predecease her, leaving her alone in old age—and perhaps wary too of the claims on their father's estate from her husband's two daughters by his first wife—Sarah's father devised a clever strategy: he purchased 23 acres of land from her husband, then willed the piece to her for the term of her life.[31]

In this transaction, all participants benefited: the husband received cash for his land; Sarah received land she could rent or lease for an income, or build a house on, should she ever need one; her father discharged a part of his testamentary obligation to her and put his mind at ease regarding her future; and it was stipulated that, after Sarah's death, the land was to go to her father's other heirs, so they were not disadvantaged by the arrangement. Sarah was treated not equally, then, but well, benefiting in five ways from her father's considerable substance. First of all, she had, according to custom, received an outset upon her first marriage and a parental gift upon her second. In addition, she had the use for life of 23 acres, the interest for life on a quarter of her father's residual estate, and as many children as her father's slave Cate might produce—a very marketable commodity.

Events proved her father's wisdom. At age fifty, Sarah was widowed again. Her two stepdaughters inherited their father's farm, one conveying her interest in it to the other—in effect, leaving Sarah homeless. By her second husband's will, Sarah inherited her choice of his female slaves, $250 in cash, her choice of his bedsteads, beds, and bedding, his cupboard, two of his cows, his psalmbook, andirons, and her choice of the spinning wheels—provided she accept these "in lieu of her dower rights," that is, her legal right to one-third of her husband's real estate. These items, added to her other resources, undoubtedly enabled this widow to live comfortably. But her story illustrates just how precarious life had become for a woman alone in the late eighteenth century. In a society that no longer regarded women as the testamentary equals of their brothers, women had to rely on men's foresight and generosity for their support and survival.

This is not to suggest that the society was becoming "sexist," but rather that sexism (then as now) may be primarily a function of economics. As economic conditions—particularly rising prices for diminishing amounts of land—put pressure on families, it was becoming expedient to enrich sons at the expense of daughters, for sons had the primary responsibility for the support of their future families. Women's economic value was to be found in secondary operations—transforming the raw materials men produced into food and clothing for the family—and even though these were important functions, they were not as vital as men's work.

FATHERS AND SONS

An important question regarding the conveyance of land and the relations between colonial American fathers and children, touched on above, is whether fathers withheld land from their sons in order to keep them on the farm throughout the fathers' old age—that is, whether they used sons as a kind of social security. The evidence is mixed.

In Andover, Mass., fathers, at least in the generation that settled on the land in the 1640s and 1650s, were not forthcoming with the means for sons to marry early and begin their own families. Instead, fathers used their economic power to exercise authority and influence over sons long after they had reached maturity. By denying them "incouragedment for a Livelyhood" (i.e., land to start their own married life upon), seventeenth-century Andover fathers forced sons to wait until their late twenties to marry. Even after sons did marry, and even if they followed a different line of work than their fathers, fathers continued to exercise economic power over sons, chiefly because they continued to own and control the land upon which the sons had settled.[32]

But in nearby Plymouth, a different situation obtained. Here, fathers did not attempt to use their economic power to keep sons dependent. Quite the opposite. Although some fathers kept ownership of their land until they died, others made gifts of all or some of it at their sons' marriage, and some even made sons independent before they married. From the beginning, the economic independence of sons was encouraged in Plymouth.[33]

127

In southeastern Pennsylvania, individual conditions rather than custom, law, or ulterior motive guided colonial and post-colonial fathers in the timing of their disposition of land. The same was true in Germantown, Pa., where parents, according to their means, freely gave their children of marriageable age something with which to start out. Most Germantown parents, however, were reluctant to part with their land—not in order to deprive children of the means to marry, but out of a desire to provide for their own old age when their children had moved on. This is because those who settled Germantown were not motivated by the concept of a cohesive, multigenerational family life, as in Tappan, and their "homeplace or community [was never] a symbol of family strength and continuity." Thus, parents held on to their land to sell for their own support in old age. Even most of those children in Germantown who did inherit land were quick to sell it and go elsewhere.[34]

Closer to Tappan, in Newtown, N.Y., few fathers actually gave their land away before death but, rather, let their sons use the land they were one day to inherit and maintain, improve, and pay taxes on. And in Flatbush, N.Y., because of the shortage of land and the availability of inexpensive land in New Jersey, parents not only encouraged but "preferred their children's departure and independence at marriage."[35]

The pattern adopted by the first generation of the Haring family in Tappan set the trend for following generations. Typically, sons were given the means to marry early and start their families under a separate roof on a farm adjoining their father's or nearby. In most cases, though, they had to wait until their father died to receive legal title to the land they worked—and, in some cases, until their mother died as well.

Haring sons seem to have been comfortable with this arrangement, if we may judge by the absence of protest to it. This reinforces the idea that, well into the eighteenth century, succeeding generations of this family continued to share their forefathers' vision of Tappan as a stable and multigenerational community of family farms. Unwilling to move to other frontiers or back to the city, Haring sons showed an amazing propensity through the fifth (and even beyond the fifth) generation of the family to keep the original dream intact. Almost none of the forty-four sons, grandsons, and great-grandsons of John Pietersen Haring left the Tappan area, and almost all of the sixty great-great-grandsons (the fifth generation) who survived to adulthood also remained. To stay meant to enjoy the comforts of a very far-flung kinship network, a privileged (though waning) economic position, deep roots in the church of their parents, grandparents, great-grandparents, and even great-great-grandparents, social prominence as a founding family in the community, access to channels of political power, and proximity to long-established markets and market mechanisms. To leave meant to abandon parents in their old age, to lose contact with brothers and sisters, to give up the emotional support and economic aid that aunts and uncles and other kin could provide, and to endure the loneliness and trials of life alone in a new place. To leave Tappan meant to contribute to the disintegration of the family, and this was an unwelcome prospect that no Haring family member had to face for more than a hundred years.

A few sons balked at parental attempts to control their destinies. Peter's son Abraham [39], for example, may have chafed at his father's attempt to keep the farm from his legal ownership until his mother died; for in 1738, two years after Peter made his will, but twelve years before he died, Abraham bought from his father for £400 the 236-acre farm he was designated to inherit.[36]

If a son showed signs of wanting to sell his lands and leave Tappan in order to further his interests elsewhere, he met with paternal disapproval. In his will Cornelius [24] instructed his eldest son, John [326], not to sell any of the land except to one of his siblings; he did not place the same restriction on his two middle sons—presumably because they did not show signs of restlessness. In the case of his youngest son, Jacob [332], however, whose only child, a daughter, had died, Cornelius instructed that if this son "Does come to Dai whithout lawfull Ears of his Body . . . the said Land shall Come to his Brodars and Sistors." Jacob did not have any more children, and he obeyed his father's wishes by conveying his inherited lands to his siblings. He then acquired a smaller property, which, as if for spite, he bequeathed to a bachelor friend.[37]

But, in general, that most third-generation sons shared their fathers' ideals and were amenable to continuing the farming life in Tappan is suggested by the fact that only these two sons, out of the eleven who lived to be mentioned in their fathers' wills, had to be instructed concerning the disposition of the land, should they not want to use it for its intended purpose.

In sum, the wills of Peter, Cosyn, Cornelius, and Abraham Haring reveal that the economic and familial considerations that had impelled the family to leave New York in 1683 to seek greater opportunity in Tappan were still, a half-century later, of paramount importance. In fact, those concerns had been the driving force in the lives of the four brothers, as they sought to accumulate enough wealth to ensure their widows' security and independence and to enhance the future of their sons and daughters. Although *their* sons—the third generation of the family—were not able to provide for their children equally without regard to gender, all fourth-generation members, male and female alike, inherited from their fathers, and all the sons inherited enough to be able to remain in the Tappan area (though some sons, as we will soon see, in less comfort than others).

Several conclusions may be drawn. The family ethic remained extremely powerful through the colonial period; it was coming increasingly into conflict with new and changing social forces; and Haring testators evinced an ambivalence toward social change. They demonstrated, on the one hand, an ability to change with the times by bequeathing their property according to the needs of their heirs. But they also attempted to sustain the values and customs of their traditional culture.

Part Three

THE FOURTH AND FIFTH GENERATIONS

Chapter Seven

Religion: "Those Who Labor in the Earth"

The eighteenth-century vision of America as a virtuous republican society was a vision that rested upon the farmer and the farming way of life—what later generations have referred to as the yeoman ideal. "Those who labor in the earth," Thomas Jefferson wrote in his *Notes on the State of Virginia* in 1785, "are the chosen people of God." In the farmer's breast, God keeps alive his "substantial and genuine virtue . . . that sacred fire, which otherwise might escape from the face of the earth."[1]

In linking human happiness with tenure on the land, eighteenth-century writers were availing themselves of a tradition that extended back to ancient Greece and Rome. The eighteenth-century American version of this conceit held that on the farm, tilling his soil, the farmer was untainted by the corruption, suffering, and vices of civilization and that, free and independent of an exploitive master or employer, he could develop the inner strength of character, discernment, and values necessary for republicanism to flourish. "Cultivators of the earth are the most valuable citizens," Jefferson wrote. "They are the most vigorous, the most independant, the most virtuous, and they are tied to their country and wedded to it's liberty and interests by the most lasting bonds."[2]

Although the eighteenth-century American farmer was undoubtedly a political creature intent on maintaining his constitutional rights and liberties, would the Haring brothers and their sons and grandsons have agreed that *nature* was the source of their virtue, inner strength, and political consciousness?

Examination of local church records and of the ecclesiastical records of the Dutch Reformed Church permits insight into the Haring family's religious life over the course of the eighteenth century, and those records suggest that, for the typical Dutch farmer in colonial America, theology, biblical interpretation, and the application of theological ideas to political circumstances—not improving hours behind the plow—were the dynamic forces in the farmer's moral life and the source of any "substantial and genuine virtue" he may have possessed.

WORSHIPING IN THE WILDERNESS

For all immigrants to America who were determined to settle into towns and form communities, the church was a central institution. The Harings and their friends wasted little time in organizing this aspect of their lives.

Few ordained ministers of any denomination in the seventeenth century were interested in serving God in the American wilderness. For the most part, the small and widely dispersed flocks who settled in the colonial hinterlands had to go unchurched or, at best had to church themselves in one another's homes. Those of the Dutch Reformed faith, if they were fortunate, might have the occasional services of an order of lay preachers call "voorlesers" (public readers) and "krankenbesoeckers" (comforters of the sick), who were authorized by the mother church in the Netherlands to console the dying, read prescribed prayers and Amsterdam-approved sermons to a gathered congregation, read aloud from the Bible, lead psalm singing, catechize children, and keep the church records. Voorlesers and krankenbesoeckers were the closest approximation to an ordained minister that most Dutch settlers in seventeenth-century America were likely to enjoy on anything like a regular basis. In New York and New Jersey in 1700, only six ordained Dutch Reformed ministers served twenty-three gathered congregations.[3]

But settlers were determined to have a religious life, despite the formidable obstacles. Their thirst was not only for sermons and sacraments, but for the fellowship that an organized church provided. Church was a respite, one of few, in the lives of farm people who six days a week were engaged in the grueling physical labor of clearing woods, planting fields, and feeding and clothing their large families. Church meant civilization, culture, and community—the society of friends, relations, and neighbors. Before and after Sunday services, men and women exchanged information and gossip, heard the latest political news that had filtered into the community from passersby or sojourners to the city, arranged to buy what they needed and sell what they did not, and kept a watchful eye on the children frolicking on the green to see that they, who would one day marry one another and have churches of their own to people, were assimilating the attitudes and habits of proper churchgoers.[4]

The importance of the church as an agency of community life cannot be overemphasized. It was the only place in the settlers' world where the traditions of the remembered past coincided with the conditions of the wilderness present and gave the colonists hope that they would persevere.

For eight years after settlement in 1686, the Tappan people met in one another's homes for Bible reading and psalm singing or traveled in good weather to congregations in New York City, Flatbush, Brooklyn, Bergen (Jersey City), and Hackensack. Marriage and baptismal records in these places document that Blauvelt, Cole, Cooper, De Vries, Haring, Harte, Keyserwyck, Meyer, Minnelay, Smith, Springsteen, Stratmaker, and Van Houten family members made the trip from Tappan down the Hudson River and, in the case of Brooklyn and Flatbush, on across New York Harbor and the East River nearly two dozen times from 1686 to 1694.[5]

They may have gone oftener, but their presence simply for worship would not have been recorded. On the other hand, they may have restricted their churchgoing during these years to the essential rites of marriage and baptism. For, as we will see below, they and many other Dutch New Yorkers were sharply at odds with the two Dutch Reformed ordained ministers in charge of the New York parishes: Dominie Henricus Selyns and Dominie Rudolphus Varick.

The trip to church required much planning and preparation. Even in the best of weather, it entailed at least one overnight stay with friends or family—more than one if the settlers took the opportunity to conduct other business. For the Tappan people, excursions to New York City, Long Island, and Brooklyn, though arduous, were less so than the alternative: the overland route through the woods to churches on the New Jersey side of the Hudson. Yet, on numerous occasions in this same eight-year period, the Tappan people hitched their horses to their wagons and rattled and bumped over the rutted "roads" to hear the Bible read

135

at Hackensack and Bergen by the lay preacher Guiliam Bertholf, a man whose Pietism (and politics) they found to their liking.[6]

GUILIAM BERTHOLF, VOORLESER AND PIETIST

A baker by profession, Guiliam Bertholf was a native of Sluis in the States Flanders, a part of the Province of Flanders conquered by the States General from the Spanish. Active in Zeeland, the "heartland" of Dutch Reformed Pietism, Bertholf emigrated to America in October 1684. What has been called the "paramountcy of conversation" clearly played a part in directing Bertholf from the Netherlands to New York. "Conversation"—usually tales of good land and golden economic opportunities but, in Bertholf's case, also opportunities to save souls and to practice his religion as he saw fit—was a strong agent in persuading men and women to take the radical step of crossing the Atlantic. Dutchmen from Zeeland already in America had heard of Bertholf's piety and calling, and word that they would welcome his presence among them had somehow reached him. Daniel De Clark, for one, was from Zeeland, and he may have been instrumental in encouraging the Pietist Bertholf to emigrate.[7]

Pietism, an impulse within Christianity almost as old as Christianity itself, helped prepare the ground in Europe for the reformers Luther, Zwingli, and Calvin, and after the Reformation it continued to extend that ground. Historically, Pietists had emphasized that the highest Christian ideal should be union with Christ, an ideal prized above the mere observance of the ecclesiastical and liturgical forms and practices devised by man. Post-Reformation Pietists applied the idea of reforming the church to an examination of how the individual Christian might reform his or her life, so that it might most nearly imitate the life of Christ.[8]

Dutch Pietism in the seventeenth century developed in relation to a theological debate within the Dutch Reformed Church between the followers of Gysbertus Voetius (1589–1676) and those of Johannes Cocceius (1603–1669) over the question of predestination and grace versus faith and good works. The Voetian conception of humankind as predestined informed the Pietist view, while the Cocceian view was that God would save his children if they had faith, obeyed the Word, and led virtuous lives. The Classis of Walcheren in Middelburg, where Bertholf was eventually ordained, was Voetian, and the Classis of Amsterdam, which had charge of the churches in New Netherland, was Cocceian. The theological debate spilled over into Dutch politics, with opposing views finding expression in the Orangist–States party division throughout the century.[9]

In New York and New Jersey during the late seventeenth and early eighteenth centuries, Dutch Pietists became a severe irritant both to the Dutch Reformed (Cocceian) clergy and to the political establishment, primarily on two accounts: they insisted that a personal conversion be experienced by all communicants, including the clergy; and they supported Jacob Leisler, a German-born New York merchant of Huguenot background and Pietist views, who in 1689 became the central figure in a successful rising against the British government, the so-called Leisler's Rebellion.[10]

Matters were more complicated even than this, because Pietism was only one force working against British government in the colonies. In New York, with its large Dutch population, economic and social factors played an important part in Leisler's Rebellion, with the middling sort supporting Leisler, and the better sort—the Philipses, Van Cortlandts, Livingstons, Schuylers, and so on—rejecting him. But in the political realm, all citizens of New York, no matter what their social standing, shared an authentic reason for resenting British rule in the 1680s; for James II, upon acceding to the throne in 1685, had revoked the colony's Charter of Libertyes, abolished representative government, annexed New York and New Jersey to the Dominion of New England, and attempted to rule the colonies by royal fiat. One of Jacob Leisler's first acts as captain of the fort was to ask the provincial towns to elect representatives to an "assembly" in the city in order to discuss their grievances.

The Harings and their fellow patentees were Pietists, as we know from their choice in 1694 of Guiliam Bertholf, now ordained, to be their first minister, and they were pro-Leisler, as we know from their connections to Leisler and the rebellion. Daniel De Clark, the Haring brothers' stepfather, was a member of the seven-man Committee of Safety that on June 8, 1689, chose Leisler as captain of the fort in New York. Other Committee of Safety members were Teunis Roelofsen Van Houten of Tappan, a Haring in-law; Samuel Edsall, the translator who had accompanied John Pietersen Haring on his excursions to negotiate with the Indians the purchase of the Tappan Patent; and John Demarest, a close Haring friend and neighbor in nearby Bergen

County, N.J. William Laurence, one of Leisler's councillors in 1690, also had Orange County connections, as did Abraham Gouverneur, clerk to the committee.[11]

"UNLESS ONE IS BORN ANEW"

Guiliam Bertholf's roots in Flanders and Zeeland had exposed him to the radical Pietism of a flourishing Mennonite community.[12] With their emphasis on a simple personal piety and their objection to the "forms" of organized religion (even the liturgy and the Lord's Prayer were in their view unnecessary for a person to approach God), the Mennonites from the fifteenth century had been preparing and inspiring hearts in Zeeland for the influential seventeenth-century ministries of four Pietist theologians who directly shaped Bertholf's thinking: Willem Teelinck and the Roman Catholic convert priest Jean de Labadie were both prominent in the Middelburg pulpit, and Jodocus Van Lodenstein and "his beloved pupil" Jacobus Koelman both occupied the pulpit in Sluis at the church to which the Bertholf family belonged. The controversial Koelman, who was to have the "greatest influence of any single Dutch Pietist on the developing points of issue among the Dutch Reformed Pietists in the [American] colonies," had been deeply influenced, like Teelinck before him, by the English Puritans and also by the New England Puritan divine Thomas Hooker, two of whose works Koelman translated into Dutch. Thus, it was through Koelman that knowledge of Thomas Hooker "passed from Connecticut to the Netherlands and back across the sea into the hands of the Dutch settlers in [New] Jersey."[13] And thus it was from Koelman, in the heady theological atmosphere of seventeenth-century Sluis, that Guiliam Bertholf acquired his particular theological views.

As suggested above, the major point on which the "Cocceian" Dutch Reformed Church in New York (which was overseen by the Classis of Amsterdam) differed from the "Voetian" Dutch Pietists, aside from the latter group's objection to the recitation of memorized prayers and rote liturgical forms, had to do with the importance of a conversion experience, or spiritual regeneration. For Pietists, belief, conviction, and faith were necessary but not sufficient conditions for salvation. Spiritual regeneration, the "putting on of the new man in Christ," was essential. For scriptural basis, they cited John 3:3: ("Jesus answered him, 'Truly, truly, I say to you, unless one is born anew, he cannot see the kingdom of God.' ") Indeed, for Pietists, not mere faith but being born again spiritually was necessary for the taking of the sacrament of Communion *and* for the administering of it. Adamant about this last point, Dutch Pietists did not hesitate to identify those ordained ministers in the church whose souls, in their opinion, had not been saved by a personal conversion to Christ. Naturally, their outspoken views and judgmental attitudes were unpopular with those church fathers who believed salvation was theirs by virtue of their faith and rectitude.

In his writings and from his pulpit in Sluis, the controversial Koelman urged his followers, Bertholf one of them, to become familiar with the whole word of God, not just with the approved texts as chosen by the church fathers. He advocated Bible study groups in homes, the practice of family devotions, public and private readings of the Scriptures, and "conventicles," private gatherings of born-again Christians for the purpose of witnessing and testifying to the glory of God. In the 1660s and 1670s, Koelman steadfastly objected to the use of the formal liturgical elements of the worship service and the prescribed rituals for the sacramental occasions, and he refused even to observe the festivals of Christmas, Easter, and Pentecost. These, having been devised by mere churchmen, were unnecessary, Koelman maintained, for direct communion between man and God. Rejecting especially the idea that salvation had anything to do with religious observance on Sunday morning, Koelman advocated spontaneous prayer, diligent study of the Word, and an evangelical spirit as the routes to communion with God. For these views he, like Labadie before him, was removed in 1674 from the pulpit at Sluis. Although Bertholf was only eighteen when Koelman lost the Sluis pulpit, there is evidence that the two men, mentor and pupil, were in touch over the next decade.[14]

After his expulsion from Sluis, Koelman moved to Amsterdam—a Cocceian stronghold—to preach to his followers and, much to the consternation of church fathers, to go out from Amsterdam to other parts of the Netherlands in order to expound his views. In 1682, he received a call from the Dutch Reformed Church in New Castle, Del., a Pietist community with Labadist connections, but the ecclesiastical authorities in Amsterdam, far from being pleased to be rid of him, refused permission for him to go. Presumably, they feared the spread of his ideas to the New World.[15] Had he been allowed to emigrate, he would have taken with him to America 250 of his followers, among them, according to the Dutch historian Albert Eekhoff, Guiliam Bertholf, now age

139

twenty-six. When the Classis of Amsterdam rejected the idea of a Koelman pastorate in America, Bertholf left for America on his own. Historians have traced the roots of Reformed Pietism within the Dutch Reformed Church in America to this man, who would shortly become the first Dutch Reformed Pietist clergyman in America and, in 1694, the founding dominie of the Tappan Reformed Church.[16]

THE PRIESTHOOD OF ALL BELIEVERS: PIETISM AND "DEMOCRACY"

If the Pietist idea that ministers as well as laypersons must experience a regenerative "warming of their hearts" for Christ was a thoroughly unwelcome one to the orthodox mainstream, Pietism's inherent democratic bias was even more so. The idea of the priesthood of all believers was repugnant to those highly educated ministers who believed their training and ordination set them above and apart from the common herd, and the discord such ideas had raised between the church establishment and Pietists in the Netherlands was apparent by the early 1680s in America. Guiliam Bertholf had no sooner arrived in New York, certified as a voorleser, than Henricus Selyns, dominie of the New York Dutch Reformed Church, wrote to Amsterdam to complain to the classis there of his sort:

> Certain men came over last year with certificates from Sluys [Sluis] in Flanders, and from Middelburg and Groode, in Zeeland. They were only tailors or shoemakers or cobblers, yet they endeavored to be promoted in this place or in that to the office of precentor and schoolmaster [Bertholf filled both roles at Hackensack].
>
> Some of them were assisted by me because of their great zeal; but how is it possible to agree with most of them? They speak against the church, public prayer, and the liturgy. They say [they] are Coelmanists, catechize, have private exercises and special prayers; and almost say, that the public prayers are spurious. True believers are grieved at these things and look forward to very great troubles therefrom to the church of God.[17]

Bertholf had arrived in America just as what were to become very great troubles, indeed, had begun to brew in the Dutch church. His zeal and the wide following he began to create among the yeomanry of New Jersey did nothing to assuage concern about him among the ordained clergy.

By 1693, Bertholf was serving the combined congregation of Hackensack and Acquackanonck (Passaic) as voorleser and schoolmaster, visiting the sick in both places, and traveling "over land and water" to such distant parishes as Staten Island and Brooklyn. Bertholf's far-flung congregations objected not only to the Cocceian theological views of the ordained dominies Henricus Selyns and Rudolphus Varick, as mentioned above, but to the dominies' politics, particularly their opposition in 1689 to the elevation of Jacob Leisler to the head of the government in New York. While those of Pietist leanings in New York rejoiced at Leisler's takeover, others, including Selyns, Varick, and Dominie Godfriedus Dellius in Albany, denounced the Leislerian effort and waited for the new monarchs in England, William and Mary, to appoint their own chosen governor. So strong was the support of the Pietists for Leisler, however, and so firm were their Voetian views, that not even Leisler's overthrow, treason trial, and death by hanging in 1691 could persuade them to enter the Cocceian fold. In 1693, Guiliam Bertholf—determined to seek ordination from the Voetian Classis of Walcheren in Zeeland—sailed back to the Netherlands.[18]

TAPPAN AND THE ITINERATING APOSTLE OF NEW JERSEY

No sooner had Bertholf preached his trial sermon in Zeeland ("Come to me, all who labor and are heavy laden, and I will give you rest") than he was again aboard a vessel bound for America, where his flock in Hackensack received him, he recorded, "with great affection."[19] Bertholf's ordination at first did little to improve the attitude of the American establishment toward him. On October 7, 1694, the Reverend Dellius of Albany, the third of three anti-Leislerian ministers in New Netherland to write against Bertholf, shot a letter off to Amsterdam to make known that "Mr. Selyns and myself will experience great difficulty in recognizing him as a minister and as a colleague."[20] Two weeks later, almost before Dellius's letter was out of New York harbor, the settlers in Tappan also risked the dominies' displeasure and engaged Guiliam Bertholf to form a church for them and be their part-time minister.

The eleven founding members of the Tappan Reformed Church were Cosyn and Cornelius Haring and their wives, Lambert Smith, Teunis Van Houten, Teunis Talman and their wives, and Johannes Blauvelt.[21] That they called Bertholf to their pulpit indicates that, like him, they too spurned official orthodoxy for evangelical Pietism, sought a religion that emphasized the necessity for personal spiritual rebirth, and rejected dead "forms," lifeless traditions, and "unregenerated" clergymen. Like him, they acted in what they perceived as their own spiritual interests, rather than as church authority dictated.

Their choice of Bertholf deepens our understanding of the community that the Harings and their fellow patentees hoped to create in the wilderness of Tappan. In good Dutch fashion, as we saw above, the farming community was to be a trading hub and a haven of family stability. In good Pietist fashion, it was to be a new Jerusalem, a "city set upon a hill" such as the English Puritans envisioned building in Massachusetts. And, in the tradition of Dutch republicanism, it was to be a place where men would feel secure in questioning authority—both ecclesiastical and political. With this background, it was almost ordained that the community would be a seedbed—and it was—for revolutionary sentiment when economic, social, political, and religious impulses fused later in the century into a coherent desire for freedom from British rule.[22]

BERTHOLF'S PARISHIONERS: AN ECONOMIC PROFILE

Although they were Leislerians, Bertholf's parishioners were not an economically deprived or embittered underclass, as Leislerians have often been portrayed. Public records indicate that the patentees were people of the middling sort with a history in both Europe and New Netherland of property owning, church affiliation, and civic participation. Many became substantial farmers in the New World, relatively wealthy in land, slaves, and cattle. On the other hand, Bertholf's parishioners in Tappan were not a homogeneous lot, as the Dutch in the Hudson and Hackensack valleys have often been described. A correlation of information on slaveholding in the census of 1702 with information on church-giving patterns reveals, in fact, that as society as a whole was characterized by social stratification, so in microcosm did this little community comprise at least three distinct economic strata.

To take the church financial records first, starting in the year of the church's organization, 1694, and continuing for three decades, excellent records were maintained of what each head of family gave to support the church. Contributors in Tappan fell into three groups (high, middle, and low), and characteristics of these groups generally correlated with such other important indicators of wealth as slaves and land. In other words, church members known to be richer in land and slaves gave more to the church than others known to have less land and no slaves.[23]

Eighty-six members of the church gave at least once during the three decades 1694–1723. In 1694, the first year of the church's existence, 24 members contributed. Of these, 2 gave three florins; 1 gave four florins; 16 gave six florins; 2 gave eight florins; 2 gave twelve florins, and 1 gave eighteen florins. Proceeding on the assumption that giving was based on financial ability, the 16 members who gave six florins represented the middle range of members in economic standing. Three gave less than the middle range, and five gave more than the middle range, one of these, Teunis Talman, contributing the most, eighteen florins. Talman must thus have been the member of the community judged most able to contribute that year. (A florin was worth six shillings. Wheat at this time was four shillings, six pence a bushel; corn, three shillings per bushel; butter, four pence a pound. Carpenters received two shillings a day; bricks cost twenty shillings per thousand.)

After Talman (who was a brother-in-law of the Harings), the next four highest givers the first year were Cornelius Cooper and Peter Haring, followed by John De Vries, Sr., one of the free-black patentees from the Out-ward, and Johannes Meyers, a son-in-law of one of the original patentees from New Jersey, Ide Van Vorst. (Van Vorst had died in 1683, before settlement; his daughter inherited his share.)

The three members on the low side of the annual giving for the year 1694 were Hendrick Blauvelt (three florins), Isaac Blauvelt (four florins), and Jacob Flierboom (three florins). Apparently, being related to a patentee family, as these three men were, did not necessarily ensure that one would share in the experience of "rising"; for neither of these two Blauvelts improved his economic position sufficiently to be able to increase his contribution as the years passed, Hendrick giving on the average less than one florin per year in the thirty-year period (through he may have died before it was over), and Isaac giving less than two florins. Jacob Flierboom (another brother-in-law of the Harings) doubled his giving in 1696 and was able to give six florins annually for most years, but his assessment was never among the highest in the congregation.

In the high range, Peter Haring gave twelve florins in 1694 and increased this to just over thirteen florins the following year, an amount he gave every year but three for as long as the record continues. During the thirty-year period for which these records survive, he and his brother-in-law Teunis Talman were consistently the two highest individual contributors, and the same eight families were consistently the highest givers (Harings, Talmans, Blauvelts, Coopers, Smiths, De Vries, Van Houtens, and Minnelays).

Always bearing in mind that "wealth" in rural, early-eighteenth-century communities is not precisely determinable, and that this particular community was composed almost entirely of obscure farmers, none of whom was wealthy by the standards of New York and New Jersey's great land barons and merchants, a picture nonetheless emerges from the church financial accounts of an economically and socially stratified society with the wealthier, less wealthy, and least wealthy levels clearly discernible.

A look back at the census of 1702 (Figure 3.1) confirms this general picture of stratification.[24] Among high-contributing church families, the Harings, Coopers, and Talmans also owned the most slaves, each of these families possessing from two to four adult slaves. Although neither Smiths, Blauvelts, nor De Vries owned any slaves in 1702, these families may have had enough male members to do all the work, or they may have employed indentured labor and seasonal workers.

To set slaveownership in sharper perspective as an indicator of wealth, the largest slaveowner in the county in 1702 was Englishman William Merritt with five, or 25 percent, of the total adult slave population of twenty. But if the two slaves owned by Daniel De Clark, the Haring brothers' stepfather, are added to the three owned by Cornelius, Cosyn, and Peter Haring, then this family owned as many adult slaves as Merritt—that is, also 25 percent of the total.

In 1712, another census was taken of Orange County. In the intervening decade, the free population had grown from 235 to 385, and the black population from 33 to 53.[25] The Harings were prospering. In 1712 they now owned four adult slaves, and De Clark, their stepfather, owned three. Among other leading church contributors, Smiths owned two adult slaves in 1712; Talmans, two; Coopers, two; and Blauvelts, one. Again, Harings (with seven, including De Clark's three) were richer in slaves than any of their other neighbors except Captain John Corbet, with nine. (William Merritt had died.)

Only some of Bertholf's parishioners belonged to this upper stratum in the community. A middle stratum comprised lesser landowners, those able to contribute in a small way to the church's support, but not able to own slaves, and younger unmarried sons yet to come into their property. And there was also a much less affluent, even poor, class in the community, as we know from references in the church records to funds set aside for the poor, Orange County court records concerning arrangements for the support of the poor, the existence of church members who did not contribute to the church's support, and the presence in the community of a transient population of bachelors who probably hired themselves out as day laborers, never acquired the means to settle down in the community, and did not affiliate with the church. The poverty of this nonlandowning sector of the community stands in sharp contrast to the affluence of men like Peter and Cosyn Haring, Daniel De Clark, Lambert Smith, and Johannes Blauvelt, who in 1729 were able to give nearly a hundred acres of first-class land to the community—the land on which the church stood, land nearby for a manse, and meadow and pasturage for the minister's support; as well as other land for a courthouse, jail, and stocks.[26]

CHURCH MEMBERSHIP

Stratification in society was reflected in the "stratification" in church membership—of which there were four categories in the Dutch Reformed Church: one for the clergy, requiring the most stringent self-examination and self-discipline; a second for the elders and deacons; a third for the regenerate; and a fourth (informal) category for the unregenerate (who were not admitted to the Lord's Table). Elders and deacons, like ministers, were called to their office by God, and thus it was an important and solemn one. Elders were "to give attention to the whole flock and to feed the same . . . to cast their eyes over the whole congregation, to rebuke irregularities, to instruct the ignorant, comfort the feeble-minded, support the weak . . . to be patient to all . . . and to help and support" the pastor.[27] Ordinary members also had a responsibility for examining their conduct and their thoughts and for rebuking the godless in the congregation.

Election to the church offices of deacon and elder constituted public recognition of one's leadership qualities, sense of responsibility, moral rectitude, state of grace, and general eminence in the congregation and the community. In Tappan, those offices were closely held by members of the founding church families. Conversion, which was a prerequisite for full, communicating membership, was, of course, also essential for church office. Tappan Reformed Church records document the leading roles played by Haring men as deacons and elders. In the first thirty-six years of the church's existence, the four brothers, three of their sons, and their stepfather were officers fifteen times, or nearly 42 percent of the time.[28]

WOMEN IN THE TAPPAN REFORMED CHURCH

The Pietist belief in the priesthood of all believers extended to women, and women played a prominent and visible part not only in the organization and early membership of the Tappan Reformed Church in 1694, but always thereafter as well (although they were never permitted to serve as elders or deacons). Five women were among the eleven founders in 1694. In 1695, the second year of the church's existence, forty-one persons joined, among whom were sixteen married couples, two married women, six single women, and a single man—in all, seventeen men and twenty-four women. No new members were taken in for another seven years—until 1702 and 1703, when eight women joined (and no men). Thereafter, women consistently comprised slightly more than half of the Tappan membership.[29]

A general surplus of women full members over men in the first years suggests that self-examination and conversion may have come more readily to women than to men. It may be that the relatively high standing Dutch women enjoyed in the seventeenth century imbued them with a confidence in their acceptability—both to humanity and to God. But whether the process that has been called "feminization" was taking place in the Tappan church in the late seventeenth and early eighteenth centuries is not clear. Historians of religion in colonial America have found that, in

146

some denominations and regions, women formed a large majority of the congregation. But in 1724, thirty years after its founding, membership rolls in the Tappan church continue to show a rather even balance between the sexes: 52 percent of those owning sittings in 1724 were female, 48 percent male, almost the same ratio as in the church's first years, whereas in the New York Dutch Reformed Church in the same period, 65 percent of the communicants were women.[30]

The Dutch church in New York had strong professional ministers leading it for many years, however, and some historians—noting that colonial churches with an ordained resident clergy often had high female membership—have suggested that power relationships within a church may have changed when male lay leaders had to hand over their influence to a higher clerical authority. In 1724, although the Tappan church was thirty years old, the Tappan people still did not have a resident pastor. (Bertholf lived in Hackensack and preached at Tappan only four times a year.) Yet, a glance at the Tappan church membership figures for the 1727–1749 period, the years of the first resident pastor, Frederick Muzelius, shows little change in the male-female membership ratio. Over these twenty-two years, 130 men joined, as compared to 151 women—that is, 46 percent of the new members were men, 53 percent women. This represents a definite surplus of women over men, but it is not evidence of "feminization" in the same sense that the phenomenon seems to be present in other places.

An analysis of church-joining patterns in the Haring family over a somewhat longer span of years, 1694–1751, does suggest, however, that men and women joined the church at different stages in their lives and perhaps for different reasons. For instance, Table 7.1 shows at a glance that, of the nineteen Haring second-, third-, and fourth-generation males joining from 1694 to 1751, ten were married and already had baptized children of their own at the time, and nine were single. The nine single men were twenty to twenty-six years old at joining, but the age at which the ten married men joined varied considerably from young (twenty-two) to middle-aged (thirty-five). Two of the latter group were married for longer than a decade before they took the plunge, and had five and six children apiece, whereas four had been married for fewer than four years before joining and had but one or two children each.

Men seem to have been able to exercise a great deal of freedom with respect to when they joined, although none waited until

Table 7.1. *Haring Men Who Joined the Tappan Reformed Church, 1694–1751*

	Year joined	Age at joining	Marital status	Children at time of joining
Cosyn [23]	1694	23	M*	1
Cornelius [24]	1694	24	M*	1
Peter [21]	1695	31	M*	4
Abraham [27]	1704	23	S	0
John [315][a]	1717	24	S	0
Abraham P. [39][b]	1729	25	M* (4 yrs.)	2
John [326][c]	1729	35	M (11 yrs.)	5
John [335][d]	1729	20	S	0
Abraham [336][d]	1729	21	S	0
Cornelius [331][c]	1730	22	M (1 yr.)	1
Harmanus [337][d]	1732	20	S	0
Jacob [332][c]	1733	23	M* (1 yr.)	1
Daniel [330][c]	1739[e]	35	M* (12 yrs.)	6
Theunis [311][b]	1740	32	M (6 yrs.)	3
Daniel [342][d]	1741	21	S	0
Johannes [451][f]	1746	26	S	0
Cornelius [462][g]	1746	24	S	0
Abraham [461][g]	1747	26	S	0
Cornelius [344][d]	1751	26	M* (4 yrs.)	2

SOURCES: Records of the Tappan Reformed Church, Tappan, N.Y.; David Cole, *History of the Reformed Church of Tappan, N.Y.* (New York, 1894).

*Joined with wife.
[a] Son of Cosyn [23].
[b] Son of Peter [21].
[c] Son of Cornelius [24].
[d] Son of Abraham [27].
[e] Joined Schraalenburgh Reformed Church.
[f] Son of John [315].
[g] Son of John [326].

after age thirty-five, and all took this step well before their own parents had died. On the other hand, for men, there appear to be patterns of joining that are consistent within individual families. Table 7.1 indicates that the sons of Peter (*b*) and Cornelius (*c*) waited until after marriage to join, whereas Cosyn's son (*a*) and four of Abraham's five sons (*d*) joined while single, the latter at age twenty or twenty-one. Perhaps some branches of this family were more pious than others, or perhaps fathers had something to

Table 7.2. *Haring Woman Who Joined the Tappan Reformed Church, 1694–1751*

	Year joined	Age at joining	Marital status	Children at time of joining
Brechtje [25]	1694	19	M	—
Maria [26]	1695	15 (?)	M	—
Grietje [31]	1706	18	S	0
Brechie [33]	1710	18	S	0
Pietertie [35]	1714	18	S	0
Marytie [325]	1715	20	S	0
Marytie [316]	1717	21	S	0
Grietie [318]	1717	17	S	0
Grietie [327]	1717	20	S	0
Fijtie [328]	1719	19	S	0
Vroutje [329]	1722	20	S	0
Maria [320]	1726	21	M	2
Claesie [312]	1731	20	M	2
Margrithje [338]	1732	18	S	0
Maria [450]	1738	20	M	1
Brechie [343]	1742	19	S	0
Catalyntie [460]	1742	23	S	0
Annetje [452]	1742	20	S	0
Grietje [463]	1745	21	M	0
Grietje [440]	1751	17	S	0
Maria [464]	1751	26	M	2

SOURCES: See Table 7.1. Also "Records of the Reformed Dutch Churches of Hackensack and Schraalenburgh, New Jersey," in Holland Society of New York, *Collections* (1891); "Baptisms from 1639 to 1730 in the Reformed Dutch Church, New York," in New York Genealogical and Biographical Society, *Collections* (1901); "Marriages from 1639 to 1801 in the Reformed Dutch Church, New Amsterdam, New York City," in New York Genealogical and Biographical Society, *Collections* (1890), vol. 1.

say about when their sons approached the Lord. In any case, differentiation from family to family within the larger kin network is clear. (If church-joining required that members make a contribution to the minister's salary and the support of the church, there may have been an economic element to the decision.)[31]

Haring women, on the other hand (see Table 7.2), not only joined in slightly greater numbers in these years (twenty-one women joined as compared to nineteen men), but two-thirds of them joined before marrying, most at age eighteen to twenty-one.

Figure 7.1. Tappan in 1778. Watercolor by British Lieutenant General Archibald Robertson. Courtesy Spencer Collection, New York Public Library, Astor, Lenox and Tilden Foundations.

Only one of the seven who joined after marrying was older than twenty-three. Three had not yet borne children, and the other four had only one or two infants at the time of their joining. Women seem to have been more conforming and conventional than their brothers in religious matters, less willing to postpone their confession of faith. Perhaps they were more aware of the perils of womanhood and their own mortality as they approached their childbearing years.

THE TAPPAN CHURCH BUILDINGS, 1694–1835

The farmers of Tappan were interested not only in arguing theological points of issue, but also in actively worshiping. The first church building in the community was erected at about the time of formal organization, 1694, by the congregation's first members. As the church financial records indicate no large influx or outflow of funds to pay for the construction, members presumably contributed the material and labor as needed. This building remained in service, with improvements and enlargements, until 1788, when much of it was replaced. Its original two-foot-thick stone walls were left intact even in 1788, however, being pulled down by teams of oxen only in 1835, when the present church— the third on the site—was built. Archibald Robertson, an engineer in the service of the British army, sketched Tappan in 1778 from a nearby hill, and the original hip-roofed church, built around 1694, appears in the sketch.[32] (See Figure 7.1.)

In 1665, the Duke's Laws had prescribed that churches accommodating two hundred people be built in areas where the population so merited, and evidence reveals that the Tappan people followed this prescription quite literally.[33] A list of sittings in the Tappan church, compiled by the voorleser in 1724, indicated that 192 congregants owned sittings, and there was extra space on benches for those who did not. From the voorleser's descriptions, it is clear that men and women were not seated together, for the men are described as sitting around the periphery of the sanctuary—in the "southwest," "west and North," "on the right side" of the entrance, on the "southwest side of the door," and so on— while the women occupied rows of stools on both sides of a center aisle and faced the minister in his wineglass-shaped pulpit on the north wall.[34]

Figure 7.2. Tappan Reformed Church. The building above stood from about 1694 to 1788; that below from 1788 to 1835. Courtesy Tappantown Historical Society.

The angles at which some of the men's benches were placed suggest that furniture was arranged to give the interior an illusion of octagonality. Octagon-shaped churches were popular in seventeenth-century rural Netherlands communities. Just as the settlers had brought their Pietist ideas with them to the Middle Colonies, so did they bring their styles of church architecture. Octagonal churches were built in Flatbush in 1663, Bergen in 1680, Hackensack in 1696, New Utrecht in 1700, and Bushwick in 1705. Records show that the Tappan church was improved in 1726 with glass windows set into "iron-work" frames. When the church was rebuilt in 1788, the interior was painted in imitation of mahogany, the columns that supported the roof in imitation of marble, and the pulpit's sounding board decorated, appropriately for a farming community, with a sheaf of golden grain.[35] (See Figure 7.2)

A TYPICAL WORSHIP SERVICE, CIRCA 1724

Worship in a Pietist congregation, according to the liturgical historian Howard G. Hageman, on most Sundays of the church year would have consisted of preaching, as opposed to Communion services. As it was considered the gravest sin to partake of Communion unless one was quite sure of his or her regeneration, "infrequent communions were the rule in pietist churches because of the awesomeness of the occasion." Even so, only a few members of the congregation might participate on a given occasion—that is, only the "spiritually elite who did not fear to eat and drink damnation to themselves," as they surely would if they partook without grace.[36]

The voorleser, or lay reader, would begin the service by reading passages from the Bible. A psalm or several would then be sung, the voorleser singing a line, the congregation repeating it or reading the text from small, leather-bound, and sometimes silver-clasped psalters (those who had them).[37] Singing was a vital part of worship, reminding the congregation of those martyrs of the faith who had gone to the stake singing psalms. Hymns or "spiritual songs," in addition to psalms, would also be sung during the service. Although spiritual songs were controversial, on the grounds that they were not drawn directly from the Bible, Pietists advocated them anyway as an important means of expressing the personal religious feelings and emotions of the worshiper.[38]

During the singing, the minister entered the church and ascended to the pulpit. Either he or the voorleser would then read the Ten Commandments, and the minister would pray. Although Bertholf's churches were Pietist in spirit, they were also correctly orthodox in liturgy and form. Therefore, they would not have dispensed with liturgical prayers, and the presermonic prayer would have included both the general liturgical confession of sin and the Apostle's Creed.

This can be known from Bertholf's own words. Few have survived, but in their 1721 "Recommendation" of three sermons by Theodore Frelinghuysen that were being published, Bertholf and his colleague Dominie Bernhardus Freeman took the opportunity to endorse explicitly the orthodox order and forms of the Dutch Reformed Church: "In accordance with our office and bounden duty, we faithfully labor to promote the orthodox and scriptural doctrines of our Church, and oppose those which are contrary in their nature." The three sermons, they made clear, agree in the "smallest particulars . . . with the written word of God . . . our Heidelbergh Catechism . . . and the forms employed in our Dutch churches."[39]

Next came a lengthy sermon, followed by the Great Prayer. Of prodigious length, the Great Prayer in a Pietist congregation was not a read prayer, but an extemporaneous one, though often preserving, according to Hageman, a "high liturgical sense," despite its being cast in a free form. Free praying was undoubtedly an integral part of the Tappan Reformed Church worship services during the Bertholf decades (1694–1724). In his treatise titled "The Need of Reformation Regarding the Use of the Liturgy," Bertholf's mentor, Koelman, had argued that since the regenerate person was a child of God, one should speak to God as to a father, from one's own heart and needs. Bertholf's zeal, as attested to by his contemporaries from Dominie Selyns to Dominie Frelinghuysen, mark him as a man who would have disdained merely to "chatter to the Lord in a cold voice," as another eighteenth-century Dutch Pietist, Willem Schortinguis, put it.[40]

THE SERMON

The sermon took up the great bulk of the service. Bertholf, like all Dutch ministers of the day, would have relied heavily in preparing his sermons on the marginal annotations and explications in the *Staten-Bijbel*. The marginal aids were intended both for preachers and congregants, and scarcely a Dutch home was without a copy. Virtually every will of the period and almost every Haring will discovered refers to "my great Dutch Bible." James Tanis points out that the *Staten-Bijbel* and its glosses were translated into English and published in London in 1657. It was "widely used by the Puritans in New England and added one more link between the English-speaking and the Dutch-speaking Calvinists" in the New World.[41]

Surviving sermons of the day run to twenty printed pages and more, and every page is abundantly sprinkled with supporting text citations from the Bible. As the minister paused to read the cited verses themselves, not just the citations, a typical sermon in the Tappan Reformed Church during the early part of the eighteenth century would have gone on for well over an hour.

No sermons of Bertholf's have been found from his thirty years as the "itinerating apostle" of New Jersey. But some five hundred eighteenth-century American Dutch Reformed sermons are known to exist, and a thorough examination shows them to share strikingly similar characteristics of structure and content.[42] Structurally, the typical sermon hews to a standard pattern of exposition followed by application. In the exposition, the Bible verses and relevant articles in the Heidelberg catechism to be dealt with that day were read, explained, and their points and subpoints outlined. Then, in the lengthier of the two parts, the message of the verses and the catechism was "applied" to the congregation for its edification.[43]

The most salient feature of a Bertholfian sermon, assuming it to have been modeled on the typical Dutch Reformed sermon of the day, was its view of the congregation as divided into the saved and the unsaved, and its exhortation to the unsaved to seek rebirth in Christ and to the saved to stay reborn. Both elements in the congregation (sheep and goats, wheat and chaff, the good fish and the bad, the vine that bears fruit and the vine that does not, etc.) were urged to undergo minute self-examination in order to determine the state of their souls.

"The Acceptable Communicant" was one of three sermons of Theodore Frelinghuysen's published in 1721 that Bertholf had "attentively read and with the utmost care examined" in order to recommend them to the purchaser. Bertholf described this sermon as "learned, well-digested, and thrilling," its contents "highly sound and scriptural, and agreeing in the smallest particulars not only with the written word of God, but also with the teachings of our Heidelbergh Catechism."[44] Bertholf's own sermon on the subject would have reflected, one infers, the same ideas and standards. It would have outlined "who may, and may not approach the Lord's Table," and it would have recommended that the church "debar those that lead offensive and wicked lives."[45]

The sheep or the wheat, in this case, would have been "only the regenerated," "renewed persons," those who are "sorrowful for their sins" (though "mere sorrow is not of itself sufficient"), those who believe their sins are forgiven, those who accept the "divine plan of reconciling and saving sinners through Jesus Christ," those who desire to be strengthened in their faith" and "to live more holy," and those who have evidence of the "indwelling of the Holy Ghost." For those on the other side—the goats, the chaff, hypocrites, dissemblers, and deceivers—the Lord's Supper was not instituted. Even though they might have an "outward un-blamable walk," the unregenerate, those without God's grace, "may not approach [the table]; because their hearts are not right with God."[46]

The hallmark of a Frelinghuysen sermon was the anxiety en-gendered by the problem of how one could know whether or not one were really and truly saved. But in his well-meaning at-tempts to bring his congregation to greater spiritual awareness, Frelinghuysen brought instead division and near havoc to his church in Raritan. His zeal knew few bounds, his standards of "acceptability" few limitations. He went to such extremes that he was eventually admonished by the Classis of Amsterdam for his harshness.[47]

Did the same happen in Tappan? Bertholf endorsed and recom-mended Frelinghuysen's sermons and theological views, and the underlying thrust of his own sermons was, like those of his con-temporaries, self-examination to discover whether one were spiri-tually renewed or not. But Bertholf is revealed in his own words and in the testimony of those who knew him as less quick to jump to judgment than Frelinghuysen and more tolerant of the limita-tions of his human flock. Moderate yourself, Bertholf urged the younger man in 1725, for you ought to know that the congrega-tion at Raritan is "very feeble in spiritual knowledge" and that there was danger, by his (Frelinghuysen's) harsh treatment of them, of turning them into

Quakers because of his demanding of them so much "to pray from the spirit," and of "special illumination"; or into Atheists because of his threats of hell and damnation, as if there were no heaven, and also no God [to save them]; or

156

into suicides, because before regeneration, he demanded "Despair," which is the path to suicide; or into Pharisees because he demanded that they should declare whether they were regenerated or not, thus causing men to depend not on God, but on their own judgment of themselves.[48]

In sum, Bertholf's personality and philosophy seem to have combined remarkably well with the ideas and ideals of the Tappan community. Independent and adventurous on the one hand, he and they seemed on the other hand to have valued harmony, tolerance, cooperation, and order—the virtues he was ordained to practice and they were meant to imitate. "[We encourage you] very heartily and brotherly Your Reverence," the Classis of Walcheren wrote to Bertholf in 1695, "to harmony and mutual peace, which is the great lesson, warning and commandment of Our Lord Jesus: to love each other, bring in your part by all means, avoid all the opportunities of displeasure, Yield rather every time pursueing the peace in that way and show always the gentle spirit of Jesus Christ." If this was the spirit of the Tappan community in its earliest decades, it was a spirit to be sorely tried, as we will see.[49]

For thirty years, Bertholf evangelized to his Dutch congregations. Besides Hackensack, Passaic, and Tappan, he organized and supervised churches in Raritan (now Somerville), Ponds (Oakland), Pompton Plains, Schraalenburgh (Dumont), Second River (Belleville), and Tarrytown, across the Hudson River from Tappan. To get to his congregation in Tarrytown, Bertholf had to be rowed across the Tappan Zee. The Hudson River at the Tappan Zee is three miles wide, strongly tidal, with swift currents and a deep channel. That such a perilous passage was taken regularly in a rowboat is striking testimony to the people's thirst for religion and Bertholf's determination to satisfy it. It is in addition, striking testimony to the intimate relations between religion and politics in the Leisler and post-Leisler era, for the oarsman who got Bertholf to the church on time was none other than Teunis Roelofsen Van Houten, a member of the Committee of Safety that had helped put Jacob Leisler into power.[50]

THE CONGREGATION IN 1724

In 1724, the last year of Bertholf's pastorate, Voorleser William Van Dalsen compiled a list of "sittings" in the Tappan church. All four Haring brothers (now ages sixty, fifty-five, fifty-two, and forty-three) owned places in the little stone church, as did, in their own names, their four wives, seven of their thirteen surviving sons, and ten of their daughters and daughters-in-law. Five of the non-seatowning sons alive that year were age fifteen or younger and thus probably were thought too young to own a seat. The ages of the seven seatowning sons suggests that boys of sixteen, deemed by the government old enough to serve in the militia, were also considered old enough to own their own sitting in the church. The cousins John P. [37], John C. [315], and John C. [326] were twenty-four, thirty-one, and thirty years old and married in 1724. Abraham P. [39] and Daniel [330] were single and twenty. And Theunis [311] and John A. [335] were a mere sixteen.[51] A glance back at Tables 7.1 and 7.2 will show that church membership was not a prerequisite for seatowning.

Of the Haring daughters and daughters-in-law who owned their own seatings, Aeltie and Rencie were the wives of John [315] and John [326]. The other eight can be identified as daughters of Peter, Cosyn, and Cornelius. (Abraham's daughters are not represented, as the eldest was only ten in 1724.) Inquiry into the ages and marital status of these eight Haring women reveals that, although they are recorded under their maiden names, seven of the eight were married in 1724 and were affiliated, except in two cases, with other churches. The eighth, Claesie [312], a daughter of the patentee Peter Haring, was a tender thirteen years old in 1724. For females, apparently, the onset of adolescence conferred the status and recognition that mature women enjoyed in this milieu; thus, young women were allowed the social prestige of owning a seat before they had undergone the deeper experience of committing to Christ. (Claesie joined in 1731. See Table 7.2.) Claesie's sister Catlyna (Meyer) was twenty-two, married, and affiliated with the New York Dutch Reformed Church in 1724. All three of Cosyn's married daughters—Marytie (Bogert), age twenty-eight; Margrietie (Demarest), age twenty-four; and Marie (Eckerson), age nineteen—owned sittings at Tappan, though Margrietie was affiliated with the Hackensack church. And three of Cornelius's married daughters—another Margrietie Demarest, age twenty-seven; Fytie (Westervelt), age twenty-four; and Vrouwtie (Demarest), age twenty-two—were affiliated variously with the churches in Schraalenburgh and Hackensack.

Clearly, the Tappan-area population was growing so fast that seats in the church were at a premium. Families, it appears, acquired as many sittings as they could, then held on to them even after their owners married and moved away, so that younger siblings and siblings-in-law would be able to participate in the worship service. In this sense, married women literally saved seats for their younger siblings. It also appears that married women normally left their home church for their husband's when they married out of Tappan—a natural consequence of geographic distance in the horse-and-wagon era.

The sittings list, even though it presents a snapshot of the Harings at only one instant in time and in one place, yields a wealth of sociological information about this yeoman-class family. For instance, although they spoke English in the public areas of their lives, they retained Dutch for the private areas of family and church. Voorleser Van Dalsen's list, like all the seventeenth- and eighteenth-century records of the Tappan Reformed Church, is in Dutch, and the entire church service the year it was made and for many years after would have been conducted in the Dutch language. Dutch was used for preaching in Tappan almost longer than anywhere else in America, sermons being preached in Dutch on alternate Sundays there until 1835, when the present church on the original site was consecrated.[52]

The list also reveals that in 1724, the matriarch of the family, Grietje Cosyns, was still alive. Now eighty-three years old, she appears on the voorleser's list as Margrietje, with the De Clark family. Surrounded in the sanctuary by her four sons, her four daughters-in-law, seven of her grandsons, two granddaughters-in-law, and ten granddaughters, seven of them married and already producing great-grandchildren, Grietje could be well satisfied that her family was successful in the most fundamental sense of that term in that it was reproducing itself with unabated vigor. Church baptismal records indicate that nine Haring children, Grietje's great-grandchildren, were born in the year 1724 alone. These nine babies add their own interesting perspective to the family portrait, for on Grietje's side of the Haring family they were already, in 1724, fifth-generation Americans.

Grietje could be content that her family was successful, too, in managing to pursue its goal of cohesiveness and harmony. Although some granddaughters had left Tappan proper for their husband's community, they were still in the vicinity and could congregate easily with their kin. At least twenty-five Haring mothers and fathers, sisters and brothers, aunts, uncles, and first cousins gathered under one roof each week to worship the Lord. (Others may have stood around the sides of the sanctuary, or morning attenders may have given their seats to seatless relatives

159

for the afternoon service.) If the actual seatowners themselves were worshiping at another church in another community, their places were readily filled by younger siblings.

Surrounding the Harings in 1724 were their old friends and fellow patentees. Seven of the original families who had ventured into the wilderness with them forty years before were still prominent in the community in 1724, though some in greater numbers than others. On the sittings list were thirty-four Blauvelts, nine Coopers, seven De Clarks, one De Vries, sixteen Smiths, fourteen Meyers (descendants of Ide Van Vorst), and seven Straatmakers, joined by a number of the Haring in-law families—Bogerts, Flierbooms, Talmans, Van Dalsens, and Van Houtens—as well as by in-laws of the other patentees—Coles, Croms, De Graws, Lents, Perrys, and so on.

Slaves were permitted to attend worship services, where they sat in the galleries, and to participate in at least some of the rites and rituals of the church. Some slaves were baptized; they were probably catechized; and they were buried in the church-owned cemetery, albeit in a segregated area of it. There is no evidence, on the other hand, that slaves partook of Communion or were encouraged to marry in the church.

TRIBALISM

This glimpse into the Tappan sanctuary in 1724 might suggest that the process which has been called "tribalism" had set in. In his study of the seventeenth-century Puritan family in New England, Edmund Morgan found that the churches there turned away from society at large and in upon themselves, increasing their numbers by recruiting members from original families rather than by incorporating newcomers. Ministers spent their energies on the churched and on the children and grandchildren of the churched, neglecting newcomers, with the result that the New England churches eventually diminished and declined. Other denominations—the Anglicans and the Quakers—also practiced religious inbreeding, treating new entrants to the community as less worthy than those descended from the founding families and their offspring.[53]

What about Tappan? Were the Dutch-descended churchgoers in this community any different from their brethren in New England and Pennsylvania? An examination of the baptismal rolls of the Tappan Reformed Church in the first thirty-one years of its existence shows that 461 infant baptisms (and four of "aged persons") were performed by the Reverend Bertholf—an average of about fifteen a year. Besides the usual patentee surnames, 130 new names appear in the rolls during these years. (All surnames have been included in this count—those of both parents and those of both sponsors.)[54] Of these 130 nonpatentee family names associated with Tappan baptisms between 1695 and 1724, 72, more than half, also appear in the membership rolls of 1694– 1730. Similar findings are associated with marriage records.[55]

The Tappan church, in other words, far from being closed to the outside world, seems to have been a veritable mecca for new young couples wishing to marry, for new families wishing to have their children baptized, and for those families who actually settled in the vicinity and entered into full membership, as shown by other public records. Deed indexes for the period 1694–1730, for instance, reveal a strong overlap between ownership of land in the area and some level of affiliation with the Tappan church. Far from declining as the founding generation aged and their children and grandchildren came to maturity, the church continued to grow vigorously in membership.

It is noteworthy, however, and it may be evidence of "tribalism" on some level, that only eight nonpatentee surnames occur in the rolls of deacons and elders during this same period (and, looking another twenty years beyond to 1750, only twelve more new surnames occur among the elected leadership). The core families, though welcoming newcomers to worship, sacraments, and fellowship, maintained tight control over the forms of piety and over finances, administration, discipline, and outreach policy. In a case on June 22, 1713, even an infant who appears to have been illegitimate was incorporated into the church family by baptism, Voorleser Jan Van Dalsen acting as sponsor. But whether that same child, grown to maturity, would have been considered just as worthy of a deaconship as the legitimate child of a founding family is highly doubtful.[56]

In "aging" New England towns, it has recently been noted, churches became the "preserves of kin groups that expressed through religious activities their aspirations for their families and their communities . . . and the church there was the established kin group writ large."[57] Many of the scores of families who constituted the Tappan Reformed Church by 1730 were related by bonds of marriage and blood, and it seems clear that some degree of tribalism was at work. But the real issues that convulsed and divided the Tappan church and its sister Dutch Reformed churches in the years from about 1730 to 1770 were not matters of kin and tribalism. They were ecclesiastical and political issues, which as we will see in Chapter 9 nearly destroyed the church and, along with it, the old family ideals of closeness and community harmony.

DISSENSION IN THE NEW JERUSALEM

One final look at the Tappan church during the Bertholf years (1694–1723) reveals not only that not all inhabitants of Orange County affiliated with the church, but also that not all church-affiliated men supported it financially. The Dutch communities in the Hudson and Hackensack valleys have often been described and thought of as inhabited by men and women who were monolithically of like mind on religious matters, with all dutifully dressing in their best and riding off in wagons to church on Sunday. And certainly we have seen a great interest in churchgoing in colonial Tappan. In 1702, however, the year of the Orange County census, only seventeen of fifty-four men older than sixteen are recorded as having contributed that year to the Tappan Reformed Church. (There was no other public house of worship in the county in 1702.) To look at it from another perspective, forty-one heads of family were counted in the census, but nine of these (22 percent) appear neither as contributors to the church nor as affiliates in any other way. Some of these nine may have been Sunday attenders, of course, but as there is no sign of this, one looks for another answer.[58]

Eleven bachelors whose surnames identify them as being from church families, when added to the recorded seventeen who contributed, account for twenty-eight out of the fifty-four men in the census; presumably these eleven men would contribute once they married. But what of the remaining twenty-six men? Where did they fit in? Were they so poor that they could not spare a florin for the church? Were they excluded from the community's central institution by their apathy toward religion? Were they excluded because the church was perceived as the province of only the land- and slave-owning elite? Or was there some other, possibly political reason?

Three of these twenty-six noncontributors—Gerrit Huijbrechtz, Poulus Tjurckssen, and Jurian Melgertssen—were bachelors who do not appear either in the church membership lists, the baptismal or marriage records, the financial records, or in another census taken in 1712. Apparently, they did not linger in Tappan, but moved on to some other place, or they died. Tjurckssen seems to have been the orphaned son of Jacobus Jurckssen. Melgertssen had parents in Tappan but did not marry and remain there himself. Huijbrechtz may have been an indentured servant or a seasonal worker in the community when the census of 1702 was taken. Evidently at the bottom of the economic and social scale in the community was Frans Wey, with his unnamed Indian "wiffe."

Some of the remaining twenty-three men were of English origin and may have been affiliated with an English church in New York or elsewhere. One of them, Colonel William Merritt, born in England, was a former mayor of New York and one of the founders of Trinity church. Edward Mek, Merritt's nephew, was the son of the widow Sarah Crab by her first husband. To judge from their names, James Weller and Isaac Brett may also have been of English origin.

This still leaves nineteen married men unaccounted for. Some, John Waard and Conraet Hansen, for instance, had affiliated with the Tappan church in 1694 and 1695, respectively, but Waard never contributed to its support after 1696, and Hansen never once contributed, suggesting that they died, moved away, were too poor to be assessed, or for some other reason withheld their support. (Waard borrowed fifty-five florins from the church in 1698.) Other names—Reynerssen, Janzen, Perry, and Cool—occur in the church lists prior to 1702 or later, but evidently these men were too poor to pay anything to its support in 1702. Some who cannot be accounted for were perhaps from the lower social echelons in the community and felt no connection with its central institution.

On the other hand, Samuel Conklin was affluent enough to own a slave, yet he was neither a contributor to the church nor a member of it. (His wife, Annetje Joachims, was a noncontributing member.) Was he disaffected? Many years later, in 1775, nine of thirteen Conklin family members refused to sign the Continental Association.[59] Rynier Van Ditmarsen paid twelve florins to the church's support in 1696, but thereafter had no recorded contact with it, even though he was still in Orange County in 1712 when another census was taken. Was he disaffected?

Perhaps in some cases nonaffiliation with the church was based not on apathy, nor on economic or social grounds, but on political/ theological differences. As noted above, politics and religion clashed violently in America during the Leisler era, and a number of the men on the Committee of Safety that officially appointed Jacob Leisler as captain of the fort in June 1689 had close ties with Tappan and nearby Bergen County: Daniel De Clark, Teunis Roelofsen Van Houten, John Demarest, and Samuel Edsall. All were men of strong Pietist views, as was Leisler. All were strenuously opposed to Roman Catholic influence in New York. And a number of them were members of churches led by Dominie Guiliam Bertholf, who in Dominie Varick's words had "violently urged on" the Leisler party.[60] It may be that the politics of such men and their friends and relations were offensive enough to others in Tappan to prevent their embracing the church.

It is reserved for the next chapter to explore how Pietism would translate itself into an enthusiasm for home rule that would split the Dutch Reformed Church in the coetus-conferentie controversy after midcentury and divide families for generations. Here it is merely suggested that, in the decades to come, Guiliam Bertholf and Jacob Leisler would be remembered as men who had challenged authority when it became oppressive.

In sum, the foregoing examination of the religious life of the Harings suggests that this yeoman-class family took both theology and worship seriously. If any particular virtue adhered to the American yeoman, its source was as likely his religion as it was his contact with "nature" or his physical distance from the wicked city and the ills of civilization.

The patentee and patentee-related families constituted a self-conscious and, through their marital alliances, self-perpetuating elite that thought of the church as its natural social center and of the community as a place where they could hope to prosper for generations to come in a spirit of lawful order and harmony. Along with some of the outsiders to whom they sold land, or who acquired it from other owners in the area, this elite also shouldered the burden of administering county affairs and representing the county on the provincial level. Indeed, the enthusiasm with which they assumed secular responsibilities nearly matched their zeal for the sacred.

Chapter Eight

POLITICS: SEEDS OF THE REPUBLIC

Essential to the development of Jeffersonian republicanism was a citizenry that enjoyed economic independence through the ownership of land. "The small land holders," Jefferson wrote, "are the most precious part of a state" because ownership of land instilled in men good judgment, self-reliance, a sense of responsibility, an inclination for order and regularity, strength of character, and a desire for political freedom. A man "by his property . . . is interested in the support of law and order. And such men may safely and advantageously reserve to themselves a wholesome control over their public affairs."[1]

A close examination of a single farming-class family such as the Haring family over five generations in America, from the 1680s to the end of the eighteenth century, confirms the Jeffersonian view of the farmer as deeply interested and involved in the political process, but it also reveals that, at least for this family and their neighbors in Tappan, it was difficult from the beginning to achieve the conditions that inclined the farmer to self-governance, independence, and order. In moving away from British New York to the Tappan wilderness in the 1680s, the Harings and their fellow patentees expected to govern themselves in the township organization to which their charter entitled them; and, with the division of New York Province into counties in 1683, they anticipated having a voice in county-level and province-level politics.[2] As with the physical and legal settlement of the patent itself, however, these political expectations met with obstacles and frustration.

"EACH CITTY TOWN AND COUNTY"

Sparsely settled Orange County needed only a very rudimentary governing structure at first, and this it got in 1686 in the person of a sheriff and a justice of the peace appointed by the governor of New York in the name of the British monarch. The patentees, in their domain in the southern part of Orange County, were entitled by their charter to all the "Priviledges, benefitts, customes, Practices, Preheminences, & Immunityes . . . used or Excercised, Practiced or belonging, unto any Towne within the Government"; so, in addition, they formed the Towne of Orange and elected a supervisor, "highway" masters, a constable, and perhaps a few other officials to attend to matters in their part of the county. As the population of the county grew, other townships or precincts formed so that the Towne of Orange was in time joined in Orange County by the Haverstraw, Goshen, Minesink, and Highlands precincts.[3]

On the county and province level, the farmers of Tappan discovered that finding a forum for their voice was not so easy. In 1691, the New York Assembly provided for the counties to be governed, English-style, by courts of common pleas presided over by appointed judges and justices of the peace. But even though the Judiciary Act of 1691 provided that courts be set up "for the Ease and benefitt of each respective Citty Town and County" within the province, Orange County was not at this time permitted its own local court of common pleas.

What was the reason? It seems likely that Orange County was being punished for the aggressive role its inhabitants had played in Leisler's Rebellion—the overthrow, two years earlier, of James II's New York government. On May 31, 1689, an Orange County company of soldiers led by Captain Cornelius Cooper, a Tappan patentee, and including commissioned officers Johannes Blauvelt and Teunis Talman, were among those rebels who had captured the fort and who had served there under Leisler during his brief tenure as commander in chief. Some of the men on the Committee of Safety that commissioned Leisler as captain of the fort on June 8, 1689, also had strong connections to Orange County—particularly Daniel De Clark, Samuel Edsall, John Demarest, and Teunis Roelofsen Van Houten. Others with Orange County associations—William Laurence, Abraham Gouverneur, Peter Bogert—as well as many unidentifiable Orange County inhabitants had supported the uprising in other important ways. In June

1689, the freeholders of the county had themselves, according to a deposition given by Daniel De Clark, responded to a written request from those holding the fort to elect two "fit and experienced" commissioners and send them to New York to "Consult what might be best & most advantageous for the welfare of the country & the protestant religion." This they did, Daniel De Clark swore, after mature deliberation "freely and unanimously."[4]

When the uprising was suppressed by Governor Henry Sloughter in 1691, De Clark described how the Orange County men in the fort "were disarmed and had their swords taken from them." And shortly after Sloughter had secured the fort, De Clark went on, the soldiers "fled from thence . . . out of fear that they should be ill used."[5]

They were not ill-used physically, but it appears that they and their countrymen in Orange County were made to bear the brunt of official British wrath for seven full years afterward: from 1691 to 1698 New York County was empowered to keep a tight rein on the affairs of its rural sister. Orange County court cases had to be tried in a New York County court; wills of Orange County inhabitants had to be proved in New York; estimates of Orange County tax ratables were to be made by New York County assessors; the sheriff and justices of the peace of New York County were authorized to act as such in Orange County as well; and Orange County militiamen were placed under the command of a New York County regiment.[6]

This was an ignominious position for the farmers of Tappan to be in, for when the patentees supported the revolt against the British government in New York, they had done so out of a highly developed sense of themselves as political beings—politically enfranchised and politically active members of society who had for centuries had a say in their own government. Determined not to submit to a king "bound in Conscience [as a Catholic] to indeavour to Damn the English Nation to Popery and Slavery," these pro-Leislerian Dutch American farmers viewed themselves not as a rabble of "mad and franticq humour," a "parcel of ignorant and innocent people, almost none but of the Dutch Nation," but rather as "gentlemen [moved] to be early in shaking off their Tyrants, and declaring for their Deliverer." What a subsequent century would think of as a romantic link between nature, landowning, and political independence, was—in seventeenth-century New York—Protestant farmers of Dutch background standing up for their constitutional rights.[7]

Orange County was not permitted to send a representative to the New York Assembly until 1699, when its population had grown sufficiently to warrant representation. Thus, the Harings and their fellow patentees had little say in county- and province-level political affairs for almost two decades after settlement.

By 1703, the system of governance in New York Province allowed for greater local autonomy on a county level, and at this time Orange County finally got its own court of common pleas, although court officials were still appointed, not elected. The court's duties were supposed to be strictly judicial; administrative matters (including the substantive ones that had been performed by New York County in the first years) were to devolve upon locally elected officials acting as a supervisory board. This did not actually happen in Orange County, however, until 1723, when population growth warranted the formation of other precincts within the county, and annually elected supervisors from each township formed a board of supervisors to regulate all county matters. Between the time of the establishment of the court of common pleas in 1703 and the formation of the board of supervisors in 1723, the administrative tasks of the county continued to be carried out by the court, which ordered elections, supervised election returns, assessed taxes, audited the returns, granted tavern licenses, ordered road repairs and the laying out of new roads, recorded cattle brands and earmarks, and so on.

In the twice-yearly sessions of the court, justices and jurors heard, now on home turf at least, cases of "petet Larcenys, thefts, trespasses, forestallings, regrettings, and Extorcons . . . and all . . . other misdeeds and offences," including "Disturbance of the people . . . Lain in wait . . to maim or kill . . . and alsoe of Inholders . . . who have offended . . . in the abuse of weights or measures or in the sale of victualls . . . and alsoe all sherriffs, Bayliffs, Constables, [and] Gaolers . . . who . . . [are] careless, remiss or negligent."[8]

Surviving court records indicate that most of the misdeeds and offenses dealt with by the court were less colorful than these—mainly illegitimate births, bothersome dogs, horse thefts, straying cattle, and the like. These court records, though they exist for only a few of the earliest years (1703–1708), show that in no case is any Haring a litigant. Rather, Harings are in the jury box, just as in the following decades they are on the bench, the Orange County Board of Supervisors, the Bergen County Board of Justices and Freeholders, or somewhere on the side of law and order serving as constables, sheriffs, justices of the peace, judges, and representatives to the New York Assembly. With the exception of their suit to preserve the patent from Lancaster Symes—a step they took only after years of provocation and after all other remedies had failed—they seem to have settled their legal differences out of court.

"Men of Good Life . . . & Not Necessitous"

What were the qualifications for officeholding, and who among the county's population was eligible? No formal property qualifications existed in New York for officeholding, but people, as they did everywhere, sought to be governed by "Men of Good Life . . . & of Good estates & Ability, & not Necessitous."[9] Although the ownership of property did not always go hand in hand with good character, as we will see, in the eighteenth-century mind they were of a piece. In Newtown, on Long Island, 100 of the 106 men holding office in the years 1692–1723 were propertyowners, and most officials came from the upper half of the economic spectrum. In Ulster County, N.Y., a rural area on the west side of the Hudson River consisting of small towns, farms, and villages, most officials were of the middling sort. For instance, of twenty-one justices of the peace in the years 1711–1776, fourteen were farmers and artisans. In those New York communities with a larger elite, the more affluent were appointed or elected to the higher offices—as assemblymen, justices and judges, supervisors, county clerks, and county treasurers—and lesser officials came from the middling sort. In Orange County, all appointed officials in the first decade were either patentees, patentee in-laws, or other large landowners in the area; and in 1690, when Orange County petitioned the governor to appoint a county clerk, the petitioners recommended Dirck Storm, "inasmuch as his capability and reliability is well known to us." Storm had been a voorleser in Flatbush and was a man of learning, character, and "good estate."[10]

Orange County justices of the peace, as set forth in their commissions, were to be men with enough credibility to enforce the laws and ordinances made for the "peace and quiet rule" and government of the people, to chastise and punish all persons breaking the law, summon before the court all lawbreakers, find good and lawful men to testify to the truth—and in all ways to "dilligently Intend . . . all that which to Justice appurteineth." The six justices chosen to sit on the first court held in Orange County, in

1703, were all men whose property and ability and experience disposed them to authority. Colonel William Merritt and his son Major John Merritt were wealthy Englishmen whose estate on the Hudson nearby was one of the choicest in the area. Colonel Merritt had been a member of the New York Assembly, an alderman, and mayor of New York from 1695 to 1698. Justices Cornelius Cooper and Teunis Van Houten, one a patentee and the other a patentee in-law, were both prominent landowners. In addition, Van Houten was a thriving merchant at the Tappan Slote, and both men had earlier held other positions. Two nonresident justices, Thomas Burroughs and Michael Hawdon, were New York City merchants and Orange County land speculators on a large scale.[11]

Although the patentees seem to have been somewhat slighted in their representation on the first bench in Orange County in favor of those of British background, this may have been in part because they were younger in years than Merritt, Burroughs, and Hawdon. The patentees and their in-laws made up nine of the thirteen members of the first grand jury chosen that year; and, as we will see, the most able of them shortly rose to more prestigious county posts.

Literacy in English was another important characteristic of officeholders in British New York. In 1694, a Dutch-speaking tax collector in Newtown was relieved of his duties because he did not understand English; another was dismissed in 1703, when it was found he was illiterate. Three men were expelled from the Eighth Assembly (1701–1702) for their "gross Ignorance and unacquaintedness . . . of the English language." Court minutes in ("Dutch") Orange County were kept in English from 1703; and, in 1724, the Orange County Board of Supervisors ordered that their minutes be kept in English "for our better understanding and Satisfaction."[12]

Learning Accountability

Public officials had to be trustworthy. If they betrayed their trust, the law provided remedy, as Orange County Sheriff Thomas Husk, Esq., found to his regret in 1719. A "person of a very ill behavior a Comon breaker of the Peace and an encourager of all manner of wickedness," he was accused by Justice Cornelius Cooper before the Council of the Province of New York of taking "very Exorbitant and unreasonable fees contrary to all Law and to the great dammage of the Subjects, nay he so farr forgetts the duty of his office that he takes upon himself when any persons refuse to obey his illegal and extrajudiciall commands to assault and wound them to [their] great Terror."[13]

And when the Orange County supervisors in 1730 discovered the "great neglect" of the tax collectors in not paying over their moneys to the treasurer, they indignantly ordered that a lawyer be employed immediately to "issue out Writs for every collector that shall neglect, refuse or delay to pay." In 1743, when a tax collector, who had "elopd from ye County" with his revenues, later absconded from the county jail, the sheriff was held accountable for the escape owing to his "good Youmore . . . [in] not Locking the . . . door of the Gaol."[14]

Accountability was fiercely guarded. Even Assemblyman Cooper ran afoul of the board of supervisors when he presented them with a pay voucher from the speaker of the Twenty-first Assembly certifying that he had served for 118 days. But it appearing, the supervisors noted, that he was absent 24 days, and considering that they "thought it unreasonable that he should be paid in addition for 13 Sundays when the Assembly was not in session," they were willing to pay him for only 81 days and 4 days travel.[15]

Accountability worked both ways. People expected their officials to be reliable, and officials expected the same of the people they served. The patentee Peter Haring [21] in October 1726 submitted to the board a voucher for Assembly service for £30 8s (152 days service at four shillings per day). The bill was not paid, nor would it be paid for thirteen years, despite Haring's repeated attempts to have the voucher honored. In 1738, he lost his patience and besought his son, Judge Abraham Haring [39], to serve the supervisors with a court order, at which point the board requested that the "lait treasuer" appear with his records to explain. Perhaps most telling is not Haring's thirteen-year campaign to be paid for services rendered, but the treasurer's insistence that the clerk make it clear in the record that the error was an honest one, so that his reputation might not be impugned.[16]

Learning to Share Power

As might be expected, the patentee and patentee-related families, Harings prominent among them, served in all of the offices that needed to be filled—younger men in the lesser posts, more affluent and older men in the higher. But a check of census, deed, and

171

probate records, among others, indicates that men from many nonpatentee-related families also participated in the politics and administration of Orange County. Officeholding in the political sphere was not and could not be nearly so closely guarded as it was in the religious, and men from a great many outside families were from the beginning able to play a role in county affairs.

In 1702, for instance, most of the families in Orange County were Dutch. But ten years later, in 1712, a census of Orange County showed sixty-seven separate families living in the three townships, and many were not Dutch. In Orangetown were forty-two separate nuclear households with twenty-five different family surnames, mostly Dutch. In Haverstraw were seventeen families with sixteen different surnames, many English. And in Minnesink were eight families with five different surnames, mixed. In all, forty-six different family surnames occur in the census, and most of those names were present in the county during the first two decades of the eighteenth century. By comparing these names against the "Civil List of Orange County, New York, from the Erection of the County to the Year 1723" and other public records, it can be determined that, besides the sixteen or so now-familiar patentee and patentee-related names that are all associated with officeholding of some type, at least one member of nine other families—Crum, Denn, Hanson, Harte, Holly, Husk, Keyserick, Minnelay, and Ten Eyck—held office at least once during the years 1686–1723. Moreover, twenty-one family names—Blagge, Burroughs, Bush, Caniff, Clowes, Cole, Corbett, Gouverneur, Halstead, Hawden, Honan, Huddleston, Hutchins, Jewell, Merritt, Osborn, Perry, Smith, Storm, Vanderburgh, and Ward—which do not appear in the 1712 census, but do appear in other local records of the period (deeds, probate, court, church), are also associated with officeholding.[17]

In the first three decades of this period (1723–1750), twenty-five men served in a possible 105 openings as supervisor. Ten of the twenty-five served only once or twice. Whether these ten chose not to stand for office a second or third time for personal reasons, or whether they were not reelected for a second or third term because of voter perception that they were deficient in some way cannot be determined. The other fifteen men served from three to as many as twelve terms as supervisor over these twenty-eight years, returning to office (presumably) out of a sense of duty and a desire to be involved in decisionmaking and administration—as well as out of the voters' sense that they were effective in office.[18]

172

From a count of the English names in the records, it is clear that, by 1723 at least, in what has been traditionally thought of as a clannish and sleepy Dutch enclave of New York Colony, Dutch origins were not a prerequisite for officeholding. Nor was church affiliation. Only eleven of the twenty-five men who served as supervisor from 1723 to 1750 had an affiliation with the Tappan Reformed Church, the only church in the county, and of those eleven, only six were deacons or elders. Three others were full members, and two were affiliated with the church in only a tenuous way. Four men with no affiliation to the church were either militia captains or a justice of the peace, bringing to fifteen the number of supervisors who had either a church affiliation or a public position of trust and responsibility. To these fifteen may be added one man whose repeated election to the board (and to other posts) identifies him as a solid citizen.[19] But this still leaves nine men of twenty-five who were elected to the board of supervisors between one and three times from 1723 to 1750 but who had no affiliation with the church, no militia or other political post of record, no recorded land and, in short, left no trace of themselves in the public record beyond having served on this board.[20]

If a man did not have to be of any particular ethnic background, a large landowner, affluent, a churchgoer, or even experienced, what did determine his qualification for county office? It seems likely that one important factor was a basic sense of fair play. So many different interests were coming to make up Orange County's population—Dutch and English, Reformed and Anglican, people of different social rank and degrees of wealth, and with differing allegiances to the factions that vied for power in the New York Assembly—that elected county officials had to be capable of accommodating all without alienating any. Even in the location of its meetings, the board had to demonstrate a sensitivity to Orange County's settlement patterns and diverse interests, moving from Tappan to Haverstraw to Kakiat in order to spread the inconveniences of travel equitably among the supervisors.

The Board's Work

As required by law, the board of supervisors met once a year in October. Business matters came first, as the board examined the treasurer's accounts and settled the quotas to be collected from each precinct in order to pay the tax due the government and cover local expenses: salaries of local officials and of representatives to the Assembly, reimbursements to workmen for county-related jobs, such as constructing bridges, animal pounds, and stocks, repairing the jail and courthouse, and such.

Every three or four years, the board reviewed the tax assessments of the precincts, in case, as they put it, one place should have grown faster than another. Orange County records indicate that the supervisors kept a vigilant eye on one another's assessment quotas and took pains to ensure strict and fair proportional obligation. As they did in 1729 and whenever they found "them Selfs not in a Method," they worked out an agreement "whereby . . . any precincts [that] have bin overtax . . . Shall be allowed for the Same." Inequity carried powerful emotional value long before taxation without representation became a rallying cry of the Revolution. If disproportion was perceived, or even suspected, the supervisors of Orange County addressed it until they could "unanimisly," "unanemusly," "younamusly," or "younanimissly" and, for good measure, "*nemine contradicente*" agree to an adjustment. The concern of these obscure eighteenth-century New York farmers for equity illustrates Bernard Bailyn's observation that the "intellectual position [on taxation and representation] worked out by the Americans [in the two years of the Stamp Act controversy] . . . had deep historical roots; it crystallized, in effect, three generations of political experience" on the local level.[21] In Orange County, those historical roots had an emotional component in the natural rivalries among townships settled by groups of different ethnic backgrounds and political outlooks.

Once business matters were taken care of, the board addressed the county's social problems: crime, poverty, and disease. From its earliest days, the community maintained stocks and a jail at Tappan, where lawbreakers could be punished and incarcerated; but the worst offenders—even murderers—were conveyed (in the characteristic eighteenth-century solution to problems) out of the county under paid escort, to become another community's burden. By court order, "lunaticks," vagabonds, thieves, and troublemakers suffered the same fate—and often the county judges who signed their fates were Harings. The dumping ground of choice for Orange County was Philipsburgh Manor in Westchester County, to which the unwanted were escorted by boat across the Hudson River and abandoned to the tender mercies of the inhabitants there. The other favorite place to transport undesirables was West Jersey (Haring judges never sent them to East Jersey, where the Harings had close friends and relations).

As well as filling judgeships and serving as justices of the peace, Harings took their turn both in Orange and, later, in Bergen County as elected overseers of the poor—of whom there were increasing numbers as the population grew. In 1751, the Orange County overseers paid for "roofing to provide a place for a Lunatick for one year," and Doctor Gale attended a vagrant lodged in the jail. In 1752, another vagrant was boarded out, and three different residents in turn sheltered a troublesome lunatic. In 1754 alone, a vagrant and his wife and five children, a lunatic woman, and two other vagrants were conveyed away; another lunatic was boarded at county expense; the county paid the funeral expenses for a schoolmaster who had hanged himself; the board ordered a tub made for the prisoners in the Goshen jail, so that they might "ease themselves"; and blankets were provided for prisoners "on account of the winter's cold." The insane continued to be boarded out around the community, and in 1758, when illness struck, orphaned children in the Seely and Williams families were boarded out "till [they] come to be 18," while the ill and dying were ministered to by doctors whose fees were paid by the county. In the 1760s, the social welfare efforts of the board occupied the lion's share of its attention.[22]

"A Great Deal of Trouble and Fategue"

Officeholding took time, and it thus incurred an opportunity cost. That is to say, in order to serve, especially in the more demanding posts, a man either had to forfeit the opportunity to tend to his own business, or he had to hire someone else to do his work for him. Some historians have found evidence in town records that men often refused office on these grounds.[23] In Orange County, however, office seems to have been sought, not spurned—or at least it was readily accepted. A reading of the board of supervisors records for the years from 1723 to 1750 indicates that a broad population of potential officeholders was called upon to carry out the county's business, that many served more than once in the same or in a variety of offices, and that in general the county was fortunate to have a responsive citizenry, there being no evidence that anyone refused office or tried to shirk responsibility.

There are, however, occasional clues as to how men felt about the time required to carry out the duties of office. In 1730, the Orange County supervisors pointed out that, as it would be a

Table 8.1. *New York Assembly Service by Haring Family, 1701–1768*

	Assembly	No. of sessions[a]	Total days in session
Peter [21]	8th (1701–1702)	2	73
Peter [21]	12th (1709)	2	158
Cornelius [24]	15th (1713–1714)	3	228
Cornelius [24]	16th (1715)	1	80
Peter [21]	17th (1716–1726)	15	803
Cornelius [24]	18th (1726)	1	46
Cornelius [24]	19th (1727)	1	57
Cornelius [24]	20th (1728–1737)	11	530
Abraham [39]	24th (1745–1747)	5	737
Abraham [39]	28th (1759–1760)	4	316
Abraham [39]	29th (1761–1768)	13	530

SOURCES: *Journal of the Votes and Proceedings of the General Assembly of the Colony of New York, 1691–1765*, 2 vols. (New York, 1764–1766); *Journal of the Votes and Proceedings of the General Assembly of the Colony of New York, from 1766 to 1776 Inclusive* (Albany, 1820); *Records of the Board of Supervisors, Orange County, New York, 1723–1978*, Budke Collection, Section 9, Mss. Division, New York Public Library.

[a]Total sessions = 58; average session length = 61 days.

"great deal of trouble and Fategue" to collect a special tax that had been levied, they would postpone the collection until the regular tax time came around. And in 1734, the county treasurer politely acquainted the supervisors with the information that he had "bin Treasuer for Severall [actually ten] years, and that he did decline to be Treasuer any longer, [and] therefore Desired [them] to nominate another." But that no sign exists of anyone refusing office suggests a high interest on the part of the inhabitants in managing their local affairs.[24]

Nor is there evidence that some men tried to monopolize a particular office, although certain men did tend to stay in the same posts for several years at a stretch, and some offices tended to be passed on from father to son to grandson, particularly in the more prominent families. The Harings, for instance, had family members serving as sheriff, supervisor, board treasurer, county and Supreme Court judges, and/or assemblyman in any given year throughout the colonial period. And they tended to pass the office on. As John Pietersen Haring had been a schepen in the Out-ward, so his eldest son Peter [21] was a judge and assemblyman; *his* son Abraham P. [39] was a judge and assemblyman; and *his* sons Peter [412] and John [415] were judges and representatives to the assemblies of New York and New Jersey.[25]

In a country with no aristocracy and no long established native gentry, officeholding was one of the ways by which a man could rise in the world. There were other strategies for rising, and the Harings, we have seen, aggresively followed all of them: marrying well, acquiring real estate, and getting the education that would open doors to judgeships, church office, and militia commissions.

Military office carried with it a great deal of prestige, and the Harings were officers in the militia throughout the eighteenth century.[26] But it was on the political scene that Haring men made their main contribution to the community. As they rose through the ranks from grand jurors and highway masters to sheriffs, tax assessors, supervisors, commissioners, justices, and judges, they began to be elected, starting in 1701, to the New York Assembly, where they represented Orange County in eleven of twenty-two assemblies from 1701 to 1768 (see Table 8.1).

THE NEW YORK LEGISLATIVE ASSEMBLY

In the early eighteenth century, the privilege of holding a seat in the New York Assembly was of no small importance. That there were only twenty-one, later twenty-four, twenty-seven, and (in 1773) thirty-one members in all meant that each one was a person of some consequence. Assemblyman was the highest elected position to which a farmer of Dutch origin from a rural district in British New York might realistically aspire, and in fact this was the highest position attained by any of the Harings up to the time of the Revolution.

The Assembly met in New York City in lengthy sessions, almost never of less than a month in duration and often much longer. Thus, assemblymen were away from home for long stretches of time and often at times of the year when planting and sowing were going on. Although the Assembly usually requested adjournment for the harvest, governors often insisted they complete their business first: to "bear some inconveniency in your private Affairs, [rather] than put the Country [sic] to needless Charge for tedious or too frequent Sessions."[27]

Yet, good attendance on the part of Assembly representatives was expected both by the governors themselves and by the voters. Assemblymen had to request permission to go home when family

177

business demanded, and were expelled from the session if they were absent without leave. As we have seen, their local officials refused to pay them for days absent.[28]

Representatives from Orange County received four shillings a day for this service in a period (1690–1730) when unskilled farm labor was earning about three shillings per day, so there was no direct financial profit in public service. The seventeenth- and eighteenth-century farmer served at considerable personal inconvenience and expense, and did so because he wanted a voice in the political decisions that would affect his life.

In the case of the Harings, what was this voice? How did these obscure farmer-politicians, representing a rural constituency, address the issues that faced the New York Assembly in the early years of the eighteenth century? How much attention did that voice get among the many voices clamoring for notice? And, beyond this, how might the earliest political experiences of the Haring family have affected its political thinking as the country moved toward its rupture with Great Britain?

Three consecutive generations of Harings served in the New York Assembly. The brothers Peter [21] and Cornelius [24] plunged into the factious partisan issues of the post-Leislerian era. Peter's son Abraham [39] participated in the stormy events that led to the colony's final break with the Crown. And, in May 1776, John Haring [415], Abraham's son and Peter's grandson, helped draft the document that came to be called New York's "virtual" declaration of independence—some six weeks before the Congress in Philadelphia drafted its declaration. (See Chapter 9.) Today, of course, these men are totally forgotten. But in the records of the votes and proceedings of the Assembly, we find them speaking with a clear voice and playing a surprisingly active role in the colony's legislative affairs.

Divided We Stand, 1701–1737

A multitude of interests and factions vied for power in eighteenth-century New York. Contemporaries and historians have given these factions many different names—names that changed as issues and interests changed over the century: Leislerians and anti-Leislerians; landed and merchants; country and court; Livingstons and Delanceys; upriver and seaboard; radicals and conservatives; church and dissenting; Republicans and Episcopalians; and, just before the Revolution, popular Whigs and moderate Whigs.[29]

As might be expected, Peter and Cornelius Haring, who served in the Assembly for most of the 1701–1737 period, aligned themselves with the Leislerian, landed, country, upriver, and dissenting interests. An early event in Peter Haring's first term makes clear that economics, not ethnicity, bound farmers of all backgrounds in joint action. Peter Haring first entered the Assembly in 1701, during the tenure of Lieutenant Governor John Nanfan, who was sympathetic to the Leislerian and upriver position. No sooner was Haring in office than the anti-Leislerians in the Assembly attempted to oust Abraham Gouverneur as speaker on the grounds that he was an alien. (Gouverneur, we recall, was a friend of the Harings and was Orange County's first representative to the Assembly in 1699.) In their angry letter of protest to the king, Haring and thirteen of his fellow pro-Leislerian assemblymen aired their views on this attempt to expel one of their number and, identifying themselves as Dutch and "some of us English by birth," made known their strong objection to attempts by the opposition—"some English, French and Dutch Merchants of this City"—to alter the source of tax revenue in a way detrimental to country interests. The notion that the American farmer in the eighteenth century was not market- and profit-oriented can be dispelled by even a cursory reading of the proceedings of colonial legislatures, which are replete with evidence that farmers were vitally involved in tax policy and were vocal and consistent in demanding that governments respond to their needs.[30]

During the period when the Leislerians enjoyed a superiority in numbers as well as the governor's support, Peter Haring was appointed (on April 30, 1702) to a committee to consider whether and how to augment the number of upriver representatives to the Assembly. The following day, his brother, Cornelius Haring [24], was made a tax commissioner to examine the receipts gathered to pay the debts of the government that were incurred "in the time of the late happy Revolucon"—the debt involved being a payment of £2,700 to the heirs of Jacob Leisler.[31]

It was no coincidence that these two appointments were made only two days before the advent of Edward Hyde, Lord Cornbury, to the governorship, for it was rightly anticipated by the Assembly that Cornbury would turn out to be unsympathetic to the Leislerian faction. In the third in this series of hasty actions, the upriver majority, seeing the handwriting on the wall, voted to

179

adopt the committee's recommendation to entitle Orange County to two representatives, a step designed to enhance the rural faction's power. (Within six weeks of his arrival, however, Cornbury questioned Orange County's right to more than one representative and ordered a census to determine the exact population—with the result that Orange County continued to be entitled to only one representative until 1716.)[32]

Cornbury was one of a succession of anti- and pro-Leisler governors who, in the eighteen years following Leisler's treason trial and hanging, muddied the political waters—pro-Leislerians by granting upriver land grants and lucrative patronage positions to their favorites, and anti-Leislerians by canceling the grants and giving the positions to others. As a result, New York politics from 1692 to 1710 was a rapid series of policy and party reversals that "pitted 'ins' against 'outs' and interest against interest, making factional strife an almost endemic condition of the colony's public life."[33]

No matter whom they supported, two main administrative matters concerned all colonial royal governors: the defense of the colony—its cities, ports, and frontiers—and the expenses of government. And, as might be expected, the proper source of revenue was a chronic matter of hot dispute between the two main factions in the Assembly and between that body and the governor. Traditionally, the greatest portion of the government's revenue (about 85 percent) was raised by commercial duties and excises on imports. Because imported items were luxuries purchased mainly by wealthy folk in the city, the landed faction in the Assembly argued that the chief burden of the colony's support should fall on the more affluent. The aim of the merchant or commercial faction, on the other hand, was to shift the burden from themselves to the upriver faction by means of additional property taxes—a goal stoutly resisted by farmers and other landowners. Assembly factions differed over how expenses were to be funded, but they were united in insisting on their inherent right to set fees and to determine the governor's salary. In the name of their autonomy, they refused to surrender control over the disbursement of funds to governors' agents, and on occasion they refused to pay the governor's salary at all, forcing him to cover the colony's expenses out of his own pocket.[34]

During the unsettled period following Cornbury's departure, Peter Haring served on committees to consider acts dealing with election irregularities, the supervision of intestate estates, and the settling of the boundaries of Orange County. But Haring's main activities were directed toward various revenue bills for supporting and financing a land expedition to Canada in order to protect the frontier. He served on a committee to "proportion" the men to be raised for the Canadian expedition, on a committee to compute expenses for the defense of the frontier during the advancing winter, and on a committee of ways and means to raise funds for the Canadian expedition.[35]

The upriver side continued strong through Governor Robert Hunter's tenure (1710– 1719), and when Hunter called for new elections in 1713, his upriver supporters voted six new members to the Fifteenth Assembly.[36] One of these new members was Cornelius Haring [24], and over the next twenty-four years, through six governors and eight assemblies, either he or his brother Peter represented Orange County in the Assembly.[37] In these years, the two brothers served on dozens of committees charged with considering all the issues of the day. As did every member in the Assembly, both brothers had to take their turn preparing bills on such "housekeeping" matters as regulating highways and fences, settling boundary disputes, destroying wolves, determining ferry fares and hours, preventing the "fraudulent marking and taking up and selling of horses," and acts enabling towns to require their inhabitants to pay for the repair of churches and courthouses. But both brothers were also appointed to committees concerned with the "more general interests of the country": raising revenue to pay the expenses of the government and to defend the colony's frontiers.

Perhaps most important, however, both served on committees that saw diverse interests in the legislature join together to demand that the Crown recognize the colony's constitutional rights and prerogatives. In the Fifteenth Assembly, for instance, Cornelius Haring joined in three unanimous votes to require Governor Hunter to grant a naturalization bill affecting foreign-born persons who had owned property in New York in 1683; to assent to the disbursement of colonial funds by the Assembly's treasurer, rather than by the colony's receiver general; and to grant the colony the right to an agent in London to lobby for colonial interests. Cornelius Haring carried this last bill to the Legislative Council for approval.[38]

In William Burnet, governor from 1720 to 1728, the upriver faction enjoyed another partisan whose efforts to reorganize the Indian trade in favor of Great Britain, undermine the French-Indian alliance, and strengthen the frontier were made at the expense of the merchant faction, which in a Burnet-inspired act of

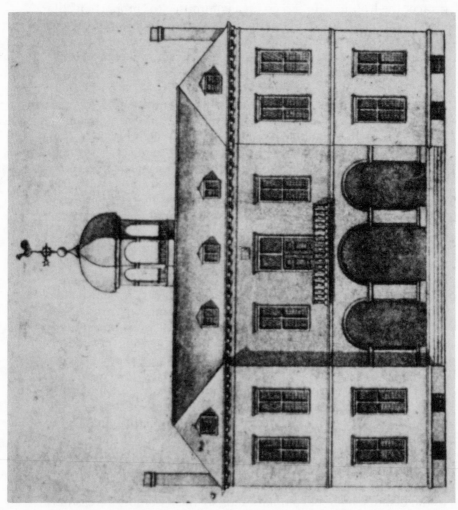

Figure 8.1. Old City Hall, New York City. The New York Assembly met in this

November 3, 1720, was prohibited from selling Indian goods to the French. Other restrictive trade policies advanced by Governor Burnet and the rurals—imposts, liquor taxes, tonnage duties—further disadvantaged the commercial interests and in these years completely polarized the upriver and merchant factions.[39]

Yet, on numerous occasions the diverse groups in the Assembly united to defend their common interests against encroachment by the Crown. Cornelius Haring was one of the rurals in the Assembly in September 1731 who unanimously rose up to join the merchant faction against a bill favoring the "Sugar Islands" in their trade with North America. Such a bill, the assemblymen claimed, "would deprive us of the Means to vend the Produce of this Colony, cramp and diminish our Navigation, lay it under unreasonable Clogs and Hardships, and disable us from taking off and consuming such large Quantities of the British Manufactures as we annually do." Whatever "indulgence" the king might grant to the Sugar Islands, the Assembly requested that it might not be at the "Cost and Ruin of . . . the Northern Colonies."[40] (See Figure 8.1)

Cornelius Haring was sixty-five years old in 1737, his last year of many in the New York Assembly. During those years—particularly during the stormy tenure of Governor William Cosby—the opposition to the Crown that the Assembly had mustered on many occasions in the past challenged again and again some of the fundamental underpinnings of British rule in America and foreshadowed in important ways the constitutional struggles that lay ahead.

The historical significance of the political experience of farmer-politicians like the Haring brothers was twofold. On the local level, by participating in government in their own communities, they were exposed to the demands of public office, formed attachments to local prerogatives, and experienced the pluralism toward which the society was gradually moving. On the provincial level, their close involvement in the daily affairs of the colony provided yeomen like Peter and Cornelius Haring with a valuable education in negotiation, conflict management, cooperation with men of diverse interests, and consensus-building. Most important, exposure to politics reinforced such men in a tradition of resistance to royal authority that their sons and grandsons would jealously guard when their constitutional rights and prerogatives were threatened by that authority.

A Rising Opposition, 1745–1768

In 1745, a new generation of Harings entered politics when Abraham Haring [39], Peter's son, became a member of the Twenty-fourth (1745–1747), the Twenty-eighth (1759–1761), and the long Twenty-ninth Assembly (1761–1768). At age thirty-nine in 1745, Abraham lived in Tappan on a substantial farm inherited from his father. Married to Martynte Bogert, a granddaughter of the pro-Leislerian dominie of the Tappan Reformed Church, Guiliam Bertholf, Abraham was a leader in the Tappan church, a colonel in the New York militia, a judge of the Orange County Court of Common Pleas, and the father of eight children. What made him complicate this comfortable existence by entering the turbulent world of New York Colony politics?

Abraham's main concern, like that of the Twenty-fourth Assembly, was war. Governor George Clinton proposed to prolong King George's War (the American phase of the War of the Austrian Succession, 1740–1748, a Prussian-Austrian conflict in which England and France had taken opposite sides) by mounting an expedition to Canada to ward the French and their Indian allies off New York's borders. The membership of the Assembly was almost universally opposed to this undertaking. Governor Clinton and his chief adviser, Cadwallader Colden, on the other hand, were enthusiastically in favor of it. So intense was the conflict with the governor that, both in 1745 and 1746, the Assembly's sessions lasted right through the harvest. In 1746 alone, the Orange County Board of Supervisors paid Abraham Haring for 198 days in service, including 18 days of travel.[41] Thus he was absent from home for six months that year on Assembly business, getting to Tappan an average of only once every three weeks.

Assembly opposition to King George's War was founded on economic grounds. Predominantly Protestant, New Yorkers were, of course, highly suspicious of the Roman Catholic French presence in Canada, but economic factors were far and away the deciding consideration in their position. New Yorkers were wary of war with the French, because it was New Yorkers who would fight such a war, they who would be taxed to pay for it, and they whose profitable trade with Canada would be disrupted by it. It was in their economic interests to oppose the plan to advance against Quebec, even though this would incur the wrath of Governor Clinton.

Abraham Haring voted consistently against war during the Twenty-fourth Assembly. In August 1745, he opposed a motion to

184

increase funds for defense of the border, in December against re-
building the fort at Saratoga, and in January 1746 against a bill
to build six blockhouses on the frontier. In the last instance, he
was in a very small minority. Nineteen assemblymen voted for
the bill, and only three against it. That Abraham Haring opposed
Governor Clinton and such a large number of his colleagues suggests the depth of his opposition to the undertaking and the importance he attached, as a farmer, to the safe continuation of his
markets. In February 1746, he voted against a bill to hold a lot-
tery to pay for repairing Fort George in New York City and, although he subsequently went along with decisions to build the six
blockhouses and to repair the fort, he also voted against repairing
the stockades at Albany, against sending 30 militiamen to Saratoga, and against sending 450 militiamen and 50 Indians to the
northern frontier.[42]

In November 1746, Abraham Haring joined his Assembly colleagues in unanimously protesting the governor's request for
funds to support the effort against the French in Canada: "The
Circumstances of the Colony (of which we are the most competent
Judges) will not suffer us," the members told the Governor, "to
take one Step further; your Excellency may know how far this
War, the securing our Frontiers, and the present Expedition have
involved us and our Posterity."[43]

Although Governor Clinton wrathfully accused the Assembly of
"declining every Expence that seems necessary for the Security of
the British Colonies in North America" and observed that "the
disrespectful Behaviour to me . . . must . . . be taken as a Disrespect to the Fountain, from whence I . . . derive my Authority,"
not even the accusation of disrespect to the monarch cowed the
defiant Assembly. In October 1747, Abraham Haring and Thomas
Cornell of Queens carried a unanimous and lengthy Assembly resolution to the governor asserting the house's "undoubted" rights
and privileges to proceed upon all matters relating to the interest
and welfare of their constituents—including war with the French.
Describing the governor as an enemy whose plans to proceed
with war were irregular and unprecedented, this resolution
decried Clinton's violation of the people's liberties and the sub-
version of their constitutional rights.[44] Finally, getting no satisfaction, the governor dissolved the Assembly, angrily demanding
that his authority be respected in future.

Brought up in the eighteenth-century tradition of deference to
authority, Abraham Haring perhaps found the fray too strong for
his stomach, for he declined to stand for election to the Twenty-

fifth Assembly. Despite his popularity at home ("no man in the County has a more universal good reputation than he has & is more generally liked," Cadwallader Colden wrote of him), he refused to be a candidate. Although he was sure to have won and although "No pains were omitted to bring him over to join the [Delancey] faction in opposition to your Excellency," Haring refused "all the offers & promises that could be made to him" for a judgeship in Orange County.[45]

By 1759, though, another war had embroiled the colonies. The French and Indian War (1754–1763) was not simply a local expression of a European dynastic quarrel. As an extension of the Seven Years' War in Europe, it was an out-and-out struggle for the control of North America. Abraham Haring, now fifty-five, emerged from retirement to stand successfully for election to the Twenty-eighth Assembly, where the question of how to finance this conflict would be the uppermost concern of the legislature.

Abraham and his first cousin, Abraham A. Haring [336], were commissioned colonels of New York militia regiments charged with defending the northern boundaries of Orange County against the Indians who "infested" the area. Both Abrahams had more than one reason for accepting their commissions: they were sons of men who had supported the fiercely antipapist Jacob Leisler in 1689, and the French and Indian War had strong anti–Roman Catholic undercurrents. If religion had not played a role in New Yorkers' resistance to King George's War, now ancient fears of a Roman Catholic presence on the American continent fueled anti-French enthusiasm in the hearts of American colonists of all Protestant denominations, much as anti-Catholic fears had motivated the supporters of Jacob Leisler seventy years earlier. "Hail, Victory!" one poet wrote:

> If on our Side, give one propitious Sign,
> And lo Ten Thousand bold *Americans* will join,
> With Chearful Hearts to extirpate a Race
> of Superstitious Papists false and base.[46]

The French and Indian War ended in decisive victory for the colonists in 1763—largely owing to vast contributions of British money and British men—men whose officers scorned ragtag colonial regiments like those of the two Colonel Harings. British officers were to learn, however, that for Americans the French and Indian War, besides being a war for territory and the Protestant religion, was also a war of nationalism—what one historian has called "unquestionably the great catalyst that precipitated the most eloquent expressions of nascent American nationalism."[47]

In one of the Colonel Haring regiments that marched or, more likely, straggled off to war were 66 soldiers—including 30 common laborers, 9 weavers and tailors, 7 farmers, 7 cordwainers, 5 men in the carpentry trades, 3 blacksmiths, 1 surgeon, and 1 sailor. But this motley corps, which included three free blacks, a "Mulatta," an Indian, and men ranging in age from seventeen to fifty-one, nearly a third of whom were born in England, Wales, Scotland, Ireland, and Germany, had begun to think of themselves as Americans by 1759.[48]

Further, they were led by a man whose father had supported the successful overthrow of a British governor in 1689, who himself now marched against a French king, whose father and uncle, like himself, had been successfully challenging the British Crown in the New York Assembly for more than half a century, and whose young officers—Harings, Blauvelts, Smiths, and Van Houtens among them—shared with him the same long tradition of political and religious dissent and the same distaste for British arrogance. This concatenation of people and historical circumstances would have a shaping effect on the next generation to go to war.

Choosing Sides, 1769–1776

In 1769, the long-disputed boundary between New York and New Jersey was finally settled. At least twenty-five Haring farms, including one that belonged to New York Assemblyman Abraham Haring, lay in the territory that changed hands. The Harings and those of their neighbors who were affected by the change were not pleased with the new division line. In fact, they viewed it with unqualified abhorrence: "Tho' by this Decree the Court House and Church in Orange Town, is left a few Rods to the Northward of the Line decreed," they lamented, "yet upwards of 150 Families settled in that ancient County Town will, if the Decree be confirmed be dismembered from this Colony, and exposed to utter Ruin."[49]

How could a legal decision affecting only an invisible geographic line utterly ruin 150 families? The only answer is a political one: the Harings, with their long tradition of service in the New York Assembly would now, as residents of New Jersey, be ineligible for office in New York. Cut off from a say in the policies

187

of the government they had served over the entire eighteenth century—and from the constituents who had repeatedly voted them into office and the political allies and benefactors they had cultivated over seven decades—they saw themselves rendered politically impotent, utterly ruined indeed, and their constituents agreed. Even on the local level, they would now have to compete for office against longtime New Jersey candidates, build new constituencies, and forge new alliances in a township and county where they had many friends, of course, but no political leverage in the legislature.

Just months before the boundary decision became final, John Haring [415], the thirty-year-old grandson of Peter [21] and the son of Abraham [39], had stood for his ailing father's seat in the New York Assembly. Continuance of the family's voice in that body was so important that, in order to ensure that he would be a legal resident of New York after the expected decision, John Haring built himself at this time a new house on the New York side of the division line on property he was designated to inherit from his father.[50]

Haring's efforts were unavailing, for he and Henry Wisner—"Livingston" candidates—lost the Orange County election of 1769 to the DeLanceyites John Denoyelles and Samuel Gale. Both Haring and Wisner charged the winners with vote fraud, and with good reason. Other losing candidates also made the same charges against their opponents, and indeed the election of 1769 has been called the most vicious in New York's colonial history: "The Livingstons stirred up religious dissenters against the DeLanceys and gladly considered the use of force. One reported that 'if there is not fair play shown there will be bloodshed, as we have by far the best part of the Bruisers on our side.' DeLancey supporters called the Livingstons 'a pack of hypocritical, cheating, lying, canting, ill-designing scoundrels,'" but did not scruple about sending their agents into the countryside to stir up tenants and small farmers against the large landholders.[51]

The underlying issue at stake as the revolutionary era developed in colonial New York was "who should rule at home," and it was in the Assembly elections of both 1768 and 1769 that this issue came to a head, with old allegiances that dated back to the age of Jacob Leisler sharpening and taking on new vigor. The Livingstons, who had been in power since 1761, attracted to their camp the upriver, landed, dissenting elements in the population, and the DeLanceys the merchant, urban, and Anglo-Episcopalian. Both factions pursued electoral victory aggressively, using every tactic in the book to win voters to their side. The DeLanceys won in 1769, probably because they insisted on a strict interpretation of the election laws that permitted only propertyowners to vote. (Customarily, the franchise had been extended to unpropertied freemen.) Although Haring and Wisner protested, as did the Livingston candidate Lewis Morris (who lost in the borough of Westchester) as well as other Livingston candidates, the charges of fraud were dismissed by the heavily pro-DeLancey Assembly.[52]

After his defeat in 1769, John Haring set up as a merchant for a time in his new house on Tappan Road, developed his law practice on the side, and committed himself to the effort of the progressives in the Dutch Reformed Church to making a success of Queen's College, a long-sought theological seminary where Reformed ministers could be educated on home ground and in the English language. By 1774, however, he was committed to ending British oppression in America and, as we will see in Chapter 9, had by 1776 become an active revolutionary, dedicating all of his considerable abilities to the American cause.

Chapter Nine

"A Spirit of Independency"

So far, examination of the public records pertaining to this farming-class family over the course of a hundred years has revealed that, from the Harings' origins in America during the mid-seventeenth century, they perceived religion, politics, and economics to be of vital self-interest. To maximize their economic position, the Harings farmed for profit; they joined a successful revolt against the British government in 1689 for a complicated mix of political, economic, social, and religious reasons; they challenged Dutch Reformed orthodoxy on deeply felt theological grounds; and they forcefully used their voice in the legislative assembly to further the economic and political interests of the family. The simple yeoman dreaming at his plow of the virtuous republic-to-be is a less accurate picture of reality than the scrappy, market-oriented farmer-businessman determined to force government to respond to his needs and desires. As the American Revolution approached, religion, politics, and economics continued to motivate the American farmer—as the experience of the Harings indicates.

RELIGION

To take religion first, long before the American Revolution, Dutch families in New York and New Jersey had fallen into dissension and disarray over religious matters that would take on political force as the Revolution approached. Thus, in a real sense, the picture presented in the foregoing chapters of the Harings as a family characterized by harmonious relations, unity, cooperation, and Christian love has another dimension—and a darker one. By

1727, when Dominie Fredericus Muzelius mounted the Tappan pulpit to replace Guiliam Bertholf, recently deceased, a furor had arisen in the Dutch Reformed Church concerning issues that would soon blast both family and congregational peace.

The Coetus-Conferentie Conflict and the Great Awakening

The incendiary issues that roiled the Dutch in America were the Dutch Reformed Church's relationship to the mother church in the Netherlands and a resurgence of the ages-old Pietist impulse—the Great Awakening, or New Light, revival of the 1730s and 1740s. One group of Dutch American ministers supported the idea of a measure of home rule for the Dutch church in America and the "true piety" of the New Light revival, whereas a more conservative group of ministers insisted that the American churches maintain a subordinate relationship to the mother church and rejected New Light preaching and spontaneity or "enthusiasm" in worship.[1]

Writing in 1827 with the events of the revolutionary period still fresh in many minds, the Reverend Cornelius Demarest, a friend and relation of the Harings, traced the eighteenth-century discord among the Dutch in America to the year 1720 and the advent in New Jersey of the Pietist preacher Theodorus Jacobus Frelinghuysen. "The commencement of faithful [i.e., Pietist] preaching was the . . . signal for war. . . . [T]he radical ground of the whole difference was, nature and grace, the kingdoms of darkness and of light, the children of God and of the devil, the friends or foes of the saving work of the Holy Ghost."[2]

Although Cornelius Demarest believed that the problem in the Dutch church in America had arisen during the 1720s, the division can in fact be traced to a much earlier era—ultimately back to the post-Reformation Cocceian-Voetian split in the Dutch Church in the Netherlands. In 1720, it is true, this division was exacerbated when Frelinghuysen excommunicated certain members of his Raritan, N.J., congregation for what he judged to be their unregenerate condition. Difficulties in communicating the complexities of the situation to Amsterdam and in reconciling the two Raritan factions led the American churches, Tappan included, to propose to the Classis of Amsterdam, their overseer, that they form a fraternal organization, or "coetus," in America for the purpose not only of creating peace and unity among themselves, but of furthering the work of the church in America and educating and ordaining ministerial candidates on American soil.[3]

The Classis of Amsterdam readily agreed to a coetus, although it balked at the idea that ministers might be educated and ordained anywhere but in the Netherlands—a reservation meant to ensure the quality of ministerial training, but one that in effect permitted Amsterdam to maintain control over most aspects of the American Dutch Reformed churches.[4]

After nearly a decade of fits and starts, a coetus was formed in 1737 to which eight congregations, including Tappan, sent delegates; on September 12, a set of fundamental articles was drafted by the fledgling organization. Although the articles did not include the right to educate and ordain ministers in America and clearly recognized the "inviolable" subordinacy of the coetus to the Classis of Amsterdam, one week later, on September 19, 1737, Frederick Muzelius, now a decade into his pastorate at Tappan, avowed himself an opponent of the coetus and wrote to Amsterdam to warn that the coetus would soon begin to consider itself equal to the classis. The voluminous ecclesiastical records on the matter make it clear that the American coetus ministers accepted, at least in the 1730s, subordinate status to the Classis of Amsterdam and, beyond the classis, to the Synod of North Holland. Nevertheless, Muzelius and several other like-minded dominies soon formed the "conferentie"—a group that was to oppose the coetus and all attempts to liberalize the Dutch church in America for the next three decades and more.[5]

The dominies' opposition was motivated less by fears of a maverick and irregular American classis arising out of the coetus than by their deep dislike of Theodorus Jacobus Frelinghuysen and his zealous, unflagging efforts to convert all Dutch men and women to his Pietist views. As the Great Awakening approached, the resurgence of the Pietist spirit among the Dutch gave new force to Frelinghuysen's influence—and to his opposition. Roundly despised by the orthodox for what they interpreted as his departures from the doctrinal and liturgical Netherlands church order, Frelinghuysen was now criticized also for urging his Pietist views upon a younger generation of zealous ministers and ministerial candidates.[6]

By the 1740s, an "extensive dispute and division . . . rage[d] in the Dutch Reformed churches, principally in the country districts," and centered around the aging Frelinghuysen's protégé John Henry Goetschius, who had run afoul of the anti-coetus ministers and had become the object of their implacable hatred. This is not the place to go into the tribulations Goetschius suffered at the hands of his enemies. He was "like a bird in a snare, attacked by many," and his troubles are documented at great length in hundreds of pages of testimony and countertestimony in the ecclesiastical records. The general thrust of the accusations against him was that his ordination had been "irregular," which was true, and that he had endeavored to convert his congregation to the views he had imbibed from Frelinghuysen: "for this reason, chiefly . . . most of the agitation of his opponents, if not all, [had] sprung up."[7]

"A Form of Government for Our Dutch Churches"

The dissenting dominies saw the existence of the coetus as a political issue and any degree of autonomy on the part of the American church as the first step toward a total break with the mother church. In 1737, Frederick Muzelius, writing to the classis, claimed that

> some on this side have undertaken to establish a Form of Government for all our Dutch Churches here. Consequently, if it were possible, they would become independent, or, at least, they would become estranged from the Rev. Classis as our immediate and most competent Judge. Thus would our churches run great risk of degenerating into Independency.[8]

Ten years later, in 1747, Muzelius still saw the matter as a political one, forecasting, in language usually reserved for strictly political issues, that if encouraged to act independently in any matter the American church would in time make a "total defection from our dear Netherlandish Church." For Muzelius and the conferentie, this was an intolerable prospect. "I write to you," Muzelius informed the coetus in 1747, again using political imagery, "that in ecclesiastical matters I have subjected myself to the Classis of Amsterdam, and in political matters to the Protestant Crown of Great Britain."[9]

Muzelius's anxieties were not shared by the Classis of Amsterdam, which over the years had consistently encouraged the formation of a (subordinate) coetus—in 1747 even giving it permission to ordain a minister. "Worthy brother," they wrote to him, "only think . . . how fruitful of good it may be, for the overseers of [the American churches] . . . to unite . . . and assemble fraternally from time to time. . . . The political subordination to your lawful authorities is not thereby taken away, because civil matters [will not be discussed] in such a coetus."[10]

The Tappan church was not represented in the coetus meeting in 1747, because Muzelius refused to participate; the following year, however, Abraham Haring [27] and Cornelius Cooper, elders at Tappan, were admitted to membership, attending without their obstinate pastor. This Abraham Haring, the youngest Haring brother in the settler generation, was thirteen years old when Guiliam Bertholf founded the Tappan church in 1694, and Cornelius Cooper was the son of the Cornelius Cooper who, under the command of Jacob Leisler, had occupied the fort at New York in 1689. That these two men supported the coetus suggests not only their theological but their political orientation and illustrates how the old frictions between religion and politics of the Bertholf-Leisler era reemerged as impetus and inspiration of a new generation of Dutch Americans in the Great Awakening.[11]

As relations in the church deteriorated, Muzelius continued to conduct himself "very badly," according to Dominie Gualterus Du Bois, who in 1748 wrote privately to the Classis of Amsterdam that the "Dutch churches here are gradually beginning to languish; both on account of [nearly three decades of] internal strife in some of them, and because of the distaste for true piety in others."[12] Muzelius was so opposed to any liberalizing action at all and so hostile to the "true piety" pervading the Tappan congregation in the 1740s that, on the request of the Classis of Amsterdam, he was investigated by the coetus in 1748. On November 8, 1749, the coetus suspended him from office for three months and, when he did not conform his behavior during this period, required him to preach one last penitential sermon and thereupon declared him emeritus.[13]

Samuel Verbryck: "Sound in the Faith and of Edifying Walk"

In the years between 1747 and 1754, the American coetus was permitted to ordain four ministers who had received their theological training in America. One of these was the successor to

Muzelius in Tappan, Samuel Verbryck, a New Light protégé both of Theodorus Frelinghuysen, Jr., and of John Henry Goetschius. Verbryck was recommended to the coetus by his mentor, Frelinghuysen, as a "most diligent scholar, and of fine promise," a young man with "excellent testimonials" who had studied Greek, Hebrew, philosophy, and theology for eight years under Freling-huysen, Goetschius, and Reinhard Erickson (at Hackensack), and also under a "certain English minister" unnamed. "Sound in the faith and of edifying walk," he "belonged to the company" of Dominies Johannes Leydt and Benjamin Van der Linde (his future brother-in-law) and "could be examined even in Holland with praise," wrote Frelinghuysen to the Classis of Amsterdam in August 1748. So great was Verbryck's promise, indeed, that Frelinghuysen "demanded" that the classis give permission for Verbryck to be examined in America, rather than require him to make the perilous journey across the Atlantic during this era of King George's War. The classis, in May 1749, granted permission to the coetus to "examine this one young man, but no more," and the following year Samuel Verbryck was ordained by Dominies John Henry Goetschius and Antonius Curtenius of the coetus. On September 12, 1750, he was appointed by the coetus to serve the Tappen congregation.[14]

As Guiliam Bertholf had imbibed Pietism at the knee of the controversial Jacobus Koelman, the Pietist minister of Bertholf's home church in Sluis, so Samuel Verbryck, born in Raritan in 1721, had first been spiritually awakened by his minister there, the aging Theodorus Jacobus Frelinghuysen. (Frelinghuysen, we recall, had come to America in 1720, probably at the suggestion of Bertholf and Bernhardus Freeman.)[15] Thus, the Pietist tradition in Tappan can be seen as having passed over the course of the eighteenth century from Bertholf to Verbryck via Frelinghuysen and Goetschius, encompassing as it did four generations of Tappan churchgoers—and the divisive tenure of Frederick Muzelius.

Infuriated at his removal from the Tappan pulpit, and at the choice of the New Light minister as his successor, Muzelius now entered upon a phase of his career that was to last for the rest of his life. He remained at Tappan in a house supplied to him as emeritus by the Tappan consistory and proceeded to vilify Samuel Verbryck, setting as many of the congregation against him as he could for the next thirty-three years. In his thirty-four-year pastorate, Verbryck had but one year of peace from his tormentor, the year before he died in January 1784.[16]

No sermons of Verbryck's have survived, but his views on the

American Dutch church's relationship to the Netherlands church are well documented in the ecclesiastical records, which reveal him as an outspoken coetus leader. In 1754, he was one of two ministers to write to the Classis of Amsterdam proposing the formation of an independent classis in America, and he was in the forefront of the long and ultimately successful effort to found Queen's College (Rutgers) for the purpose of educating Dutch ministers in America.[17]

RELIGION AND POLITICS

Like the other coetus ministers—Theodore Frelinghuysen, Jr., John Frelinghuysen, John Henry Goetschius, Dirck Romeyn, Johannes Leydt, Jacob Hardenbergh, John Livingston, and Solomon Froeligh—Samuel Verbryck was a staunch patriot during the Revolution. Thus, as a Pietist minister had been their spokesman and spiritual leader during the Leisler era, so during the most violent decades of the coetus-conferentie conflict and continuing throughout the entire revolutionary period, the farmers in Tappan found the spokesman for their political ideas in another Pietist minister.

Schism was inevitable, given the coetus's continual effort to establish Queen's College—an effort enthusiastically supported throughout the 1750s and into the 1760s by Verbryck. In 1761, the enraged Muzelius and his conferentie colleagues, writing to Amsterdam to complain of Verbryck and the "notable division" that had occurred in Tappan, described him as a "turbulent fellow . . . [who] without direction from the congregation or Consistory, [has] engaged with other ministers of the so-called Coetus to obtain from the Governor of New Jersey a charter for the erection of an academy for that province." Thirty-eight heads of families, Muzelius went on, "took [Verbryck's involvement in the aborning Queen's College] so ill that they refused to pay the Domine's salary [and] were all put under censure." In April 1762, these thirty-eight families organized a "Schismatic" church of their own at Tappan with Muzelius as their pastor.[18]

In 1765, Muzelius and the conferentie ministers again appealed to the Classis of Amsterdam—this time asking that it intervene on their behalf with the king of England: "We see no other resort," they wrote, "[than to request the protection of the King and to let him know] that the Netherlandish Churches in North America [meaning the schismatic conferentie churches] are oppressed in their privileges and liberties by a band of ministers who, through a spirit of independency, have torn them away from the Netherlandish Church. . . . That such a request would be listened to by the King we feel assured, because our . . . Church has always been regarded by the Episcopalians as a national church" and because the monarch had always provided them with charters to manage their own affairs.[19]

It was too late. As Thomas Wertenbaker wrote, fifty years ago:

> The Conferentie might enlist in their cause all the weight of Church law, all the influence of Synod and Classis, all the force of tradition, all the love of mother country; their cause was hopeless. Their real opponents were not the Coetus group, but the forces which created the Coetus group, the three thousand miles of water between America and the Netherlands, the proximity to other races and other faiths, the difficulties of communication.[20]

And, one might add, the growing "spirit of independency" in America.

The governor of New Jersey granted the coetus ministers a charter to establish Queen's College in 1766. Samuel Verbryck and Abraham Haring [39] were named to its first board of trustees.[21]

Historians from Cornelius Demarest in 1827, to Thomas Wertenbaker in 1938, to those of the present time have seen the struggle of the Dutch church in America against the authority of the mother church in the Netherlands as foreshadowing the colonies' rebellion against Great Britain. Not only Dutch Reformed New Lights helped shape the republican tradition in America, of course. Americans of all denominations saw in Anglican Great Britain a threat to their religious liberty, and from there it was only a step to think of political liberty. But in New York and New Jersey, the religious issue had taken on added urgency with the establishment in 1754 of King's College (Columbia University) as a specifically Episcopalian rather than nondenominational institution, thus giving new impetus to the Dutch proponents of Queen's College—and fueling Dutch dissatisfaction with British rule.[22]

More interesting—but less noticed—is that the theological and ideological roots of the American Revolution go deeper in the Dutch church than those of the coetus-conferentie conflict—and likewise so do the political roots. Coetus proponents in support of

197

the War of Independence were the spiritual direct descendants of their Leislerian and Pietist forefathers who had supported the overthrow of another British monarch in 1689. In the Middle Colonies, it can be seen in retrospect, the ideological and theological seeds of the American Revolution were sown during the 1680s and 1690s from the nine country pulpits filled by the "itinerating apostle" of the Pietist spirit, Guiliam Bertholf.

A Closer Look

Religion and politics were inextricably related in the eighteenth-century Dutch American mind, a connection with origins in the sixteenth-century Dutch Wars of Independence against Catholic Spain (1565–1590). By the time of the American War of Independence, this connection had already been superbly encapsulated for the Haring family for two hundred years. On October 12, 1573, during a fierce battle between the Spanish fleet and a swarm of patriot vessels for control of the Zuider Zee, John Haring of Hoorn was shot and killed in the act of hauling down the colors of Admiral de Bossu's man-of-war, *La Inquisición*. The politically fragile little Netherlands against the might of imperial Spain; a ragtag Dutch flotilla against the seemingly invincible Spanish navy; the local citizen Haring against the great royalist stadtholder, the Count de Bossu; the Protestant martyr against the papist tyrant: the images were riveting, unforgettable, and eminently repeatable. If the Haring family looked to a "reference" ancestor, they looked to John Haring of Hoorn, their Calvinist forebear, who had defied the Catholic king of Spain and single-handedly humiliated his admiral.[23]

In the New World, the descendants of Dutch Calvinists continued to be jealous of their civil and religious liberties and sensitive to the relation between religion and politics. In 1689, as we saw in Chapter 7, now Pietists in rebellious New York Colony, they responded to England's Glorious Revolution by resisting Stuart claims to the divine right and absolute authority of kings and insisting on their political and religious liberty. During Leisler's Rebellion, politics and religion were such familiar bedfellows to the Harings and other Dutch Pietists in New York and New Jersey that the spokesmen for their political views was a Dutch Reformed minister. Guiliam Bertholf not only encouraged the antipapist Leisler, he "violently urged [him] on."[24]

Later, in prerevolutionary America, religion and politics again went hand in hand. Evangelical Calvinism and religious rational- ism "did not carve separate channels but flowed as one stream toward the crisis of 1776." Those Harings who were New Light descendants of their Dutch Pietist forefathers continued to believe that America was the promised land God had led them to. For them, the Revolution was an expression of their covenant theol- ogy—the view that they and their forefathers had entered into an agreement with God. God's part of this covenant was to uphold and preserve them by his providential might; their part was to acknowledge no other sovereign, to observe the law as contained in God's Word, to work to prepare the way for the Second Coming of Christ and the establishment of the kingdom of God on earth. It was a promise not taken lightly. Resistance to the king of En- gland was practically an imperative, for he had set himself against God as a competing sovereign demanding their obe- dience.[25]

The Dutch in the Hudson and Hackensack valleys were hardly so otherworldly as to think solely in spiritual terms. By 1760, the Harings were also confirmed children of the Enlightenment. Some of them certainly viewed the American Revolution as a nec- essary evil, a just war to preserve their sacred covenant with God. Others saw it as a necessary instrument of their political exis- tence. For many, it was both. To revolt against the king was not only their Christian duty but a matter of their natural rights, of the social contract, of the sanctity of common law, of constitu- tional government as they believed it applied to them as English citizens, and of republican principles as they had been living them in their American communities for a hundred years and more. Both those who felt themselves in covenant with God and those who merely felt endowed by God with inalienable rights that the king of Great Britain wished to curtail shared a common desire for resolution and rectification of this conflict. Indeed, a decade before the Declaration of Independence, the "right, the need, the absolute obligation to disobey legally constituted au- thority had become the universal cry."[26]

But civil disobedience was not revolution, and the cry for revo- lution was far from universal in 1766. Revolution was the answer to British oppression only for some Americans, even in 1776. For others, a change of the magnitude called for was a threat to the most elemental principles of order and discipline in society. For these Americans, the idea of overthrowing authority and the pros- pect of the social chaos that would result were truly feared and dreaded.[27]

Both patriots and loyalists saw the dangers of civil disobedience, of course, and both dreaded the specter of mobs and committees taking over the courts and the government. But as the Revolution approached, if Tory pulpits thundered with the message that obedience to government was every citizen's duty, patriot pulpits resounded with an opposite message. Some members of the Haring family listened to Tory preaching; most did not. First cousins John Haring [415] and Peter T. Haring [441] heard the call differently.

John Haring

In the eighteenth century, republican virtue was associated with the ownership of land, the cultivation of the earth, and an improving contact with nature. A glance at the background of John Haring, however, suggests that his Dutch origins, the history of the Dutch Republic, his theological views, and his family's long record of political participation at the town, county, and province level were more significant shaping factors in his republican views than the fact that he owned land and benefited by his contact with it.

John Haring [415], born September 28, 1739, was the fourth child of eight, the second of four sons born to his parents, Abraham [39] and Martyntie Bogert. Not a farmer, but certainly versed in rural interests, John Haring, like his father and grandfather (patentee Peter Haring), was attracted to politics; and in 1769, at age thirty, he stood for election to his ailing father's seat in the New York Assembly. As noted above, John Haring and Henry Wisner, pro-Livingston candidates, after losing this election, charged the victors, pro-DeLancey John Denoyelles and Samuel Gale, with vote fraud. Although Haring called no fewer than forty-eight witnesses to testify in his behalf, his charges were dismissed by the DeLancey-dominated Assembly.[28]

A few months later, John Haring was appointed a trustee of Queen's College—the newly formed theological seminary that would soon begin to graduate a formidable company of radical Whig ministers. He was now embarked upon a long career that would involve him in the politics of the Revolution.

Like most ambitious men of the day, John Haring had several sources of income, for he had received enough education to qualify both as a surveyor and as a lawyer. (His own lawyer was John Morin Scott, the radical politician and friend of William Livingston.) As a surveyor, he could count on work—at least until politics made them enemies—from the large landowner William Bayard, whose family had owned the farm next to the Haring farm in Manhattan for several generations, and who himself had accumulated extensive property on the west shore of the Hudson.[29]

Besides the patronage and encouragement of well-placed friends, a propitious marriage assisted the rise of a young eighteenth-century gentleman, and John Haring's fortunes visibly blossomed in 1773 when he married his cousin Mary, Elbert Haring's daughter. Elbert died a few weeks after the wedding, and John, his nephew and now son-in-law, suddenly became at age thirty-four one of Elbert's executors and the owner and manager of his bride's sizable assets in Manhattan.

To support his growing family, John Haring entered upon yet a third career, this as a merchant operating out of his new house on Tappan Road. But "following commerce," as he called it, evidently did not long appeal, for in 1774 he sought and received an appointment as Orange County Judge from Governor William Tryon. This appointment was opposed by Oliver DeLancey's "tool" in the Assembly, John Denoyelles, who protested that Haring's "Promosion would give the Dominion of the County to 2 or 3 People." William Smith, recording in his memoirs Denoyelles' opposition, noted that he "knew no Man in the County opposed" to Haring except Denoyelles himself, and he voted with the majority in the Legislative Council to approve the appointment. (Oliver DeLancey voted in the minority.)[30]

Events moved quickly for John Haring (and for America) after his March 1774 appointment to the judgeship. In Tappan three months later, on July 4, 1774, he signed the so-called Orangetown Resolutions, a remonstrance to the king in protest of taxation without representation and other policies of the British government. Politics and the patriot cause became for the next decade the consuming interest in his life. Also in July, Haring was named to a Committee of Correspondence for the Town of Orangetown, and the next month he and Henry Wisner were elected delegates from Orange County to the First Continental Congress at Carpenter's Hall, Philadelphia.[31]

Haring arrived at Carpenter's Hall on September 26, 1774, three weeks after the Congress had begun to meet, only to find it in dissension over a plan by the pro-Tory delegate Joseph Galloway of Pennsylvania for accommodation with Great Britain. The New York delegation of eight was split four to four on the matter. The Galloway Plan was formally introduced two days later, on

September 28, and New York voted against it five to four—Haring casting the ninth and deciding vote. New Yorkers Isaac Low, John Alsop, James Duane, and John Jay voted for the defeated plan; and Haring, Philip Livingston, Henry Wisner, Simon Boerem, and William Floyd voted against.[32]

The whole Congress finally defeated the Galloway Plan by six colonies to five. It then voted to form a Continental Association banning the importation of all goods from Great Britain and of tea, molasses, coffee, syrups, and pimento from the British West Indies, of wine from Madeira, and slaves. Export to Great Britain of all goods, except rice, was absolutely banned.[33] Apparently satisfied that he had made his contribution, John Haring returned home (before signing the Articles of the Continental Association) only to find that, back in New York, the pro-Tory Thirty-first New York Assembly had refused to recognize the Continental Congress.

That Assembly adjourned on April 3, 1775; lacking popular support, it never fully functioned as a body again. In the name of the people, a Whiggish ad hoc government coalesced and called for the election in the counties of deputies to a Provincial Convention that would elect delegates to the Second Continental Congress. Haring was chosen to be deputy for Orange County.

Out of this Provincial Convention, which met on April 20, 1775, arose a Provincial Congress, whose formation the freemen, freeholders, and inhabitants of Orange County—or at least most of them—were quick to approve. On April 29, Orange County citizens resolved to

> associate under all the ties of Religion, Honour and Love to our Country, to adopt and endeavour to carry into execution whatever measures may be recommended by the Continental Congress or resolved upon by the Provincial Congress for the purpose of . . . opposing the execution of the several arbitrary and oppressive acts of the British Parliament, until a reconciliation . . . on constitutional principles . . . can be obtained.[34]

The Provincial Congress, though a more permanent revolutionary body than the Convention that had called for its formation, was not a legitimate one in the eyes of the British. It nevertheless assumed all the duties of a duly constituted government and met in a series of four separate congresses in New York from May 1775 to July 1776. John Haring was a member of all four provincial congresses and was president pro tem of the second and third. In the recesses between sessions, a Committee of Safety, of which he was chairman, served as the executive branch of government.[35]

The New York Provincial Congress, as a de facto and extralegal revolutionary body, derived its putative legitimacy from its defense of the rights of the people in opposition to the oppressive acts of king, Parliament, Governor Tryon, and the pro-Tory Thirty-first Assembly, which remained in adjournment throughout most of the year. Like the provincial congresses in New Jersey and in other colonies, the New York Provincial Congress at this point was intent not on independence from Great Britain but on the "Defense and Re-establishment of the Constitutional Rights of the Colonies," an intent it declared in an address to the people of New York as late as February 13, 1776.[36]

When pro forma elections to the old colonial assembly were called by Governor Tryon and a new colonial assembly with a Whiggish cast was elected early in 1776—with John Haring and Henry Wisner this time winning in Orange County—the political climate made this new body confident that its goals would prevail. As it prepared to convene and consider the question of how New York should vote on independence, however, it was prorogued by Governor Tryon. Tryon signed the writ of prorogation from the *Dutchess of Gordon* in New York Harbor, where for fear of his safety he had taken refuge the previous October.

By April 1776, George Washington had arrived in New York to take command of military operations, and the clamor for separation from Great Britain was growing in all the colonies. In May the New York delegation to the Second Continental Congress, of which John Haring had been appointed a member, traveled to Philadelphia to settle the burning question of the colonies' relation to Great Britain. John Haring did not accompany the delegates to Philadelphia, but stayed (along with John Jay and others) in New York, where Haring was acting as president pro tem of the Third Provincial Congress—in effect, as head of the revolutionary government in New York. By this time, separation from Great Britain was a genuine intent of many colonists, and of many in the Second Continental Congress, though not yet of the majority.[37]

In New York, the Provincial Congress met on May 27, 1776, to hear the report of an internal committee concerning the resolution of the Continental Congress "relating to a new form of government." This committee, appointed by the Provincial Congress three days before, on May 24, 1776, consisted of John Haring,

John Jay, John Morin Scott, Henry Remsen, Francis Lewis, Jacob Cuyler, and John Broome. It had taken only three days for the committee to deliver its recommendation that New York declare its independence from Great Britain. The colonial government was dissolved, the committee declared, "by the voluntary abdication of . . . Governor Tryon, the dissolution of our Assembly for want of due prorogation, and the open and unwarrantable hostilities committed against the . . . inhabitants . . . of all the United States."[38]

Tantamount to a declaration of New York's independence from Great Britain, the committee's recommendation anticipated by six weeks the Continental Congress by going on to state that the "said old form of government is become, *ipso facto*, dissolved; whereby it hath become absolutely necessary for the good people of this Colony to institute a new and regular form of internal government and police."[39]

A week or so later, on June 8, 1776, the New York delegation in Philadelphia appealed to its parent body, the Third Provincial Congress, for instructions on how to vote concerning independence. (The delegates' uncertainty stemmed from the fact that the previous year's instructions were to vote for restoring harmony with the mother country—instructions that they, mainly lawyers, believed might still be legally binding on the colony.) On this point, however, the Third New York Provincial Congress could or would provide no clear advice, for it was on the verge of a new election that would give that body, it was hoped, full legislative legitimacy as New York's official government, absolving it of any legal commitment to the Thirty-first Assembly's decisions. To this fourth (and last) New York Provincial Congress, elected in June 1776, and consisting of 106 men, Orange County sent 8 delegates: 3 loyalists and 5 patriots, among whom were John Haring and again his old friend Henry Wisner. The New York Congress did not instruct its delegates at Philadelphia how to vote on the independence question, but the position of at least some of its members on that issue had already been made clear, of course, on May 27, 1776, in the committee report of John Haring, John Jay, John Morin Scott, and others recommending a "new form of government."

Peter T. Haring

Although John Haring was among this small group of radicals who recommended that New York declare its independence from

Great Britain six weeks before the Continental Congress in Philadelphia so declared, Haring had to tread carefully, for within his
own and his wife's family close relatives had decided to espouse
the Tory cause.

Peter T. Haring and John Haring [415], his cousin, were almost
exact contemporaries. Peter was baptized in the Tappan church
by Frederick Muzelius in 1737, John in 1739. Twelve and ten
years of age when Muzelius was finally ousted from the Tappan
pulpit in 1749, the two cousins spent their formative years
steeped in the controversy and enmity that gripped the Tappan
congregation throughout the 1740s and 1750s. But whereas one
cousin was imbued with the coetus's spirit of progressivism, the
other imbibed the conservatism of Muzelius and the conferentie.
In 1762, when Muzelius and thirty-eight pro-conferentie families
broke away from Verbryck's congregation to form their own
schismatic church, they chose Peter T. Haring, now twenty-five
years old, as their voorleser.[40]

The Haring family illustrates well the observation that the
coetus-conferentie conflict not only divided family branches, but set
brother against brother within the same branch. It also illustrates
the almost perfect correlation *in this family* between conferentie
membership and Toryism on the one hand and between coetus
affiliation and the American revolutionary cause on the other. In
most families, there were exceptions to this correlation as a general pattern. Conferentie and Tory sympathizers crossed over to
the American side or took a neutral stance, and opportunistic patriots embraced the British cause when convenient. In the Haring
family, however, only nine Tory (and conferentie) adherents can
be discovered in all.[41] In overwhelming numbers, Harings were
patriots and pro-coetus; and they remained so throughout the entire period, just as the nine Tory and conferentie Harings likewise
maintained a consistent position. As they matured, then, it is not
surprising that the two cousins, following in the paths of their
fathers, the brothers Abraham [39], a patriot, and Theunis [311],
a loyalist, found themselves on opposite sides of the religious as
well as the political conflict.[42]

The War Years

The coetus-conferentie conflict in the Dutch churches in America
finally came to a resolution in 1771, but in the Tappan church
the rift was so wide—and Muzelius, on the sidelines, was so

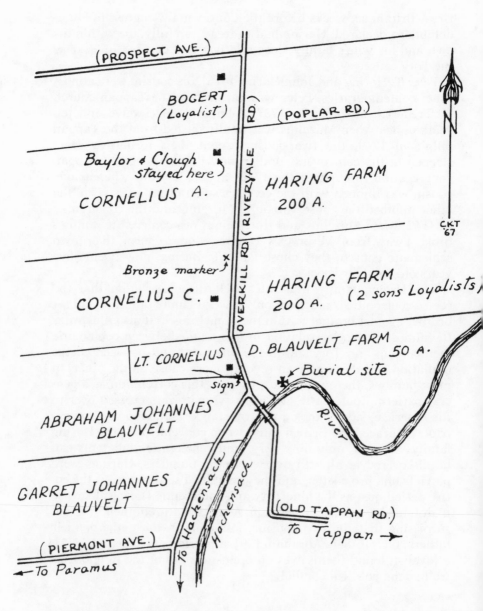

BAYLOR MASSACRE NEIGHBORHOOD

Figure 9.1. Neighborhood of the Baylor Massacre. Courtesy C. K. Tholl.

determined not to let it close—that the two sides found it impossible to reconcile their differences.

The records show that the Irregular Tappan Church continued to meet until late 1778 or January 1779. If the feelings of its members were so strong, why did the congregation dissolve at this time?

A brutal British massacre of American troops at Tappan in the fall of 1778 apparently shocked the members of the Irregular congregation into an awareness of the dangerous path they had chosen. In this violent episode, known in history as the Baylor Massacre, more than a hundred American troops and their twelve officers, quartered for the night in six barns and three houses along Overkill Road a half-mile from Tappan village, were attacked at three in the morning by rampaging British troops under the command of General Charles Grey. Nicknamed No-Flint Grey for his habit of ordering that the "Charges [be] . . . drawn from their Firelocks & the Flints taken out that the Men might be constrained to use their Bayonets only," Grey ordered that no quarter be given to the Americans. The barns the Americans slept in that bloody night of September 28, 1778, belonged to certain of the Irregular church's own members; the American officers slumbered in the stone farmhouses of the neighborhood—two of them in the house of Cornelius A. Haring [344], a founder and elder of the Irregular church.[43] (See Figure 9.1.)

These two American officers, Major Alexander Clough, George Washington's chief of intelligence, and Colonel George Baylor, a favorite young friend and neighbor of Washington's in Virginia, tried to conceal themselves from the British light infantry in the ample chimney of Cornelius Haring's fireplace, but were discovered and mercilessly bayoneted, later dying of their wounds. Clough expired the day after the massacre in the Tappan church, which was turned into a hospital to accommodate the scores of wounded, and Baylor died six years later of complications from the wound inflicted that night by the British troops. Worse, eleven soldiers were stabbed to death during the massacre, four died soon after of their wounds, and by October 23 another seven had expired. Militiaman John A. Haring [5113] was among the men whose duty it was to bury the murdered soldiers.[44]

How the British came to know that Clough and Baylor and their men were quartered in the neighborhood of Cornelius A. and Cornelius C. Haring has never been determined. But both cousins had been arrested the previous year as Tories (along with Peter T. Haring), and all who have studied the episode have pointed out

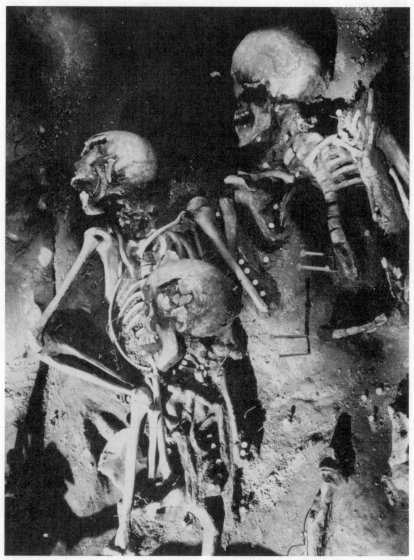

Figure 9.2. Excavated Dragoon Skeletons, Baylor Massacre Site.
Courtesy C. K. Tholl.

the likelihood that someone, probably Cornelius A. Haring or a member of his household, alerted the British to the fine opportunity that awaited them in the barns on Overkill Road.[45] (See Figure 9.2.)

The members of the Irregular church, no doubt sickened by such a ghastly massacre (the blood of the American troops flowed so freely from the haylofts where they slept that it collected in pools on the barn floors), decided in the ensuing weeks to meet no more. Some members of the defunct congregation began to reaffiliate with the regular Tappan congregation, but Peter T. Haring, the schismatic congregation's voorleser, was not among them.

Along with his relatives, Cornelius A. and Cornelius C. Haring, Peter had been found guilty of disloyalty to the American government in 1777 and was sentenced to jail in Morristown, N.J. In August 1777, he was sent to New York in exchange for a patriot prisoner of the British, and he was soon allowed to return home. But his troubles were far from over: his land and homestead in Old Tappan were confiscated by the American authorities in March 1779, and he died soon after, forty-three years old and childless.[46]

To glimpse the struggles of men like John Haring and Peter T. Haring is to understand a part of history as the ordinary man probably understood it. For some, the Revolution was a wrongful war against a legitimate sovereign. For others, it was a just war against a sovereign who would tread on their rights and liberties—civil and religious. For men of Dutch background, it was also an extension of the religious war within their own denomination, and thus it was a conflict with a peculiar emotional context whose roots led back to the furor caused by seventeenth-century Pietist preachers like Guiliam Bertholf and by the Pietist political figure Jacob Leisler.

The emotionalism and fervor of the New Light revivalists embarrassed the conferentie, outraged their Augustan sense of propriety, decorum, deference, and balance—much as the enthusiastic Pietism of Bertholf and Leisler had offended decorous dominies a century earlier. As the conferentie-Tory side considered separation from either mother church or the motherland unthinkable, and revolutionary spirit no less misguided than revivalist spirit, so did they also reject the political revolution and the new Pietism, with its call for personal spiritual "revolution."

One of the ironies of the Haring family and those Dutch families like it in the Hudson and Hackensack valleys is that their hopes for family harmony and Christian cooperation fell victim, in effect, to the differences in individual temperaments and psychological constitutions. Some could tolerate the anxiety of separation from their parent institutions and release themselves into political and cultural freedom, just as they could let the Holy Spirit release them from what they called the forces of darkness into the grace of light. Others found political separation intolerable and the New Light emphasis on the "freedom" of the new man in Christ a misreading of the Gospels.

The greater irony is that the same Gospels were cherished alike by both sides.

ECONOMICS: THE DESTRUCTIVE HAND OF WAR

From the point of view of its other goal—to prosper economically—the Revolution was for the Haring family an unmitigated disaster. Essential markets were interrupted well before the war, valuable property was destroyed during the war, and an economic depression continued to frustrate the farmers' hopes for recovery for five years after the war.

Correspondence between Colonel Thomas Ellison, a farmer and sloopowner in Newburgh, Orange County, and his son Thomas, Jr., his trading partner in Manhattan, illustrate the effect on wheat prices of supply and demand, which in turn were affected by the seasons, the weather, the size of the crop, price actions by city authorities, and the mood of the farmer—but especially, as the Revolution approached, by political events. We might well imagine a similar correspondence between the Harings in Orange and Bergen counties and their nephew Elbert [310] in New York, who in 1732 had married his first cousin, Elizabeth Bogert, and entered into the Bogert family's bolting and baking business with his brothers-in-law. Like the Ellisons, the Harings in Tappan had in the patentee Peter Haring's son Elbert a trusted connection in the city to whom they could sell their wheat and flour and who could act as their ears and eyes for the best prices.[47]

Supply and demand were a constant factor in price, and whether the farmer was of Dutch or, as were the Ellisons, of English background, he was affected by the same fluctuating market conditions. In the summer of 1764, the harvest was in, and "There is not quite so great a Call for flower as was Last Week," wrote Thomas Ellison, Jr., in the city to his father, Colonel Ellison, upriver. "There has Been plenty a long the Docks this Week, The

210

Esopus [Kingston] men [primarily of Dutch background] all sold @ 14/ The Demand for Spain is over as you'll see by the paper. Whether Real or not is a little Check to the Market" (August 28, 1764).

The following winter, supply was down and the price was up: "Flower is 17/ tho not very quick Wheat 5/," the son reported. Three weeks later, Colonel Ellison paid more for the wheat he purchased from his upriver neighbors for resale in New York than his son thought prudent, given the demand in the city: "I heard . . . that you had given 5/6 for wheat, which is . . . more then it has been here this Winter, & am pretty sure more then the market will Bear the fore part of the year" (February 6 and 28, 1765).

But the local farmers had something to say about the price that Colonel Ellison, even with his access to the New York trade, had to pay for their wheat. "Deare Childe," he explained to his son in New York in the winter of 1766, "our Country [meaning the small farmers whose wheat he bought for resale] has Got upon thare High Hors a bout the Price of wheat & [barrel] Staves that none of it Can be got at a resenabel Price."

The farmers might get on their high horse, but they knew they were at the buyer's mercy to some extent, for Colonel Ellison had his own recourse: he could, "as Sune as Snow Coms . . . set the price of wheat @ 5/6 & the Staves as a Gree abal to what you Rite a Bout them [.] [I]f the markets shold Prove Dole at York at the time . . . wee may Get Some at the price a bove as money is Scarse." On the other hand, the farmers might take satisfaction from knowing that, as the middleman, Colonel Ellison was subject to pressures from his buyers, too: "As wee have So many wheat Byars on Credit . . . [till] June it may obledge me to give somthing more [in] In Corragment of a market In the fore part of the Summor" (December 23, 1766).

The wheat trade was further complicated by the fact that the processing of wheat had long been a monopoly of the bolters in New York City. To prevent the bolters from cheating on weight and purity, a chamber of commerce had been established in 1768 to regulate the industry, to the displeasure of the bolters. "Last Evening," Thomas wrote to his father, the Bolters & flower Sellars Came to a Resolution not to Sell flower Barrells Under 28/ a Tun . . . which I Suppose will Ruffle some of the Chamber of Commerce." In retaliation, Thomas warned, the latter "insist on having all the flower weigh[ed] here again, & they find some parcels that falls short 2 or 3, so that it will be necessary to be Careful" (October 29, 1768).

But the main threat to the stability of the wheat market, and the main anxiety of both the American farmer and the city trader, was the growing tension between Great Britain and the American colonies, as the correspondence of this father and son from the time of the Stamp Act in 1765 to the verge of Revolution in 1775, illustrates.

In October 1765, opposition to the Stamp Act, scheduled to take effect on November 1, rose to fever pitch. Delegates from nine colonies gathered in New York in the so-called Stamp Act Congress, forming a united front against this British tax and all taxes "not granted by ourselves." At the same time, more than two hundred merchants of the city also united to resolve on a general boycott of all goods, wares, and merchandise shipped from Great Britain unless the act were repealed.[48]

The British, however, were slow to take a hint. On the twenty-third, when the ship carrying the stamps arrived, Lieutenant Governor Cadwallader Colden insensitively heralded its appearance by having celebratory cannons fired from British men-of-war, which escorted the ship into the harbor "with great parade." According to one observer, Robert R. Livingston, "A vast number of people beheld this sight, and . . . appeared most furiously inraged."[49] On the night of November 1, a mob, the "most formidable imaginable," hanged and burned Colden in effigy, burned the army's stables, and looted and burned the house of a British major who had rashly announced his intention to "cram down the Stamp Act upon [the People] with a hundred men."[50]

Livingston, a Whig justice of the New York Supreme Court and a former assemblyman from Dutchess County, delivered his opinion loud and clear to General Robert Monckton about the effects of the Stamp Act not only on civil order but on trade:

> [T]he enforcing the Stamp Act will be attended with the destruction of all Law Order & Government in the Colonies, and ruin all men of property, for such is the temper of people's mind. . . . Therefore, we beg, as for life and all its comforts . . . that this Act may be repealed. If it be not, it is impossible for the wisest man on earth to tell how far its mischievous consequences will extend. Britain will suffer more by it, in one year, in her trade, than this tax, or any other . . . can ever recompence. Merchants have resolved to send for no more British manufactures, Shopkeepers will buy none, Gentlemen will wear none . . . [for] he that does not appear in Homespun . . . [already] is looked on with an

evil eye. The Lawyers will not issue a writ. Merchants will not clear out a vessel. These are all facts not in the least exagerated; and it is of importance that they should be known. But the worst of all is this; that should the Act be enforced there is the utmost danger, I speak it with the greatest concern imaginable, of a civil war.[51]

A few days later, Thomas Ellison described to his father the events of the first days of the despised measure. The populace "have been greatly Raised by fortifying the fort in so strong a manner & Spiking all the Cannon on the Battery," he wrote. "The governour has made a great manny Enemies by this proceeding, it is Dangerous to Say any thing in his Behalf[.] I Expect the City will be quiet unless the new governour [Sir Henry Moore] when he arrives Should Endeavour to put the Stamps in . . . which is Impossible, with what troops are here—they say the Custom house & Secretary's office are open as usual, & say will clear out Vesells without stamps[.] [T]he Collector's Behaviour is very well approved" (November 1765).

That same week, and on the same anxious topic, Thomas wrote to his father again about the "Disturbances in . . . Regard to the Stamp Papers & the Extraordinary fortifying [of] the fort . . . which greatly Rais'd the Minds of the people. The most of the familys near the fort have moved their Effects, & I Believe there would [have] been a great Disturbance in the City Last Night had not the Stamps been Deliver'd to the Mayor & Corporation, who have placed them in the City hall which was not Don till after Dusk last Night, which Quieted the Minds of the people, so that believe there never was the 5 Nov. kept with Less Noise [November 5 was the anniversary of the execution of Guy Fawkes for attempting to blow up Parliament.]" (November 6, 1765).

The British repealed the obnoxious Stamp Act in March of 1766, but the government, which still badly needed funds to finance its debts and to support the troops who were defending British territory against the French and Indians, could think of no better way of raising those funds than by introducing a new series of levies—the Townshend Acts—on British paper, printer's ink, glass, lead, paints, and tea.

Again, the colonists united to resist with a boycott, and merchants in Boston, New York, and Philadelphia joined in August 1768 in a nonimportation agreement that within eighteen months forced Parliament to revoke these odious duties—except the one on tea. By 1770, even the tea tax was generating division, with

213

the radicals still clamoring for a total ban on all British imports, the moderates urging a boycott on tea only, with many merchants importing the tea despite the ban, and with the general public mostly for importation. "The Importation Committees went about yesterday to take the Sence of the City," Thomas, Jr., reported. The house-to-house convass indicated that a majority of the merchants were for nonimportation, but "Doubt if a majority of the whole city is for it. . . . About sun set yesterday a Party against Importation Began to Parade the City. . . . [When they were stopped and their flags taken], Blows with Sticks & Throwing of Stones Insued. . . . Several People were hurt but none Dangerous, Mr. Gab'l Wm Ludlow [a pro-British, proimportation merchant from Orange County] had his head Broke by some of the non Importers, & his [brother] . . . got several Blows. Its Expected the Magistrate will Bind some of the Principles Over, which Expect will put a Stop to such Mobs & Riots" (July 8, 1770).

Thomas's hopeful expectations were realized for a few years of relative calm in the early 1770s, but not after the Boston Tea Party in December 1773 and especially not after the Coercive Acts, particularly the Port Act closing Boston Harbor to commerce until the sunken tea was paid for. Even so, at the end of May 1774, Thomas reported to his father that, although the radicals in New York were for a tea party of their own, many New Yorkers and others were still ambivalent. "[Regarding] the Boston affair—The Philadelphian [newspaper] Does not think it Advisable for them [the merchants] to Enter into a nonImportation & nonExportation without Consulting the Country [the farmers] as well as the City[.] [I]f the Principle merchants of this City have not a Right, (which they do not assume) to Determine for the City, the City has not more Right to Determine for the whole Province" (May 31, 1774).

The threat of a boycott that would extend to wheat and flour was a temporary spur to the wheat trade: "I have more Business this Summer than Ever had as I have Engaged another 1000 Bu[shels] of wheat to Come Down," Thomas reported. "Your flour [I] have put in store, as Could not sell it, as the Weather is hot. . . . Our City in general are for prudent measures[.] Some would be for a nonImportation from great Brittain, but believe there will nothing be don till the [First Continental] Congress meets" (June 11, 1774).

Something was done when the First Continental Congress met in the late summer and early fall of 1774. With the signing of the

Continental Association, the importation and exportation of all goods, including wheat and flour, to and from Great Britain, was banned—the ban to take effect on December 1.

Now, except for domestic sales, the wheat trade languished. "Was there Vessells," Thomas wrote to his father, "Belive wheat woud be 6/9 or 7/, What Comes to market is Bought at 6/6 & put in Store which makes 2d [twopence] a Bu[shel] Expense, so that I Believe you may venture to give 6/ for all You Can get. . . . Markets woud be much Quicker if we had Vessells, I never knew so few in the Harbour as at present" (April 1, 1775).

As ambivalence over the question of independence from Great Britain began to dissipate, and as Parliament grew more intent on suppressing insurrection, the situation was becoming very tense. In April, Thomas hastened to inform his father of some important news, "lest you should be one Day without [it], for if the Country [farmers] should hear of it before you, they might Run Down & Sell you a large Quantity of Wheat." The news was that "Parliament was for pursuing Vigours measure with Collonies, & that a Bill was to be Brought in to prevent our Sending any produce out of the Kingdom [i.e., to the West Indies or to Europe] which no Doubt will Effect the Prise Considerable here. . . . I wish with all my hearth those Unhappy Disputes was settled" (April 9 and 12, 1775).

But the unhappy disputes were to grow even more acrimonious, and when, at the end of April, redcoats shot and killed American farmers in Lexington, Mass., few doubted that war would be long in coming. "Our Commotions are not yet over," Thomas wrote, "for after the [New York] Provincial Congress had Published, to keep peace & not Disturb . . . & had got those Replaced that was Removed at Turtle Bay, Last Sunday Night they were taken out . . . again . . . by some New England men & . . . Carryed up the Sound. . . . [The King's Man-of-War] went in persute, but is Returned without meeting with them." Now if a ship came into the formerly bustling harbor, it was news: today, he went on, a "ship from Ireland & a Brig from South Carolina Came up which Expect will Load with Wheat & Flour" (June 13, 1775).

The following month, Thomas reported that the "Market State keeps Up—Wheat 6/9 & Scarse flour 17/. . . . [Y]esterday the Man of War turned several of the Jersey Boats Back will not let them Bring any Iron & Some other things to town, but hear will let flour & provisions Come" (July 26, 1775).

The last ominous letter in this correspondence brought melancholy news to Colonel Ellison, and to all the wheat growers in the

Hudson and Hackensack valleys: "The sale for Country produce is now over, Unless it be some flour for our Army—there is several Parcels of wheat at market which will not Sell. Smith from Pough-kepsey . . . [is] Expected to Carry his wheat Back" (September 9, 1775).

A year later, Haring farms in Bergen and Orange counties would be plundered by armies foraging for food for their troops and oats for their horses, laying waste what they could not use. The sale for country produce was over, indeed.

WAR IN THE NEUTRAL GROUND

In the so-called neutral ground between British-held New York City and American-held territory in the Hudson and Hackensack valleys, the Harings and their neighbors in Orange and Bergen counties were fair game not only for British and Continental armies marching through their lands, but also for the gangs of marauders who plundered, raped, and robbed and who burned farms, fields, and fences at their will.[52]

War arrived in Tappan three years before the Declaration of Independence when the Tappan courthouse was burned to the ground—on October 11, 1773, probably by Tory enemies of the patriot sheriff who lived in the building. And war continued to agitate Tappan until May 6, 1783, when George Washington met with the British commander in Chief, Sir Guy Carleton, in the De Clark (De Wint) house in order to arrange the British evacuation of New York and the exchange of prisoners.[53]

In the summer of 1776, the British, convinced of the "utility and absolute necessity" of cutting the lines of communication and supply between the Americans in the highlands and the Americans encamped at the mouth of the Hudson, sailed up the river to effect that strategy. On July 12, five weeks after independence was declared, Orangetown families were thrown into turmoil and fear by the sudden appearance in the river of two British frigates (with their sixty-four guns), accompanied by an armed schooner and two tenders. On board were about four hundred men, a complement of Royal Marines, and highly trained commanding officers. This was only the beginning of the frightened inhabitants' years-long effort to defend themselves against British attack by sea and by land, and to fend off the depredations of foraging armies, unscrupulous friends, turncoat patriots, and thieving neighbors.[54]

216

The British naval foray up the Hudson River in July 1776 was followed in August by General William Howe's attack on the American army on Long Island. By the fall, Sir William had driven the Americans out of lower Manhattan; Paulus Hook and Bergen Neck in New Jersey were evacuated; and the Americans were attempting to hold the Hackensack Valley, with General Nathanael Greene in command on the Palisades at Fort Lee. Fort Washington, across the Hudson from Fort Lee, fell to the British on November 16, 1776, and four days later Fort Lee was hastily abandoned when several thousand British troops landed at lower Closter Dock and scaled the perpendicular, four hundred-foot-high Palisades—considered unassailable and therefore left unguarded. (See Figure 9.3.)

A week later, now occupying Hackensack, the British army visited the house of the pro-coetus patriot minister Dirck Romeyn, sacked it and his barns, stole his livestock, furniture, and clothing, and broke all the windows and doors in his house. That same day, the homes and barns of two members of Romeyn's church met a similar fate. Samuel Verbryck fled for his life to the safety of Clarkstown, whose church he also served, but one of his sons was captured by the British and confined to a jail in New York City where he nearly died. Almost every patriot in the precinct suffered heavy losses—and, for the rest of the war, continued to pay a price for allegiance to the American cause. In New Jersey, the fighting, much of it perpetrated by American Tories upon their friends and neighbors, "never left the state . . . [which] was the scene of seemingly interminable raids, patrol actions, and skirmishes." Much fighting, too, was perpetrated by the British. A New Jersey minister in April 1777 described their ravages: "The murder, robbery, ravishments, and insults, they were guilty of are dreadful. When I returned . . . the town . . . looked more like a scene of ruin than a pleasant well cultivated village." Governor William Livingston of New Jersey spoke of the "Gothic Ravages" of the British army, their indiscriminate rapine and unparalleled barbarity: "They have butchered the wounded asking for Quarter; mangled the dying weltering in their Blood; refused to the Dead the Rites of Sepulture; suffered Prisoners to perish for Want of Sustenance; violated the Chastity of Women; disfigured private Dwellings of Taste and Elegance; and in the Rage of Impiety and Barbarism, profaned Edifices dedicated to Almighty God."[55]

Inhabitants of New Jersey, by an act of December 20, 1781, were allowed to claim compensation for possessions lost to the armies, and although no claimant ever received compensation

Figure 9.3. The Landing of the British Troops in the Jerseys, November 1776. Courtesy Emmet Collection, Miriam & Ira D. Wallach Division of Art, Prints and Photographs. New York Public Library, Astor, Lenox and Tilden Foundations.

from the government, the claim records are extant and permit a glimpse into the losses suffered. To take but one example in the Haring family, John D. Haring [474] of Harington Precinct filed a claim in October 1778 for damages attributed to the British, probably during the Baylor Massacre the previous month. Four slaves were carried off—a man of twenty-eight, a woman of twenty-three, a seventeen-year-old woman, and a child of four—valued together at £250. One "fatt Cow," two young cattle, and twenty-five sheep, the "flower" of ten bushels of rye and four of wheat, a bushel of Indian meal, thirty pounds of butter, and miscellaneous clothing and home furnishings brought this victim's losses from this one raid to more than £300—a small fortune. Two years later, when the American army encamped in Tappan for the trial of the British spy Major John André, the same John Haring sustained losses by his own countrymen of forty bushels of Indian corn, a hog, and a ram, and he was required to pasture seventy-two of the army's horses for a day.[56]

Worse than losing one's slaves, livestock, and personal belongings was to lose one's house and barns—a favorite target. Dozens of homes and barns from Hackensack to Tappan were burned, although not one blackened shell, Adrian Leiby notes, was owned by a Tory.[57]

By late 1778, the Tappan people had nearly given up hope: "We have every reason to expect we must, unless immediately relieved fall a sacrifice to the enemy," they wrote to New York Governor Clinton. "We have every reason to believe no aid will be afforded from the Continental army."[58]

One militia captain warned New Jersey Governor Livingston in the spring of 1780 that "the inhabitants . . . of this County [Bergen], already plundered, diffused and worn out with fatigue and watching, and who for their spirit of perseverance deserve a better fate, must unless speedily saved, soon fall a sacrifice to [enemy] violence."[59] And three days into the American army's stay in Tappan in August 1780, John Haring [415], now a brigade major in the Ulster and Orange County militia, delivered a note to Washington at the De Clark house to advise him that the Tappan people were "being brought to a starving condition. . . . Cornfields, buckwheat, orchards, meadows, etc. etc. are laid waste [by the American army], and we know not where it will end."[60]

Certainly it had not ended a year later when (in August 1781) Simeon De Witt, writing to his friend John Bogart, a teacher at Queen's College, described the once "delightful" Tappan area as a Country which bears the melancholy Vestiges of War; The whole is almost one vast common in which Weeds, Briars and grass promiscuously cover its surface and not a creature to disturb its growth . . . not a hand to cut down the overgrown meadows. Even the high ways were lost and not to be known but by the Ruins of the stone fences which formed the lane—What cruel changes does the destructive hand of war make where ever it approaches! . . . The land mourns.[61]

Two months after De Witt wrote this letter, the British were defeated at Yorktown, and there was little official fighting after that; but Tory raids into the Hackensack Valley continued throughout 1782 and into 1783, as did an illicit trade between the Tories in New York and those sympathizers willing to supply them with produce grown in Bergen and Orange counties. The militia, by this time "too weak and too much worn down with service and suffering," could not contain Tory plunderers, much less Tory traders. Just how weak and worn down may be glimpsed in the recitation by a Haring cousin of his militia activities. Abraham Blauvelt took part in an

engagement . . . under Captain Blanch at which time he was one of the party who took a sentinel from one of the enemy's picket guards. . . . [H]e was in an engagement with the Refugees [Tories] at Closter at which time he assisted in taking about sixty sheep and about fifty head of horned cattle and killed one of their party. . . . [H]e was also engaged with the Refugees in the English Neighborhood at which time he was one of a party which succeeded in retaking a Continental team drive and four horses from the enemy. . . . [H]e was also engaged with the Refugees at Schraalenburgh at which time they retook five horses and killed two Refugees. . . . [H]e was also one of the party that succeeded in taking John Berry, a Regular Refugee who had been advertised as an outlaw for the several murders and depredations he had committed. . . . [H]e was also engaged with the Refugee horse thieves near the New Bridge . . . at which time he received a wound from a musket ball passing through the fleshy part of his hip which confined him for three months. . . . [H]e was also in a battle with the Refugees at . . . the Liberty Pole at which time they succeeded in retaking about 150 head of horned cattle.[62]

Leiby places this man also at (today's) Snedens Landing in June 1780, during the attack on the blockhouse there, and in the battle at Fort Lee in 1781.[63]

The war ended officially in 1783 with the meeting of the two commanders in chief, Washington and Carleton, at the house Daniel De Clark had built in Tappan in 1700.[64] For the Harings, fittingly, it ended where in one sense it had begun one hundred years before, when in 1683 they settled in Tappan to farm, raise their families, practice their religion, participate in their own governance—and enjoy the constitutional rights and privileges they had already insisted upon for at least a hundred years before that.

Chapter Ten

Getting on for One's Self

If the Harings after the war were more secure in their rights and privileges than they had been when they began to fight it, they were poorer in the material things they had sought. At the time of the Revolution, Colonel Abraham A. Haring [336] was the wealthiest man in Harington Township, and his brother Daniel [342] was not far behind. Neighbors on what is today Tappan Road in Northvale, both brothers also owned other large working farms in the area. Each had £750 at interest generating a comfortable annual income, and each owned numerous slaves (Abraham eight adults, according to his inventory). Their stone houses, commodious barns, flat fertile meadows, and healthy cattle, visible from the main road to Hackensack, constituted the farms so often admired by contemporary travelers through the area.

But Abraham and Daniel were of the third generation. What about their sons and nephews—the great-grandson generation? How well did they live in comparison?

All twenty-nine married male members of the fourth generation continued to enjoy a living standard that placed them well within the so-called prosperous minority, but wealth differentials among them, as determined from their wills and inventories, were far wider than those among their fathers and grandfathers (see Table 10.1). A closer look at some of these testators suggests that the disparities among them reflect the following factors: what a man had inherited from his own father; the wealth his wife had brought to the marriage; the number of children he had to support; how much of his property had been lost during the Revolution; and such intangible factors as luck, health, intelligence, talent, and ambition.[1]

222

Table 10.1 *Disposition of Property, Real and Personal, Fourth Haring Generation*

Testator	Will[a]	To widow	To children	Value of personal property (per inventory)
Peter A. [412]	1807; 1807; Bergen Co., bk. A, p. 170.	Marriage portion plus 1 slave, in lieu of dower (L/D). Also: eight-day clock, etc.; use of homestead.	Farm to be sold. Proceeds in five equal parts to one son & four daughters.	$5,246 (Bergen Co., bk. A, p. 207)
John [415]	1808; 1809; Verbryck Papers, Historical Society of Rockland Co.	Bedstead & beds, 1 slave, $800 in L/D. Also use of 2 rooms.	Two properties to three sons equally. Bequests and personal residue to fourth son & three daughters equally.	$5,895 (Verbryck Papers)
Abraham [416]	1799; 1807; Bergen Co., bk. A, p. 138.	Bed, cupboard, spinning wheel, Bible, 1 slave, 2 cows, $250 in L/D.	One farm in two equal shares to two daughters.	$4,097 (Bergen Co., bk. A, p. 175)
Johannes T. [442]	1810; 1813; Bergen Co., bk. A, p. 485.	Room in house; goods she chooses; wagon, 2 horses & best cow; all flax and linen; maintenance in L/D.	One farm to three sons equally; $900 each to three daughters, paid by sons.	$1,003 (Bergen Co., bk. B, p. 217)
Johannes [451]	1797; 1798; N.J. State Library, lib. 37, p. 286, file 2895B.	All while widow	Two farms equally to two sons and two grandsons. Personal in equal fifths to	$3,369 (Bergen Co., June 30, 1798)

Table 10.1 (continued)

Testator	Will[a]	To widow	To children	Value of personal property (per inventory)
			two sons, daughter & three grandsons. Daughter and one grandson $1,250 equally; one son to pay $750.	
Frederick [455]	1800; 1807; Bergen Co., bk. A, p. 148.	All money & goods that were hers when joined in matrimony; 1 room or £50; support by sons.	Lands unequally to four sons. $1,000 each to five daughters; sons to pay.	$1,677 (Bergen Co., bk. A, p. 185)
Abraham J. [461]	Unrecorded	—	—	$2,987 (Bergen Co., bk. B, p. 69)
Cornelius [462]	1806; 1807; Unrecorded, transcribed in Durie, *Kakiat*, pp. 39–40.	Predeceased	One farm equally to two sons. Sons to pay three daughters £73 each. Single daughter to get extra £50 plus an outset.	—
John [466]	1795; 1802; Bergen Co., docket 1, p. 40.	£266 (amount I received with her); her own furnishings; 2 cows; use of 2 rooms; maintenance.	Real and personal equally to son and three daughters.	—
Cornelius [470]	1794; 1803; N.Y. Co., liber 44, p. 334.	All while widow. Then to brother, except for £2 to son.	£2 to son	—

Jacob [473]	1807; 1809; Bergen Co., bk. A, p. 269.	Slave; 1/5 of personal property; support by two youngest sons.	50 acres to each of three sons; they to pay daughters $300 total; two younger sons to have seats in church, horse, cow, plow & tackling in return for support of their mother.	$843 (Bergen Co., bk. B, p. 31)
John [474]	1815; 1823; Bergen Co., bk. B, p. 400.	A "genteel support and maintenance" from children	Land to one daughter & four sons, two grandchildren; two other children to share with all in remainder. "Bed compleate" and cupboard to daughter.	$471 (Bergen Co., bk. C, p. 273)
Hendrick [475]	1822; 1825; Bergen Co., bk. C, p. 120.	All while widow. Then to nephews/nieces.	Childless. Land to three nephews; money to two nieces, minister, and minister's daughter.	(Bergen Co. Historical Society, Mss. Coll., reel 4, pp. 281–284)
Roelef [4135]	1837; 1837; Bergen Co., bk. E, p. 181.	$100, a cow or value of; use of half of dwelling; as much furniture as needed. Also a good livelihood & support by son plus $16 per year.	Two sons each 100 acres	—
Abraham [4136]	1817; 1817; Bergen Co., bk. B, p. 151.	All while widow. Then to brother.	Childless	$2,148 (Bergen Co., bk. C, p. 50)

SOURCE: Wills and inventories, as cited in cols. 2 and 5.

"Year written; year proved; location.

Table 10.2 Comparison of Wealth, Third and Fourth Haring Generations, Selected Testators

Testator	Year of inventory (I)	Year of ratables (R)	Acres	Slaves	Horses & horned cattle	Money at interest	Value of personal property[a]
Abraham A. [336]	1791	1790	224 (R); c. 600 (will)	$960[b]	$1,032 (I)[b]	$942 (I)[b]	$2,502 (I)[b]
Peter A. [412]	1807	1802	140 (R)	$600 (I); 1 (R)	$490 (I)	$3,418 (I)	$5,246 (I)
Abraham A. P. [416]	1807	1802	150 (R)	$290 (I); 4 (I), 1 (R)	$799 (I)	$2,369 (I)	$4,097 (I)
Johannes [451]	1798	1796	212 (R)	$270 (I)[b]; 3 (I), 0 (R)	$510 (I)[b]	$1,800 (I)[b]	$3,369 (I)[b]
Frederick [455]	1807	1802	100 (R)	$505 (I); 6 (I), 1 (R)	$252 (I)[b]	none (I)	$1,677 (I)
Johannes T. [442]	1813	1802	50 (R)	$137 (I); 2 (I), 1 (R)	$132 (I)	$207 (I)	$1,003 (I)
Jacob [473]	1809	1802	80 (R)	$250 (I); 1 (R)	$115 (I)	none (I)	$843 (I)

SOURCES: See Tables 6.3 and 10.1.

[a]Includes slaves, livestock, money at interest, and household goods.

[b]For purposes of comparison, pounds have been converted to dollars at a rate of $3 per pound.

Table 10.2 compares the worldly possessions of Abraham [336], aside from Elbert the most prosperous member of the third generation, with those of six fourth-generation Harings. These six were selected out of the known testators because they were born within one generation of Abraham and died within half a generation of him—a short enough period that prices and values remained nearly constant. Also, all six are found in ratables lists for years shortly before their deaths; in addition, wills, inventories, or their houses and other evidence exist for examination. In the variations in their wealth, moreover, the six are representative of the variations for their generation of the family, in general, as seen in Table 10.1.[2]

Two of the fourth-generation members in Table 10.2 equaled or improved on Abraham A. Haring's position, two fell far below it, and two were in the middle. The two most affluent were Judge Peter A. Haring [412] and his brother Captain Abraham A. P. Haring [416].

Peter, whose main source of income was from his fees as a judge of the Bergen County Court of Common Pleas, had entered politics and was a member of the New Jersey Legislative Council from 1784 to 1790 and from 1792 to 1795. His career followed that of his grandfather, the patentee Peter Haring [21], an Orange County judge and representative to the New York Assembly, and his father, Abraham [39], also a county judge and a New York assemblyman. In 1807, Peter left personal property (exclusive of his real estate) of about $5,200. (Personal property includes slaves, livestock, money at interest, and personal and household effects.)[3]

Peter's brother, Abraham A. P. [416], a captain in the militia, lived on a neighboring farm on Tappan Road. Abraham died the same year as his brother and left around the same amount of personal property (i.e., about $5,000). His detailed eight-page inventory mentions five bedsteads, suggesting that his house was a relatively large one.

Besides the bedsteads and the usual tables, chairs, cupboards, chest, and stands, Abraham owned looking glasses, books, and silver items. Livestock included a brindle cow, a herd of nine red cows, two fat calves, a sorrel horse, three bay mares, a red mare, a bay colt, and two roan horses. He also owned four adult slaves, Jo, Cate, Nanny, and Cuff. That 170 ells of flax linen (an ell is three-quarters of a yard) and another 72 ells of tow were counted, as well as thirteen pounds of tow thread, six and a half pounds of

Figure 10.1. Twin-Door House of Frederick Haring [455], c. 1753. Courtesy C. K. Tholl.

yarn, nineteen pounds of flax yarn, five pounds of hetcheled flax, seventy pounds of flax, and a "lot of baskets with tow" suggests that the women in this household had a lively business turning the farm surpluses into manufactured goods. Twenty-three tow sheets and thirty-nine shirts were ready for sale at the time of inventory.

A few miles west of the farms of Peter and Abraham were the farms of two of their cousins, the brothers Johannes [451] and Frederick [455]. These two men fall into a middle category in the group of seven in Table 10.2. Yet even so, Johannes seems to have been considerably more prosperous than his younger brother Frederick, who lived nearby (see Figure 10.1).

Both men had started out life with the same advantages, but Johannes ended with a farm of 212 acres (according to ratables from two years before he died) and Frederick with one of only 100 acres. Johannes had fewer slaves than his younger brother (whose inventory reported six), but the fact that he had more livestock suggests that these two men may have shared these valuable commodities as needed. Still Johannes's personal property was valued at more than twice his brother's, according to the two men's inventories, and Johannes had nearly £600 (about $1,800) at interest, giving him an annual income from his lending activities of about £36—more than enough to provide for all of his household's basic needs. Frederick had no money at interest.

Perhaps Frederick's case illustrates the handicap that a large number of offspring presented in the late eighteenth century. Although he started out with the same resources as his brother, the fact that he had ten children to raise—twice as many as Johannes—probably accounts for his inability to prosper to the same extent. Also, Frederick lost more in the war than his brother: in one British foray into his neighborhood, he was relieved of two horses, six milk cows, two steers, one bull, a yoke of oxen, two guns, a carbine, and a musket—worth £92 total. It may be that in a preindustrial agricultural economy, losses sustained on this scale were never recouped.[4]

Johannes and Frederick decidedly fall into the "prosperous minority." Even so, their inventories indicate that they owned very few of the luxury items of the day, such as the pictures and imported rugs and quantities of silver that graced Elbert Haring's house in Manhattan. Johannes's most valuable possession was an eight-day clock worth £20 4s; Frederick's were a bedstead and bedding valued at £20, sheets and pillowcases worth £33 5s, and a corner cupboard, eight silver teaspoons, and a pair of silver shoe buckles worth £18 15s.

Both men were deacons and elders in the Tappan Reformed Church but appear not to have played any wider role in community life. Unlike their politically and militarily active cousins Peter and Abraham, they seem to have had little desire to participate in the increasingly diverse economic and political opportunities of the age, inclining instead to the old ways, even as the times changed in ways that would profoundly affect their lives.

This also seems to have been true of the two least prosperous fourth-generation Harings in Table 10.2, Johannes T. [442] and Jacob [473]. Both were considerably less affluent than their relatives. They had little or no money at interest; their farms were smaller (they paid tax on 50 and 80 acres, respectively); they owned little livestock; and they had fewer slaves (Johannes two, Jacob one). Although they were not in danger of declining into the unprosperous majority, they were closer to it than any other member of their family had been in Tappan.[5]

229

WIDOWS AND CHILDREN

The wills noted in Table 10.1 are a source of social as well as economic information and bear witness to the persistence of familiar themes from the preceding generation—and to the persistence of Dutch material culture. Thus, testators specify that, in lieu of her dower rights, the widow receive her "marriage portion," the "goods she brought," the "amount I received with her," or the "money and goods she had when we joined in matrimony." As it had in earlier generations, the bride's outset functioned not only as a dowry to attract a husband and as a way of contributing to the establishment of a new household, but also as her "social security" in old age. All testators are careful to mention where and how the widow is to be maintained. According to the means of the husbands, and probably also the age, health, and competence of their wives, these widows were given the whole "use of the homestead," the right "personally to occupy and enjoy the two northerly rooms in my present dwelling house," one room in the house, one room or £50, a "genteel support and maintenance," the "use of one half of my dwelling house," or a "good livelihood and support by my son."

Wealthier testators were able to supply their widows with a personal slave. Poorer ones, such as Jacob [473], whose inventory in 1809 totaled only $842.80, left his widow a slave, but no private quarters of her own and no cow to provide her with even a small source of independent income. Johannes [442] promised his "Beloved wife Sarah . . . a Negro woman Which she selects if any there are Belonging to me at that time." But as the time approached and it became clear that this promise would not be kept, Johannes had to add a codicil to his will specifying that certain items previously bequeathed to his sons be given to Sarah instead: "Unto my Loving wife Sarah the oldest waggon of my Two waggons . . . and a Team of my best horses . . . a set of Tackling and also my best milch Cow . . . [and] all my flax and Tow linen which is unbleached [formerly] Bequeathed . . . unto my Three Sons." Roelef [4135], who had been married three times, could give his third wife only $16 a year and had to charge his son with the responsibility for her support.

Two childless testators, Hendrick [475] and Abraham [4136], left all to their widows, then after their death or remarriage to siblings or nieces and nephews. Only one fourth-generation testator with children, Johannes [451], followed earlier practice and left his whole estate to his wife. We are reminded that the four

Haring grandfathers of these men left their whole substantial property to their widows' ownership and management in two cases, and in two others provided their widows with the means for a livelihood that makes the circumstances of these fourth-generation widows look quite reduced, indeed.

Children, of course, were likewise endowed according to their fathers' means. Wealthier testators could afford to revert to seventeenth-century practice and treat sons and daughters equally. Judge Peter A. [412], for instance, specified that the home farm be sold (with his widow's permission) and the proceeds divided in equal parts among his sons and four daughters. The less affluent bestowed their lands equally on sons and designated cash legacies for their daughters as they were able.

For children in special situations, special arrangements were made. Frederick [455], who shared his house with a married and an unmarried son, allowed the latter his choice of the feather beds, bedstead, and bedding and did not require him to pay any legacy to his sisters in return for the land he farmed. This bachelor, age thirty-five when his father wrote his will in 1800, never married, and in 1829, left what was probably the same feather bed, "with blankets, pillows, pillow cases and sheets and every thing," to his sister-in-law, no doubt in recognition of all the meals, laundry, and cleaning she had provided him all his bachelor life. Harmanus was also grateful to the brother he lived with, and he willed the remainder of his estate, which totaled $713, to him and his son.

In the case of a son who had disappointed his father in some unnamed way, the father had recourse in his will: Cornelius [470], "utterly disallowing all former wills," left his whole estate to his wife and after her death or remarriage to his brother, "except the sum of Two pounds which I will shall be paid to my son Jacob within one year after my decease." One wonders if this was the same Jacob who, fifteen years later in 1818, petitioned the Bergen County Court of Common Pleas "to hear what can be alleged for and against my liberation from confinement pursuant to the acts of the legislature relative to insolvent debtors."[6]

Some fathers attempted to direct the use of their lands from beyond the grave. Apparently concluding that Harmanus would never marry, Frederick in 1807 added a codicil to his will reducing Harmanus's share of his lands from one-fourth to one-eighth and making it clear that "Harmanus shall not be at liberty to sell his land to strangers, but to any of my other sons." When Cornelius [462] in 1806 at age seventy-eight wrote his (unrecorded) will, his daughter, "Elizabeth single woman," was thirty-three years old and probably expected never to marry. Her father provided her, so that she should not be a burden on her siblings, with a legacy equal to that of her married sisters, as well as with the equivalent of an outset: £50 and the "bilested [sweet gum] cupboard of her Mother and a good bedstead, bedding and all that belongs to a bed fit for use, as blankets, sheets, etc., and the remainder of an outset according as my other daughters [received]." Elizabeth must have surprised her family when, at age thirty-nine, she married her first cousin, Peter A. Haring [5112].[7]

When predeceased by a son or daughter with children, testators by law (and natural inclination) bequeathed the deceased's share to the grandchildren. Johannes [451] left to his two orphaned grandsons, Johannes [6116] and Casparus [6117], an equal fifth of his personal estate to divide between them and, as tenants in common, "that part of the farm or plantation I now Occupy and Live on," as well as a pasture, a Salt Meadow, and "a piece of ground I have in a Swamp commonly called the Old Tappan Green bush" (or all that their father would have received to start out farming if he had lived).

Piety is still a feature of wills. Hendrick [475] directed that his heirs pay the "usual sum of money yearly and every year as a I have and so yearly pay to the reverend James Romine [Romeyn] as part of his salary . . . as long as he shall remain the minister of the Schralenburgh congregation." To the Reverend Romeyn's daughter, Hannah, Hendrick also gave $100.

The comparatively straitened means of some of these fourth-generation testators can be seen as resulting, in part, from their having received smaller inheritances from their fathers than some of their cousins had received. Again, though, other factors— a lack of talent or ambition, a diminishment of energy and vitality, a certain conservatism, a desire to "stay down on the farm"— undoubtedly played a part. Johannes [442] had received enough education to be commissioned an ensign in the Orangetown militia, and Jacob [473] had a source of non-farm-related income as a weaver; but both these occupations or offices were far lower in status than those attained by some of their cousins and by many of their forebears. Jacob's brother John [474] was also a weaver; Daniel [478], another brother, was a tailor. Many in this generation identify themselves in documents simply as yeoman or farmer.[8]

The revolutionary war was also a factor. As we saw in Chapter 9, many families in the so-called neutral ground, including many

Harings, suffered major losses of real property, livestock, slaves, and personal property during the Revolution and apparently were unable to recoup those losses.

THE MELANCHOLY VESTIGES OF WAR

Ten men in this fourth generation of thirty-two died intestate. A look into the circumstances reveals that the Haring family was no stranger to tragedy, grief, and heartbreak—and, again, that the war was a factor in cases of intestacy.

Peter [427], Elbert's oldest surviving son, who in legal documents identifies himself as "gentleman" and who was disinherited by his father, shot and killed himself in Tappan in 1787, at age forty-nine—without doubt a most shocking event in this pious family and community. "About a fortnight since, at Tappan, Peter Haring shot himself.—Desperate [man]! to arrogate to [himself] the prerogative of the Deity, and thus affront God, and the wrath of Heaven defy," The *New Jersey Journal* exclaimed. Gerrit [453] died, probably unexpectedly, at age forty-three, leaving a wife and six children at home, the youngest only eight years old. Cornelius [484], a "farmer," enlisted in 1758 at age twenty-two in the French and Indian War and presumably was killed in action. Captain Abraham A. [4111] died intestate in a British military prison in New York in 1779, at age forty-five, leaving three children and a pregnant wife. His younger brother, John [4114], age thirty-six and the father of a son, died the same year, perhaps also a casualty of war. Yet a third brother in this family, David A. [4113], died intestate in 1798. Finally, Cornelius [4125] died unexpectedly at age forty-one in 1801, leaving a wife and three daughters, ages nine, eleven, and thirteen.[9]

The fourteen children left fatherless by these various misfortunes received their fathers' shares of their grandfathers' estates as well as their due share, under the laws of intestacy, of their fathers' personal property. But a fatherless child was inevitably poorer in the long run for being deprived of the full lifetime earning power of his parent, and so these fourteen fifth-generation Harings faced their adult lives with fewer resources and fewer prospects than they might have.

Finally, some of the fourth-generation Harings who failed to prosper were those who chose the Tory side in the American Revolution. Three of the ten Haring men who died intestate in this

Figure 10.2. Hoebuck Ferry House, Hoboken, N.J., 1772. Courtesy Museum of the City of New York.

generation did not make wills, presumably because they had no property of importance to will. As accused Tories, Peter T. [441] and his cousins John C. [485] and Abraham C. [489] saw their farms confiscated in 1779 by the American authorities—among whom were other cousins who had chosen independence.

FORMERLY A FERRYMAN

As social change quickened, a man who would rise in the increasingly populous, heterogeneous, and competitive world of the late colonial period had to be resourceful, ambitious, and adventurous—as the career of Cornelius Haring [417] illustrates. Cornelius, the brother of Judge John Haring [415] and Peter [412] and Abraham [416] (above), had, while still in his twenties, persuaded his father to give him his share of the estate. His father's will, written in 1771 when Cornelius was twenty-seven, specifically excludes this son from any land or legacy: "My son Cornelius Haring hath already had all his share out of my whole Estate."

Farming held no allure for Cornelius, and with his share of his father's estate, he first obtained an education (he was a surveyor) and then entered upon various business ventures. The most colorful of these was the ferry he opened in May 1775, soon after receiving his inheritance, in partnership with a family friend, William Bayard, plying the waters between Hoboken and Manhattan. With a flourish, Cornelius Haring begged leave "to present his most respectful compliments to the public and to inform them that he intends . . . to open the new established ferry from the remarkable pleasant and convenient situated place of William Bayard, Esq. at the King's-Arms Inn" in Hoboken. As war clouds gathered, however, Cornelius Haring, a patriot, and William Bayard, a loyalist, found themselves in opposite camps. Less than a year after the ferry opened, Bayard advertised for a new manager for his "pleasant situated and convenient House, Out-Houses, Stables, Barn and Grounds, at Hoebuck, lately established into a Ferry."[10] (See Figure 10.2.)

For Cornelius, ever resourceful, the war offered opportunities for advancement, and he found at around this time in the new American government a patron more palatable to him than the Tory Bayard. First as paymaster to Bergen County recruits, then as a contractor for the purchase of flour for the troops and as a captain in the Bergen County militia, Cornelius acquitted himself well enough by 1779 to win the job of Commissioner of Seized Estates. He pursued this latter role with vigor, petitioning the Legislative Council and the General Assembly of New Jersey in 1782 for power to sell the seized estates and, again the same year, petitioning for funds to enable him to collect debts due the state from prisoners who had fled its borders. It was not only the coffers of New Jersey that motivated Cornelius in these petitions. For their trouble, commissioners were allowed to keep for themselves, over and above reasonable charges and expenses, 5 percent of every estate sold or leased.[11]

William Bayard now came to regret the encouragement he had once provided to Cornelius Haring, for when Cornelius secured appointment as Commissioner of Seized Estates, he confiscated Bayard's handsome spread at Hoboken. "Sir," Cornelius wrote to Bayard's overseer, on May 8, 1783, "You will please to Deliver the possession of Hobock to the Bearer hereof . . . [or] expect to abide by the Consequences." Bayard, in a panic, appealed the next day to Major George Beckwith, begging him to intervene with George Washington: "[I] am apt to believe," he wrote, "this fellow Herring who was formerly my Ferryman from this Place has done it more from a wish to get on for himself . . . than from [an] . . . order [from above]." But Bayard's pleas were in vain. Cornelius seized not only Bayard's 564-acre estate at Hoboken, but also his six smaller properties in Bergen County.[12]

Indeed, Bayard spoke truth. A man who would rise in late-eighteenth-century America needed more than his native talents, an inheritance, some education, a wife with a good dowry, and an influential patron or mentor. In a world of competition for advancement, of a many who would rise and the few who could, he needed that particular drive to "get on for himself" that a wealthy man like Bayard could deride.

THE FIFTH GENERATION

By the end of the eighteenth century, when the fifth generation was coming to maturity and the sixth and seventh generations were being born, the Haring family had become so large that no one, coherent family could any longer be said to exist. Instead of one large family, there were now many discrete families, the branches of which very likely knew little about one another or about what their particular kin relationship was, even though they still occupied the same basic square miles.

Seventy-five male children and an almost equal number of females were born to the Harings in the fifth generation over the years from 1752 to 1800. Of the sons, sixty (80 percent) survived to adulthood and can be traced to the end of their lives in tax, land, church, cemetery, town, and probate records. Almost incredible to report, fifty-six of these men, or 91 percent, remained in Tappan or within a fifteen-mile radius of it for their entire lives. (The exceptions are the sons of Abraham [436], who were born and reared in New York City, and the sons of Cornelius [417], who had settled in upstate New York during the 1790s.)

As they married and needed land, the fifth generation moved out from the Hackensack and Hudson valleys to land watered by the Ramapo, the Passaic, and the Saddle rivers; but expansion into new areas represented more a need for space than a desire for a new and different way of life. Where they established new communities, these bore striking resemblances to the communities of their parents. Networks of kinship remained precious, bonds with the Dutch Reformed Church remained strong, and fifth-generation male members of the family continued to be active in local—though not in state or national—politics. Their lives, as Thomas Bender has said of New England townspeople, "remained overwhelmingly bounded by local and intimate patterns of human interaction,"[13] and those with whom they interacted were often kin in some degree.

Their material culture also showed remarkable persistence. They continued to build and furnish their houses in traditional styles; and, as they shared in Tappan until 1812 the same burial cloth their ancestors had shared, so too they continued to bequeath their worldly goods as their fathers had.

A CLOSER LOOK

The will of Abraham Haring [5221] is a particularly telling document, for it reveals how many of the themes and characteristics of his forefathers' lives were still operative in his own in 1800—170 years after his great-great grandfather had emigrated to New Netherland.

On Christmas Day, 1800, Abraham called his family around his bedside and proceeded to dictate his last will and testament. He was thirty-three years old and either fatally ill or injured; he died three days later.[14]

Though young, Abraham, who identified himself as a yeoman,

237

had a substantial estate, part of it inherited from his grandfather [336] only nine years before and part assembled on his own. Because his three children were only thirteen, seven, and five years of age, he bequeathed all of his considerable property to his wife, Elizabeth Van Dalsen (Sickles)—who had already been widowed once—so long as she remained his widow. Abraham apparently had great confidence in Elizabeth's ability to manage, for he specified that she was to have full control and use of the rents and profits of all his real and personal property, and he specifically forbade his executors from selling any of his slaves, horses, cattle, sheep, swine, household goods, or furniture during the time that Elizabeth remained his widow, except with her consent or in the case of "absolute necessity." He also trusted her to relinquish control of his property to his sons when they came of age. His farm in Hackensack and Saddle River was designated for his elder son, and the remainder—his grandfather's farm in Tappan—for his younger son, five years old at the time of the will. Ann, his daughter, age seven, was to be paid $2,000 by her brothers at age twenty-one or on the day of her marriage—a generous outset. Of this amount, William, the younger brother, was charged to pay $1,200; John, the elder, then thirteen, only $800. John paid less either because he was expected as the elder son to assume greater obligations to the mother of this family or because his property was less valuable. Although the will does not describe Ann's share as equal to her brothers', it surely represented a substantial and equitable portion of her father's worldly goods.

Abraham chose close family relatives—his father-in-law and his cousin (but not his wife)—as his executors, and their inventory of his goods, chattels, and credits reveals that, in addition to his livestock, plate, household goods, and grain, this young husband and father owned slaves worth nearly $500 and was owed interest and bonds of $1,831.82.[15] Surely one explanation for the remarkable persistence of the customs and patterns among descendants of the early settlers was the comfortable and prosperous life that Dutch ways seemed to afford.

The tried-and-true ways did not always lead to the good life as the nineteenth century dawned, however, and Haring men of the fifth generation did not always succeed, even as farmers. That only one fifth-generation Haring played any role at all on the stage of the new republic suggests that the yeoman ideal, the notion of America as a republic of small farmers, was indeed "theory only," as Jefferson had acknowledged in 1785 (in a letter to the Rev. James Madison). Elbert [536] was graduated from

238

Princeton, went on to study law in the office of his uncle, Judge Samuel Jones, was admitted to the New York bar, and served in the administration of President Andrew Jackson—a career possible only to men who had rejected farming as a way of life and got an education. For men who persisted in traditional patterns and clung to the farm, prosperity was elusive, failure awaited many, obscurity was almost assured. Abraham D. [5209] was able to bequeath "Roseland," his handsome stone house, still standing, to two of his sons, money to his daughter, and the rest of his real estate, his gristmill, and other possessions to a third son; but not all Harings of this generation were so fortunate.[16]

In 1801, David A. [5203], age forty-one, like his cousin the year before, sickened and died shortly after making his will. David was able to leave his wife only $375 and had to direct that a meadow and part of his farm be sold to pay his debts. The remaining part of his farm of 101 acres had to be divided among five children. Misfortune stalked other men in this generation as well. In 1826, the Tappan church was obliged to pay a doctor $27 "for services rendered as Phicician to the family of Peter D. Haring" [5165]; one Jacob Haring was confined to jail in 1818 for insolvency; and when John C. [5117] died in 1815, at age sixty-one, his inventory was valued at only $218.[17]

From what can be learned from the public record of the men of the fifth generation, in short, their economic lot varied—often dramatically. Some prospered. Some simply persevered. Some failed as they attempted with varying degrees of success to "get on for themselves." Their forefathers' substance could no longer insulate them from the vagaries of fate and fortune, and a changing world made it ever more difficult to maintain their comfortable Dutch traditions and customs. Change, though sure, was slow, however—and the surprise is not so much that the Harings and their fellow congregants listened to Dutch preaching in the Tappan church until 1835, but that Dutch preaching ended in that church once and for all in 1835.

THE AMERICAN DREAM: A RETROSPECTIVE

By 1802, Harington Township ratables document that, although there were now forty-three Harings taxed on land, as compared with twenty-five a quarter-century earlier, in 1779, total family landholdings had dropped from 3,571 acres to 3,070 acres. The family had not only not increased its landholdings in this township, it had seen them dwindle at the same moment that they had to be divided among more family members.[18]

In 1779, 7 percent of all the polls taxed were Harings owning 12 percent of the total land; by 1802, however, they represented 10 percent of the polls taxed, but owned only 9 percent of the land. (A total of 31,021 acres of improved and unimproved land was taxed in 1802.)

The average size of all properties in the township was drastically smaller in 1802—in fact, half as large, down from 122 acres to 61. The average Haring property at 71 acres was still somewhat larger than the township average, but in 1802 it was also only half the size it had been a quarter-century before (143 acres). Still, these Harings continued to enjoy the land advantage their head start in the area had given them; for twenty of their forty-three farms, or 46 percent, were in the "larger than average" category in 1802.

As we saw above, many fifth- and sixth-generation members moved after the Revolution to newly developing townships farther out in Bergen County, and these men owned farms in their new locales; in Harington Township, however, the Harings who remained were demonstrably less well off than they had been, with eighteen additional family members owning 11 percent (as opposed to an earlier 13 percent) of the township's horses and 11 percent (as opposed to an earlier 14 percent) of the cattle. As for slaves, they owned exactly the same number as in 1779, thirteen, but a much smaller percentage of the total—down from 22 percent to 12.6 percent. (Money at interest was not taxed in 1802, so this important indicator of wealth cannot be compared with the 1779 figures, which had shown the Harings holding 32 percent of the township's surplus funds.)

The richest 10 percent in Harington Township in 1802 owned farms as much as four times the size of the average farm in the township. Yet, only five Harings, or 1 percent of the total 505 polls in Harington Township that year, were among the richest inhabitants, or top 10 percent.

A "CURIOUS OLD DUTCH PLACE"

In 1833, when Washington Irving and Martin Van Buren—on what is referred to in Irving's journal as his "Esopus [Kingston] Dutch Tour"—traveled down the Hudson Valley from Albany to

Jersey City, with stops in Tappan and Harrington, they perceived the local farmers as being culturally not American but Dutch—a puzzling designation for two reasons. First, by then these families had been in America for two centuries, seven or eight generations. Second, most of these Dutch families had taken an extremely active part in the American Revolution, primarily on the patriot side. Yet, in 1833, the farmers lived in what Irving described as "very neat Dutch stone houses," their wagons were "Dutch" wagons, their speech was Dutch, and the women wore Dutch sunbonnets. Later, Irving spoke of the "curious old Dutch places and Dutch families" he had visited, including one family in Jersey City, the Van Hornes, a "primitive [Dutch] family . . . living in patriarchal style in the largest and best house of the place."[19]

What explains such persistent "Dutchness"—particularly among people only about half of whom had been ethnically Dutch to begin with? Were the Dutch ways simply considered to be "better," as one historian has suggested?[20] Was the social ideal of their fathers and grandfathers—a harmonious community characterized by stability, continuity, and order and revolving around the old themes of family, field, and friendship, church, local politics, and a "Yearly profitt"—that strong? Or was the farmer's economic situation so unfavorable in the new order that he had no hope or opportunity to participate, but was left behind to molder in his small republic, Irving's quaint Dutchmen in calico pantaloons?

Answers to such questions about the Dutch farmer in the Hackensack and Hudson valleys have often been in the affirmative. But such answers ignore the fact that the Dutch were at best only half Dutch: many considered to be Dutch were in fact of French, German, Flemish, Walloon, Scandinavian, or Polish origin. They ignore also what the preceding chapters have amply demonstrated—that the Dutch farmer's social ideal, though enduring, had in fact been compromised at every level from the beginning of his sojourn in America. Moreover, they ignore that in the early national period the Middle Colony farmer was in general an important participant in economic life, for European demand for American grain had created at this time an "unusually favorable opportunity" for ordinary men to produce for the Atlantic trade world.[21]

Perhaps, then, other explanations for the persistence of Dutch culture in America are in order. Three possibilities suggest themselves.

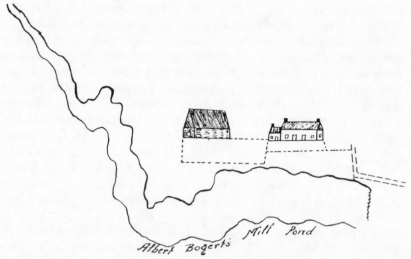

Figure 10.3. Twin-Door House, Surrogate Map no. 39, September 15, 1810.

THE TWIN-DOOR HOUSE: A LOST "GOLDEN AGE"?

First of all, some of these Dutch families may have attempted to re-call their Dutchness after the American Revolution, or even to reinvent it, as they nostalgically looked back to what seemed to be the golden age of their forefathers. One intriguing clue in this regard is that, after the Revolution, in the area settled by the Har-ings and their friends, some families began, for some reason, to build houses again in the twin-door style of an earlier generation.[22]

The early twin-door house (known, as pointed out in Chapter 4, mainly from survey sketches such as that in Figure 10.3) had dis-appeared from the area for a time in favor of the single-entry/center-hall house as families became more conversant with evolv-ing architectural modes, as they became more able to afford the extra expense of material and labor involved in the center-hall style, and as family size declined. The early style, we recall, was rare in the Netherlands, where family size was small; but it was quite common in the Hudson and Hackensack valleys, where the Dutch Pietists, who had large families, settled in the seventeenth century. Form follows function: the twin-door house could accommodate under one roof two generations of a family, affording privacy and communication to both by means of an interior door connecting its two halves; it could also suit one large family with many children, ranging in age from infancy to adulthood.

In a sense, then, the twin-door house was a unique architectural expression of the values especially cherished by the early generations of Harings and their friends and relations in Tappan. Like the kas, which they revered for its association with mother, wife, home, and plenty, the twin-door house resonated with memories—whether accurate or not—of family closeness and cooperation and of the communal and community spirit of pioneer days in the wilderness.

As the schism in the Dutch church was finally resolved, and as the dust of the Revolution settled, the simple bygone era of their fathers and grandfathers must have seemed to men like Abraham D. Haring [4121] very like a lost utopia. And the twin-door house—an ephemeral form linked in memory to a fleeting, perhaps even entirely imagined, golden age of their history—must have seemed an appropriate style to resurrect. No sooner had the war ended than Abraham, age thirty-five and the father of four, engaged his friend and relation, the carpenter Dowe H. Talman, to build a four-room house (two rooms deep) with a modern gambrel roof—and old-fashioned twin exterior doors on the façade.[23]

From 1783 to about 1810, at least eight such twin-door houses were built in a two-square-mile radius in the locality known as Upper Pascack, which straddles today's Bergen and Rockland counties northwest of Tappan—and at least four such houses outside this locale. (Others may exist, and still others have undoubtedly disappeared.)[24]

This house style, as its historian suggests, obviously had a basic appeal in order to have been used so frequently earlier in the century and then to have made a reappearance after the war.[25] If the appeal of the twin-door house to the first generations was a particular one, based on the style's function, then the appeal after the revolutionary war, it is suggested here, was a nostalgic one—a means of regaining what was interpreted as a lost Eden, a time in the remembered "Dutch" past when the Harings and their friends and relations in the area had enjoyed those qualities of friendship, intimacy, and family harmony which were destroyed in the church schism and in the Revolution.

Dowe Talman and Abraham Haring certainly had good reason to long for a simpler era. In May 1779, when John Haring [5113], their cousin, reported to Governor George Clinton of New York

that "Mr. Dowe Tallman [the carpenter's ninety-year-old grand-
father], who was stabbed by the Tories last Sunday morning, died
of his wounds on Tuesday last," he was reporting only one of
scores, perhaps hundreds, of brutalities committed by former
friends against one another. The Tories John Haring spoke of
were neighbors of his own and Talman's, many of them descendants of the Tappan patentees themselves.[26]

TO BE OR NOT TO BE AMERICAN:
AN AMERICAN DILEMMA

A second possibility for the persistence of Dutch culture in America
also suggests itself. Because of the violence America had inflicted
on every aspect of their social ideal, some Dutch may have been
so ambivalent about becoming American at all that they had con-
sciously rejected Americanization almost from the beginning,
willing themselves to retain both their material culture and those
religious and political virtues they had brought with them from
Europe. In other words, they opted for ethnicity rather than as-
similation out of disappointment with the way their social and
moral ideal had been compromised and violated in America.

Certainly Dutch farmers like the Harings had reason to be ambivalent about America. From the beginning, their experience in
the New World had been characterized by ambiguity, uncertainty, conflict, and irony. To review, within one generation or
less, the British conquest of New Netherland had irrevocably al-
tered the course of Dutch destiny in America. Resettlement on land
away from British New York was fraught with unhappy conflicts.
For the Tappan people, these were conflicts with, for example,
Frederick Philipse, Lancaster Symes, and the governmental officials who had claimed part of their New Jersey lands for New York.
Political revolution and religious controversy in the 1680s and
1690s divided their families and their churches and foreshadowed
greater troubles to come in the eighteenth century. At the outset,
political participation in the affairs of the province was circumscribed, with the Orange County families having no representation in provincial politics for two decades after settlement.
Throughout the colonial period, political participation was characterized by the struggle to maintain rights and privileges that as
Dutchmen they had already fought to secure in the Netherlands—
and that were now supposed to be secured for them by British
institutions. Family harmony soon fell victim to divisive religious

issues. Slavery, from the beginning of settlement, presented an additional troubling contradiction to the values of a pious community. And finally order, harmony, stability, and a hard-won prosperity perished at the "destructive hand of war." America was no Eden.

After independence had been secured, a new source of ambivalence toward America appeared in the proposed Constitution. As Anti-Federalists, the Harings—and rural interests in New York and New Jersey generally—viewed the Constitution as unrepublican, counterrevolutionary, less democratic than the Articles of Confederation and the state constitutions, and protective of the elite and its property to the detriment of the ordinary citizen. In the debates in New York over ratification of the Federal Constitution and in the final vote on July 26, 1788, John Haring, Esq. [415], a radical patriot in the 1760s and 1770s, voted with the Anti-Federalist minority, thirty to twenty-seven, against ratification.[27]

The Anti-Federalist position was itself fraught with ambivalence. As Herbert Storing has pointed out, "The Anti-Federalists were committed to both union and the states; to both the great American republic and the small, self-governing community; to both commerce and civic virtue; to both private gain and public good." But in the end, they came down on the conservative side:

> The Anti-Federalists did not deny the need for some change, but they were on the whole defenders of the status quo. They deplored departures of the Constitution from "the good old way" or "the antient and established usage of the commonwealth." They shook their heads at "the phrenzy of innovation" sweeping the country. . . . They warned that constant change would leave Americans "always young in government." . . . In the main, they saw in the Framers' easy thrusting aside of old forms and principles threats to four cherished values: to law, to political stability, to the principles of the Declaration of Independence, and to federalism.[28]

If the Dutch farmer was ambivalent about America, if the persistence of his material culture—for instance, the hundreds of sandstone houses in the "Dutch" style built in Bergen and Rockland counties even long after the Revolution—represents his misgivings about America and about "becoming American," it seems inescapable that America itself had something to do with the reason: by rejecting America's demand for newness, innovation, and change, the Dutch farmer was rejecting the very spirit of progressivism that had impelled him to America. But in doing so, he was rejecting as well the violence that newness, innovation, and change had wreaked upon an older ideal and that had ended by dividing and damaging his family, his church, and his community.

EDUCATION

A third explanation for the persistence of Dutchness lies in geography, for the relative isolation of the Dutch farmer in the rural backwaters of the Hudson and Hackensack valleys increasingly separated him from new ideas and opportunities in New York City, and the relatively inferior education available to him in the country increasingly ensured his inadequacy for a role on the stage of the new republic. With a few exceptions—Martin Van Buren being the most prominent—middling farmers, especially on the more remote and relatively inaccessible west side of the Hudson River, simply could not obtain an education of high enough quality to prepare them for officeholding in the modern era on anything but a local level. The rural life did not necessarily uplift and improve, then, as contact with the "green world" was supposed to do, according to the Greeks, the Romans, the Elizabethans, and eighteenth-century romantics, but rather had the reverse effect: it produced parochialism, inwardness, and provincialism. As provincialism became a mode of thinking—of looking to the past rather than to the future, of hewing to the old Dutch ways and self-consciously shunning the new anglicized ways—Dutch farmers were increasingly left behind and left out. Martin Van Buren could become president of the United States, just as he could hobnob with Washington Irving, not only because he was relatively well educated, but because he did not act Dutch. After the war, farmers in Bergen County and today's Rockland County continued to build houses on the old Dutch country model; Van Buren built himself a stylish Italianate house in (Dutch) Kinderhoek.

In the long run, however, whether the Dutch American farmer rejected America or whether America rejected him, America was home, for better or for worse, and the resurgence of the twin-door house may, in the end, be a positive manifestation of what

246

Thomas Bender has described as the eighteenth-century American's ability to "bridge" in informal ways the abstract theological differences that had threatened to destroy his community during the Revolution.[29]

That is to say, the stone houses and other enduring objects of Dutch material culture may embody the Dutch descendants' nostalgia for the traditions of their forefathers. But they are also reminders today of the persistence of Dutch spiritual culture in America. Built by men and women mindful that their forefathers had come to America determined to maintain their political and religious liberties—however they viewed them—they stand today as eloquent testimonies to our national history and as hardy symbols of the ability of such ordinary folk as the Harings and their friends and neighbors to adapt to changing times.

In the end, then, the longing for continuity prevailed over the sources of conflict; and the yeoman ideal, though on some level only an ideal or a theory of how men might live in the new republic, yet continued on other levels in rural America as the real-life paradigm of community for another century. Just as the Dutch Reformed Church survived another wave of schisms in the Second Great Awakening at the turn of the century, just as local governments, peopled by local citizens, continued to assert their needs and protect their rights as they always had, so did the Dutch families endure and carry on. Atlases of Bergen and Rockland counties published in 1876 to commemorate the centennial of the Declaration of Independence reveal that scores of Harings, Blauvelts, Smiths, Van Houtens, Coopers, and others still lived at the end of the nineteenth century as neighbors on the same farms and in the same communities their forefathers had created in the seventeenth.

Appendix

Male Descendants of
John Pietersen Haring
through the Fifth Generation

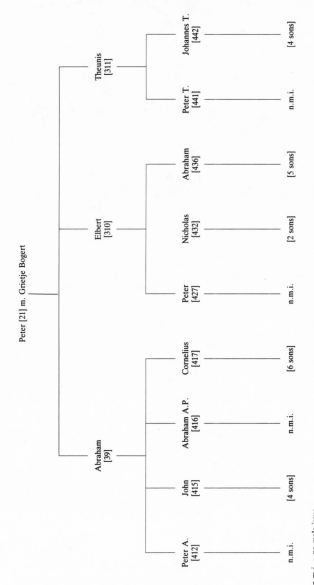

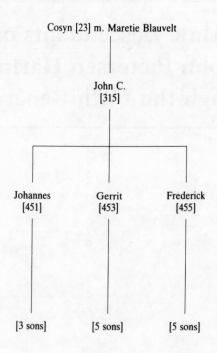

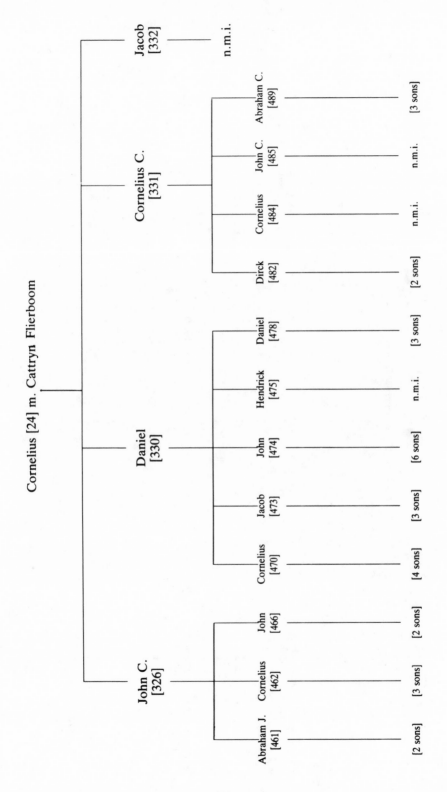

Cornelius [24] m. Cattryn Flierboom

John C. [326]
   Abraham J. [461] — [2 sons]
   Cornelius [462] — [3 sons]
   John [466] — [2 sons]

Daniel [330]
   Cornelius [470] — [4 sons]
   Jacob [473] — [3 sons]
   John [474] — [6 sons]
   Hendrick [475] — n.m.i.
   Daniel [478] — [3 sons]

Cornelius C. [331]
   Dirck [482] — [2 sons]
   Cornelius [484] — n.m.i.
   John C. [485] — n.m.i.
   Abraham C. [489] — [3 sons]

Jacob [332] — n.m.i.

Abraham [27] m. Dircktie Talman

Abraham A. [336]

    Abraham A.A. [4111] — [3 sons]

    David [4113] — [2 sons]

    John [4114] — [1 son]

Daniel [342]

    Abraham [4121] — [2 sons]

    John D. [4123] — n.m.i

    Cornelius D. [4125] — n.m.i

Cornelius A. [344]

    Roelef [4135] — [2 sons]

    Abraham [4136] — n.m.i

    John [4138] — n.m.i

Notes

Chapter 1. New Netherland Beginnings

1. Franklin Burdge, "A Notice of John Haring: A Patriotic Statesman of the Revolution" (1878), unpaginated ms., Mss. Division, New York Public Library. The subject of Burdge's notice was a great-grandson (1739–1809) of John P. Haring and Grietje Cosyns (see Chapter 9).

Burdge had access to a family Bible, location today unknown, with biographical information in it. On the subject of John Pietersen Haring's ancestry, Burdge states that Haring was a descendant of the John Haring who in 1573 had distinguished himself against the Spanish at the Battle of Diemerdyk in the Zuider Zee off Hoorn. Accounts of the two military incidents in which Haring figured during the Dutch revolt against Spain are in John L. Motley, *The Rise of the Dutch Republic: A History*, 5 vols. (New York, 1900), vol. 3, pp. 359, 420–422. See also Richard H. Amerman, "Highlights of History of Hoorn, North Holland," *de Halve Maen* 44, no. 2 (1969), 9–10, 16.

One Pieter Janszen from Hoorn, North Holland, is described in various genealogies of the Harings and related families as the grandson of the sixteenth-century hero. Diligent search in the Netherlands fails to document descendants of John Haring of Hoorn, however, suggesting that he was childless at his death and stood in a collateral rather than a direct relation to the Haring line in America. The Hoorn archives indicate that a Pieter Janszen and Mary Pieters, both from Hoorn, had a son, Jan, baptized there on December 18, 1633; in the Dutch way of naming, this child would have been known as John Pietersen (son of Pieter).

Pieter Janszen (son of John), a farmer, is mentioned in A.J.F. van Laer, ed., *Van Rensselaer Bowier Manuscripts* (Albany, N.Y., 1908), as being in Rensselaerswyck on December 17, 1648, and he was still there in 1666 (pp. 829, 838).

Cosyn Gerritsen van Putten was born circa 1608. (In 1644, he testified in court that he was "about 36 years of age." *New York Historical Manuscripts, Dutch*, 4 vols., trans. and annot. A.J.F. van Laer (Baltimore, 1974), vol. 2, p. 109a; hereafter, *N.Y. Hist. Mss. Dutch*. With his wife Vroutje, he had four children.

2. *Ecclesiastical Records of the State of New York*, 7 vols., ed. E. T. Corwin (Albany, 1901–1916), vol. 1, pp. 487–488.

3. Daniel Denton, *A Brief Relation of New York* [1670] (New York, 1937), p. 3.

4. *Documents Relative to the Colonial History of the State of New York,* 15 vols., eds. E. B. O'Callaghan and Berthold Fernow (Albany, 1853–1887), vol. 3, pp. 38–39; hereafter, *Docs. Rel. Col. N.Y.*

5. Article 21, *N.Y. Colonial Mss., Holland Documents,* 4 vols., trans. and ed. A.J.F. van Laer (Baltimore, 1974), vol. 1, pp. 1603–1656.

6. The Manatus map is reproduced, with a detailed discussion, in I. N. Phelps-Stokes, *The Iconography of Manhattan Island, 1498–1909,* 6 vols. (New York, 1915–1928), vol. 2, pl. 41.

7. Article 22, *N.Y. Colonial Mss., Holland Documents,* vol. 1, pp. 1603–1656. After ten years, a quitrent of one-tenth of the produce and increase of the cattle was charged—a system known as free and common socage. The terms of the original Charter of Freedoms and Exemptions (1629) were improved in 1638 and 1640 to encourage settlement, and in the following five years the population of New Netherland doubled. For Gerritsen, see *New York Historical Mss.: Dutch, Land Papers, GG, HH, II,* ed. and trans. Charles T. Gehring (Baltimore, 1980), p. 52; and confirmation of May 26, 1668, Liber Patents, III:50 (Albany), quoted in Phelps-Stokes, *Iconography,* vol. 6, p. 129.

8. Having an occupation in addition to farming was important to success in the colonies, and double occupations were common. In New Netherland, skilled tradesmen were in such demand that Van Rensselaer paid a premium of 25 percent to obtain them. Of the 102 emigrants to Rensselaerswyck in the period 1630–1644, 14 percent were carpenters, masons, wheelwrights, millwrights, and carpenters' apprentices; the services of cobblers, tailors, brewers, coopers, bakers, weavers, blacksmiths, surgeons, and ministers were slow in coming to the New World but were urgently needed. Oliver A. Rink, "The People of New Netherland: Notes on Non-English Immigration to New York in the Seventeenth Century," *New York History* 62 (1981), 23, 26. In Albany, N.Y., 126 of the 178 first-generation settlers had two or more occupations or sources of income and future profit. Donna Merwick, "Dutch Townsmen and Land Use: A Spatial Perspective on Sixteenth-Century Albany, New York," *The William and Mary Quarterly,* 3rd ser., 37 (1980), 70–71. The continuing need for labor was a strong stimulus to population recruitment and settlement throughout the colonial period. Bernard Bailyn, *The Peopling of British North America* (New York, 1986), pp. 60–64.

In June 1643, Cosyn Gerritsen hired Albert Cornelissen "to make wheels and wagons [and] whatever is connected therewith, for [the term] of one year." If they should not "agree together," the indenture reads, Albert "is to be released at the end of six months; for which he is to be paid in addition to his board, per annum, by Cosyn Gerritsen, one hundred and ten guilders, and fourteen days are to be allowed in harvest time when Albert shall be at liberty to seek his own advantage." *N.Y. Hist. Mss. Dutch,* vol. 2, p. 139.

9. See recitation in Phelps-Stokes, *Iconography,* vol. 6, p. 129; vol. 2, pp. 238, 369; vol. 6, p. 162. See John A. Kouwenhoven, "Key to the Castello Plan," in *The Columbia Historical Portrait of New York* (New York, 1953),

pp. 41 and 42. The Van Twiller farmhouse was visited in 1704, about fifteen years after Cosyn's death, by Madame Sarah Kemble Knight, who wrote: "Old Madame Dowes [whose husband Gerard Douwes owned it then], a Gentle-woman that lived at a farm House, . . . gave us a handsome Entertainment of five or six Dishes and choice Beer and metheglin, Cyder, etc. all which she said was the produce of her farm." *The Journal of Madam Knight* (New York, 1825; repr. 1935). See also Phelps-Stokes, "The Van Twiller Homestead Plot," in *Iconography*, vol. 6, p. 162. Bernard Bailyn confirms that land speculation was a "universal occupation" from the beginning. "Land speculation was everyone's work," he writes, and "every farmer with an extra acre of land became a land speculator." Bailyn, *Peopling*, pp. 66–67; the full discussion is on pp. 65–87.

10. Thomas J. Archdeacon, *New York City, 1664–1710: Conquest and Change* (Ithaca, N.Y., 1975), pp. 51, 30.

11. Joyce D. Goodfriend, " 'Too Great a Mixture of Nations': The Development of New York City Society in the Seventeenth Century" (Ph.D. diss., UCLA, 1975), table 29, p. 163, table 21, and p. 168. Most of the mayors of New York until 1691 were Dutch. From 1689 to 1733, 32 percent of the New York Common Council were lay officials in the Dutch Reformed Church, and in the period 1734–1775 this percentage increased. Bruce M. Wilkenfeld, "The New York City Common Council, 1689–1800," *New York History* 52 (1971), 249–273.

12. James Riker, *Harlem: Its Origins and Early Annals*, rev. ed. (New York, 1904).

13. Documents are missing, but Phelps-Stokes believed that Haring purchased this property directly from one Solomon Pieters, who for speculative reasons had bought considerable land in the neighborhood from Pieter Stuyvesant. Phelps-Stokes, *Iconography*, vol. 6, p. 106. Stokes notes that deeds for surrounding property mention John Pieterson Haring as a boundary owner, sufficient evidence to document his presence in the neighborhood.

14. *The Records of New Amsterdam from 1653 to 1674*, 7 vols., comp. Berthold Fernow (New York, 1897), vol. 7, p. 127. From 1652 to 1664, the year of the first British conquest, a schout, three burgomasters, and five schepens sat together in council in New Amsterdam and "resolved" upon all subjects relating to the city. Burgomasters were to be chosen by the common burghers from the "honestest, richest, and most capable men" in the city, and schouts and schepens also had to be of good character and "understanding." Schepens were empowered to give final judgment on all cases involving sums of less than a hundred guilders and had full power in all criminal cases. See New-York Historical Society Collections, *The Burghers of New Amsterdam and the Freemen of New York* (New York, 1886).

15. *Records of the Reformed Dutch Church in New Amsterdam and New York*, 2 vols. (New York, 1890 and 1901).

16. No tax records have survived for the Out-ward for any year that John Pietersen Haring was alive. Three references in unpublished tax records

for the Out-ward, 1699–1710 and 1721–1733, show the estate of a John Haring being taxed long after John P. Haring was dead. In 1702, "John Harine house" in the Out-ward was valued at £15, which put it on level 4 (2 being the lowest) of the ten levels of all properties taxed, according to a scale devised using the 1677 tax rolls and a published roll from 1703.

The original handwritten records in bound volumes are at the Hall of Records, 31 Chambers St., New York. They are also on microfilm, reel AR-1, in the Historical Documents Collection, Queens College. The scale is Archdeacon's in *New York City, 1664–1710*, p. 161. After establishing "population rosters" for the city in 1677 and 1703, Archdeacon translated tax assessments (which were based not on actual wealth but on an estimated proportion of property value) into scales of economic standing. In 1703, those taxed up to £5 were assigned to level 2 (the lowest); up to £10, level 3; up to £15, level 4; up to £20, level 5; up to £30, level 6; up to £45, level 7; up to £70, level 8; up to £110, level 9; and more than £110, level 10.

In January 1708, "Mr. Haring" was taxed on £5; the following month, the "John Haring Estate" was taxed on £5 again. As late as 1721, the "John Haring Estate and house" were taxed on £5. This property appears to have been the nucleus of the much larger Haring, or Herring, farm discussed in Chapter 5 below.

17. The deed from the Tappaen Indians is recorded in *East Jersey Patents* (Trenton, N.J.) liber 4, pp. 17 and 18. The date of purchase was March 17, 1681 (old style).

18. From the legend on a map of the Province of West Jersey, 1677, John Carter Brown Library, Providence, R.I.

19. Sung Bok Kim, *Landlord and Tenant in Colonial New York: Manorial Society, 1664–1775* (Chapel Hill, N.C., 1978), Chap. 4.

20. Frank B. Green, *The History of Rockland County* (New York, 1886), p. 39. To build a trading city on the Hudson to rival all others in New Jersey was hardly an absurdity in 1683, given the location and rich natural resources of the area, the energy of the settlers, and the small size of the existing "cities." See also Wilfred B. Talman et al., *Tappan: 300 Years, 1686–1986*, ed. Firth Fabend (Tappan, N.Y., Tappantown Historical Society, 1988), p. 22.

Chapter 2. "A Cartaine trackt of Landt named ould tappan"

1. Most of the Tappan patentees and the families they married into had arrived in New Netherland in the 1630s; by 1680 they were in their second and even, in some cases, their third generation. Gerrit Hendricksen, the first Blauvelt in New Netherland, emigrated in 1638. In 1646, he married Marie Lambert Moll—like Grietje Cosyns, native-born. The Coopers were among the earliest settlers of New Jersey. Related by marriage to the Van Vorst family, they owned tracts of land in present-day Bayonne,

Weehawken, Jersey City, and Orange County long before the Tappan Patent was envisioned. The Van Houtens, who were in Rensselaerswyck by 1638 and were related by marriage to the Coopers and the Van Vorsts, owned good riverland in Orange County by 1682. The patentee Ide Van Vorst's father, Cornelius Van Vorst (d. 1638), had come to New Netherland as director of the patroonship of Pavonia in present Hudson and Bergen counties, N.J. Besides the real estate of his father, this Tappan patentee inherited from his mother in 1641 a portion of her substantial personal estate, consisting of cash, wampum, fine clothing, silver spoons, a silver goblet and brandy cups, jewelry, furs, cattle, and household furnishings of good quality.

For more biographical information on these and some of the other patentees, see "Patents Granted for Lands in the Present County of Rockland, New York, with Biographical Notices of the Patentees," comp. George H. Budke, Budke Collection, Section 67, Mss. Division, New York Public Library; hereafter, BC 67.

2. *The Colonial Laws of New York from the Year 1664 to the Revolution,* 5 vols. (Albany, 1894), vol. 1, p. 149, hereafter *Col. Laws N.Y.;* Irving Mark, *Agrarian Conflicts in Colonial New York, 1711–1775* (New York, 1940), pp. 103–104. In the Indian culture, the concept of man's *ownership* of land did not exist.

The deed with the Indians is dated March 17, 1681 (old style). It was recorded in *East Jersey Patents* (Trenton, N.J.), liber 4, pp. 17 and 18, on July 1, 1682. The patent was granted by the New York Provincial Council on October 13, 1685—New York in the years between the signing of the deed and the granting of the patent having laid claim to Tappan and environs. See "Calendar of Council Minutes, 1668–1783," New York State Library, *Bulletin* 58 (1902), 45. The patent was formally confirmed by New York Governor Thomas Dongan on March 24, 1687. The original document is in the Budke Collection. A transcription by George H. Budke appears in BC 67.

3. The death date of John Pietersen Haring at age forty-nine is given in Franklin Burdge, "A Notice of John Haring: A Patriotic Statesman of the Revolution" (1878), unpaginated ms., Mss. Division, New York Public Library. Ide Van Vorst was buried in New York on December 28, 1683. Holland Society of New York, *Year Book* (1915), vol. 3, p. 25. Haring witnessed the will of his friend Blauvelt, who was "lying sick in bed," on November 28, 1683, only nine days before he himself died. That three of the four men died in the same month of 1683 and the fourth not long after ("before 1686") suggests that they may well have been victims of a common tragedy or contagious disease. On the other hand, that Haring died intestate suggests that he had no reason to anticipate an untimely death.

4. *Minutes of the Common Council of the City of New York, 1675–1776,* 8 vols. (New York, 1905), vol. 1, pp. 130–131.

5. Dongan's report to the Privy Council, February 22, 1687: *Documents Relative to the Colonial History of the State of New York,* 15 vols, eds. E.B.

O'Callaghan and Berthold Fernow (Albany, 1853–1887), vol. 3, pp. 391–393; hereafter, *Docs. Rel. Col. N.Y.*

6. "Marriages from 1639 to 1801 in the Reformed Dutch Church: New Amsterdam, New York City," in New York Genealogical and Biographical Society, *Collections* (1890), vol. 1, p. 56. They married on February 7, 1685. A census of the New York Reformed Dutch Church membership in 1686 places them in the Out-ward for that year. George O. Zabriskie, "Daniel De Clark (De Klerck) of Tappan and His Descendants," *The New York Genealogical and Biographical Record* 101, no. 3 (1965), 194–205.

7. By order of Governor Thomas Dongan soon after he was installed, the oath of allegiance was administered to all residents in the province. The list on September 26, 1687, by residents of Orange County, into which the Tappan Patent fell, contains the names of the thirty-one first settlers in the county. Tappan patentee or patentee-related signers included Adriaen and Lambert Smith, Huybert, Johannes, Abraham, and Hendrick Blauvelt, Peter Haring, Daniel De Clark, John De Vries, Claes Manuel, and Staats De Groot. Cornelius Cooper also signed, but he was living on another patent in the county, not in Tappan. *Calendar of Historical Manuscripts in the Office of the Secretary of State, Albany, N.Y.*, 2 vols. (Albany, 1866), vol. 2, p. 170.

8. Unless otherwise noted, this and all following Haring baptismal and marriage dates in the present chapter come from the records of the New York Reformed Dutch Church and the Tappan Reformed Church. The identification numbers in brackets after names are those assigned by Herbert S. Ackerman. The first digit signifies the generation; the subsequent number(s) signify birth order within the generation, relative to one's nuclear family. Ackerman's "Haring Family" (bound typescript, 1952) is at the New York Public Library, the New York Genealogical and Biographical Society Library, and the Johnson Free Library in Hackensack, N.J. This work should be used with extreme caution, as it contains many errors, especially in the fourth generation and beyond, but the numbering system is useful.

9. Zabriskie, "Daniel De Clark," p. 195. By marriage to Grietje Haring, De Clark came by law into her dower share of Haring's real estate—that is, one-third of three-sixteenths of the Tappan Patent and one-third of whatever real estate Haring owned in Manhattan. According to the Dutch law of intestate succession, however, this share had to be divided at Grietje's death so that each of Haring's seven children or their heirs would receive an equal portion. By law, De Clark was entitled to receive a one-eighth share of the patent, and apparently he did, for Grietje's children's and even her grandchildren's land papers well into the eighteenth century refer to one or the other's one-eighth share in the three-sixteenths of the patent lands.

10. Cathy Matson, "Commerce after the Conquest: I. Dutch Traders and Goods in New York City, 1664–1764," *de Halve Maen* 59, no. 4 (1987), 11, 12. See also part II of this article: ibid., 60, no. 1 (1987), 17–22. Kammen has noted that violations of Dongan's laws and grants of exclusive privi-

lege during the 1680s became a "way of life" for small farmers and traders whose economic hopes were adversely affected by his policies. Michael Kammen, *Colonial New York: A History* (New York, 1975), p. 107.
11. Proprietors of East Jersey to George Lockhart, February 7, 1685, *East Jersey Patents,* liber B, p. 34. For biographical information on Lockhart, see BC 67. Also see Lockhart to Frederick Fillipson [Philipse], February 20 and February 26, 1985, in *Calendar, the Stevens Family Papers,* 2 vols. (Newark, N.J., 1940), vol. 1 (1664–1750), pp. 8–9, 98; this collection is at the New Jersey Historical Society.
12. See shipping records, London Public Record Office, on microfilm at the New-York Historical Society; and Patricia U. Bonomi, *A Factious People: Politics and Society in Colonial New York* (New York, 1971), pp. 60–68. The 67 acres were confiscated from Philipse's great-grandson, a Tory, during the Revolution. They appear on a map, drawn by the surveyor David Pye in 1784, on file in the County Clerk's Office, New City, N.Y.
13. "The Controversy between the Proprietors of the Tappan Patent and McEvers and Symes," BC 67. Also, *Journal of the Votes and Proceedings of the General Assembly of the Colony of New York, 1691–1765,* 2 vols. (New York, 1764–1766), vol. 1, pp. 427, 487, 490, 498, 525, 547, 551, 552; hereafter, *Votes and Proceedings, 1691–1765.* On five occasions during the nine years that Symes pressed his claim and the patentees defended theirs, Peter Haring [21], who for almost exactly the same years was one of Orange County's two representatives to the Seventeenth New York Assembly, was excused to return home "on extraordinary business"— perhaps, as he was also a judge of the court of common pleas, to take part in the diverse suits, controversies, and debates over the disputed land.
14. Although good records exist of what merchants sold, no records have survived to identify their suppliers. Jacobus Van Cortlandt, "Shipping Book, August 12, 1699–June 30, 1702," New-York Historical Society; Jacobus Van Cortlandt, "Letter Book, 1698–1700," New-York Historical Society. On June 8, 1698, Jacobus sold a slave for £37 10s. See census of 1702, in *The Documentary History of the State of New York,* 4 vols., ed. E. B. O'Callaghan (Albany, 1849–1851), vol. 1, p. 365; and the census of 1712, *Calendar of New York Colonial Manuscripts, Indorsed Land Papers; in the Office of the Secretary of State of New York, 1643–1803* (Albany, 1864).
15. See Philip J. Greven, Jr., *Four Generations: Population, Land, and Family in Colonial Andover, Massachusetts* (Ithaca, N.Y., 1970), p. 45; and Sumner Chilton Powell, *Puritan Village: The Formation of a New England Town* (Middletown, Conn., 1963), p. 45. See also David G. Allen, *In English Ways: The Movement of Societies and the Transferral of English Local Law and Custom to Massachusetts Bay in the Seventeenth Century* (Chapel Hill, N.C., 1981); John W. Reps, *The Making of Urban America: A History of City Planning in the United States* (Princeton, N.J., 1965), p. 117; and Douglas R. McManis, *Colonial New England: A Historical Geography* (New York, 1975), pp. 53, 55. Bailyn has noted that "examination of the settle-

ment and development patterns for the whole of British North America reveals not uniformity, but highly differentiated processes." Bernard Bailyn, *The Peopling of British North America* (New York, 1986), p. 49.

16. Glenn T. Trewartha, "Types of Rural Settlement in Colonial America," *Geographical Review* 36 (1946), 569–572, 580, 581; Thomas Bender, *Community and Social Change in America* (New Brunswick, N.J., 1978), p. 69; William John McLaughlin, "Dutch Rural New York: Community, Economy, and Family in Colonial Flatbush" (Ph.D. diss., Columbia University, 1981), p. 75; Bernard H. M. Vlekke, *Evolution of the Dutch Nation* (New York, 1945), pp. 20, 28–29.

17. Vlekke, *Evolution of the Dutch Nation*, pp. 31–32, 87.

18. B. H. Slicher Van Bath, *The Agrarian History of Western Europe, A.D. 500–1850* (New York, 1963), chap. C, pt. 3.

19. Ibid.

20. BC 67.

21. See John Demos, *A Little Commonwealth: Family Life in Plymouth Colony* (New York, 1970), pp. 9–11; Powell, *Puritan Village*, p. 122; Greven, *Four Generations*, p. 57; and James T. Lemon, *The Best Poor Man's Country: A Geographical Study of Early Southeastern Pennsylvania* (Baltimore, 1972), p. 98.

22. Kammen, *Colonial New York*, pp. 128–129; Herbert A. Johnson, "The Advent of Colonial Law in Colonial New York," in George A. Billias, ed., *Law and Authority in Colonial America* (Barre, Mass., 1965), p. 75; Mark, *Agrarian Conflicts*, pp. 77–78; *Col. Laws N.Y.*, vol. 2, pp. 329, 336, 337; *Docs. Rel. Col. N.Y.*, vol. 5, pp. 807, 808, 809.

23. McLaughlin, "Dutch Rural New York," p. 67.

24. Jessica Kross, *The Evolution of an American Town: Newtown, N.Y., 1642–1775* (Philadelphia, 1983), pp. 58–60.

25. "Documents Relating to the Division of the Tappan Patent," comp. George H. Budke, Budke Collection, Section 71, Mss. Division, New York Public Library.

26. Ibid., p. 43.

27. Ibid., p. 46.

28. *Orange County Deeds* (Clerk's Office, Rockland County Court House, New City, N.Y.), bk. 1, no. 166, p. 299.

29. Ibid., bk. 1, no. 150, p. 269.

30. Ibid., bk. 1, no. 146, p. 259.

31. Ibid., bk. 1, nos. 141 and 142, pp. 251 and 253.

32. Bergen County ratables, 1779, New Jersey State Library; available on microfilm in many New Jersey public libraries.

33. "Orangetown Precinct Assessment Roll for the Year 1779," box 1, folder 13, Lansing Papers, New York State Library.

Chapter 3. First Families

1. John Demos, "Families in Colonial Bristol, Rhode Island: An Exercise in Historical Demography," *The William and Mary Quarterly*, 3rd ser., 25

(1968), 40, and Philip J. Greven, Jr., *Four Generations: Population, Land, and Family in Colonial Andover, Massachusetts* (Ithaca, N.Y., 1970), p. 33, are two important works that point out some of the misconceptions and simplifications in Arthur W. Calhoun, *A Social History of the American Family from Colonial Times to the Present*, 3 vols. (Cleveland, 1917–1919); Edmund S. Morgan, *The Puritan Family: Essays on Religion and Domestic Relations in Seventeenth-Century New England*, rev. ed. (New York, 1966); Oscar Handlin, *The Americans: A New History of the People of the United States* (Boston, 1963); and Curtis P. Nettels, *The Roots of American Civilization* (New York, 1938). Daniel Blake Smith, "The Study of the Family in Early America: Trends, Problems, and Prospects," *The William and Mary Quarterly*, 3rd ser. 39 (1982), 4, notes that the earlier scholars based their interpretations on laws, court records, newspapers, sermons, tracts, and the correspondence and diaries of the Puritan elite, whereas the new generation explored church records, land, probate, and tax records, census records, and other public demographic information. See also John Murrin, "Review Essay," *History and Theory* 11 (1972), 226–275.

2. Records and documentation for these statements follow.

3. Alice P. Kenney, "Private Worlds in the Middle Colonies: An Introduction to Human Tradition in American History," *New York History* 51 (1970), 8. In rural France, "one always married the same people," and marriage "was always a matter of fields." Tina Jolas and Françoise Zonabend, "Tillers of the Fields and Woodspeople," in Robert Forster and Patricia M. Ranum, eds., *Rural Society in France: Selections from the Annales* (Baltimore, 1977), p. 134. Also see Jacob Cats, *Houwelijck* (Amsterdam, 1655).

4. Simon Schama, *The Embarrassment of Riches: An Interpretation of Dutch Culture in the Golden Age* (New York, 1987), p. 388.

5. Except where otherwise noted, biographical data in this chapter are from the records of the Tappan Reformed Church. The identification numbers in brackets after names are those assigned in Herbert S. Ackerman's "Haring Family" (bound typescript, 1952). Concerning this and all further references, see Chapter 2, n. 8, above for an explanation and a caveat. For individuals in relation to the Haring family as a whole, see the genealogical charts in the Appendix, above.

6. James Riker, *Harlem: Its Origins and Early Annals*, rev. ed. (New York, 1904), p. 491.

7. Cornelius B. Harvey, ed., *Genealogical History of Hudson and Bergen Counties, N.J.* (New York, 1900), p. 158.

8. In 1675, one Harman Dowesen Tallman moved to lands acquired by his father in present-day Nyack, N.Y., probably to trade with the Tappaen Indians. See George H. Budke, ed., "Rockland County, N.Y., First Settled in 1675: A Short Account of the Earliest Occupation of the Lands," *Proceedings* of the Historical Society of Rockland County, vol. 2 (1931–1932), p. 51.

9. Will of Teunis Quick, Historic Documents Collection, Queens College, New York liber 15, pp. 137–140. Archdeacon places bakers in the top

rank of professions, under merchants, bolters (wheat processors), and goldsmiths, all of whom were entitled to call themselves "gentlemen." Thomas J. Archdeacon, *New York City, 1664–1710: Conquest and Change* (Ithaca, N.Y., 1976), pp. 52, 53. This prosperous baker ordered an unusually large, two-handled silver bowl from the American silversmith Cornelius Kierstede. Bearing the initials of Teunis and Vroutje, it is in the Metropolitan Museum of Art in New York. *New York Sun*, April 9, 1938.
10. Teunis Quick's sister was the wife of Gerrit Cosyn, Vroutje's maternal uncle. Arthur C. Quick, *A Genealogy of the Quick Family in America* (South Haven, Mich., 1949), p. 22.
11. Haring to Flierboom, *Orange County Deeds* (Clerk's Office, Rockland County Court House, New City, N.Y.), bk. 1, p. 54; Smith (Lambertse) to Bogert, ibid., bk. 1, p. 102; Blauvelt to Van Houten, ibid., bk. 1, p. 95; De Groot to Meyers, ibid., bk. 1, p. 124; De Groot to Flierboom, ibid., bk. 1, p. 126; De Vries to Flierboom, ibid., bk. 1, p. 140.
12. L. L. Blauvelt, *The Blauvelt Family Genealogy*, rev. ed. (1987); Herbert S. Ackerman, "Five Bogert Families," 2 vols. (bound typescript, 1950), at the New York Genealogical and Biographical Society Library.
13. Ackerman, "Haring Family."
14. Blauvelt, *Blauvelt Family.*
15. Joyce D. Goodfriend, " 'Too Great a Mixture of Nations': The Development of New York City Society in the Seventeenth Century" (Ph.D. diss., UCLA, 1975), pp. 78–85, describes how marriage patterns of 151 second-generation sons in New York City "ensured the continuance of a stable and firmly rooted old-settler segment in the city throughout the seventeenth century. Men consistently chose to marry women with roots in the city or some tie within the Colony." In colonial Guilford, Conn., one-third of 135 taxpayers came from five families, and in 27 percent of the families at least one child married a cousin, while another 12 percent exchanged siblings in marriage. In all, 39 percent of the families were re-related. John J. Waters, Jr., "Family, Inheritance, and Migration in Colonial New England: The Evidence from Guilford, Connecticut," *The William and Mary Quarterly*, 3rd ser., 39 (1982), 66.
16. Bernard Bailyn, *Education in the Forming of American Society: Needs and Opportunities for Study* (Chapel Hill, N.C., 1960).
17. See Goodfriend, "Too Great a Mixture," pp. 73, 80; Greven, *Four Generations*, pp. 32–38; John Demos, *A Little Commonwealth: Family Life in Plymouth Colony* (New York, 1970), p. 275; Kenneth A. Lockridge, *A New England Town, the First Hundred Years: Dedham, Massachusetts, 1636–1736* (New York, 1970), p. 330. Community studies of Flatbush, N.Y., Chester County, Pa., Germantown, Pa., and Middlesex County, Va., do not report on marriage age.
18. Philip J. Greven, Jr., found that, in seventeenth-century Andover, a son's marriage often depended upon the "willingness of the settler father to allow the marriage to take place and to provide for the new couple's economic subsistence, most generally in the form of land. Without the

means to support a wife, marriage was virtually impossible." Greven, *Four Generations*, p. 37.

19. Rev. Henricus Selyns, in *Ecclesiastical Records of the State of New York*, 7 vols., ed. E. T. Corwin (Albany, 1901–1916), vol. 2, p. 829; William Penn, quoted in Albert Cook Meyers, ed., *Narratives of Early Pennsylvania, West-New Jersey, and Delaware, 1630–1707* (New York, 1912), p. 238.

20. Stephanie Grauman Wolf, *Urban Village: Population, Community, and Family Structure in Germantown, Pennsylvania, 1683–1800* (Princeton, N.J., 1976), pp. 260–261. She quotes a contemporary observer: "If a man gets a woman with child and he marries her . . . he has expiated his guilt and is not punished by the authorities" (p. 261). In Germantown, about 25 percent of married couples in the years 1740–1800 produced a child within nine months after marriage (p. 259).

21. Daniel Scott Smith and Michael S. Hindus, "Premarital Pregnancy in America, 1640–1971: An Overview and Interpretation," *Journal of Interdisciplinary History* 5 (1975), 537 and 549–550. The authors' study of marriages and baptisms in the Dutch Reformed Church in Bergen, N.J., indicates that in 1681–1700 nearly 20 percent of all baptisms occurred within six months after marriage; in the 1700–1720 period, the figure was only slightly lower, but it later rose to 25 percent within eight and a half months after marriage (p. 563).

22. Rev. John Miller, *A Description of the Province and City of New York; with Plans of the City and Several Forts as They Existed in the Year 1695*, p. 43, in Cornell Jaray, ed., *Historic Chronicles of New Amsterdam, Colonial New York, and Early Long Island*, 2 vols. (Port Washington, N.Y., 1968), vol. 1, p. 43. John Demos points out that in Plymouth "courtships fell considerably short of 'Puritanical' standards." Fornication was a familiar problem to the courts, as were paternity cases. Demos, *A Little Commonwealth*, pp. 152–153.

23. See Donald Haks, *Huwelijk en Gezin in Holland in de 17de en 18de eeuw* (Assen, 1982), pp. 102, 127; J. Le Francq van Berkhey, *Naturlyke Historie van Holland*, 4 vols. (Amsterdam, 1769–1779); and Schama, *The Embarrassment of Riches*, pp. 438–440.

24. Minutes of the Orange County Court of Common Pleas, April and October 1703, County Clerk's Office, Goshen, N.Y. John Demos found that in Plymouth, too, bastardy was an expense the community did not like bearing. Demos, *A Little Commonwealth*, p. 153.

25. Cadwallader Colden, quoted in John Duffy, *A History of Public Health in New York City, 1625–1866* (New York, 1968), pp. 34 and 35. An epidemic in New York in 1668, thought to have been malaria or typhoid, was so bad that Governor Francis Lovelace proclaimed a "General Day of Humiliation" for the many who were "dayly swept away & many more lying on their languishing bedds, expecting each houre their dissolution." In the autumn and winter of 1679/80, smallpox ravaged the population. A visitor recorded going into one house "where there were two children

lying dead and unburried and three others sick, and where one had died the week before." The Harings were in the city during these years, but apparently suffered no losses from the disease.

No major epidemics were reported in New York for another decade, by which time the Harings were in Tappan, but smallpox, accompanied by a "sort of pleurisy and violent fevers," made its appearance in the city again in the spring and summer of 1690.

A much more virulent epidemic, this of yellow fever, descended in 1702 and, spreading rapidly, killed in the city "near 20 Persons dayly for some Months," literally decimating the population of about five thousand. Considering the country safer than the city, the governor (Lord Cornbury) and his council fled New York for Cheer Hall, the country estate of the former New York City mayor William Merritt, about two miles from Tappan on the Hudson River. From here the governor wrote to the Lords of Trade in London that in New York the "great mortality . . . has so much diminished our number . . . [that] in ten weeks time the Sickness has swept away upwards of five hundred people of all ages and sexes. . . . I hope the cold weather will abate the fury of it." *Documents Relative to the Colonial History of the State of New York*, 15 vols., eds. E. B. O'Callaghan and Berthold Fernow (Albany, 1853–1887), vol. 4, p. 972.

26. Darrett B. Rutman and Anita H. Rutman, *A Place in Time: Middlesex, Virginia, 1650–1750* (New York, 1984), p. 114.

27. In seventeenth-century Plymouth, "Every fifth woman . . . died from causes associated with childbirth." Demos, *A Little Commonwealth*, p. 131.

28. Wolf, *Urban Village*, p. 263, n. 31; Peter Kalm, *Travels in North America*, 2 vols., ed. Adolph B. Benson (New York, 1937), vol. 1, p. 56.

29. Lawrence Stone, "Past Achievements and Future Trends," *Journal of Interdisciplinary History* 12 (1981), 60. See also Robert V. Schucher, "Elizabethan Birth Control and Puritan Attitudes," *Journal of Interdisciplinary History* 4 (1975), 656; Smith and Hindus, "Premarital Pregnancy in America"; and Schama, *The Embarrassment of Riches*, pp. 424, 524. In the Netherlands in the seventeenth century, the mean household size of 4.75 meant that couples had fewer than three children on average. See A. M. Van der Woude, "Variations in the Size and Structure of the Household in the United Provinces of the Netherlands in the Seventeenth and Eighteenth Centuries," in Peter Laslett and Richard Wall, eds., *Household and Family in Past Time* (London, 1972), p. 315.

30. Rutman and Rutman, *A Place in Time*, p. 76, note that young sons and daughters were an asset, but that too many children could "spell disaster for a family's fortunes or for individual children."

31. Bergen County Historical Society, Mss. Collection, reel 5 (emphasis added).

32. "List of the Inhabitants in the County of Orange 1702," in *The Documentary History of the State of New York*, 4 vols., ed. E. B. O'Callaghan (Albany, 1849–1851), vol. 1, p. 365. See Greven, *Four Generations*, for a discussion of the term "family" (pp. 14–16); he defines the extended fam-

ily as a "kinship network consisting, for the most part, of separate [nuclear] households" (pp. 15–16).

33. Local historians have long recognized the ethnic mix in the Dutch American community. In Harlem Village in 1661, Riker found that of the thirty-two total inhabitants that year, eleven were French, seven Dutch, four Walloon, four Danish, three Swedish, and three German. All nineteenth-century county and other local histories comment on the phenomenon, and in this century Wertenbaker, Leiby, and De Jong among many others have described it in detail. One recent attempt to quantify the multinational characteristics of the Dutch in America has discovered that, in a sample of 904 immigrants to New Netherland in the seventeenth century, only 50.8 percent were originally Dutch; the rest were from Germany, France, Belgium (the Walloon and Flemish provinces), Schleswig-Holstein (part of Denmark), and other Scandinavian countries. James Riker, *Harlem: Its Origins and Early Annals*, rev. ed. (New York, 1904), p. 190; Thomas J. Wertenbaker, *The Founding of American Civilization: The Middle Colonies* (New York, 1938), p. 35; Adrian C. Leiby, *The Early Dutch and Swedish Settlers of New Jersey* (Princeton, N.J., 1964), Chap. 9; Gerald F. De Jong, *The Dutch in America, 1609–1974* (Boston, 1975), Chap. 9; David Steven Cohen, "How Dutch Were the Dutch of New Netherland?" *New York History* 62 (1981), 52 and 53. See also Oliver A. Rink, *Holland on the Hudson: An Economic and Social History of Dutch New York* (Ithaca, N.Y., 1986); and Rink, "The People of New Netherland: Notes on Non-English Immigration to New York in the Seventeenth Century," *New York History* 62 (1981), 5–42.

34. Bernard Bailyn, *The Peopling of British North America* (New York, 1986), pp. 36–37, describes America as "an independent force acting on the demographic configurations of the Old World, a powerful and ungovernable prod outside all indigenous propulsion, created by entrepreneurship, promotion, and the sheer magnetism of economic betterment and religious toleration."

Chapter 4. "A Gallant Plentifull Country"

1. Thomas Jefferson to the Rev. James Madison, October 28, 1785, in *The Works of Thomas Jefferson*, 12 vols. (New York, Federal Edition, 1904), vol. 8, pp. 194–196; Thomas Jefferson in *Notes on the State of Virginia*, ed. William Peden (Chapel Hill, N.C., 1955), pp. 164–165. For a recent discussion of Jefferson's agrarian ideal, see Robert E. Shalhope, "Agriculture," in Merrill Peterson, ed., *Thomas Jefferson: A Reference Biography* (New York, 1986). See also A. Whitney Griswold, "The Agrarian Democracy of Thomas Jefferson," *American Political Science Review* 40, no. 4 (1946), 657–681; Griswold, *Farming and Democracy* (New York, 1948); Chester E. Eisinger, "The Freehold Concept in Eighteenth-Century American Letters," *The William and Mary Quarterly*, 3rd ser., 4 (1947), 42–59; Richard Bridgman, "Jefferson's Farmer before Jefferson," *American*

Quarterly 14 (1962), 567–577; and Joyce Appleby, "Commercial Farming and the 'Agrarian Myth' in the Early Republic," *Journal of American History* 68 (1982), 4.

2. Hubert G. Schmidt, *Agriculture in New Jersey: A Three-Hundred Year History* (New Brunswick, N.J., 1973), p. 44; Thomas Harrison to brother, in George Scot, *The Model of the Government of the Province of East-Jersey* (Edinburgh, 1685), p. 21.

3. Unsigned letter, "Methods Used in Clearing Forests for Cultivation," Livingston Papers, New-York Historical Society, undated box.

4. Disposition of the estate of Rachel Wileman, of Wilemanton, Ulster County, Orange County Miscellaneous Mss., New-York Historical Society.

5. *Documents Relative to the Colonial History of the State of New York*, 15 vols., eds. E. B. O'Callaghan and Berthold Fernow (Albany, 1853–1887), vol. 5, p. 368; hereafter, *Docs. Rel. Col. N.Y.* Dominie Michaelius of New Netherland described the pit houses in a letter reproduced in J. F. Jameson, ed., *Narratives of New Netherland, 1609–1664* (New York, 1909): "They are meanwhile [1628] beginning to build new houses in place of the huts and sheds in which heretofore they nestled rather than dwelt." See also Roderic H. Blackburn, "Dutch Domestic Architecture in the Hudson Valley," *New Netherland Studies: An Inventory of Current Research and Approaches. Bulletin KNOB* 84, nos. 2–3 (1985), 151–164.

6. Paul Huey, "Archaeological Excavations in the Site of Fort Orange, a Dutch West India Company Trading Fort Built in 1624," *New Netherland Studies: An Inventory of Current Research and Approaches. Bulletin KNOB* 84, nos. 2–3 (1985), 71–73; and, in the same issue, Lois M. Feister, "Archaeology in Rensselaerswyck: Dutch 17th-Century Domestic Sites," pp. 80–87.

7. Manatus map, in I. N. Phelps-Stokes, *The Iconography of Manhattan Island, 1498–1909*, 6 vols. (New York, 1915–1928), vol. 2, pl. 41; vol. 2, pp. 181–187. Also, Reginald McMahon, "The Achter Col Colony on the Hackensack," *New Jersey History* 89, no. 4 (1971), 221–240. This colony was in present-day Bogota, N.J. Henk J. Zantkuyl, "The Netherlands Town House: How and Why It Works," in Albany Institute of History and Art, *New World Dutch Studies: Dutch Arts and Culture in Colonial America, 1609–1776* (Albany, 1987), pp. 143–160, discusses the Winckelman barn and seven Dutch houses built in or near Manhattan in the 1640s.

8. Henk J. Zantkuyl, "Reconstructie van Enkele Nederlandse Huizen in Nieuw-Nederland Uit de 17e Eeuw," *New Netherland Studies: An Inventory of Current Research and Approaches. Bulletin KNOB* 84, nos. 2–3 (1985), 166–179.

9. Bergen County Division of Cultural and Historic Affairs, "Survey of Early Stone Houses of Bergen County," Office of Albin H. Rothe, A.I.A., field survey by Claire K. Tholl (Hackensack, N.J., 1986), pp. 44–89; hereafter, "Stone House Survey." A conjectural chronology appears as fig. 57, "Conjectural Chronological Evolution—Bergen County Stone Houses"; the twin-door houses are discussed on pp. 52–59. See also Roderic H.

Blackburn, "Transforming Old World Dutch Culture in a New World Environment: Processes of Material Adaptation," in Albany Institute of History and Art, *New World Dutch Studies: Dutch Arts and Culture in Colonial America, 1609–1776* (Albany, 1987), p. 105.

10. "Stone House Survey," pp. 44, 52, and fig. 57. Correspondence with Claire K. Tholl, April 6, 1988, and January 11, 1990. Tholl points out that more research needs to be done in order to document the date of the first appearance of these houses and their function.

11. De Clark's house in Tappan, N.Y., is operated by the Masons and is open to the public. A marker calls it the "De Wint House," after the family who owned it during the Revolution, when George Washington stayed there on four occasions, once for two weeks. The gable roof was a medieval construction type used in all the colonies during the seventeenth and early eighteenth centuries. A separate kitchen wing is one of the first visible signs of changing function within the dwelling. With cooking removed to its own unit, the main dwelling could be used exclusively for living, eating, and sleeping. "Stone House Survey," p. 59.

12. There are few examples left of jambless fireplaces, a style brought from the Netherlands. Most homeowners converted to the smaller and more efficient English, or jambed, style. "Stone House Survey," p. 47; Blackburn, "Dutch Domestic Architecture," p. 162; Peter Kalm, *Travels in North America*, 2 vols, ed. Adolph B. Benson (New York, 1937), vol. 2, pp. 611–613.

13. Sarah Kemble Knight, *The Journal of Madam Knight* (New York, 1935 [1825]), p. 53.

14. David Steven Cohen discusses such architectural borrowing in "Defining the Dutch-American Farmhouse Types," ms., Trenton, New Jersey Historical Commission.

15. "Stone House Survey," p. 61. Zantkuyl, "The Netherlands Town House," pp. 150–160, relates his seven New Netherland houses and Winckelman's barn to seventeenth-century structures in the Netherlands. Blackburn, "Dutch Domestic Architecture," p. 151, notes that Dutch "housetypes," relatively unchanged from their Netherlands prototypes, continued to be built in America until the 1760s and that Dutch architectural features appeared until the 1830s.

16. Cosyn's will: Historical Documents Collection, Queens College, liber 15, p. 60. Abraham's will: Historical Documents Collection, Queens College, liber 28, p. 238. Also see Tappan Reformed Church records, Tappan, N.Y.

17. A 1704 date was assigned to this house by Rosalie F. Bailey, *Pre-Revolutionary Dutch Houses and Families in Northern New Jersey and Southern New York* (New York, 1936), p. 292 and p. 356, pl. 89. A date of 1707 was arrived at by the Works Progress Administration, "Historic American Buildings Survey" (Washington, D.C., 1939); hereafter, HABS NJ-154. Thomas B. Demarest, on personal acquaintance with the house and its history, believes it was built "sometime before the second division of the patent" in 1721. Correspondence, April 18, 1988. (This date is

compatible with the date of the son's marriage, 1718, and also with the reference in Cosyn's will [1733] to his son's living that year "on the old farm.") Claire K. Tholl, basing her opinion on structural evidence, believes the house was built in two or three stages, the northeast room being original. Correspondence, March 26, 1988, April 6, 1988, and August 10, 1990.

18. John J. Haring, *Floating Chips: Annals of Old and New Times* (Toledo, Ohio, 1924), p. 9.

19. On the "kitchen in the garden," see Zantkuyl, "The Netherlands Town House," pp. 146–147; and Haring, *Floating Chips*, p. 10.

20. The exterior entrance served to facilitate crop storage. Blackburn, "Transforming Old World Dutch Culture," p. 105.

21. The *Oxford English Dictionary* finds the first use of the word in Old English in the year 1000. The description of the airy piazza is in James Thacher, *Military Journal of the American Revolution* (Hartford, Conn., 1862), p. 156. For Henk Zantkuyl's findings on the Schenck house, see Zantkuyl, "The Netherlands Town House," p. 157. See also Piet Van Wijk, "Form and Function in the Netherlands' Dutch Agricultural Architecture," in Albany Institute of History and Art, *New World Dutch Studies: Dutch Arts and Culture in Colonial America, 1609–1776* (Albany, 1987), pp. 161–169; and, in the same volume, Jaap Schipper, "Rural Architecture: The Zaan Region of the Province of North Holland," pp. 171–184. Also see *Boerderijen bekijken: Historisch boerderij-onderzoek in Nederland* (Arnhem, 1985) for a history of farms and combination house-barns in the Netherlands; and Eric Nooter, "Colonial Dutch Architecture in Brooklyn," *de Halve Maen*, 60, no. 1 (1987), 12–16.

22. The house Colden built in 1732 is described in Cadwallader Colden, "Journal of my Farm" (1727–1735), a ms. in the Rosenbach Museum & Library, Philadelphia.

23. Johannes's inventory: 1798, Surrogate's Office, Bergen County Courthouse, Hackensack, N.J., docket 1. The information in the caption to Figure 4.4 can be found in Reginald McMahon, "Two Haring Houses at Rockleigh, N.J." (typescript, Harrington Park Historical Society, 1974), p. 12 and n. 30.

24. Thacher, *Military Journal*, p. 156; Alice P. Kenney, "Silence Is Golden: A Survey of Hudson Valley Dutch Material Culture," *de Halve Maen* 58, no. 1 (1983), 1–4, 16; Blackburn, "Transforming Old World Dutch Culture," pp. 98–101. On the painted kas, see Patricia C. O'Donnell, "Grisaille Decorated Kasten of New York," *Antiques* 117 (1980), 1108–1111; and Firth Fabend, "Two 'New' Eighteenth-Century Grisaille Kasten," *The Clarion* (Spring-Summer 1981), 45–48. Also see Joyce Geary Volk, "The Dutch Kast and the American Kas: A Structural/Historical Analysis," in Albany Institute of History and Art, *New World Dutch Studies: Dutch Arts and Culture in Colonial America, 1609–1776* (Albany, 1987), pp. 107–117, particularly on the kas pictured in Figure 4.5.

25. Blackburn, "Transforming Old World Dutch Culture," pp. 100–101.

26. Huey, "Archaeological Excavations," pp. 74–75; Charlotte Wilcoxen,

"Household Artifacts of New Netherland, from Its Archaeological and Documentary Records," *New Netherland Studies: An Inventory of Current Research and Approaches. Bulletin KNOB* 84, nos. 2–3 (1985), 122–124.
27. Van Wijk, "Form and Function," p. 165.
28. The reconstruction is in Zantkuyl, "The Netherlands Town House," pp. 157–158. Also see John Fitchen, *The New World Dutch Barn* (Syracuse, N.Y., 1958), pp. 15–16. For a discussion of the Dutch plow, the Flemish scythe, and the Dutch wagon as used in America, see David Steven Cohen, "Dutch-American Farming: Crops, Livestock, and Equipment, 1623–1900" in Albany Institute of History and Art, *New World Dutch Studies: Dutch Arts and Culture in Colonial America, 1609–1776* (Albany, 1987), pp. 193–198.
29. Kalm, *Travels in North America*, vol. 1, pp. 118–119.
30. Verplanck family farm journal (c. 1800), 3 vols., New-York Historical Society, microfilm, vol. 3, p. 70; Hubert G. Schmidt, *Rural Hunterdon: An Agricultural History* (New Brunswick, N.J., 1945), p. 95. Constructing a proper barrack was no mean feat. A barrack eighteen feet square required that four white oak posts, twenty-four feet long, seven inches square at the butt end, and six inches at the top end, be bolted with four-inch iron pins to four stone blocks or footings, nine inches square by two and a half feet long and sunk two feet into the ground. The floor was seven feet above the ground, and the movable, raftered hip roof was of thatch nailed down by lath and underlaid by lath. Verplanck family farm journal, vol. 3, p. 79.
31. Schmidt, *Agriculture in New Jersey*, p. 73; Blackburn, "Dutch Domestic Architecture," p. 161; Kristin Lunde Gibbons, "The Van Bergen Overmantel" (M.A. thesis, Cooperstown Graduate Program, State University of New York at Oneonta, 1966).
32. Schmidt, *Agriculture in New Jersey*, p. 60; James T. Lemon, *The Best Poor Man's Country: A Geographical Study of Early Southeastern Pennsylvania* (Baltimore, 1972), pp. 150–151; anonymous, *American Husbandry* (London, 1775; repr. New York, 1939), pp. 105–106 and p. 9; and "Dutch Gardening, as Empirically Practised," in *Encyclopedia of Gardening*, 2 vols. (London, [1831], vol. 2, p. 32. See also Bridgman, "Jefferson's Farmer before Jefferson."
33. Ulysses P. Hedrick, *A History of Horticulture in America* (New York, 1950); Kalm, *Travels in North America*, vol. 1, p. 344.
34. See B. H. Slicher Van Bath, *The Agrarian History of Western Europe, A.D. 500–1850* (New York, 1963), chap. 2, esp. pp. 18–23; and Bernard H. M. Vlekke, *Evolution of the Dutch Nation* (New York, 1945). Kalm, in *Travels in North America*, vol. 1, pp. 97–98 and 307–309, speaks of careless farming and includes the Dutch among the negligent.
35. Colden, "Journal of my Farm," March 1727; March 1728; March, April, and May 1729.
36. Charles Varlo, *A New System of Husbandry* (Philadelphia, 1785); Verplanck family farm journal, vols. 1–3; Jared Eliot, *Essays upon Field Husbandry in New England* (Boston, 1760); Lemon, *The Best Poor Man's*

Country, p. 150. Other early works available to Americans were Richard Bradley, *A General Treatise of Husbandry and Gardening*, 2 vols. (London, 1726); and William Belgrove, *A Treatise Upon Husbandry and Planting* (Boston, 1755).

37. Letter, Walter Rutherford to Gouverneur Morris, August 31, 1787, Stuyvesant-Rutherford Papers, New-York Historical Society. In Pennsylvania, James Lemon estimates ten bushels of wheat per acre after 1760. Lemon, *The Best Poor Man's Country*, table 27; also see pp. 154–158.

38. Verplanck family farm journal, vol. 3, p. 95.

39. Ibid., pp. 95, 98, 99, 100, 112, 118, 116.

40. Anne MacVicar Grant, *Memoirs of an American Lady, with Sketches of Manners and Scenes in America* (New York, 1846), pp. 30–31.

41. According to his journal, this is what Colden sowed in March 1727 and in April and May 1728.

42. Colden, "Journal of my Farm," April 1728–April 1729.

43. Ibid., November 1, 1729; May and June 1728.

44. Ibid., October 1727; November 1730; May 7, 1729.

45. Haring, *Floating Chips*, pp. 14–15; Ralph Voorhees, "Franklin Township Historical Notes," *Somerset County Historical Quarterly* 6 (1917), 89–90.

46. Adriaen Van der Donck, *A Description of the New Netherlands*, ed. Thomas F. O'Connell (Syracuse, N.Y., 1968), pp. 24–25; Mahlon Stacy, letter of April 26, 1680, in Scott, *Model of the Government*, p. 22.

47. Grant, *Memoirs*, pp. 30–31; Van der Donck, *A Description of the New Netherlands*, p. 67. See also Ruth Piwonka, "Dutch Gardens in the Hudson Valley, I and II," *de Halve Maen* 49, nos. 2–3 (1974), 11–12 and 11–12, 14, 16.

48. Verplanck family farm journal, vol. 3, pp. 9–14.

49. Tappan Reformed Church records; Section 48, Budke Collection, comp. George H. Budke, Mss. Collection, New York Public Library.

50. William Wickham's account book, August 31, 1763, New-York Historical Society.

51. Letter, Rutherford to Morris (n. 37 above).

52. Will of Cornelius [24]: New Jersey State Library, liber L, p. 271; Titan Leeds, *The American Almanack* (New York, 1742), n.p.

53. Haring, *Floating Chips*, pp. 17–18.

54. James Lemon argues that the eighteenth-century farmer was entrepreneurial, competitive, and motivated by a desire for wealth. Lemon, *The Best Poor Man's Country*, chaps. 6 and 7; Lemon, "Household Consumption in Eighteenth-Century America and Its Relationship to Production and Trade: The Situation among Farmers in Southeastern Pennsylvania," *Agricultural History* 41 (1967), 59–70. Henretta argues that the farmer was community-oriented, wanting only a decent standard of living, not large profits. James A. Henretta, "Families and Farms: *Mentalité* in Pre-Industrial America," *The William and Mary Quarterly*, 3rd ser., 35 (1978), 3–32.

See also Appleby, "Commercial Farming"; and Bettye Hobbs Pruitt,

"Self-Sufficiency and the Agricultural Economy of Eighteenth-Century Massachusetts," *The William and Mary Quarterly*, 3rd ser., 41 (1984), 333–364.
Logic suggests that profits were desired by, but not accessible to, everyone.
55. Jasper Danckaerts, *Journal*, eds. Bartlett B. James and J. Franklin Jameson (New York, 1913), p. 221; *Docs. Rel. Col. N.Y.*, vol. 5, pp. 685–688.
56. Governor Cosby to Lords of Trade, December 6, 1734, *Docs. Rel. Col. N.Y.*, vol. 6, p. 20.
57. See references to Tappan in Arthur E. Peterson and George W. Edwards, *New York as an Eighteenth Century Municipality* (New York, 1917).
58. Colden, "Journal of my Farm," January and June 1733.
59. Thomas Jefferson to Charles Willson Peale, August 20, 1811, in *The Writings of Thomas Jefferson*, 20 vols., eds. Andrew A. Lipscomb and Albert Ellery Bergh (Washington, D.C., 1903–1904), vol. 13, pp. 78–80.

Chapter 5. A Prosperous Minority

1. Baptismal and marriage dates for the third generation are from the records of the Tappan Reformed Church, the Reformed Churches of Hackensack and Schraalenburgh, the Reformed Dutch Church of Flatbush, the Reformed Church of Acquackanonk (Passaic), and the New York Reformed Church. See Bibliography for full citations.
2. A comparison of childbearing patterns for the second and third generations is presented in tabular form in Firth Haring Fabend, "The Yeoman Ideal: A Dutch Family in the Middle Colonies, 1660–1800" (Ph.D. diss., New York University, 1988), table 5.1.
3. Baptismal and marriage dates for the fourth generation are the same as for the third (see n. 1 above), supplemented by records from the Irregular Dutch Reformed churches of Tappan and Kakiat, the Paramus Reformed Church, the Albany Reformed Church, the Clarkstown Reformed Church, and by information found in deed, wills, and other public records. Some of this material has been brought to light by researchers over the past sixty years, notably by George H. Budke and Howard I. Durie. The Budke Collection at the New York Public Library may be viewed only on microfilm, but much of it has been photocopied and bound by the New City Free Library, New City, N.Y. See also Howard I. Durie, *The Kakiat Patent in Bergen County, New Jersey, with Genealogical Accounts of Some of Its Early Settlers* (Pearl River, N.Y., 1970); and Howard I. Durie and George O. Zabriskie, "The Irregular Dutch Reformed Churches of Tappan and Kakiat, Rockland County, New York," *The New York Genealogical and Biographical Record* 101, nos. 2–3 (1970), 65–73 and 158–164, which digest and interpret much genealogical information not easily found or understood.
Another source of information comprises unrecorded deeds and wills in the archives of the Bergen County Historical Society, the Pascack His-

271

torical Society, the Historical Society of Rockland County, and the Tappantown Historical Society. The publications of these four societies also contain much information. Finally, the genealogies listed in the Bibliography are a source of family information in this chapter not found elsewhere, although some of these works also contain misinformation.

4. Cousin marriages were more prevalent in some branches of the family than in others. According to the testimony of one Haring in-law, Eleanor Banta, born May 4, 1786, "It was one of the rules of the society of our relatives . . . that it was wrong to marry out of the family, and almost all of the persons who married in those days, married cousins. In fact it was almost a law with us." Howard I. Durie called this document, dated December 14, 1873, Switzerland County, Ind., to my attention.

5. As above, these data are presented in Fabend, "The Yeoman Ideal," table 5.2.

6. Bernard Bailyn, *The Peopling of British North America* (New York, 1986), p. 94.

7. Jessica Kross, *The Evolution of an American Town: Newtown, N.Y., 1642–1775* (Philadelphia, 1983), chap. 8; William John McLaughlin, "Dutch Rural New York: Community, Economy, and Family in Colonial Flatbush" (Ph.D. diss., Columbia University, 1981), pp. 260, 269–270; Barry J. Levy, "'Tender Plants': Quaker Farmers and Children in the Delaware Valley, 1681–1735," in Stanley N. Katz and John M. Murrin, eds., *Colonial America: Essays in Politics and Social Development*, 3rd ed. (New York, 1983), pp. 177–178, 184–186, and 192.

8. James T. Lemon, *The Best Poor Man's Country: A Geographical Study of Early Southeastern Pennsylvania* (Baltimore, 1972), p. 69, table 13, and p. 18; Dennis P. Ryan, "Landholding, Opportunity, and Mobility in Revolutionary New Jersey," *The William and Mary Quarterly*, 3rd ser., 36 (1979), 574, 575, and table 1. The six towns considered by Ryan are Newark, Morristown, Woodbridge, Piscataway, Shrewsbury, and Middletown, all formed in the 1660s.

9. Besides the works on agricultural methods noted in Chapter 4 above, the profit-oriented farmer at this time had access to such practical works as John Dabney, *An Address to Farmers* (Newburyport, Mass., 1796); John A. Binns, *A Treatise on Practical Farming* (Richmond, Va., 1804); Timothy Matlack, *An Oration Delivered March 16, 1780* (Philadelphia, 1780); John Spurrier, *The Practical Farmer* (Wilmington, Del., 1793); and J. B. Bordley, *Essays and Notes on Husbandry and Rural Affairs* (Philadelphia, 1801). See Joyce Appleby, "Commercial Farming and the 'Agrarian Myth' in the Early Republic," *Journal of American History* 68, no. 4 (1982), 842–843.

For the boundary dispute, see *New Jersey Archives, Newspaper Extracts* (Trenton, 1901–1917), 2nd ser., vol. 7, p. 518; and the Alexander Papers and the Stevens Family Papers, both at the New Jersey Historical Society. Also see William A. Whitehead, "The Circumstances Leading to the Establishment in 1769, of the Northern Boundary Line between New Jersey and New York," *Proceedings* of the New Jersey Historical Society, 1st

ser., vol. 8 (1859), pp. 161–186. In 1769, when the boundary between
New York and New Jersey was settled, twenty-five Harings were named
in a "list of the possessions held under New York which fall south of the
northwesterly line began on Hudsons River 89 chains and 60 links south
of the old house of Madam Corbets." Another four were named on other
lists identifying them as inhabitants "who submit to the jurisdiction of
New Jersey" in Hackensack and New Barbadoes precincts.
10. "A List of the Rateables in the Township of Harington in the County
of Bergen with the Assessments Made Thereon in the Month of September 1779," New Jersey State Library; hereafter, "Harington Rateables."
Also, "Orangetown Precinct Assessment Roll for the Year 1779," box 1,
folder 13, Lansing Papers, New York State Library, Albany; hereafter,
"Orangetown Assessment." Some Harings were also buying land in other
New Jersey townships and in the Ramapo Tract in New York for future
use and in Cayuga and Montgomery counties in New York for speculative
purposes.
11. Jackson Turner Main, *The Social Structure of Revolutionary America*
(Princeton, N.J. 1965), pp. 25–28, 42, 43; Ryan, "Landholding," pp. 575–
577, and table 1, p. 576.
12. "Harington Rateables" (1779). In Chester County, Pa., the average
farm in 1710 was 245 acres; the smallest were from 129 to 190 acres. In
the 1760s and 1770s, the average farm was 125 acres. The average was
slightly larger in Lancaster County, Pa. See Lemon, *The Best Poor Man's
Country*, p. 89; and Lucy Simler, "Tenancy in Colonial Pennsylvania: The
Case of Chester County," *The William and Mary Quarterly*, 3rd ser., 43
(1986), 551.
13. Colonial tax lists must be used with caution for many reasons besides this important one: (1) based on a regressive tax system, the lists
underestimate the wealth of those in the top quarter of the wealth structure; (2) they omit those too poor to pay a tax; (3) they do not tax certain
important forms of wealth; (4) and in the cities, they do not include rural
land owned by urban dwellers—for instance, Elbert Haring [310]. Gary
B. Nash, "Urban Wealth and Poverty in Pre-Revolutionary America," in
Stanley N. Katz and John H. Murrin, eds., *Colonial America: Essays in
Politics and Social Development*, 3rd ed. (New York, 1983), pp. 450–451
and n. 7. See also Gloria L. Main, "Probate Records as a Source for Early
American History," *The William and Mary Quarterly*, 3rd ser., 32 (1975),
89–99.
14. Ryan, "Landholding," p. 578. The petition for the new township was
presented to William Franklin, royal governor of New Jersey. The undated original is in Section 76 of the Budke Collection, comp. George H.
Budke, Mss. Division, New York Public Library. The Hackensack opposition presented their petition to the King's Council at Perth Amboy, February 11, 1775: *New Jersey Archives, Journal of the Governor and Council*
(Newark, 1880–1928), 1st ser., vol. 6, p. 526. Gary Nash reports that in
Boston after 1715 half of all decedents with inventories left less than £40
in personal wealth and less than £75 in total wealth, while the bottom

quarter left only about half those amounts. "This should temper the enthusiasm of those who have argued that Colonial communities enjoyed a state of changeless prosperity down to the eve of the Revolution." Nash, "Urban Wealth and Poverty," p. 457.

15. "Harington Rateables" (1779); "Orangetown Assessment" (1779); and Nash, "Urban Wealth and Poverty," pp. 448–483. In New York City in this era, the population increased by about half, Nash reports, but the rate of poverty quadrupled and more. Between 1740 and 1773, the "rate of poverty . . . climbed from about nine per thousand to between twenty-seven and thirty-six per thousand" (p. 461).

16. William Bayard, "Memorial of William Bayard," American Loyalist Transcripts, Mss. Division, New York Public Library. See also Durie, *Kakiat*, pp. 8, 9.

17. On the other hand, because the rent charged was very small, there was an advantage to the tenant and a disadvantage to the leaseowner in this arrangement. Bayard, as leaseowner, was earning less on his investment than he could have if he had put his capital at interest. But his rationale was that he had bought the land at a low price and was "saving" it and improving it either for his descendants or for later sale at a good profit.

18. Wills and other public records document that many third- and fourth-generation Harings, besides identifying themselves as "yeomen," also described themselves as esquire, gentleman, judge, captain, colonel, assemblyman, and holders of numerous local political and church offices. A few in the fourth generation were tradesmen or millers, and some became professionals—lawyers and surveyors. Elbert [310], the wealthiest member of the Haring family, was a baker in New York City. Some would have earned a substantial income from their occupations and offices. Data on the slaves and livestock they owned, as well as on the money they had out at interest, are found in the Harington ratables for 1779, 1780, 1782, 1784–86, 1789–1794, 1796, 1802, 1813, 1815, 1818, and 1822 (New Jersey State Library); in their wills and inventories; in the Orangetown Precinct Assessment, Lansing Papers, for 1779 and 1786; and in the Orange County ratables for 1799, 1800, and 1801 (New York State Archives).

19. Elbert was baptized and married both times at the New York Reformed Dutch Church. See "Baptisms from 1639 to 1730 in the Reformed Dutch Church, New York," in New York Genealogical and Biographical Society, *Collections* (1901), vol. 2; and "Marriages from 1639 to 1801 in the Reformed Dutch Church, New Amsterdam, New York City," ibid. (1890), vol. 1.

20. Ibid. Also, Henry P. Toler, *The New Harlem Register* (New York, 1903); Herbert S. Ackerman, "Five Bogert Families," 2 vols. (bound typescript, 1950), vol. 1, at the Bergen County Historical Society, Mss. Collection, Johnson Library, Hackensack, N.J.; Bogert files, New York Genealogical and Biographical Society Library.

21. Dutch naming customs followed a particular order: first son and first

daughter were named after the father's parents, second son and second daughter after the mother's. That Elbert [310] named his first son, Elbert, after his uncle-by-marriage rather than after his father, or even his father-in-law, suggests the strategic importance of the Lieverse affiliation to him, as does his choice of the Lieverses as godparents of his first child by his wife—a role customarily played by grandparents.

22. See tax assessment books, 1699–1770 and 1721–1733, New York City Archives, 31 Chambers St.; New-York Historical Society Collections, *The Burghers of New Amsterdam and the Freemen of New York* (New York, 1886), p. 120; and Thomas J. Archdeacon, *New York City, 1664–1710: Conquest and Change* (Ithaca N.Y., 1976).

23. *Minutes of the Common Council of the City of New York, 1675–1776*, 8 vols., ed. Herbert L. Osgood (New York, 1905), vol. 3, p. 352; vol. 5, p. 464; vol. 6, pp. 3–5, 56–57, 87, 131, 149.

24. *Ecclesiastical Records of the State of New York*, 7 vols., ed. E.T. Corwin (Albany, 1901–1916), vol. 3, p. 2101; vol. 4, pp. 2749–2750, 2793, 2834–2835, 3123, 3417, 3748. The coetus-conferentie conflict will be discussed in Chapter 7.

25. Will of Peter Haring [21]: Surrogate's Office, New York County, June 27, 1750. Will of Elbert Lieverse: *New York Wills* (Historical Documents Collection, Queens College, Flushing, N.Y.), bk. 18, p. 177.

26. Besides the Ratzer map of 1767, see I. N. Phelps-Stokes, *The Iconography of Manhattan Island, 1498–1909*, 6 vols. (New York, 1915–1928), vol. 6, pp. 106, 116, 124, and 128. The farm by 1767 seems to have comprised Cosyn Gerritsen's land, John Pietersen Haring's land, and perhaps also the land of Jan Louwe Bogert (d. 1706), who was Elbert's father-in-law, as well as land purchased by Elbert himself. In 1780, it was described as containing 200 acres; in lower Manhattan, only the farms of James DeLancey, Peter Stivesant (sic), and "Ben Hogelands' heirs," at 300 acres, were larger. "A List of Farms on New York Island 1780," Bancker Collection of Mss., New-York Historical Society.

27. In 1767, the streets of Greenwich Village as they exist today were not all laid out, but a comparison of the 1767 and 1784 maps suggests that the house stood about where Cornelia Street had appeared by the latter date, between Bleecker Street (formerly Haring or Herring Street) and Waverley Place.

28. Inventory of Elbert [310]: December 14, 1773, New-York Historical Society, Mss. Collection. In a recent comment on this inventory, Ruth Piwonka notes that the household's quantities of porcelain, silver, and "food service equipage" suggest elegant entertainment and that the furnishings have an "unexpected stylishness" for an urban farmhouse. Piwonka, "New York Colonial Inventories: Dutch Interiors as a Measure of Cultural Change," in Albany Institute of History and Art, *New World Dutch Studies: Dutch Arts and Culture in Colonial America, 1609–1776* (Albany, 1987), pp. 67–68.

29. Information in this paragraph is compiled from the records of the New York Reformed Dutch Church and from the various genealogies of

the families the six daughters married into, as well as from the *Minutes of the Common Council* (for the positions occupied by their husbands). See also "Low Values Seen in Old City Deed," *New York Times*, August 11, 1929.

30. *New York Gazette*, February 26, 1776. This house, known today as the "Old '76 House Restaurant," served as a prison for Major John André between his capture and his treason trial and hanging on a nearby hill in 1780. John Haring [415], Elizabeth's nephew and son-in-law, was president pro tem of the revolutionary New York Provincial Congress in 1776 and, in pursuit of lead for patriot bullets, ordered that sash weights be sought out. *New York in the Revolution as Colony and State: A Compilation of Documents and Records from the Office of the State Comptroller*, 2 vols. (Albany, 1904), vol. 2, pp. 63–67; David Cole, "Baptisms at Tappan," in Cole et al., *History of Rockland County, New York* (New York, 1884; repr. 1986), app., pp. 31–37.

31. Locations of wills and inventories are given in Table 6.3. The five bedsteads in the inventory of Daniel [342] suggest a house the size of his brother's.

32. Will locations are given in Table 6.3; affidavit of John Haring to Chief Justice Daniel Horsmanden, March 21, 1774, Donald Clark Collection, New-York Historical Society.

33. The original receipt for Sarah's inheritance is in Section 58 of the Budke Collection, comp. George H. Budke, Mss. Division, New York Public Library. Will of Abraham A. [336], Sarah's father: New Jersey State Library, liber 32, p. 538. Will of Abraham A. P. [416], Sarah's second husband: Bergen County, book A, p. 138. Also, personal correspondence with Howard I. Durie, April 21, 1986.

34. Records of the Tappan Reformed Church; Wilfred B. Talman, "Death Customs among the Colonial Dutch, I and II," *de Halve Maen* 42, no. 4 and 43, no. 1 (1968), 9–10 and 13–14.

Chapter 6. When Flesh Must Yield unto Death

1. See R. W. Lee, *An Introduction to Roman-Dutch Law* (London, 1915); *The Colonial Laws of New York from the Year 1664 to the Revolution*, 5 vols. (Albany, 1894), hereafter *Col. Laws N.Y.*; and Herbert A. Johnson, "The Advent of Common Law in Colonial New York," in George A. Billias, ed., *Law and Authority in Colonial America* (Barre, Mass., 1965). David Evan Narrett, "Patterns of Inheritance in Colonial New York City, 1664–1775: A Study in the History of the Family" (Ph.D. diss., Cornell University, 1981), analyzes 1,572 wills from New York City and 557 Suffolk County and 288 Ulster County wills between 1664 and 1695.

2. See Hugo Grotius, *The Introduction to Dutch Jurisprudence*, 2 vols. trans. Charles Herbert (London, 1845), vol. 1, bk. 6. For a discussion of inheritance practices among Dutch settlers on Long Island, see William John McLaughlin, "Dutch Rural New York: Community, Economy, and

Family in Colonial Flatbush" (Ph.D. diss., Columbia University, 1981), chap. 6.

3. In the fifteen years after the British conquest of New Netherland in 1664, David Narrett found that 54.5 percent of the wills of persons of Dutch origin in New York City were written in Dutch; between 1700 and 1709, 96.4 percent were written in English. Narrett, "Patterns of Inheritance," table 1.2, p. 19. Further, Charles Gehring has noted that Dutch Americans adopted English *handwriting* in the eighteenth century—"a good example of social accommodation." Gehring, "The Dutch Language in Colonial New York: An Investigation of a Language in Decline and Its Relationship to Social Change" (Ph.D. diss., Indiana University, 1973), p. 5. Customs changed more slowly in some rural areas: in 1715, the Tappan patentee Johannes Blauvelt dictated his last will and testament in Dutch. Surrogate's Office, New York County, N.Y., bk. 12, p. 238.

4. Narrett, "Patterns of Inheritance," p. 40.

5. Peter's will: Surrogate's Office, New York County, N.Y., bk. 17, p. 180. Published abstracts of wills often omit important information; originals or transcriptions should be consulted. A discussion of Pietism follows in Chapter 7.

6. Abraham's will: Historic Documents Collection, Paul Klapper Library, Queens College, bk. 28, p. 238.

7. Narrett, "Patterns of Inheritance," p. 45. See also Jack Goody, Joan Thirsk, and E. P. Thompson, eds., *Family and Inheritance: Rural Society in Western Europe, 1200–1800* (New York, 1976).

8. Lee, *Roman-Dutch Law*, pp. 82, 327–339. The status at law of women in the Netherlands was higher than elsewhere in Europe. Dutch women could own property, execute contracts, participate in commerce, and make wills, leaving their property as they wished. Likewise, "Dutch women in New Netherland and early New York were 'emancipated' to a greater degree than women in other colonies." Michael Kammen, *Colonial New York: A History* (New York, 1975), pp. 93–94.

9. W. S. Holdsworth, *A History of English Law*, 3 vols. (London, 1909), vol. 3, pp. 153–165, 409–413; Narrett, "Patterns of Inheritance," pp. 116–118; and, for Articles of Capitulation, *Documents Relative to the Colonial History of the State of New York*, 15 vols., eds. E.B. O'Callaghan and Berthold Fernow (Albany, 1853–1887), vol. 2, p. 251.

10. Narrett, "Patterns of Inheritance," pp. 115, 133–135. See also David E. Narrett, "Men's Wills and Women's Property Rights in Colonial New York," in Ronald Hoffman and Peter J. Albert, eds., *Women in the Age of the American Revolution* (Charlottesville, Va., 1989).

11. Narrett, "Patterns of Inheritance," pp. 335, 336.

12. Cosyn's will: Historical Documents Collection, Paul Klapper Library, Queens College, bk. 15, p. 60.

13. Peter's will (see n. 5 above).

14. Cornelius's will: New Jersey State Library, bk. L, p. 271. This widow also got a "good room to life in" and firewood.

15. James T. Lemon has estimated that five to twelve bushels was

normal on "old" land, but that newer land (such as the Haring brothers farmed) yielded from twenty to forty bushels per acre. *The Best Poor Man's Country: A Geographical Study of Early Southeastern Pennsylvania* (Baltimore, 1972), pp. 154–156. As noted in Chapter 4 above, Gouverneur Morris in Westchester County, N.Y., expected thirty-two bushels of wheat per acre and forty bushels of barley on old land (1787), provided he manured it. Walter Rutherford to Gouverneur Morris, August 31, 1787, "Advice on How to Manage an American Farm," Rutherford-Schuyler Papers, New-York Historical Society.

16. Bettye Hobbs Pruitt, "Self-Sufficiency and the Agricultural Economy of Eighteenth-Century Massachusetts," *The William and Mary Quarterly*, 3rd ser., 41 (1984), 344.

17. "A List of the Rateables in the Township of Harington in the County of Bergen with the Assessments Made Thereon in the Month of September 1779," New Jersey State Library.

18. Dennis P. Ryan, "Landholding, Opportunity, and Mobility in Revolutionary New Jersey," *The William and Mary Quarterly*, 3rd ser., 36 (1979), p. 574. Lemon figured that a family of five in Pennsylvania needed seventy-five acres. James T. Lemon, "Household Consumption in Eighteenth-Century America and Its Relationship to Production and Trade: The Situation among Farmers in Southeastern Pennsylvania," *Agricultural History* 41 (1967), 68.

19. Abraham's will (see n. 6 above).

20. Lemon, *The Best Poor Man's Country*, p. 158. In Tappan, farmers leasing land from William Bayard in the 1770s were required to plant a hundred apple trees. "Memorial of William Bayard," American Loyalist Transcripts, New York Public Library, Mss. Division. William Strickland, passing through Bergen County in 1794–1795, noted that every farm had an "ample orchard loaded with fruit." *Journal of a Tour in the United States of America, 1794–1795* (New-York Historical Society, 1971), p. 72.

21. Lemon, *The Best Poor Man's Country*, p. 163.

22. *Col. Laws N.Y.*, vol. 1, p. 114.

23. Narrett, "Patterns of Inheritance," pp. 231, 240.

24. Abraham's will (n. 6 above).

25. Narrett, "Men's Wills and Women's Property Rights."

26. John C. [315], Cosyn's son, either died intestate or his will has not been recorded. But he seems to have provided each of his three sons with a farm or the means to purchase a farm in the neighborhood. (He died in 1771, and in the tax records for 1779 his eldest son, Johannes [451], was assessed on 200 acres, and sons Gerrit [453] and Frederick [455] were assessed on 310 and 190 acres of improved land in the same neighborhood.) Jacob [332], with no surviving issue, left his house and lot first to his wife, then to a friend, with the residue to his siblings. The 180-acre farm of Theunis [311], who died intestate, was divided between his two sons.

27. Will of Abraham P. [39]: Division of Archives and Records, New Jersey State Library, file 2303B.
28. Will of Daniel [342]: Division of Archives and Records, New Jersey State Library, file 3361B. Also see Howard I. Durie, "The Two-Door Sandstone Houses of Upper Pascack," *Relics* 26 (Pascack Historical Society, 1984), p. 5; Carol Ruth Berkin and Mary Beth Norton, eds., *Women of America: A History* (Boston, 1979); and Joan R. Gunderson and Gwen Victor Gampel, "Married Women's Legal Status in Eighteenth-Century New York and Virginia," *The William and Mary Quarterly*, 3rd ser., 39 (1982), 114–134.
29. Will of Cornelius C. [331]: *Calendar of Wills* (New Jersey State Library), bk. 25, p. 283. The sons were loyalists, and the farm was confiscated in 1779. An act of December 11, 1778, provided for the confiscation and sale of the real estate of loyalists. See *Acts of the Council and General Assembly of the State of New Jersey, 1776–1783* (Trenton, 1784); *New Jersey Archives, Newspaper Extracts* (Trenton, 1901–1917), 2nd ser., vol. 7, p. 529; and Frances A. Westervelt, ed., *History of Bergen County, New Jersey, 1630–1923* (New York, 1923), pp. 123–129. The sale price of £3,778 reflected the rampant wartime inflation; at prewar prices, the farm would have been worth about £800 (at £4 per acre).
30. Will of Abraham A. [336]: Division of Archives and Records, New Jersey State Library, file 2169B.
31. Sarah's two marriages are reported in Henry P. Toler, *The New Harlem Register* (New York, 1903).
32. Philip J. Greven, Jr., *Four Generations: Population, Land, and Family in Colonial Andover, Massachusetts* (Ithaca, N.Y., 1970), p. 98.
33. John Demos, *A Little Commonwealth: Family Life in Plymouth Colony* (New York, 1970), pp. 164, 166, 169, 170.
34. Lemon, *The Best Poor Man's Country*, pp. 91–92; Stephanie G. Wolf, *Urban Village: Population, Community, and Family Structure in Germantown, Pennsylvania, 1683–1800* (Princeton, N.J., 1976), pp. 313 and 94.
35. Jessica Kross, *The Evolution of an American Town: Newtown, N.Y., 1642–1775* (Philadelphia, 1983), p. 80; and McLaughlin, "Dutch Rural New York," p. 269.
36. Deed (Clerk's Office, Rockland County Court House, New City, N.Y.), bk. 1, p. 297. That Abraham's father may have been sympathetic to his son's desire for this measure of independence and control over his own life is suggested by the fact that money did not change hands in the transaction. Peter's will in 1736 stipulated that Abraham, after his mother's death or remarriage, would receive the "Plantation whereon I now dwell allowing fore the same to my estate the sum of £400." Of this £400, Abraham was to divide £300 among Peter's other heirs and keep £100 for himself. In this case, Peter gave his son title to the farm in 1738, but did not require him to pay for it until the other heirs' bequests were due, at which time he could keep his own share, £100, of the homestead farm's value.

37. Cornelius's will (see n. 29 above); will of Jacob [332] in New Jersey State Library, liber M, p. 46.

Chapter 7. Religion: "Those Who Labor in the Earth"

1. Thomas Jefferson, *Notes on the State of Virginia*, ed. William Peden (Chapel Hill, N.C., 1955), pp. 164–165.
2. Letter to John Jay, August 23, 1785, in *The Papers of Thomas Jefferson*, 22 vols., ed. Julian P. Boyd (Princeton, N.J., 1953), vol. 8, p. 426.
3. Gerald F. De Jong, *The Dutch Reformed Church in the American Colonies* (Grand Rapids, Mich., 1978), chap. 6.
4. Church offered "spiritual succor and cultural reinforcement" to immigrants seeking the "security of familiar ways after the stresses of emigrating." Patricia U. Bonomi, *Under the Cope of Heaven: Religion, Society, and Politics in Colonial America* (New York, 1986), pp. 74, 87–88; Darrett B. Rutman and Anita H. Rutman, *A Place in Time: Middlesex County, Virginia, 1650–1750* (New York, 1984), pp. 53, 125.
5. "Baptisms from 1639 to 1730 in the Reformed Dutch Church, New York," in New York Genealogical and Biographical Society, *Collections* (1901), vol. 2; "Marriages from 1639 to 1801 in the Reformed Dutch Church, New Amsterdam, New York City," ibid. (1890), vol. 1. Also: "Flatbush Dutch Church Records," Holland Society of New York, Year Book (1898); "First Book of Records, 1660–1719, of the Dutch Reformed Church of Brooklyn, N.Y.," ibid. (1897); "Records of the Reformed Dutch Church of Bergen, New Jersey: Baptisms," ibid. (1913); "Records of the Reformed Dutch Church of Bergen, New Jersey: Marriages," ibid. (1914); "Records of the Reformed Dutch Church of Hackensack and Schraalenburgh, New Jersey," Holland Society of New York, *Collections* (1891).
6. Primary source materials on Bertholf (also spelled Bartholf) are to be found in the *Ecclesiastical Records of the State of New York*, 7 vols., ed. E. T. Corwin (Albany 1901–1916); hereafter, *ERNY*. (See vol. 7, index, for page references.) Also see Tobias Boel, *Boel's "Complaint" against Frelinghuysen*, trans. and ed. Joseph Anthony Loux, Jr. (Rensselaer, N.Y., 1979). Secondary sources include James Tanis, *Dutch Calvinistic Pietism in the Middle Colonies: A Study of the Life and Theology of Theodorus J. Frelinghuysen* (The Hague, 1967); and Tanis, "Reformed Pietism in Colonial America," in F. Ernest Stoeffler, ed., *Continental Pietism and Early American Christianity* (Grand Rapids, Mich., 1976). Also: Howard G. Hageman, "William Bertholf: Pioneer Domine of New Jersey," *Reformed Review* 29 (1976), 73–80; Howard G. Hageman, "Colonial New Jersey's First Domine, I and II," *de Halve Maen* 54, no. 3 (1969), 55, no. 1 (1970), 9–10, 14 and 17–18; Randall Balmer, "From Rebellion to Revivalism: The Fortunes of the Dutch Reformed Church in Colonial New York,

280

1689–1715," *de Halve Maen* 56, no. 2 (1981), 6–13, 19–20, 25 and 57, no. 3 (1982), 10–12, 21; Adrian Leiby, *The United Churches of Hackensack and Schraalenburgh, New Jersey, 1686–1822* (River Edge, N.J. 1976); David Cole, *History of the Reformed Church of Tappan, N.Y.* (New York, 1894), pp. 7–20, hereafter *History of the TRC*.

7. George Zabriskie obtained some of Bertholf's correspondence with the Classis of Walcheren, and these transcripts and translations add important new information about him and correct some older accounts. For instance, Bertholf sold property in Sluis on September 5, 1684—information that fixes the date of his arrival in America more definitely than had been possible. With his wife and children, Bertholf must have set sail immediately for America, for he joined the church at Bergen on October 16, 1684. He was twenty-eight years old. These papers can be found in the Bertholf folders at the New Jersey Historical Society and in the Archives of the Sage Library, New Brunswick Theological Seminary. See also Rutman and Rutman, *A Place in Time*, pp. 47–48; and George O. Zabriskie, "Daniel De Clark (De Klerck) of Tappan and His Descendants," *The New York Genealogical and Biographical Record* 101, no. 3 (1965), 194–205.

8. J. Leslie Dunstan, ed., *Protestantism* (New York, 1962), chaps. 1–3.

9. Dutch Reformed Pietism in the Middle Colonies was a theological sister to Puritanism in New England but has received less attention from historians, owing to language and translation barriers. This situation is slowly being rectified. See James Tanis, *Dutch Calvinistic Pietism*; Tanis, "Reformed Pietism"; Tanis, "The American Dutch, Their Church, and the Revolution," in J. W. Schulte Nordholt and Robert T. Swierenga, eds., *A Bilateral Bicentennial: A History of Dutch-American Relations, 1782–1982* (New York and Amsterdam, 1982); and Randall Balmer, "The Social Roots of Dutch Pietism in the Middle Colonies," *Church History* 53, no. 2 (1984), 187–199.

10. On Leisler, see David S. Lovejoy, *The Glorious Revolution in America* (New York, 1972); Charles H. McCormick, "Governor Sloughter's Delay and Leisler's Rebellion, 1689–1691," *New-York Historical Society Quarterly* 62 (1978), 238–252; Michael Kammen, *Colonial New York: A History* (New York, 1975), chap. 5; David William Voorhees, "European Ancestry of Jacob Leisler," *The New York Genealogical and Biographical Record* 120, no. 40 (1989), 193–201; and Voorhees, " 'In Behalf of the True Protestants religion;' The Glorious Revolution in New York" (Ph.D. diss., New York University, 1988).

11. On the Orange County Leislerians, see *The Documentary History of the State of New York*, 4 vols., ed. E. B. O'Callaghan (Albany, 1850–1851), vol. 2, pp. 11, 24, 30, 405–407; hereafter, *Doc. Hist. N.Y.* Pietism's French connection should not be overlooked: Leisler was a Huguenot, as were Demarest and Gouverneur, and De Clark may have been of Huguenot background. In 1685, the Edict of Nantes, which in 1598 had established Protestantism in France, was revoked by Louis XIV—thus making the

Leislerian Huguenots in New York all the more avidly averse to the reign of Catholic James II, who came to the throne in the same year. See Tanis, "Reformed Pietism," pp. 36–41, on the "enigmatic role" of the Huguenots in American Pietism in the Middle Colonies.

12. The term "radical" here is meant to convey its literal connotation from the Latin *radix*, root: that is, proceeding from or to the root. In stressing the individual's personal relationship with Christ, Pietists were going to the original, fundamental, and inherent root and reason-for-being of Christianity. The Mennonites, in Howard Hageman's words, "represented what has sometimes been called the 'radical Reformation' in that they went far beyond Luther and Calvin in objecting to the structures and institutions of the Roman Catholic Church, replacing them with simple societies of laymen who had little use for liturgies, organizations, orders, etc., but instead claimed to rely on the direct and immediate inspiration of the Holy Spirit." Hageman, "Colonial New Jersey's First Domine, I," p. 9.

13. A prolific author, Koelman wrote widely and was widely read on the close affinities between English Puritanism and Dutch Pietism. His works were also practical in nature. (*Duty of Parents* appears in the 1791 inventory of Abraham A. Haring [336], who married one of Bertholf's granddaughters.) In the 1660s and early 1670s, when Bertholf (b. 1656) was an impressionable young member of Koelman's congregation, Koelman had gone so far as to advocate from the pulpit the separatism and communism of Labadie. Koelman later rejected Labadie's ideas, however, and wrote against them. But he never rejected his belief in the necessity for regeneration or his opposition to liturgical forms. Tanis, "Reformed Pietism," p. 43.

14. "The ardent Pietist zeal of Koelman was communicated to his young parishioner, Guiliam Bartholf . . . [and] brought up in this Koelmanist atmosphere, [he] imbibed the full spirit of it." Tanis, "Reformed Pietism," pp. 43–44.

15. *ERNY*, vol. 2, pp. 823–824. See also Leiby, *United Churches*, pp. 18–21.

16. Tanis, "Reformed Pietism," p. 43, and *Dutch Calvinistic Pietism*, p. 39. Bertholf was the source, ultimately, it might be added, for the roots of the Great Awakening itself, for it seems to have been he and his two younger colleagues in the field, Bernhardus Freeman and Cornelius Van Sandvoort, who together urged that Theodore Jacobus Frelinghuysen be called to lead the Dutch Reformed Church in Raritan in 1718. "Bertholf's success [in New Jersey] built on the conflicts within the colonial Dutch church and paved the way for Frelinghuysen's more spectacular triumphs in the ensuing decades." Balmer, "The Social Roots of Dutch Pietism," p. 198.

17. Selyns to Classis of Amsterdam, September 20, 1685, *ERNY*, vol. 2, pp. 906–909.

18. Selyns to Classis of Amsterdam, November 14, 1694, *ERNY*, vol. 2,

pp. 1106–1109. Dominie Selyns strenuously opposed Bertholf's service in Bergen, but Bertholf claimed (somewhat ingenuously) that, as it lay across the Hackensack River, and as his letter of call authorized him to "preach on water and on land and by the way," it was within his jurisdiction. See also Leiby, *United Churches*, pp. 41–43.

19. *ERNY*, vol. 2, p. 1073; Cole, *History of the TRC*, p. 12.

20. Dellius to Classis of Amsterdam, October 7, 1694, *ERNY*, vol. 2, pp. 1105–1106.

21. Records of the Tappan Reformed Church. Only men founded churches in colonial New England. Dutch women enjoyed in America the rights and privileges they had been accustomed to in the Netherlands.

22. The thirst among ordinary Dutch colonists in New Jersey for ministers of Bertholf's zeal and simple piety was very great, and in the spring of 1695 he was able to report to the Classis of Walcheren that not only had he established a new parish "two to three hours above Ackinsack, named Tappan," but that the parish of the recently deceased Dominie Varick on Long Island had called him to fill its empty pulpit. Bertholf turned down the flattering call from Varick's former parish, because, as he put it, his own parish in New Jersey was "not [financially] capable of maintaining any other minister," while the people of the Long Island parish "had enough resources to nominate another one from the mother-country." The Walcheren Classis commended Bertholf for his "charity" in staying with his New Jersey flocks, for he would have had "much more external advantage" as Varick's successor on Long Island.

That Varick's supposedly "Cocceian" congregation called Bertholf is a testimony to the grip Pietism had on the seventeenth-century New Yorker. The call is referred to in a letter from Dominie Godfriedus Dellius to the Classis of Amsterdam, October 7, 1694, *ERNY*, vol. 2, pp. 1105–1106: "I am informed that certain members of those vacant congregations wish to call him." That they did indeed call Bertholf is confirmed by the "Minutes of the Meeting of the Convention of Walcheren," October 6, 1695, transcript and translation at the New Jersey Historical Society, Bertholf folders (also Archives of the Sage Library, New Brunswick Theological Seminary).

23. Records of the Tappan Reformed Church, transcription in Section 48 of the Budke Collection, comp. George H. Budke, Mss. Division, New York Public Library; hereafter, BC 48. Although the Dutch Reformed Church was allowed by its charter of incorporation (1696) to levy rates on members to support church and clergy, it is not known whether the Tappan church assessed members according to their wealth or even whether it encouraged members to tithe. The charter of incorporation, which was in effect from 1696 to 1784, confirmed the Dutch Reformed Church's authority to find its own ministers, buy and sell property, and levy rates on members for ministers' salaries and the upkeep of the church property. Kammen, *Colonial New York*, p. 150.

24. Census of 1702, *Doc. Hist. N.Y.*, vol. 1, p. 365.

25. Census of 1712, "A Liste of the Inhabitants and Slaves in the County of Orange," *New York Colonial Manuscripts, Indorsed Land Papers, 1643–1803*, 60 vols. (Albany 1864), vol. 57, p. 117.

26. BC 48 and *Orange County Deeds* (Clerk's Office, Rockland County Court House, New City, N.Y.), bk. 1.

27. Tanis, *Dutch Calvinistic Pietism*, pp. 148–149. He quotes from sermon no. 2 in Frelinghuysen's *Drei Predikaten*, trans. William Demarest (New York, 1856).

28. See also Cole, *History of the TRC*, pp. 131–140.

29. Ibid., pp. 142–168.

30. Bonomi, *Under the Cope of Heaven*, pp. 111–115.

31. Of the 281 new members in the period 1727–1749, 100 are identified as married couples joining together. (Seventy-one of the 281, including some of the married couples, joined "by certificate"—i.e., they transferred their membership in another church to Tappan.) Of the 181 who make up the "singles" joining, 37 are identified as wives or widows, usually of men who (or whose families) were or would be affiliated in some degree with the Tappan church. The rest, the 144 whose marital status is not indicated, can often be identified as the unmarried children of members.

32. A bill adopted by the New York Assembly in 1699 allowed towns to raise funds by taxation in order to build and repair "meetinghouses," and the church may have been constructed at this time. A reference to the building occurs in the church records for 1704. The financial status of the church was secure in the early 1700s, and a congregation whose treasury contained the handsome sums of fl. 1,458 in 1703 (£145), fl. 1,754 in 1706 (£175), and fl. 1,880 in 1707 (£188) would surely have wanted a building as good as those in neighboring Dutch towns. The account of the first church as given in Cole, *History of the TRC*, states that a building was not erected until 1716; but this was written without benefit of information discovered later by George Budke. See BC 48. Also see Kammen, *Colonial New York*, p. 221.

33. Kammen, *Colonial New York*, p. 85.

34. Records of the Tappan Reformed Church.

35. De Jong, *The Dutch Reformed Church*, pp. 79–82; Alice P. Kenney, "Religious Artifacts of the Dutch Colonial Period," *de Halve Maen* 53, no. 4 (1977/1978), 2; Records of the Tappan Reformed Church; BC 48; Cole, *History of the TRC*, p. 77.

36. Howard G. Hageman, *Pulpit and Table: Some Chapters in the History of Worship in the Reformed Churches* (Richmond, Va., 1962), p. 54.

37. Kenney, "Religious Artifacts," p. 17.

38. Ibid, p. 16. Tanis, "Reformed Pietism," p. 150, quotes a contemporary on Van Lodenstein's songs: they "cannot be sung often enough. . . .[a good hymn] arms the soul against the attacks of the devil . . . stills the wandering affections, keeps the attention lively, and drives the good movements of the mind deeper into the heart." According to Howard Hageman, no one did more than the Pietists to introduce hymns into the

Reformed church. See Alice P. Kenney, "Hudson Valley Dutch Psalmody," *The Hymn* 25, no. 1 (1974), 15–26; and Hageman, *Pulpit and Table*, p. 49.

39. "Recommendation," in Theodorus Jacobus Frelinghuysen, *Sermons*, trans. William Demarest (New York, 1856), n.p. Thirty sermons by Freeman (1662–1743), a Pietist pastor at Schenectady and later on Long Island, were published as *The Scale of God's Grace* (1721), sometimes translated as *The Balance of Grace*. A copy was among the effects of Abraham A. Haring [336] in 1791.

40. Hageman, *Pulpit and Table*, pp. 57, 46, 47.

41. Tanis, *Dutch Calvinistic Pietism*, p. 154. Yet another link was typological imagery. As in the seventeenth-century Puritan sermons of England and New England, typology in Dutch Reformed sermons was an important aid to the minister in stirring the interest and imagination of his flock. Well into the eighteenth century, America in sermonic literature was the wilderness Zion and the land of milk and honey; the Atlantic Ocean was the Red Sea; the settlements were new Jerusalems; ministers were "spiritual fishermen"; and so on. See also Harry S. Stout, *The New England Soul: Preaching and Religious Culture in Colonial New England* (New York, 1986).

42. See Jack Douglas Klunder, " 'The Application of Holy Things': A Study of Covenant Preaching in the Eighteenth Century Dutch Colonial Church" (Ph.D. diss., Westminster Theological Seminary, 1985).

43. Klunder, "The Application of Holy Things," p. 75, states that "covenant theology . . . [was] the focal idea upon which the whole system of Christian doctrine rested" in the eighteenth century. "I will be your God and you shall be my people" is the covenant, fulfilled in Jesus. Sermons of Dutch Reformed ministers revolved around seven fundamental teachings: (1) the nature and extent of sin; (2) the relationship between Creator and created; (3) the bond between Christ and the human race; (4) the means of grace; (5) the doctrine of the Christian life; (6) the place of children in the church; and (7) the philosophy of history, the "end days" (p. 95).

44. Frelinghuysen, who first brought the Great Awakening to New Jersey, was introduced there by Bertholf, the "first true revivalist in the Raritan Valley" and the "key figure between Koelman and Frelinghuysen." Ibid., p. 159. For agreement, see also the works already cited of Tanis, Hageman, Balmer, and Leiby.

45. Bertholf, "Recommendation," in Frelinghuysen, *Sermons*, n.p. For the sermon itself, see pp. 51–70. This particular sermon is chosen here in order to show something of the Pietist sermonic style and to illustrate the Pietist emphasis on the necessity for spiritual regeneration as a prerequisite for receiving Communion.

46. As these phrases from "The Acceptable Communicant" suggest, Dutch Pietist ministers in the Middle Colonies, like Puritan divines in New England, grappled mightily in their sermons with the mystery and meaning of Communion and with the inexplicable contradictions

implicit in the Calvinist doctrines of election and predestination and the biblical presumption of free will. One did not have to be a theology student to perceive the enigmas central to Calvinist thought: even a farmer at the plow could question what use there was in trying to be born again, if God had already chosen those who would be saved; or what point there was in being moral and having faith and doing good works, if works and faith are the fruit of grace, and if grace is bestowed by God only on his chosen.

47. *ERNY*, vol. 4, pp. 2609–2610; Boel, *Boel's "Complaint."*
48. *ERNY*, vol. 4, p. 2319.
49. "Minutes of the Meeting of the Convention of Walcheren," October 6, 1695 (see n. 22 above), p. IIa.
50. *ERNY*, vols. 2, 3, and 4. Until 1709, Bertholf was the only Dutch Reformed preacher in New Jersey. His reputation was relayed to a descendant of a minister who knew him: "It is impossible to magnify the impulses he gave to the Lord's work in every direction. . . . His piety was deep, his judgment superior, his Biblical knowledge great, his preaching reverent and spiritual, and his intercourse with people cordial and magnetic." Leiby, *United Churches*, pp. 50–51; Cole, *History of the TRC*, p. 13.
51. Records of the Tappan Reformed Church; a transcript is in BC 48. Identifications of persons in this and the following paragraphs were made with the aid of the church records cited in n. 5 above. The identification numbers in brackets after names are those assigned in Herbert Ackerman's "Haring Family" (bound typescript, 1952).
52. Records of the Tappan Reformed Church; Leiby, *United Churches*, p. 49. Records for 1835 indicate that, among the numerous Harings in the congregation that year, Cosyn's great-great grandson, Frederick I. Haring [6166], was elected elder; David A. Haring [7461], a three-greats grandson of Abraham [27], joined; and the eighth generation of the family was being baptized. Thus, tenth-generation Haring descendants born in the area and alive today were spoken to as children in "Jersey Dutch," the local dialect, by their grandparents and great-grandparents. Leiby notes that this dialect continued to be in household use in Bergen County up to the twentieth century. See also Wilfred B. Talman, "Dying Gasp of a Language," *How Things Began*, rev. ed. (New City, N.Y., Historical Society of Rockland County, 1989), pp. 263–266.
53. Edmund S. Morgan, *The Puritan Family: Religion and Domestic Relations in Seventeenth-Century New England*, rev. ed. (New York, 1966), pp. 174–186. Also see Gerald F. Moran and Maris A. Vinovskis, "The Puritan Family and Religion: A Critical Reappraisal," *The William and Mary Quarterly*, 3rd ser., 39 (1982), 31, 49.
54. These are printed in David Cole et al., *History of Rockland County, New York* (New York, 1884; repr. 1986), app., pp. 3–50; hereafter, *History of R.C.*
55. For ready access, see David Cole, "Roll of Members," in *History of the TRC*, pp. 142–145; for marriages, BC 48.
56. David Cole, "Elders and Deacons," in *History of the TRC*, pp. 131–

133; and Cole et. al., *History of R.C.*, app., p. 5. In the Dutch church in Bergen (Jersey City), outsiders could purchase seats only after the original founders of the church and their descendants had purchased theirs.

57. Moran and Vinovskis, "The Puritan Family," p. 38.

58. It has been pointed out that there were many ways of affiliating with a church other than as a full communicating member. One could be a financial contributor, an adherent, an auditor, or an attender, or one could just use the church for the rites of marriage and baptism. Bonomi, *Under the Cope of Heaven*, p. 89.

59. The list is in Section 67 of the Budke Collection, comp. George H. Budke, Mss. Division, New York Public Library.

60. See the Rev. Rudolphus Varick to Classis of Amsterdam, April 9, 1693, *ERNY*, vol. 2, pp. 1048–1053, for Varick's view of Leisler's Rebellion and of Bertholf's politics and theology.

Chapter 8. Politics: Seeds of the Republic

1. Thomas Jefferson to the Rev. James Madison, October 28, 1785, in *The Works of Thomas Jefferson*, 12 vols. (New York, Federal Edition, 1904), vol. 8, pp. 194–196; Jefferson to John Adams, October 28, 1813, ibid., vol. 11, p. 348.

2. In 1683, the New York Assembly passed an act dividing New York into twelve counties. Tappan fell into Orange County. *The Colonial Laws of New York for the Year 1664 to the Revolution*, 5 vols. (Albany, 1894), vol. 1, p. 121; hereafter, *Col. Laws N.Y.*

3. *Calendar of Historical Manuscripts in the Office of the Secretary of State*, 2 vols. (Albany, 1866), vol. 2, pp. 143, 147. The original patent is in the Budke Collection. A transcription by George H. Budke appears in Section 67 of the Budke Collection, comp. George H. Budke, Mss. Division, New York Public Library; hereafter BC 67.

4. In August 1689, Leisler became commander in chief of New York Province. By this time, revolutionary regimes had also been established in Massachusetts, Connecticut, and Maryland. See David S. Lovejoy, *The Glorious Revolution in America* (New York, 1972); Charles H. McCormick, "Governor Sloughter's Delay and Leisler's Rebellion, 1689–1691," *New-York Historical Society Quarterly* 62 (1978), 238–252; and David William Voorhees, " 'In Behalf of the True Protestants religion;' The Glorious Revolution in New York" (Ph.D. diss., New York University, 1988). See also *The Documentary History of the State of New York*, 4 vols., ed. E. B. O'Callaghan (Albany, 1849–1851), vol. 2, pp. 11, 24, 30, 405–407; hereafter, *Doc. Hist. N.Y.* In recognition of their support, Leisler in December 1689 appointed De Clark, Roelofsen, Cooper, and Laurence as justices of the peace in Orange County, Edsall in Queens. *Doc. Hist. N.Y.*, vol. 2, pp. 347–354.

5. *Doc. Hist. N.Y.*, vol. 2, pp. 405–407. Tappan soldiers who were reimbursed for their confiscated arms included Casparus Mabie and Cornelius

Cooper. Peter Bogert, a Haring in-law, was also reimbursed. *Col. Laws N.Y.*, vol. 1, pp. 962, 973–976. Historians differ over the causes for the rebellion in New York, but economic inequities, class rivalries, and ethnic and religious tensions all played a part.

6. *Col. Laws N.Y.*, vol. 1, pp. 228, 300–308; "Calendar of Council Minutes," pp. 76, 101; *Doc. Hist. N.Y.*, vol. 1, p. 318. See also George H. Budke, "The Political History of Old Orange County, New York, from . . . 1683 . . . to 1703," *Proceedings* of the Historical Society of Rockland County, vol. 1 (1930), p. 31; and Julius Goebel, Jr., and Raymond T. Naughton, *Law Enforcement in Colonial New York: A Study in Criminal Procedure, 1664–1776* (New York, 1944).

7. See "Loyalty Vindicated from the Reflections of a Virulent Pamphlet" (Boston, 1698), in Charles M. Andrews, ed., *Narratives of the Insurrection, 1675–1690* (New York, 1915), pp. 375–401.

8. Court Records, Clerk's Register (Orange County Court House, Goshen, N.Y.), March 8, 1702.

9. The quoted phrase is from "gov. Montgomeries Instructions" (October 20, 1727), Stevens Family Papers, New Jersey Historical Society, box 1, folder 3. See also Patricia U. Bonomi, *A Factious People: Politics and Society in Colonial New York* (New York, 1971), pp. 36–37.

10. Jessica Kross, *The Evolution of an American Town: Newtown, N.Y., 1642–1775* (Philadelphia, 1983), pp. 72–73; Patricia U. Bonomi, "Local Government in Colonial New York: A Base for Republicanism," in Jacob Judd and Irwin H. Polishook, eds., *Aspects of Early New York Society and Politics* (Tarrytown, N.Y., 1974), pp. 37, 38, and app., pp. 118–131; Bonomi, *A Factious People*, pp. 36–38; *Calendar of Historical Manuscripts*, vol. 2, p. 185. The same holds true for other colonies. In Plymouth, Mass., power and position were conferred on those with ten to fifteen years as independent householders, unless they had unusual characteristics relating to family background, wealth, or character, and in Dedham, Mass., only the "most powerful" men in town were elected to public office. "Few in number," they were "old, relatively rich, and saints of the church." In Virginia, "possession of land and wealth were clearly vital elements in the selection process," and no itinerant tenant, sharecropper, common laborer, or even a Catholic, Jew, or recent newcomer was ever chosen for office. Men were selected for "skills, sagaciousness, trustworthiness, and stature," and "their prestige was based on the "degree to which they served the public." See John Demos, *A Little Commonwealth: Family Life in Plymouth Colony* (New York, 1970), p. 174; Kenneth A. Lockridge, *A New England Town, the First Hundred Years: Dedham, Massachusetts, 1636–1736* (New York, 1970), p. 42; and Darrett B. Rutman and Anita H. Rutman, *A Place in Time: Middlesex County, Virginia, 1650–1750* (New York, 1984), pp. 145, 143–144. Biographical information on the patentees and their in-laws can be found in "Patents Granted for Lands in the Present County of Rockland, New York, with Biographical Notices of the Patentees," comp. George H. Budke, Budke Collection, Section 67, Mss. Division, New York Public Library; Howard I. Durie, "Some Lesser-

Known Huguenots on the Hackensack," in *Bergen County History* (River Edge, N.J., Bergen County Historical Society, 1971); "The Founding of Jersey City," Holland Society of New York, *Year Book* (1914); and Howard I. Durie, "André's Prison—The '76 House: A History," in *South of the Mountains* (New City, N.Y., Historical Society of Rockland County, January-March 1982), pp. 13–14.

11. See George H. Budke, "The Political History of Old Orange County, . . . 1703–1723, *Proceedings* of the Historical Society of Rockland County, vol. 2 (1931–1932), pp. 13–36; and Howard I. Durie, *The Kakiat Patent in Bergen County, New Jersey, with Genealogical Accounts of Some of Its Early Settlers* (Pearl River, N.Y., 1970), pp. 2–4.

12. Kross, *The Evolution of an American Town*, p. 139; *Journal of the Votes and Proceedings of the General Assembly of the Colony of New York, 1691–1765*, 2 vols. (New York, 1764–1766), vol. 1, p. 128; hereafter *Votes and Proceedings, 1691–1765*. Also, "Records of the Board of Supervisors, Orange County, N.Y., 1723–1798," Budke Collection, Section 9, Mss. Division, New York Public Library; hereafter, BC 9, O.C. Board.

13. Petition by Cornelius Kuyper, Esq. (December 29, 1719), in *Votes and Proceedings, 1691–1765*, vol. 1, p. 435.

14. BC 9, O.C. Board, 1730, 1743.

15. Ibid., 1738.

16. Ibid., 1736, 1738, 1740.

17. Census of 1702, in *Doc. Hist. N.Y.*, vol. 1, 365; census of 1712, in *Calendar of New York Colonial Manuscripts, Indorsed Land Papers; in the Office of the Secretary of State of New York, 1643–1803*, 60 vols. (Albany, 1864), vol. 57, p. 117, hereafter *N.Y. Col. Mss.* Also see Edgar A. Werner, *Civil List and Constitutional History of the Colony and State of New York* (Albany, 1888); *Orange County Deeds* (Clerk's Office, Rockland County Court House, New City, N.Y.), bks. 1 and 2; and "List of Inhabitants West of the Highlands" (1715), in *N.Y. Col. Mss.*, vol. 60, p. 56 (Denn and Holly appear on this list).

18. BC 9, O.C. Board, 1723–1750.

19. Ibid.; David Cole, *History of the Reformed Church of Tappan, N.Y.* (New York, 1894), pp. 141–154; Cole et al., *History of Rockland County, New York* (New York, 1884; repr. 1986), app.

20. BC 9, O.C. Board, 1723–1750.

21. BC 9, O.C. Board, 1729; Bernard Bailyn, *The Ideological Origins of the American Revolution* (Cambridge, Mass., 1967), p. 162. Others also see the Revolution's success as stemming from the tradition of local government—a tradition that taught ordinary men to guard jealously their power to make the decisions that governed their own lives. As Patricia Bonomi has put it, the idea of a sovereign people, used to governing themselves from the township and precinct level, undergirded their eventual republican form of government. Bonomi, "Local Government in Colonial New York," p. 48.

22. BC 9, O.C. Board, 1723–1760.

23. Sung Bok Kim, *Landlord and Tenant in Colonial New York: Manorial*

Society, 1664–1775 (Chapel Hill, N.C., 1978), pp. 124, 125; Kammen, *Colonial New York*, p. 151.

24. BC 9, O.C. Board, 1730, 1734.

25. Historians have noticed the tendency in the eighteenth century for public office to become hereditary. See, for instance, J. R. Pole, "A Whig World of Politics and Society," in Michael Kammen, ed., *Politics and Society in Colonial America* (New York, 1967), p. 112.

26. A militia company under Captain Cornelius Cooper was first organized in Orange County as early as 1689 and served under the command of Jacob Leisler at the fort in New York City during the uprising. In 1706, all Orange County men between the ages of sixteen and sixty were ordered to enroll in the militia, and a muster roll from 1715 indicates that eighty-one Orange County men signed up. Cornelius Haring was company captain, and Cosyn Haring was captain for the precinct of Tappan in a second company that formed in 1717. Both Peter and Cornelius were colonels. Peter's eldest son, John P. [37], was commissioned a lieutenant in the militia in 1722; and his second son, Abraham [39], was a colonel, as was a cousin, Abraham A. [336]. See *Col. Laws. N.Y.*, vol. 1, 962, 973; *Calendar of Historical Manuscripts*, vol. 2, 194, 348, 428, 433, 472; and *Votes and Proceedings, 1691–1765*, vol. 1, 1720s and 1730s. The fourth and fifth generations of the family continued to produce militia officers to meet unfolding political and military events. See Lawrence H. Leder, "Military Victualing in Colonial New York," in Joseph R. Frese. S.J., and Jacob Judd, *Business Enterprise in Early New York* (Tarrytown, N.Y., 1979), pp. 16–54, for insight into the financial profitability of a military commission (esp. pp. 19–21).

27. *Votes and Proceedings, 1691–1765*, vol. 1, p. 478.

28. Orange County payment records are in BC 9, O.C. Board, 1723–1798.

29. On party labels, see Bonomi, *A Factious People*, pp. 237–239.

30. *Votes and Proceedings, 1691–1765*, vol.1, p. 136.

31. Ibid., vol. 1, pp. 141, 142 (April 30 and May 1, 1702).

32. Ibid.

33. Bonomi, *A Factious People*, p. 78.

34. Ibid., chap. 3; Mary Lou Lustig, *Robert Hunter, 1666–1734: New York's Augustan Governor* (Syracuse, N.Y., 1983), pp. 221–222.

35. *Votes and Proceedings, 1691–1765*, vol. 1 (1709).

36. Bonomi, *A Factious People*, pp. 82–87. Lustig, *Robert Hunter*, pp. 221–222, describes Hunter as securing the support of the Assembly by appealing to "large Hudson River Valley landowners and their tenants, small independent farmers, and small city merchants and artisans."

37. "Voters swung to Hunter's support because he persuaded dedicated and able men to run for office. Their election, and Hunter's appointment of honest judges, competent militia officers, and efficient officeholders, ensured peace and order in a formerly chaotic society." Lustig, *Robert Hunter*, p. 222. Also see *Votes and Proceedings, 1691–1765*, vol. 1, pp. (1710–1719).

38. *Votes and Proceedings, 1691–1765*, vol. 1 (1713–1714); Lustig, *Robert Hunter*, pp. 124–125.

39. On Burnet, see Bonomi, *A Factious People*, pp. 87–97. Again, the idea that the eighteenth-century farmer, in New York at least, was not interested in maximizing his profits is dispelled by reading the *Proceedings* of the New York Assembly.

40. *Votes and Proceedings, 1691–1765*, vol. 1, p. 635.

41. BC 9, O.C. Board, 1745–1746.

42. *Votes and Proceedings, 1691–1765*, vol. 2, pp. 72, 90, 93, 94, 104, 105, 106, 108, 111.

43. Ibid., vol. 2, p. 130 (November 4, 1746).

44. Ibid. vol. 2, p. 147 (April 24, 1747).

45. Colden to Governor George Clinton, December 1748 (?), in *The Letters and Papers of Cadwallader Colden*, 9 vols., *Collections of the New-York Historical Society, 1917–1923 and 1934–1935* (New York, 1918–1937), vol. 7, app. pp. 346–347.

46. From a poem by Nathaniel Ames, quoted in Max Savelle, "The Genesis of an 'American' Nationalism," in James Kirby Martin, ed., *Interpreting Colonial America* (New York, 1973), p. 470.

47. Savelle, "Genesis," p. 469.

48. "Men Inlisted of Coll Abrahm Haring's Regim't" (May 22, 1760), *Report of the State Historian* (Albany, 1896), vol. 3, pp. 613–615. His cousin's regiment, mustered on April 24, 1759, shared similar characteristics (ibid., vol. 2, pp. 915–917).

49. *New Jersey Archives, Newspaper Extracts* (Trenton, 1901–1917), 2nd ser., vol. 7, p. 518. Also see William A. Whitehead, "The Circumstances Leading to the Establishment, in 1769, of the Northern Boundary Line between New Jersey and New York," in *Proceedings* of the New Jersey Historical Society, 1st ser., vol. 8 (1859), pp. 161–186.

50. Affidavit of John Haring to New York Colony Chief Justice Daniel Horsmandan, March 21, 1774, Donald Clark Collection, New-York Historical Society.

51. Roger Champagne, "Family Politics versus Constitutional Principles: The New York Assembly Elections of 1768 and 1769," *The William and Mary Quarterly*, 3rd ser., 20 (1963), 57–79; Bernard Friedman, "The New York Assembly Elections of 1768 and 1769: The Disruption of Family Politics," *New York History* 46 (1965), 3–24; Lawrence H. Leder, "The New York Elections of 1769: An Assault on Privilege," *Mississippi Valley Historical Review* 49 (1963), 675–682; Patricia U. Bonomi, "Political Patterns in Colonial New York City: The General Assembly Election of 1768," *Political Science Quarterly* 81 (1966), 432–447.

52. William Smith, *Historical Memoirs of William Smith*, 2 vols., ed. William Sabine (New York, 1956), vol. 1, pp. 63, 64, 65.

Chapter 9. "A Spirit of Independency"

1. On the coetus-conferentie conflict, see *Ecclesiastical Records of the State of New York*, 7 vols., ed. E. T. Corwin (Albany, 1901–1916), vols. 4 and 5, hereafter *ERNY;* Corwin, *Manual of the Reformed Church in America*, 4th ed. (New York, 1902); and Corwin, *A History of the Reformed Church, Dutch, in the United States* (New York, 1895). On the Great Awakening, see Alan Heimert, *Religion and the American Mind: From the Great Awakening to the Revolution* (Cambridge, Mass., 1966).

2. Cornelius T. Demarest, *A Lamentation over the Rev. Solomon Froeligh* (New York, 1827), p. 61. As discussed in Chapter 7, Pietists insisted that a man or woman must be born again to gain salvation; the more orthodox members of the Reformed church relied on faith combined with a virtuous and God-fearing life to redeem them.

3. *ERNY*, vols. 4 and 5.

4. *ERNY*, vol. 4, p. 2363. As early as 1726, the Amsterdam Classis had written to dissuade the churches in America from any "ideas" they might have that a coetus would make them independent of the classis "and not subject to the judgement of the Classis; nor consequently to any Synod; and likewise from the idea that the Classis was only their adviser, of whom counsel might occasionally be sought." The Classis of Amsterdam was to be in authority over any American coetus, as decreed by the rules of church order.

5. *ERNY*, vol. 4, pp. 2679–2687. The articles appear in *ERNY*, vol. 4, pp. 2687–2689, and pp. 2706–2708; the draft of the constitution appears on pp. 2708–2710. A postscript of the draft as sent to the Classis of Amsterdam for approval indicates that the Reverend Muzelius was against this coetus, although the consistory at Tappan was not, nor "as we understand it the entire church" (p. 2710). Muzelius's letter is in *ERNY*, vol. 4, pp. 2691–2694. Three other ministers, Antonides, Boel, and Mancius, added their views in the same correspondence.

6. *ERNY*, vol. 4, pp. 2538–2540.

7. "Rev. John Ritzema to the Classis of Amsterdam. In Defense of Rev. J. H. Goetschius," in *ERNY*, vol. 4, pp. 2913–2916 ("about" June 1746). For Goetschius, see *ERNY*, vol. 4, pp. 2779–2948.

8. *ERNY*, vol. 4, pp. 2691–2694.

9. *ERNY*, vol. 4, p. 2999 and pp. 2958–2960; see also pp. 2911–2913.

10. *ERNY*, vol. 4, 2985–2986.

11. *ERNY*, vol. 4, 3028.

12. *ERNY*, vol. 4, pp. 3037–3038.

13. In response to Amsterdam's request that the coetus "take hold of this case and settle it," the coetus appointed a committee to investigate, but Muzelius refused to appear before the committee or even to answer it in writing. On two occasions, G. Hagoort, president, and John Henry Goetschius, clerk of the committee, accompanied by their consistories, went to Tappan to interview Muzelius—to no avail. Therefore, the coetus "unanimously suspended him from office." *ERNY*, vol. 4, pp. 3071–3072.

The committee, of course, sought the opinion of the Tappan consistory and congregation. One item of evidence sent to Amsterdam was a "declaration by many of the members at Tappan testifying that they were in no way induced by the elder, J. Blauvelt, to complain against Muzelius, as he had charged." *ERNY*, vol. 4, pp. 3071–3072.

14. ERNY, vol. 4, pp. 3006, 3029, 3046, 3133.

15. James Tanis, "Reformed Pietism in Colonial America," in F. Ernest Stoeffler, ed., *Continental Pietism and Early American Christianity* (Grand Rapids, Mich., 1976), pp. 43–49. See also Tanis, *Dutch Calvinistic Pietism in the Middle Colonies: A Study of the Life and Theology of Theodorus J. Frelinghuysen* (The Hague, 1967); Howard G. Hageman, "William Bertholf: Pioneer Domine of New Jersey," *Reformed Review* 29 (1976), 73–80; and Randall Balmer, "The Social Roots of Dutch Pietism in the Middle Colonies," *Church History* 53, no. 2 (1984), 187–199.

16. David Cole, *History of the Reformed Church of Tappan, N.Y.* (New York, 1894), p. 44. Besides being unalterably opposed to all attempts to liberalize the Dutch church in America, Muzelius was possessed of an unsavory character. Known far and wide for his drunkenness (even Cadwallader Colden and Governor George Clinton spoke of it), he shocked his pious congregation by drinking and bowling "in a company" in a local taphouse one Monday morning, after having offered Communion only the previous evening, and by his "odious cursing and swearing," the drunkenness of his wife, his neglect of church duties, and "misbehaviour in reference to housekeeping." *ERNY*, vol. 4, pp. 3071–3072. See Colden to Clinton, December 1748 (?), in *The Letters and Papers of Cadwallader Colden*, 9 vols., *Collections of the New-York Historical Society, 1917–1923 and 1934–1935* (New York, 1918–1937), vol. 7, app., p. 346.

17. *ERNY*, vol. 5, pp. 3493, 3547–3554, 3624–3633, 3674–3677, 3638. (Amsterdam's scorn for this latter idea was boundless: the classis, "not having been at all consulted in the matter, is not obliged to weary its brains in seeking to interpret this enigma . . . [but] to wait for . . . this new phenomenon [to] . . . appear in the American Ecclesiastical Heavens.")

18. *ERNY*, vol. 6, pp. 3811–3812; Howard I. Durie and George O. Zabriskie, "The Irregular Dutch Reformed Churches of Tappan and Kakiat, Rockland County, New York," *The New York Genealogical and Biographical Record* 101, nos. 2–3 (1970), 65–73 and 158–164.

19. *ERNY*, vol. 6, pp. 3928–3929, 4013–4014.

20. Thomas J. Wertenbaker, *The Founding of American Civilization: The Middle Colonies* (New York, 1938), p. 101.

21. *ERNY*, vol. 6, pp. 4085–4086.

22. James Tanis, "The American Dutch, Their Church, and the Revolution," in J. W. Schulte Nordholt and Robert P. Swierenga, eds., *A Bilateral Bicentennial: A History of Dutch-American Relations, 1782–1982* (New York and Amsterdam, 1982), p. 119; Adrian C. Leiby, *The Revolutionary War in the Hackensack Valley: The Jersey Dutch and the Neutral Ground, 1775–1783* (New Brunswick, N.J., 1962), p. 23; Heimert, *Religion and the*

American Mind; Patricia U. Bonomi, *Under the Cope of Heaven: Religion, Society, and Politics in Colonial America* (New York, 1986); Harry S. Stout, *The New England Soul: Preaching and Religious Culture in Colonial New England* (New York, 1986).
23. John L. Motley, *The Rise of the Dutch Republic: A History,* 5 vols. (New York, 1900), vol. 3, pp. 359, 420–422; Geoffrey Parker, *The Dutch Revolt* (Ithaca, N.Y., 1977); Willem J. van Balen, " 'Bossu Song' Celebrated Naval Victory of 1573," *de Halve Maen* 44, no. 3 (1969), 11–15; "Nooks and Bays around the Zuider Zee," *National Geographic Magazine* 64, no. 3 (1933), pl. 1, facing p. 300. Bernard Farber, *Kinship and Class: A Midwestern Study* (New York, 1971), defines a "reference" ancestor as one venerated and emulated by all descendants as a means of perpetuating the identity of the family—even though some of the ancestor's accomplishments may be exaggerated.
24. *ERNY,* vol. 2, p. 1051.
25. The quotation is from Bonomi, *Under the Cope of Heaven,* p. 188. On the connection between religion and the Revolution, see Heimert, *Religion and the American Mind.* For the connection in New England, see Sacvan Bercovitch, *The Puritan Origins of the American Self* (New Haven, Conn., 1975); and Stout, *The New England Soul.* For the connection among the Dutch Reformed, see Tanis, "American Dutch, Their Church, and the Revolution." Melvin B. Endy, Jr., distinguishes between holy wars and just wars, and argues that clergy supported the war effort more for political than for religious or millennial reasons, their sermons warning of the "adverse consequences" that a British victory would have for religious liberty. The "Revolutionary clergy for the most part," he states, "presented themselves not as priests of a holy people but as the religious and moral leaders of a body politic fighting what they perceived to be a just war." Endy, "Just War, Holy War, and Millennialism in Revolutionary America," *The William and Mary Quarterly,* 3rd ser., 42 (1985), 4, 10.
26. Bernard Bailyn, *The Ideological Origins of the American Revolution* (Cambridge, Mass., 1967), p. 304.
27. Ibid., p. 310.
28. Information in this paragraph comes from the records of the Tappan Reformed Church. Also see William Smith, *Historical Memoirs from 16 March 1763 to 9 July 1776 of William Smith,* 2 vols., ed. William Sabine (New York, 1956), vol. 1; and Franklin Burdge, "A Notice of John Haring: A Patriotic Statesman of the Revolution" (1878), an unpaginated manuscript containing some misinformation, at the New York Public Library, Mss. Division.
29. Records of the Supreme Court of New York County, Division of Old Records, 39 Chambers St., New York; field book of John Haring and S. Metcalfe for a survey of Man of War Ridge (1771), Bayard-Campbell-Pearsall Papers, Orange County (box 3), New York Public Library.
30. Affidavit of John Haring to New York Colony Chief Justice Daniel Horsmandon, March 21, 1774, Donald Clark collection, New-York Historical Society; letter from John Haring to Governor William Tryon, n.d.,

but probably March 23, 1774, ms. item 15026, New York State Library; Smith, *Historical Memoirs*, p. 180 (March 23, 1774).
31. David Cole et al., *History of Rockland County, New York* (New York, 1884; repr. 1986), pp. 27–28; hereafter, *History of R.C.*
32. Bernard Mason, *The Road to Independence: The Revolutionary Movement in New York, 1773–1777* (Lexington, Ky., 1966), pp. 35–36.
33. Ibid., p. 36.
34. *Calendar of Historical Manuscripts Relating to the War of the Revolution*, 2 vols., ed. E. B. O'Callaghan (Albany, 1865–1866), vol. 1, p. 5.
35. Division of Archives and History, *The American Revolution in New York: Its Political, Social, and Economic Significance* (Albany, 1926), pp. 52–53.
36. Ibid., p. 61; Donald L. Kemmerer, *Path to Freedom: The Struggle for Self-Government in Colonial New Jersey, 1703–1777* (Princeton, N.J., 1940), pp. 331–334.
37. Division of Archives and History, *The American Revolution in New York*; Patricia U. Bonomi, *A Factious People: Politics and Society in Colonial New York* (New York, 1971), p. 310; Edward Countryman, *A People in Revolution: The American Revolution and Political Society in New York, 1760–1790* (Baltimore, 1981), p. 102 and chap. 4.
38. *Journals of the Provincial Congress*, 2 vols. (Albany, 1842), vol. 1, p. 460; and Mason, *The Road to Independence*, pp. 152–155.
39. *Journals of the Provincial Congress*, vol. 1, pp. 462–463.
40. Records of the Tappan Reformed Church; Durie and Zabriskie, "The Irregular Dutch Reformed Churches of Tappan and Kakiat," pp. 66–67.
41. Durie and Zabriskie, "The Irregular Dutch Reformed Churches of Tappan and Kakiat," p. 68, also count seven Haring wives and other female relatives in the Irregular church records, for a total of sixteen.
42. Three Haring third-generation men left the regular Tappan church in 1762, among them Peter's father, Theunis [311], and Theunis's first cousins, Cornelius C. [331] and Cornelius A. [344]. Joining them, besides Peter and his brother Johannes [442], were John C. [485], the son of Cornelius C. above, and (as they came of age) John's brother Abraham C. [489] and Ralph [4135], son of Cornelius A. above. In New York, at least one of Elbert's sons, Abraham [436], was also a Tory. See Durie and Zabriskie, "The Irregular Dutch Reformed Churches of Tappan and Kakiat," pp. 72–73 and 158–164. See also Cole, *History of the Reformed Church of Tappan, N.Y.* pp. 25–68.
43. The most complete account of this grisly episode is Thomas B. Demarest, "The Baylor Massacre: Some Assorted Notes and Information," in *Bergen County History* (River Edge, N.J., Bergen County Historical Society, 1971), pp. 29–93. See also Leiby, *The Revolutionary War in the Hackensack Valley*, pp. 163–172; and D. Bennett Mazur and Wayne M. Daniels, "The Massacre of Baylor's Dragoons, September 28, 1778: Excavation of the Burial Site," a report to the Board of Chosen Freeholders, Bergen County, N.J., February 1968; repr. October 1972.
44. Demarest, "The Baylor Massacre," pp. 67–69; affidavit of John A.

Haring, Revolutionary War Pension Records, S6980, National Archives, Washington, D.C.

45. For the arrests, see *Minutes of the Council of Safety of the State of New Jersey* (Jersey City, 1872), hereafter *MCSNJ;* and Leiby, *The Revolutionary War in the Hackensack Valley,* pp. 122–125 and 204–207. See also Ruth M. Keesey, "Loyalism in Bergen County, N.J.," *The William and Mary Quarterly,* 3rd ser., 18 (1961), 558–576.

46. *MCSNJ;* Leiby, *The Revolutionary War in the Hackensack Valley,* pp. 122–125 and 204–207. Baptisms, October 6, 1782: "Records of the Reformed Dutch Churches of Hackensack and Schraalenburgh, New Jersey," in Holland Society of New York, *Collections* (1891).

47. The following excerpts from this correspondence are in the Ellison Papers, collection 313, New-York Historical Society.

48. *Journal of the Votes and Proceedings of the General Assembly of the Colony of New York, 1691–1765,* 2 vols. (New York, 1764–1766), vol. 2, pp. 776–779; *New York Mercury,* November 7, 1765.

49. Robert R. Livingston to Gen. Robert Monckton, November 8, 1765, in *Aspinwall Papers* (Massachusetts Historical Society Collections), vol. 10, pp. 559–567.

50. Ibid., pp. 561–562.

51. Ibid., p. 567.

52. Again, these happenings are fully described and documented in Leiby, *The Revolutionary War in the Hackensack Valley.* See also Cole et al., *History of R. C.,* chaps. 5–13.

53. See Isabelle K. Savell, *Wine and Bitters: An Account of the Meetings in 1783 at Tappan, N.Y., and Aboard H.M.S. Perseverance, between George Washington and Sir Guy Carleton* (New City, N.Y., Historical Society of Rockland County, 1975).

54. The fullest account of these events is Richard J. Koke, "The Struggle for the Hudson: The British Naval Expedition under Captain Hyde Parker and Captain James Wallace, July 12–August 18, 1776," in *Narratives of the Revolution in New York* (New York, New-York Historical Society, 1975), pp. 36–79.

55. Leiby, *The Revolutionary War in the Hackensack Valley,* p. 84; "Damages by the British Army, Hackensack Precinct," Revolutionary Documents, Mss. Collection, New Jersey State Library, p. 72; Larry R. Gerlach, ed., *New Jersey in the American Revolution, 1763–1783: A Documentary History* (Trenton, 1975), p. 281; Rev. Alexander MacWhorter, *Pennsylvania Evening Post,* April 26, 1777, quoted in Gerlach, ed., *New Jersey,* pp. 296–297; Livingston to New Jersey State Legislature, *Votes and Proceedings,* August 27, 1776–June 7, 1777 (Burlington, N.J., 1777), pp. 85–89, quoted in Gerlach, ed., *New Jersey,* pp. 368–372.

56. "Damages by the British Army"; "Damages by the Continental Army," Revolutionary Documents, Mss. Collection, New Jersey State Library.

57. The houses were often substantial in size. For some dimensions, see Leiby, *The Revolutionary War in the Hackensack Valley,* p. 209.

58. *Public Papers of George Clinton, First Governor of New York, 1777–*

1795, 1801–1804, 10 vols. (New York and Albany, 1899–1914), vol. 4, pp. 170–171.

59. Militia Captain Peter Ward to Livingston, April 20, 1780, Livingston Papers, Mss. Division, New York Public Library.

60. Leiby, *The Revolutionary War in the Hackensack Valley*, p. 265; *The Writings of George Washington*, 39 vols., ed. J. C. Fitzpatrick (Washington, D.C., 1931), vol. 19, p. 358.

61. De Witt to Bogart, August 1, 1781, Leiby Collection, Sage Library, New Brunswick Theological Seminary.

62. Affidavit of Abraham Blauvelt, Revolutionary War Pension Records, S2080, National Archives, Washington, D.C.

63. Leiby, *The Revolutionary War in the Hackensack Valley*, p. 291.

64. On May 4, 1783, Sir Guy Carleton and his party sailed up the Hudson River in the frigate *Perseverance* and, on May 6, went ashore at Piermont. After welcoming ceremonies, Washington and Carleton rode together in a four-horse carriage the three miles to Tappan. Though the three matters on the agenda were not satisfactorily resolved, the meeting is significant in representing the first official recognition of the United States of America as a sovereign power by Great Britain. Savell, *Wine and Bitters*, pp. 20–22, 28–34.

Chapter 10. Getting on for One's Self

1. "Wealth" is, of course, relative. Looking at these individuals, we might keep in mind the class structure of New York Colony in the revolutionary era, as described by one observer, Cadwallader Colden. The "People of New York," wrote Colden, "are properly distinguished into different Ranks": (1) landowners with 100,000 acres or more; (2) lawyers and judges, who "are of the most distinguished Rank in the Policy of the Province"; (3) merchants, "many . . . suddenly rose from the lowest Rank . . . to considerable fortunes and chiefly in the last war, by illicit Trade"; and (4) "Farmers & Mechanics . . . This last Rank comprehend[ing] the bulk of the People and in them consisting the strength of the Province. They are the most usefull and the most moral."

By this account, the Harings were in the very numerous fourth rank, albeit at its upper level, which corresponds roughly to what Ryan has called in New Jersey the "prosperous minority." Some Harings in every generation were also lawyers, judges, and merchants, as we have seen. "Mr. Colden's Account of the State of the Province of New-York," in *Documents Relative to the Colonial History of the State of New York*, 15 vols., eds. E. B. O'Callaghan and Berthold Fernow (Albany, 1853–1887), vol. 7, p. 795; Dennis P. Ryan, "Landholding, Opportunity, and Mobility in Revolutionary New Jersey," *The William and Mary Quarterly*, 3rd ser., 36 (1979), 571–592.

2. Wills for fifteen of the thirty-two men in this generation have been located. Ten men died intestate. Wills for the other seven may exist but

have not been found. To set the six considered here in their lines of descent, Peter A. [412] and Abraham A. P. [416] are brothers, grandsons of the patentee Peter Haring through his son Abraham [39]. Johannes T. [442] is a grandson of the patentee Cosyn Haring [23] through his son Theunis [311]. Johannes [451] and Frederick [455] are brothers, sons of John C. [315] and grandsons of Cosyn. Jacob [473] is a grandson of the third Haring brother, Cornelius [24], through his son Daniel [330].

3. Peter was a judge from at least age thirty-four in 1762, when "judge herring of Tappon" ordered a "pair of silver Buckels for himself," until at least 1797, when he tried John Tice for breaking and entering the "house of Jost Kough and taking and Carrying away the goods and Chattles" of Kough to the damage of £200. Mss. Collection, Bergen County Historical Society, reel 4. About forty cases heard by him appear in this collection.

In New Jersey, the Legislative Council (or upper house) included one member from each of thirteen counties. Property qualifications called for councillors to be worth £1,000 in real and personal property. The thirteen-member council shared legislative power with the Assembly, made up of thirty-nine men, three from each county. Together these bodies formed the General Assembly, wielding almost total legislative power in the state and enjoying considerable appointive and judicial power. The Privy Council served the governor in an advisory capacity. Richard P. McCormick, *New Jersey from Colony to State, 1609–1789*, rev. ed. (Newark, 1981), pp. 122–123; *New Jersey Archives, Minutes of the Governor's Privy Council, 1777–1789* (Trenton, 1974), 3rd ser., vol. 1.

4. Damages by the British in New Jersey, 1776–1782, New Jersey State Library. In Guilford, Conn., John Waters found family size and wealth to be related; Hingham, Mass., families with fewer children were better off than those with many; and some branches of Newtown, N.Y., families fared better than others because of fewer children. See John J. Waters, Jr., "Family, Inheritance, and Migration in Colonial New England: The Evidence from Guilford, Connecticut," *The William and Mary Quarterly*, 3rd ser., 39 (1982), 64–86; Daniel Scott Smith, "Parental Power and Marriage Patterns: An Analysis of Historical Trends in Hingham, Massachusetts," *Journal of Marriage and the Family*, 35 (1973) 419–428; and Jessica Kross, *The Evolution of an American Town: Newtown, N.Y., 1642–1775* (Philadelphia, 1983).

5. Although the ratables lists are invaluable for studying the economic structure of a community, wealth is often underreported, particularly in slaves, because only male adults were taxed. For instance, a comparison of the ratables with inventories reveals that in 1790, when Abraham [336] paid tax on two slaves, he actually owned more; for when he died the following year, eight slaves were listed in his inventory. Eighty slaves were declared to the tax collector in Harington Township in 1790. If a more accurate total count of slaves is desired, inventories must be consulted.

An informal comparison of wills and inventories reveals the following, for instance. Peter A. [412], according to the 1802 ratables (see Table 10.2), owned one slave; but five years later, in 1807, his inventory indicated that he owned slaves to the value of $600. His brother [416] paid tax in 1802 on one slave, yet his 1807 inventory lists four slaves. Others: Johannes T. [442], 1802 ratables show one slave, 1813 inventory shows two slaves; Johannes [451], 1796 ratables show no slaves, 1798 inventory shows three slaves; Frederick [455], 1802 ratables show one slave, 1807 inventory shows six slaves; Jacob [473], 1802 ratables show one slave, 1809 inventory shows more than one ($250). Prices varied considerably, according to the "commodity's" utility. Frederick's inventory (1807) prices his six slaves at from $225 for a man to $10 for a female child; a boy was valued at $100, and a girl and a wench at $70 and $75, respectively.

The same is true of livestock. Young stock were not taxed. Simler suggests that if an inventory reports eight cows, one can assume an additional four young. If seven horses are reported, assume an additional three young. Lucy Simler, "Tenancy in Colonial Pennsylvania: The Case of Chester County," *The William and Mary Quarterly*, 3rd ser., 43 (1986), 558.

6. Mss. Collection, Bergen County Historical Society, reel 4.

7. Unrecorded will of Cornelius [462]: June 16, 1800, in Mss. collection of A. M. Blauvelt. The text is given in Howard I. Durie, *The Kakiat Patent in Bergen County, New Jersey, with Genealogical Accounts of Some of Its Early Settlers* (Pearl River, N.Y., 1970), pp. 39–40.

8. Jacob, John, and Daniel are identified by occupation in receipts for their shares of their father's estate found in Section 34 of the Budke Collection, comp. George H. Budke, Mss. Division, New York Public Library.

9. For Peter, see *New Jersey Journal*, May 16, 1787; for Gerrit, "Haring Family Notebook" (1810), Bergen County Historical Society; for Cornelius [484], Durie, *Kakiat*, pp. 158–159; for Abraham, affidavit of James Riker for pension application of Maria Blauvelt [widow of Paul Powles], Revolutionary War Pension Applications, W15877; for John, David, and Cornelius [4125], Tappan Reformed Church cemetery records.

10. *New Jersey Archives* (Newark, 1880–1928), 1st ser., vol. 31, pp. 124–125; ibid. (Trenton, 1901–1917), 2nd ser., vol. 1, pp. 88–89.

11. Revolutionary War Records, New Jersey State Library, box 15; Frances A. Westervelt, ed., *History of Bergen County, New Jersey, 1630–1923*, 3 vols. (New York, 1923), vol. 1, pp. 123–129.

12. Bayard to Beckwith, May 9, 1783, Carleton Papers, 7647, Institute of Early American History and Culture, Williamsburg, Va.; Bergen County Courthouse, bk. D, p. 437; Westervelt, *History of Bergen County*, vol. 1, pp. 127–129.

13. "Kinship networks and the local community continued to shape social experience and, because of intermarriage over the years, may have become, in some respects, even tighter." Thomas Bender, *Community and Social Change in America* (New Brunswick, N.J., 1978), p. 71.

14. Abraham I.'s will: Archives, New Jersey State Library, liber 39, p. 207. Death date, December 28, 1800: Herbert S. Ackerman, "Haring Family" (bound typescript, 1952), p. 60.

15. Abraham's inventory: Archives, New Jersey State Library, file 3203B.

16. Thomas Jefferson to the Rev. James Madison, October 28, 1785, in *The Works of Thomas Jefferson*, 12 vols. (New York: Federal Edition, 1904), vol. 8, pp. 194–196. Samuel Jones Papers, Mss. Division, New York Public Library. Abraham D.'s will: Archives, New Jersey State Library, liber E., p. 442.

17. David's will: Archives, New Jersey State Library, liber 39, p. 341. Section 48 of the Budke Collection, comp. George H. Budke, Mss. Division, New York Public Library; hereafter, BC 48. Mss. Collection, Bergen County Historical Society, reel 4. John's will and inventory: Archives, New Jersey State Library, file 3669B.

18. Ratables, Harrington Township, Bergen County, June–August 1802, New Jersey State Library, box 1. Because of the 1769 boundary decision giving to New Jersey that part of New York where many Haring farms lay, few Harings actually lived any longer in Orangetown. Orangetown ratables for 1801 show that, of the 221 polls taxed on real and personal property that year, only Isaac [582] and John [4123] were residents. Another 10 Harings, out of 58 nonresidents who were taxed, owned land in Orangetown but lived elsewhere. The richest 10 percent in Orangetown—those 22 polls with real and personal property worth more than $2,500—included Isaac ($3,830) but not John, whose house, mill, and farm in Tappan were valued at $1,805 and whose personal property was valued at $307. "Orangetown Assessment Roll for the Year 1801," Archives, New York State Library.

19. Washington Irving's journal: Mss. Division, New York Public Library. Also see Isabelle Savell, "Martin Van Buren and Washington Irving in Rockland County," in *South of the Mountains* (New City, N.Y., Historical Society of Rockland County, October-December 1983 and January-March 1984).

20. Adrian C. Leiby, *The Early Dutch and Swedish Settlers of New Jersey* (Princeton, N.J., 1964), p. 109.

21. Joyce Appleby, "Commercial Farming and the 'Agrarian Myth' in the Early Republic," *Journal of American History* 68 (1982), 836.

22. Howard I. Durie, "The Two-Door Sandstone Houses of Upper Pascack," *Relics* 26 (Pascack Historical Society, 1984), 3–5.

23. The date of construction, 1783, and the builder (D.H.T.) of this house at 341 South Pascack Road, South Spring Valley, N.Y., are carved in a stone under the eaves. Ibid., p. 5.

24. Ibid., p. 3. More research is needed on the early twin-door houses in order to determine their extent, locales, and function. Of the 225 early stone houses of Bergen County studied by the architectural historian Claire K. Tholl, 36 or so were of the twin-door type; of these, a maximum of 9 were prerevolutionary. See Bergen County Division of Cultural and Historic Affairs, "Survey of Early Stones Houses of Bergen County," Of-

fice of Albin H. Rothe; field survey by Claire K. Tholl (Hackensack, N.J., 1986); and correspondence, January 11, 1990.
25. Durie, "The Two-Door Sandstone Houses," p. 3.
26. *Public Papers of George Clinton, First Governor of New York, 1777–1795, 1801–1804,* 10 vols. (New York and Albany, 1899–1914), vol. 4, p. 817.
27. See John P. Kaminski, "New York: The Reluctant Pillar," in Stephen L. Schecter, ed., *The Reluctant Pillar: New York and the Adoption of the Federal Constitution* (Albany: New York State Commission on the Bicentennial of the United States Constitution, 1987), pp. 48–117.
28. Herbert J. Storing, ed., *The Complete Anti-Federalist,* 7 vols. (Chicago, 1981), vol. 1, pp. 6, 7. See also H. James Henderson, *Party Politics in the Continental Congress* (New York, 1974); Edward Countryman, *A People in Revolution: The American Revolution and Political Society in New York, 1760–1790* (Baltimore, 1981); and Gordon S. Wood, *The Creation of the American Republic, 1776–1787* (Chapel Hill, N.C., 1969), esp. chaps. 1–3.
29. Thomas Bender, *Community and Social Change in America,* p. 76.

Select Bibliography

Printed Archival and Documentary Sources

Acts of the Council and General Assembly of the State of New Jersey, 1776–1783. Trenton, 1784.

Acts of the General Assembly of the Province of New Jersey, 1702–1775. Burlington, N.J., 1776.

The Acts of the General Assembly from 1753 to 1761. 2 vols. Woodbridge, N.J., 1761.

American Archives, 4th and 5th ser. Ed. Peter Force. 6 vols. and 3 vols. Washington, D.C., 1837–1853.

Archives of the State of New York; New-York in the Revolution. Albany, 1887.

Bergen County Historical Society. *Minutes of the Justices and Freeholders of Bergen County, 1715–1795.* 1924.

"Calendar of Council Minutes, 1668–1783." New York State Library. *Bulletin* 58 (1902).

Calendar of Historical Manuscripts in the Office of the Secretary of State, Albany, N.Y. 2 vols. Albany, 1866.

Calendar of New York Colonial Manuscripts, Indorsed Land Papers; in the Office of the Secretary of State of New York, 1643–1803. Albany, 1864.

The Colonial Laws of New York from the Year 1664 to the Revolution. 5 vols. Albany, 1894.

The Documentary History of the State of New York. Ed. E. B. O'Callaghan. 4 vols. Albany, 1849–1851.

Documents Relating to the Colonial History of the State of New Jersey (New Jersey Archives). Eds. William A. Whitehead, William Nelson, and F. W. Ricord. 42 vols. Newark, Trenton, and Passaic, 1880–1886.

Documents Relative to the Colonial History of the State of New York. Eds. E. B. O'Callaghan and Berthold Fernow. 15 vols. Albany, 1853–1887.

Ecclesiastical Records of the State of New York. Ed. E. T. Corwin. 7 vols. Albany, 1901–1916.

Bibliography

Journal of the Legislative Council of the Colony of New York, 1691–1775. 2 vols. Albany, 1861.

Journal of the Votes and Proceedings of the General Assembly of the Colony of New York, 1691–1765. 2 vols. New York, 1764–1766.

Journal of the Votes and Proceedings of the General Assembly of the Colony of New York, from 1766 to 1776 Inclusive. Albany, 1820.

Minutes of the Common Council of the City of New York, 1675–1776. Ed. Herbert L. Osgood. 8 vols. New York, 1905.

Minutes of the Provincial Congress and the Council of Safety of the State of New Jersey, 1774–1776. Trenton, 1879.

New York Historical Manuscripts. Ed. A.J.F. van Laer. New York, 1974.

Public Papers of George Clinton, First Governor of New York, 1777–1795, 1801–1804. 10 vols. New York and Albany, 1899–1914.

The Records of New Amsterdam from 1653 to 1674. Ed. Berthold Fernow. 7 vols. New York, 1897.

Van Rensselaer Bowier Manuscripts. Ed. A.J.F. van Laer. Albany, 1908.

Votes and Proceedings of the General Assembly of the State of New Jersey. Newark, 1848.

Manuscript Collections

Bergen County Historical Society, Hackensack, N.J.
  Mss. Collection
Historical Society of Rockland County, New City, N.Y.
  Verbryck Family Papers
  Wilfred B. Talman Papers
New Jersey Historical Society, Newark, N.J.
  Stevens Family Papers
New Jersey State Library, Trenton
  Damages by the Americans in New Jersey, 1776–1782
  Damages by the British in New Jersey, 1776–1782
  Revolutionary Documents, Mss. Collection
  Revolutionary War Records
  Tax Records, Bergen County, 1779–1827
New-York Historical Society, New York
  Donald Clark Collection
  Ellison Papers
  Inventories of Estates, 1708–1815
  Livingston Papers
  Stuyvesant-Rutherford Papers
  Verplanck Family Papers
  Wickham Papers
New York Public Library, New York
  American Loyalist Transcripts
  Budke Collection
  Emmet Collection
  Samuel Jones Papers

Bibliography

New York State Library, Albany
Lansing Papers
Queens College, Flushing, N.Y.
Historical Documents Collection
Original Inventories, 1st and 2nd ser.
Original Wills, 1st and 2nd ser.
Will Libers, 1665–1800

Church Records

"Baptisms from 1639 to 1730 in the Reformed Dutch Church, New York." Vol. 2 of New York Genealogical and Biographical Society *Collections*, 1901.
"First Book of Records, 1660–1719, of the Dutch Reformed Church of Brooklyn, N.Y." Holland Society of New York *Year Book*, 1897.
"Flatbush Dutch Church Records." Holland Society of New York *Year Book*, 1898.
"Marriages from 1639 to 1801 in the Reformed Dutch Church, New Amsterdam, New York City." Vol. 1 of New York Genealogical and Biographical Society *Collections*, 1890.
"Records of the Reformed Dutch Church of Bergen, New Jersey: Baptisms." Holland Society of New York *Year Book*, 1913.
"Records of the Reformed Dutch Church of Bergen, New Jersey: Marriages." Holland Society of New York *Year Book*, 1913.
"Records of the Reformed Dutch Churches of Hackensack and Schraalenburgh, New Jersey." Holland Society of New York *Collections*, 1891.
"Records of the Reformed Protestant Dutch Church of Albany." Holland Society of New York *Year Book*, 1904.
"Staten Island Church Records." Vol. 4 of New York Genealogical and Biographical Society, *Collections*, 1909.
Tappan Irregular Church records: original, Tappan Reformed Church Office, Tappan, N.Y.
Tappan Reformed Church records: original, Tappan Reformed Church Office, Tappan, N.Y.; transcribed, Budke Collection, New York Public Library; baptismal and marriage records, transcribed and bound, New City Free Library, New City, N.Y.

Genealogies

Ackerman, Herbert S. "Five Bogert Families." Bound typescript. 2 vols. Ridgewood, N.J., 1950.
———. "Haring Family." Bound typescript. Ridgewood, N.J., 1952.
Blauvelt, L. L. *The Blauvelt Family Genealogy.* Association of Blauvelt Descendants. Rev. ed. 1987.
Demarest, W.H.S. *The Demarest Family.* New Brunswick, N.J., 1938.

305

Bibliography

Durie, Howard I., comp. *The Durie Family: Jean Durier of the Huguenot Colony in Bergen County, New Jersey, and Some of His . . . Descendants.* Pomona, N.Y., 1985.

Quick, Arthur C. *A Genealogy of the Quick Family in America.* South Haven, Mich., 1949.

Zabriskie, George O. *The Zabriskie Family.* Salt Lake City, 1963.

Books, Pamphlets, and Dissertations

Anburey, Thomas. *Travels through the Interior Parts of America.* Vol. 2. Boston, 1923.

Andrews, Charles M. *The Colonial Period of American History.* New Haven, Conn., 1937.

———, ed. *Narratives of the Insurrections, 1675–1690.* New York, 1915.

Archdeacon, Thomas J. *New York City, 1664–1710: Conquest and Change.* Ithaca, N.Y., 1976.

Ariès, Philippe. *Centuries of Childhood: A Social History of Family Life.* Trans. Robert Baldick. New York, 1962.

Bailey, Rosalie F. *Pre-Revolutionary Dutch Houses and Families in Northern New Jersey and Southern New York.* New York, 1936.

Bailyn, Bernard. *Education in the Forming of American Society: Needs and Opportunities for Study.* Chapel Hill, N.C., 1960.

———. *The Ideological Origins of the American Revolution.* Cambridge, Mass., 1967.

———. *The Origins of American Politics.* New York, 1968.

———. *The Peopling of British North America.* New York, 1986.

Bender, Thomas. *Community and Social Change in America.* New Brunswick, N.J., 1978.

Bidwell, Percy W., and John I. Falconer. *History of Agriculture in the Northern United States, 1620–1860.* Washington, D.C., 1925.

Biemer, Linda Briggs. *Women and Property in Colonial New York: The Transition from Dutch to English Law, 1643–1727.* Ann Arbor, Mich., 1983.

Billias, George A., ed. *Law and Authority in Colonial America.* Barre, Mass., 1965.

[Boel, Tobias]. *Boel's "Complaint" against Frelinghuysen.* Trans. and ed. Joseph Anthony Loux, Jr. Rensselaer, N.Y., 1979.

[———]. *A Complaint against Rev. Theodore Jacobus Frelinghuysen and His Consistory.* Pamphlet printed by William Bradford and J. Peter Zenger. New York, 1721.

Bonomi, Patricia U. *A Factious People: Politics and Society in Colonial New York.* New York, 1971.

———. *Under the Cope of Heaven: Religion, Society, and Politics in Colonial America.* New York, 1986.

Brown, Dale W. *Understanding Pietism.* Grand Rapids, Mich., 1978.

Bibliography

Burnaby, Rev. Andrew. *Travels through the Middle Settlements in North America, in the Years 1759 and 1760.* 3rd ed. New York, 1904.

Burr, Nelson R. *Education in New Jersey, 1630–1871.* Princeton, N.J., 1942.

———. *A Narrative and Descriptive Bibliography of New Jersey.* Princeton, N.J., 1964.

Clayton, W. Woodford, comp. *History of Bergen and Passaic Counties, New Jersey.* Philadelphia, 1882.

Cohen, David Steven. *The Folklore and Folklife of New Jersey.* New Brunswick, N.J., 1983.

Cole, David. *History of the Reformed Church of Tappan, N.Y.* New York, 1894.

Cole, David, et al. *History of Rockland County, New York.* New York, 1884; repr. 1986.

Corwin, Edward T. *A History of the Reformed Church.* 4th ed. New York, 1902.

———. *Manual of the Reformed Church in America.* 4th ed. New York, 1902.

———. *Tercentenary Studies, 1928. A Record of Beginnings, Reformed Church in America.* New York, 1928.

Countryman, Edward. *A People in Revolution: The American Revolution and Political Society in New York, 1760–1790.* Baltimore, 1981.

Cousins, Peter, H. *Hog Plow and Sith: Cultural Aspects of Early Agricultural Technology.* Dearborn, Mich., 1973.

Craven, Wesley F. *New Jersey and the English Colonization of North America.* Princeton, N.J., 1964.

De Jong, Gerald F. *The Dutch in America, 1609–1974.* Boston, 1975.

———. *The Dutch Reformed Church in the American Colonies.* Grand Rapids, Mich., 1978.

Demarest, Cornelius T. *A Lamentation over the Rev. Solomon Froeligh.* New York, 1827.

Demarest, David D. *The Reformed Church in America: Its Origin, Development, and Characteristics.* New York, 1889.

Demarest, William H. *A History of Rutgers College, 1766–1924.* New Brunswick, N.J., 1944.

Demos, John. *A Little Commonwealth: Family Life in Plymouth Colony.* New York, 1970.

Denton, Daniel. *A Brief Description of New York* [1670]. New York, 1937.

De Vries, Jan. *The Dutch Rural Economy in the Golden Age, 1500–1700.* New Haven, Conn., 1974.

Duffy, John. *A History of Public Health in New York City, 1625–1866.* New York, 1968.

Durie, Howard I. *The Kakiat Patent in Bergen County, New Jersey, with Genealogical Accounts of Some of Its Early Settlers.* Pearl River, N.Y., 1970.

Eager, Samuel W. *An Outline History of Orange County.* Newburgh, N.Y., 1846–1847.

Bibliography

Fabend, Firth Haring. "The Yeoman Ideal: A Dutch Family in the Middle Colonies, 1660–1800." Ph.D. diss., New York University, 1988.

Farber, Bernard. *Kinship and Class: A Midwestern Study.* New York, 1971.

Flick, Alexander C., ed. *History of the State of New York.* 10 vols. New York, 1933–1937.

Frelinghuysen, Theodorus Jacobus. *Sermons* [1721]. Trans. Rev. William Demarest. New York, 1856.

Frese, Joseph R., S.J., and Jacob Judd. *Business Enterprise in Early New York.* Tarrytown, N.Y., 1979.

Gehring, Charles Theodor. "The Dutch Language in Colonial New York: An Investigation of a Language in Decline and Its Relationship to Social Change." Ph.D. diss., Indiana University, 1973.

———. *A Guide to Dutch Manuscripts Relating to New Netherland in United States Repositories.* Albany, N.Y., 1978.

———., trans and ed. *New York Historical Manuscripts: Dutch, Volumes GG, HH, and II, Land Papers.* Baltimore, 1980.

Gerlach, Larry R., ed. *The American Revolution: New York as a Case Study.* Belmont, Calif., 1972.

———, ed. *New Jersey in the American Revolution, 1763–1783: A Documentary History.* Trenton, N.J., 1975.

———. *Prologue to Independence: New Jersey in the Coming of the American Revolution.* New Brunswick, N.J., 1976.

Geyl, Pieter. *The Netherlands in the Seventeenth Century: Part One, 1609–1648.* New York, 1961.

———. *The Revolt of the Netherlands, 1555–1609.* London, 1958.

Goebel, Julius, Jr., and Raymond T. Naughton. *Law Enforcement in Colonial New York: A Study in Criminal Procedure, 1664–1776.* New York, 1944.

Goodfriend, Joyce D. " 'Too Great a Mixture of Nations': The Development of New York City Society in the Seventeenth Century." Ph.D. diss., University of California at Los Angeles, 1975.

Goody, Jack, Joan Thirsk, and E. P. Thompson, eds. *Family and Inheritance: Rural Society in Western Europe, 1200–1800.* New York, 1976.

[Grant, Anne MacVicar]. *Memoirs of an American Lady, with Sketches of Manners and Scenes in America.* New York, 1846.

Green, Frank B. *The History of Rockland County.* New York, 1886.

Greene, Jack, and J. R. Pole, eds. *Colonial British America: Essays in the New History of the Early Modern Era.* Baltimore, 1984.

Greven, Philip J., Jr. *Four Generations: Population, Land, and Family in Colonial Andover, Massachusetts.* Ithaca, N.Y., 1970.

Griswold, A. Whitney. *Farming and Democracy.* New York, 1948.

Grotius, Hugo. *The Jurisprudence of Holland.* Trans. and ed. R. W. Lee. Oxford, 1926.

Hageman, Howard G. *Pulpit and Table: Some Chapters in the History of Worship in the Reformed Churches.* Richmond, Va., 1962.

Hall, Michael G., Lawrence H. Leder, and Michael G. Kammen, eds. *The*

Bibliography

Glorious Revolution in America: Documents on the Colonial Crisis of 1689. Chapel Hill, N.C., 1964.

Haring, John J. *Floating Chips: Annals of Old and New Times.* Toledo, Ohio, 1924.

Harvey, Cornelius B., ed. *Genealogical History of Hudson and Bergen Counties, N.J.* New York, 1900.

Hedrick, Ulysses P. *A History of Horticulture in America.* New York, 1950.

Henderson, H. James. *Party Politics in the Continental Congress.* New York, 1974.

Heyrman, Christine Leigh. *Commerce and Culture: The Maritime Communities of Colonial Massachusetts, 1690–1750.* New York, 1984.

Holdsworth, W. S. *A History of English Law.* 3 vols. London, 1909.

Jameson, J. F., ed. *Narratives of New Netherland, 1609–1664.* New York, 1909.

Janvier, Thomas A. *In Old New York.* New York, 1894.

Jefferson, Thomas. *Notes on the State of Virginia.* Ed. William Peden. Chapel Hill, N.C., 1955.

———. *The Works of Thomas Jefferson.* Federal Edition. 12 vols. New York, 1904.

———. *The Writings of Thomas Jefferson.* Eds. Andrew A. Lipscomb and Albert Ellery Bergh. 20 vols. Washington, D.C., 1903–1904.

Jones, Alice Hanson. *Wealth of a Nation to Be: The American Colonies on the Eve of the Revolution.* New York, 1980.

Judd, Jacob, and Irwin H. Polishook, eds. *Aspects of Early New York Society and Politics.* Tarrytown, N.Y., 1974.

Kalm, Peter. *Travels in North America.* Ed. Adolph B. Benson. 2 vols. New York, 1937.

Kammen, Michael. *Colonial New York: A History.* New York, 1975.

Katz, Stanley N., and John M. Murrin, eds. *Colonial America: Essays in Politics and Social Development.* 3rd ed. New York, 1983.

Kemmerer, Donald L. *Path to Freedom: The Struggle for Self-Government in Colonial New Jersey, 1703–1777.* Princeton, N.J., 1940.

Kenney, Alice P. *The Gansevoorts of Albany: Dutch Patricians in the Upper Hudson Valley.* Syracuse, N.Y., 1969.

———. *Stubborn for Liberty: The Dutch in New York.* Syracuse, N.Y., 1975.

Kim, Sung Bok. *Landlord and Tenant in Colonial New York: Manorial Society, 1664–1775.* Chapel Hill, N.C., 1978.

Klein, Milton M., ed. *The Independent Reflector; or, Weekly Essays on Sundry Important Subjects More particularly Adapted to the Province of New-York, by William Livingston and Others.* Cambridge, Mass., 1963.

Klein, Randolph Shipley. *Portrait of an Early American Family: The Shippens of Pennsylvania across Five Generations.* Philadelphia, 1975.

Klunder, Jack Douglas. " 'The Application of Holy Things': A Study of Covenant Preaching in the Eighteenth Century Dutch Colonial Church. Ph.D. diss., Westminster Theological Seminary, 1985.

Bibliography

Knight, Sarah Kemble. *The Journal of Madam Knight.* New York, 1825.

Kross, Jessica. *The Evolution of an American Town: Newtown, N.Y., 1642–1775.* Philadelphia, 1983.

Landesman, Alter F. *A History of New Lots, Brooklyn, to 1887.* Port Washington, N.Y., 1977.

Laslett, Peter. *The World We Have Lost.* New York, 1965.

Launitz-Schurer, Leopold S., Jr. *Loyal Whigs and Revolutionaries: The Making of the Revolution in New York, 1765–1776.* New York, 1980.

Leeds, Titan. *The American Almanack.* New York, 1742.

Leiby, Adrian C. *The Early Dutch and Swedish Settlers of New Jersey.* Princeton, N.J., 1964.

——. *The Revolutionary War in the Hackensack Valley: The Jersey Dutch and the Neutral Ground, 1775–1783.* New Brunswick, N.J., 1962.

Lemon, James T. *The Best Poor Man's Country: A Geographical Study of Early Southeastern Pennsylvania.* Baltimore, 1972.

Lockridge, Kenneth A. *A New England Town, the First Hundred Years: Dedham, Massachusetts, 1636–1736.* New York, 1970.

Lustig, Mary Lou. *Robert Hunter, 1666–1734: New York's Augustan Governor.* Syracuse, N.Y., 1983.

McCormick, Richard P. *Experiment in Independence.* New Brunswick, N.J., 1950.

——. *New Jersey from Colony to State, 1609–1789.* Princeton, N.J., 1964.

McCoy, Drew R. *The Elusive Republic: Political Economy in Jeffersonian America.* Chapel Hill, N.C., 1980.

McCusker, John J. *Money and Exchange in Europe and America, 1600–1775: A Handbook.* Institute of Early American History and Culture. Chapel Hill, N.C., 1978.

McLaughlin, William John. "Dutch Rural New York: Community, Economy, and Family in Colonial Flatbush." Ph.D. diss., Columbia University, 1981.

McMahon, Reginald. *Ramapo: Indian Trading Post to State College.* Pamphlet. Mahwah, N.J., 1977.

Main, Jackson Turner. *The Social Structure of Revolutionary America.* Princeton, N.J., 1965.

Mark, Irving. *Agrarian Conflicts in Colonial New York, 1711–1775.* New York, 1940.

Motley, John L. *The Rise of the Dutch Republic: A History.* 5 vols. New York, 1900.

Muhlenberg, Henry Melchior. *The Journals of Henry Melchior Muhlenberg.* 3 vols. Philadelphia, 1942–1958.

Narrett, David Evan. "Patterns of Inheritance in Colonial New York City, 1664–1775: A Study in the History of the Family." Ph.D. diss., Cornell University, 1981.

Nooter, Eric, and Patricia U. Bonomi, eds. *Colonial Dutch Studies: An Interdisciplinary Approach.* New York, 1988.

Pennington, William S. *Diary. Proceedings* of the New Jersey Historical Society, 63 (1945) and 64 (1946).

Bibliography

Peterson, Arthur E., and George W. Edwards. *New York as an Eighteenth Century Municipality.* New York, 1917.

Peterson, Merrill, ed. *Thomas Jefferson: A Reference Biography.* New York, 1986.

Phelps-Stokes, I. N. *The Iconography of Manhattan Island, 1498–1909.* 6 vols. New York, 1915–1928.

Piwonka, Ruth, and Roderic H. Blackburn. *A Remnant in the Wilderness.* Exhibit catalogue for "New York Dutch Scripture History Paintings of the Early Eighteenth Century," Albany Institute of Art. Albany, N.Y., 1980.

Pomfret, John E. *Colonial New Jersey.* New York, 1973.

———. *The Province of East New Jersey, 1609–1702.* Princeton, N.J., 1962.

Powell, Sumner Chilton. *Puritan Village: The Formation of a New England Town.* Middletown, Conn., 1963.

Raesly, Ellis L. *Portrait of New Netherland.* New York, 1945.

Riker, James. *Harlem: Its Origins and Early Annals.* Rev. ed. New York, 1904.

Rink, Oliver A. *Holland on the Hudson: An Economic and Social History of Dutch New York.* Ithaca, N.Y., 1986.

Schama, Simon. *The Embarrassment of Riches: An Interpretation of Dutch Culture in the Golden Age.* New York, 1987.

Schmidt, Hubert G. *Agriculture in New Jersey: A Three-Hundred Year History.* New Brunswick, N.J., 1973.

Scot, George. *The Model of the Government of the Province of East-Jersey in America.* Edinburgh, 1685.

Smith, Samuel. *The History of the Colony of Nova Caesaria, or New Jersey . . . to the Year 1721. . . .* Burlington, N.J., 1765.

Smith, William. *Historical Memoirs from 16 March 1763 to 9 July 1776 of William Smith.* Ed. William Sabine. 2 vols. New York, 1956.

Stoeffler, F. Ernest. *Continental Pietism and Early American Christianity.* Grand Rapids, Mich., 1976.

Storing, Herbert J., ed. *The Complete Anti-Federalist.* 7 vols. Chicago, 1981.

Talman, Wilfred B., et al. *Tappan: 300 Years, 1686–1986.* Ed. Firth Fabend. Tappantown Historical Society. Tappan, N.Y., 1988.

Tanis, James. *Dutch Calvinistic Pietism in the Middle Colonies: A Study of the Life and Theology of Theodorus J. Frelinghuysen.* The Hague, 1967.

Thacher, James. *Military Journal of the American Revolution.* Hartford, Conn., 1862.

Toler, Henry P. *The New Harlem Register.* New York, 1903.

U.S. Bureau of the Census. *A Century of Population Growth, 1790–1900.* Washington, D.C., 1909.

Van der Donck, Adriaen. *A Description of the New Netherlands.* Ed. Thomas F. O'Donnell. Syracuse, N.Y., 1968.

Van Laer, A.J.F., ed. *The Van Rensselaer Bowier Manuscripts.* Albany, N.Y., 1908.

311

Bibliography

Van Rensselaer, Maria G. *History of the City of New York in the Seventeenth Century.* 2 vols. New York, 1909.

Varlo, Charles. *A New System of Husbandry.* Vol. 1. Philadelphia, 1785.

Vlekke, Bernard H.M. *Evolution of the Dutch Nation.* New York, 1945.

Voorhees, David William. " 'In Behalf of the True Protestants religion;' The Glorious Revolution in New York." Ph.D. diss., New York University, 1988.

Wacker, Peter O. *Land and People: A Cultural Geography of Preindustrial New Jersey, Origins and Settlement Patterns.* New Brunswick, N.J., 1975.

Wertenbaker, Thomas J. *The Founding of American Civilization: The Middle Colonies.* New York, 1938.

Westervelt, Frances A., ed. *History of Bergen County, New Jersey, 1630–1923.* 3 vols. New York, 1923.

White, Philip L. *The Beekmans of New York in Politics and Commerce, 1647–1877.* New York, 1956.

Winfield, Charles H. *History of the County of Hudson, New Jersey, from Its Earliest Settlement to the Present Time.* New York, 1874.

Wolf, Stephanie Grauman. *Urban Village: Population, Community, and Family Structure in Germantown, Pennsylvania, 1683–1800.* Princeton, N.J. 1976.

Wood, Gordon S. *The Creation of the American Republic, 1776–1787.* Chapel Hill, N.C., 1969.

Woodward, Carl Raymond. *Ploughs and Politics: Charles Read of New Jersey and His Notes on Agriculture, 1715–1774.* New Brunswick, N.J., 1941.

Wright, William C., ed. *Economic and Social History of Colonial New Jersey.* Trenton, N.J., 1974.

Wrigley, E. A., ed. *An Introduction to English Historical Demography from the Sixteenth to the Nineteenth Century.* New York, 1966.

Zuckerman, Michael. *Peaceable Kingdoms.* New York, 1970.

Articles, Typescripts, and Theses

Amerman, Richard H. "Dutch Life in Pre-Revolutionary Bergen County." *Proceedings* of the New Jersey Historical Society, 76 (1958), 161–181.

———. "Treatment of American Prisoners during the Revolution." *Proceedings* of the New Jersey Historical Society, 78 (1960), 257–275.

Appleby, Joyce. "Commercial Farming and the 'Agrarian Myth' in the Early Republic." *Journal of American History* 68 (1982), 287–309.

———. "What Is Still American in the Political Philosophy of Thomas Jefferson?" *The William and Mary Quarterly*, 3rd ser., 39 (1982).

Archdeacon, Thomas J. "The Age of Leisler—New York City, 1689–1710: A Social and Demographic Interpretation." In Jacob Judd and Ir-

Bibliography

win H. Polishook, eds. *Aspects of Early New York Society and Politics*. Tarrytown, N.Y., 1974.

Auwers, Linda. "History from the Mean—Up, Down, and Around: A Review Essay." *Historical Methods* 12 (1979).

Balmer, Randall. "Anglo-Dutch Wars and the Demise of Dutch Reformed Power, 1664–1682." *de Halve Maen* 58, no. 1 (1983), 5–8.

———. "From Rebellion to Revivalism: The Fortunes of the Dutch Reformed Church in Colonial New York, 1689–1715." *de Halve Maen* 56, no. 2 (1981), 6–13, 19–20, 25 and no. 3 (1982), 10–12, 21.

———. "The Social Roots of Dutch Pietism in the Middle Colonies." *Church History* 53, no. 2 (1984), 187–199.

Beitzinger, A. J. "Political Theorist." In Merrill Peterson, ed., *Thomas Jefferson: A Reference Biography*. New York, 1986.

Bergen, James J. "The 'Rebellion' at Raritan in 1723." *Somerset County Historical Quarterly* 3 (1914), 172–184.

Bergen County Division of Cultural and Historic Affairs. "Survey of Early Stone Houses of Bergen County." Office of Albin H. Rothe, A.I.A.; field survey by Claire K. Tholl. Hackensack, N.J., 1986.

Blackburn, Roderic H. "Dutch Domestic Architecture in the Hudson Valley." *New Netherlands Studies: An Inventory of Current Research and Approaches. Bulletin KNOB* 84, nos. 2–3 (1985), 151–165.

———. "Dutch Material Culture: Architecture." *de Halve Maen* 52, no. 1 (1977), 1–5; "Furniture," 54, no. 1 (1979), 3–5; "Paintings," 54, no. 3 (1979), 6–10; and "Silversmiths" 55, no. 3 (1980). 5–11.

———. "Transforming Old World Dutch Culture in a New World Environment: Processes of Material Adaptation." In Albany Institute of History and Art, *New World Dutch Studies: Dutch Arts and Culture in Colonial America, 1609–1776*. Albany, N.Y., 1987.

Bonomi, Patricia U. "'A Just Opposition': The Great Awakening as a Radical Model." In Margaret Jacob and James Jacob, eds., *The Origins of Anglo-American Radicalism*. London, 1984.

———. "Local Government in Colonial New York: A Base for Republicanism." In Jacob Judd and Irwin H. Polishook, eds., *Aspects of Early New York Society and Politics*. Tarrytown, N.Y., 1974.

———. "The Middle Colonies: Embryo of the New Political Order." In Alden T. Vaughan and George A. Billias, eds., *Perspectives on Early American History: Essays in Honor of Richard B. Morris*. New York, 1973.

———. "Political Patterns in Colonial New York City: The General Assembly Election of 1768." *Political Science Quarterly* 81 (1966), 432–447.

Bonomi, Patricia U., and Peter R. Eisenstadt. "Church Adherence in the Eighteenth-Century British American Colonies." *The William and Mary Quarterly*, 3rd ser., 39 (1982), 245–286.

Budke, George H. "The Political History of Old Orange County, New York, from . . . 1683 . . . to 1703." *Proceedings* of the Historical Society of Rockland County, 1 (1930), 23–36.

313

Bibliography

————. "The Political History of Old Orange County, New York, from . . . 1703 to . . . 1723." *Proceedings* of the Historical Society of Rockland County, 2 (1931–1932), 13–35.

Champagne, Roger. "Family Politics versus Constitutional Principles: The New York Assembly Elections of 1768 and 1769." *The William and Mary Quarterly*, 3rd ser., 20 (1963), 57–79.

————. "New York's Radicals and the Coming of Independence." *Journal of American History* 51 (1964), 21–40.

Cohen, David Steven. "Dutch-American Farming: Crops, Livestock, and Equipment, 1623–1900." In Albany Institute of History and Art, *New World Dutch Studies: Dutch Arts and Culture in Colonial America, 1609–1776.* Albany, N.Y., 1987.

————. "How Dutch Were the Dutch of New Netherland?" *New York History* 62 (1981), 43–60.

De Jong, Gerald F. "Minister Johannes Megapolensis: Minister to New Netherland." *New-York Historical Society Quarterly* 52 (1968), 7–47.

————. "The 'Ziekentroosters' or Comforters of the Sick in New Netherland," *New-York Historical Society Quarterly* 54 (1970), 339–359.

Demarest, Thomas B., "The Baylor Massacre: Some Assorted Notes and Information." In Bergen County Historical Society, *Bergen County History.* River Edge, N.J., 1976.

Demos, John. "Families in Colonial Bristol, Rhode Island: An Exercise in Historical Demography." *The William and Mary Quarterly*, 3rd ser., 25 (1968), 40–57.

Durie, Howard I. "The Two-Door Sandstone Houses of Upper Pascack." *Relics* 26 (Pascack Historical Society, 1984), 3–5.

Durie, Howard I., and George Olin Zabriskie. "The Irregular Dutch Reformed Churches of Tappan and Kakiat, Rockland County, New York." *The New York Genealogical and Biographical Record* 101, no. 2 (1970), 65–73, and 101, no. 3 (1970), 158–164.

Endy, Melvin B., Jr. "Just War, Holy War, and Millennialism in Revolutionary America." *The William and Mary Quarterly*, 3rd ser., 42 (1985), 3–25.

Fabend, Firth. "Two 'New' Eighteenth-Century Grisaille Kasten." *The Clarion* (Spring-Summer 1981), 45–49.

Feister, Lois M. "Archaeology in Rensselaerswyck: Dutch 17th-Century Domestic Sites." *New Netherland Studies: An Inventory of Current Research and Approaches. Bulletin KNOB* 84, nos. 2–3 (1985), 80–88.

Friedman, Bernard. "The New York Assembly Elections of 1768 and 1769: The Disruption of Family Politics." *New York History* 46 (1965), 3–24.

————. "The Shaping of the Radical Consciousness in Provincial New York." *Journal of American History* 16 (1970), 781–801.

Fussell, G. E. "Low Countries' Influence on English Farming." *English Historical Review* 74 (1959), 611–622.

Gampel, Gwen Victor, and Joan R. Gundersen. "Married Women's Legal

Status in Eighteenth-Century New York and Virginia." *The William and Mary Quarterly*, 3rd ser., 39 (1982), 114–134.

Gibbons, Kristin Lunde. "The Van Bergen Overmantel." M.A. thesis. Cooperstown Graduate Program, State University of New York at Oneonta, 1966.

Greenberg, Douglas. "The Middle Colonies in Recent American Historiography." *The William and Mary Quarterly*, 3rd ser., 36 (1979), 396–427.

Griswold, A. Whitney. "The Agrarian Democracy of Thomas Jefferson." *American Political Science Review* 40, no. 4 (1946), 657–681.

Hageman, Howard G. "William Bertholf: Pioneer Domine of New Jersey." *Reformed Review* 29 (1976), 73–80.

Hareven, Tamara K. "The History of the Family as an Interdisciplinary Field." *Journal of Interdisciplinary History* 2 (1971), 399–414.

Henretta, James A. "Families and Farms: *Mentalité* in Pre-Industrial America." *The William and Mary Quarterly*, 3rd ser., 35 (1978), 3–32.

Huey, Paul. "Archaeological Evidence of Dutch Wooden Cellars and Perishable Wooden Structures at Seventeenth- and Eighteenth-Century Sites in the Upper Hudson Valley." In Albany Institute of History and Art, *New World Dutch Studies: Dutch Arts and Culture in Colonial America, 1609–1776*. Albany, N.Y., 1987, 13–35.

———. "Archaeological Excavations in the Site of Fort Orange, a Dutch West India Company Trading Fort Built in 1624." *New Netherland Studies: An Inventory of Current Research and Approaches. Bulletin KNOB* 84, nos. 2–3 (1985), 68–79.

Institute on Man and Science. "Cultural Mosaic of New Netherland, Seminar II." Typescript. Rensselaerswyck, N.Y., 1972.

Jolas, Tina, and Françoise Zonabend. "Tillers of the Fields and Woodspeople." In *Rural Society in France: Selections from the Annales*, eds. Robert Forster and Patricia M. Ranum; trans. Elborg Forster. Baltimore, 1977.

Jones, Alice Hanson. "Wealth Estimates for the American Middle Colonies, 1774." *Economic Development and Cultural Change* 18 (1970), 127–140.

Keesey, Ruth M. "Loyalism in Bergen County, N.J." *The William and Mary Quarterly*, 3rd ser., 18 (1961), 558–576.

Kenney, Alice P. "Hudson Valley Dutch Psalmody." *The Hymn* 25, no. 1 (1974), 15–26.

———. "Private Worlds in the Middle Colonies: An Introduction to Human Tradition in American History." *New York History* 51 (1970), 5–31.

———. "Religious Artifacts of the Dutch Colonial Period." *de Halve Maen* 53, no. 4 (1977/78), 1–2, 14, 16, 19.

———. "Silence Is Golden: A Survey of Hudson Valley Dutch Material Culture." *de Halve Maen* 58, no. 1 (1983), 1–4, 16.

Leder, Lawrence H. "The New York Elections of 1769: An Assault on Privilege." *Mississippi Valley Historical Review* 49 (1963), 675–682.

Bibliography

———. "The Politics of Upheaval in New York, 1689–1709." *New-York Historical Society Quarterly* 44 (1960), 413–427.

Lemon, James T. "Household Consumption in Eighteenth-Century America and Its Relationship to Production and Trade: The Situation among Farmers in Southeastern Pennsylvania." *Agricultural History* 41 (1967), 59–70.

Lemon, James T., and Gary B. Nash. "The Distribution of Wealth in Eighteenth-Century America: A Century of Change in Chester County, Pa., 1693–1802." *Journal of Social History* 2 (1968), 1–24.

Lockridge, Kenneth. "Land, Population, and the Evolution of New England Society, 1630–1790." *Past and Present* 39 (1968), 62–80.

———. "The Population of Dedham, Massachusetts, 1636–1736." *Economic History Review* 19 (1966), 329–339.

McMahon, Reginald. "The Achter Col Colony on the Hackensack." *New Jersey History* 89, no. 4 (1971), 221–240.

———. "Two Haring Houses at Rockleigh, N.J." Typescript. Harrington Park Historical Society. Harrington Park, N.J., 1974.

Main, Gloria L. "Probate Records as a Source for Early American History." *The William and Mary Quarterly*, 3rd ser., 32 (1975), 89–99.

Moran, Gerald F., and Maris A. Vinovskis. "The Puritan Family and Religion: A Critical Reappraisal." *The William and Mary Quarterly*, 3rd ser., 39 (1982), 29–63.

Morris, Richard B. "Spotlight on the Plowmen of the Jersies," *Proceedings of the New Jersey Historical Society*, 67 (1949), 106–123.

Murrin, John. "Review Essay." *History and Theory* 11 (1972), 226–275.

Mutch, Robert E. "Yeoman and Merchant in Pre-Industrial America: Eighteenth-Century Massachusetts as a Case Study." *Societas* 7 (1977), 279–302.

Nash, Gary B. "Urban Wealth and Poverty in Pre-Revolutionary America." In Stanley N. Katz and John M. Murrin, eds., *Colonial America: Essays in Politics and Social Development*, 3rd ed. New York, 1983.

Piwonka, Ruth. "Dutch Gardens in the Hudson Valley, I and II." *de Halve Maen* 49, nos. 2–3 (1974), 11–12 and 11–12, 14, 16.

———. "New York Colonial Inventories: Dutch Interiors as a Measure of Cultural Change." In Albany Institute of History and Art, *New World Dutch Studies: Dutch Arts and Culture in Colonial America, 1609–1776*. Albany, N.Y. 1987.

Prince, J. Dyneley. "The Jersey Dutch Dialect." *Dialect Notes* 3, pt. 6 (1910), 459–484.

Pruitt, Bettye Hobbs. "Self-Sufficiency and the Agricultural Economy of Eighteenth-Century Massachusetts." *The William and Mary Quarterly*, 3rd ser., 41 (1984), 333–364.

Rink, Oliver A. "The People of New Netherland: Notes on Non-English Immigration to New York in the Seventeenth Century." *New York History* 62 (1981), 5–42.

Runcie, John D. "The Problem of Anglo-American Politics in Bellomont's

Bibliography

New York." *The William and Mary Quarterly*, 3rd ser., 26 (1969), 191–217.
Rutman, Darrett B. "The Mirror of Puritan Authority." In George A. Billias, ed., *Law and Authority in Colonial America*. Barre, Mass., 1965.
Ryan, Dennis P. "Landholding, Opportunity, and Mobility in Revolutionary New Jersey." *The William and Mary Quarterly*, 3rd ser., 36 (1979), 571–592.
Schipper, Jaap. "Rural Architecture: The Zaan Region of the Province of North Holland." In Albany Institute of History and Art, *New World Dutch Studies: Dutch Arts and Culture in Colonial America, 1609–1776*. Albany, N.Y., 1987.
Schucher, Robert V. "Elizabethan Birth Control and Puritan Attitudes." *Journal of Interdisciplinary History* 4 (1975), 655–667.
Shalhope, Robert E. "Agriculture." In Merrill Peterson, ed., *Thomas Jefferson: A Reference Biography*. New York, 1986.
Simler, Lucy. "Tenancy in Colonial Pennsylvania: The Case of Chester County." *The William and Mary Quarterly*, 3rd ser., 43 (1986), 542–569.
Smith, Daniel Blake. "The Study of the Family in Early America: Trends, Problems, and Prospects." *The William and Mary Quarterly*, 3rd ser., 39 (1982), 3–28.
Smith, Daniel Scott, and Michael S. Hindus. "Premarital Pregnancy in America, 1640–1971: An Overview and Interpretation." *Journal of Interdisciplinary History* 5 (1975), 537–570.
Tanis, James. "The American Dutch, Their Church, and the Revolution." In J. W. Schulte Nordholt and Robert P. Swierenga, eds., *A Bilateral Bicentennial: A History of Dutch-American Relations, 1782–1982*. New York and Amsterdam, 1982.
———. "Reformed Pietism in Colonial America." In F. Ernest Stoeffler, ed., *Continental Pietism and Early American Christianity*. Grand Rapids, Mich., 1976.
Trewartha, Glenn T. "Types of Rural Settlement in Colonial America." *Geographical Review* 36 (1946), 568–596.
Van der Woude, A. M. "Variations in the Size and Structure of the Household in the United Provinces of the Netherlands in the Seventeenth and Eighteenth Centuries." In Peter Laslett and Richard Wall, eds., *Household and Family in Past Time*. London, 1972.
Van Wijk, Piet. "Form and Function in the Netherlands' Dutch Agricultural Architecture." In Albany Institute of History and Art, *New World Dutch Studies: Dutch Arts and Culture in Colonial America, 1609–1776*. Albany, N.Y., 1987.
Varga, Nicholas. "Election Procedures and Practices in Colonial New York." *New York History* 41 (1960), 249–277.
Volk, Joyce Geary. "The Dutch Kast and the American Kas: A Structural/Historical Analsysis." In Albany Institute of History and Art, *New World Dutch Studies: Dutch Arts and Culture in Colonial America, 1609–1776*. Albany, N.Y., 1987.

Wacker, Peter O. "Dutch Material Culture in New Jersey." *Journal of Popular Culture* 11 (1978), 948–958.

Waters, John J., Jr. "Family, Inheritance, and Migration in Colonial New England: The Evidence from Guilford, Connecticut." *The William and Mary Quarterly*, 3rd ser., 39 (1982), 64–86.

Wilcoxen, Charlotte. "Household Artifacts of New Netherland, from Its Archaeological and Documentary Records." *New Netherland Studies: An Inventory of Current Research and Approaches. Bulletin KNOB* 84 nos. 2–3 (1985), 120–129.

Wilkenfeld, Bruce M. "The New York City Common Council, 1689–1800." *New York History* 52 (1971), 249–273.

Zantkuyl, Henk J. "The Netherlands Town House: How and Why It Works." In Albany Institute of History and Art, *New World Dutch Studies: Dutch Arts and Culture in Colonial America, 1609–1776.* Albany, N.Y., 1987.

———. "Reconstruction of Some 17th-Century Dutch Houses in New Netherland." *New Netherland Studies: An Inventory of Current Research and Approaches. Bulletin KNOB* 84, nos. 2–3 (1985), 166–179.

Index

References to figures are in italics. Tables are indicated by an italic *t*.

319

Index

also children; Haring family;
Haring family (individuals);
inheritance customs; widows
farmers: Dutch, 21, 24; Dutch
American, 76–78;
entrepreneurial or subsistence,
12, 84–85, 270n54. *See also*
Tappan patentees: economic
motives of
First Continental Congress, 201–
202, 214–215
free blacks, 49, 50–51
Freeman, Dominie Bernhardus,
154, 195, 282n16
Frelinghuysen, Theodorus
Jacobus, 154, 155–157, 191–193,
282n16
Frelinghuysen, Theodorus, Jr., 195
French and Indian War, 186–187

Gale, Samuel, 82, 188, 200
Galloway Plan, 201–202
Gerritsen, Cosyn, 3–8, 254nn8, 9
Goetschius, John Henry, 192–193,
194, 195, 196
Goodfriend, Joyce D., 9
Gouverneur, Abraham, 138, 166,
179
Grant, Mrs. Anne, quoted, 78–79
Great Awakening, 191–193

Hackensack River, as disputed
boundary of Tappan Patent, *16*,
22–23; and Tappan Patent, 12,
15, 17; and Tappan patentees'
trading strategy, 12, 17
Haring family: demographics of,
86–89; and disposition of land,
89–92; economic position after
the Revolution, 222–235; fifth
generation, 236–239; fourth
generation, 87–89; and politics,
165–189; and religion, 133–164;
and Revolutionary War, 190–
221, 233–235; second
generation, 35–51; third

generation, 86–87. *See also*
Haring family (individuals);
inheritance customs; marriage
Haring family (individuals)
—Abraham [27]: career, 178, 184–
188, 290n26; family, 40, 44, 47,
48; house, 62; land, 19, 32, 33,
56; marriage, 37, 39, 41, 45;
relation to Tappan Reformed
Church, 146, 148*t*, 158, 194; will,
62, 71, 102, 105, 106–107, 111,
115, 117, 118, 129
—Abraham [39], 120*t*, 123, 129,
148*t*, 158, 171, 176*t*, 184–187,
188, 197, 200, 205, 290n26
—Abraham [5221], 237–238
—Abraham A. [336], 85, 93, 99–
102, 103–104, 120*t*, 125–127,
148*t*, 186–187, 222, 290n26,
226*t*, 227–228
—Abraham A. P. [416], 123, 126,
223*t*, 226*t*, 227–228, 235
—Abraham G. [592], 63–65
—Cornelius [24]: career, 176*t*,
178–183, 290n26; family, 40, 44,
47, *48*, 94; house, 63; land, 19,
32, 33, 56; marriage, 37, 39, 41,
45; slaves, 50, 144; relation to
Tappan Reformed Church, 142,
145, 146, 148*t*, 158; will, 83, 105,
111, 115, 117, 129
—Cornelius [417], *234*, 235–237
—Cornelius A. [344], 103, 120*t*,
148*t*, *206*, 207–209
—Cornelius C. [341], 103, 120*t*,
124–125, 148*t*, *206*, 207, 209
—Cosyn [23]: career, 290n26;
family, 40, 44, 47, *48*; house, 62–
63, *64*, 65–66, 73–74; land, 19,
31, 32, 33, 37, 56; marriage, 37,
38, 39, 41, 45; slaves, 50, 144;
and Tappan Reformed Church,
142, 145, 146, 148*t*, 158; will, 62,
105, 110, 117, 129, 267n17
—Daniel [342], 101, 120*t*, 123–
124, 148*t*, 222
—Elbert [310], 86–87, 93, 94–102,

sort," 7, 12; East Jersey, 11;
Manhattan, 7, 10–11
religion: factor in Revolution,
190–191, 196–200, 209–210. *See
also* Bertholf, Guiliam; Dutch
Reformed Chruch; Leisler's
Rebellion; Tappan Reformed
Church
Revolutionary War: coetus
ministers, 195, 196; economic
losses, 210–221, 222–247
passim; events of, 190–221
passim; prelude to, 187, 188–
189; religion as factor in, 190–
191, 196–200, 209–210. *See also*
Baylor Massacre
Ryan, Dennis P., 91, 272n8

Scott, John Morin, 200, 204
Second Continental Congress, 178,
201, 204–205
second occupations, 7, 254n8
Selyns, Dominie Henricus, 3, 39,
135, 140, 141, 154
slavery, 23–25; 298n5; in Tappan,
24
slaves: in census of 1702, 24, *48*,
142–144; in census of 1712, 24,
144–145; and family, 50; as
index of wealth, 9, 23, 142–145;
labor of, 14; in Tappan
Reformed Church, 160; trade in
21, 23
Sloughter, Governor Henry, 167
Smith, William, 201
Stamp Act, 212–214
Stone House Survey, 58–59,
266n9, 267nn10, 11, 12, 15
Stuyvesant, Peter, 3
Sudbury, Mass., distribution of
land in, 25, 28
Symes, Lancaster, 22–23, 30, 169,
244

Talman, Teunis, 44, 142, 143, 144,
166
Tanis, James, 155, 281n9

Tappaen Indians, 11, 15; deed to
Tappan Patent, 15
Tappan Patent, 5, 11, 12, 19, 20,
49; conceptualization of, 25–27;
description of, 15–17; division
of, 28, 30–34; free blacks in, 49;
and Lockhart Patent, 20–22;
map of, *16*; Old World model
for, 25–27; purchase of, 14–15;
settlement patterns, 33; slavery
in, 49; suit against, 22–23;
today's towns within original
perimeter, 17
Tappan patentees: delay in
dividing land, 29–30; economic
profile, 142–145; economic
motives of, 12, 17–18, 19, 84–85,
129–130, 142; ideals, 11–13, 27,
29–30, 31, 33–34, 36, 37–38, 87,
88, 128–130, 142; identified by
name, 15, 256n1, 258n7; as
Leislerians, 137–138, 142, 166–
167, 194, 198, 281n11, 287nn3,
5; marriage, patentee
generation, 36–39; marriage,
third and fourth generations,
86–89; officeholding, 165–177;
politics, 12–13, 20–21, 165, 166–
169
Tappan Reformed Church, 62, 99;
buildings (1694–1835), *150*, 151,
152, 153, 284n32; dissension in,
162–164; economic profile of
members, 142–145;
"feminization" in, 146–147;
formation of, 137–138, 140,
141–142, 146; giving patterns,
142–145; joining patterns, 146–
151, 148*t*, 149*t*; pall, 104;
stratification in, 142–145;
"tribalism," 160–162; women in,
142, 146–151, 149*t*, 157–160;
and worship, 153–157. *See also*
Bertholf, Guiliam; Verbryck,
Rev. Samuel
Tappan Reformed Church
(Irregular), 205, 206, 209